SCIPIO

Other Books by The Author

This Righteous War (The Hull 92nd Brigade – 1914 to 1919)

The Sign of the Double 'T' (The 50th Northumbria Division in Sicily and
    North West Europe – 1943 to 1944)

Known to the Night (Reckitts Factory of Hull and The Great War)

OPERATION SCIPIO
(The 8th Army at the Battle of the Wadi-Akarit, 6th April 1943, Tunisia)

B. S. BARNES

SENTINEL PRESS

First Published in 2007 by Sentinel Press

© B. S. Barnes

ISBN: 0-9534262-2-X

Printed by The Amadeus Press, Cleckheaton

Page Layout by Highlight Type Bureau Ltd, Bradford

Published by Sentinel Press
6 Sandfield Close, Market Weighton
York YO43 3ET

Dedicated to the men who marched and fought with the Desert Army.

Their drills were bloodless battles and their battles bloody drills

Contents
(The 8th Army at the Battle of Wadi Akarit - 6 April 1943)

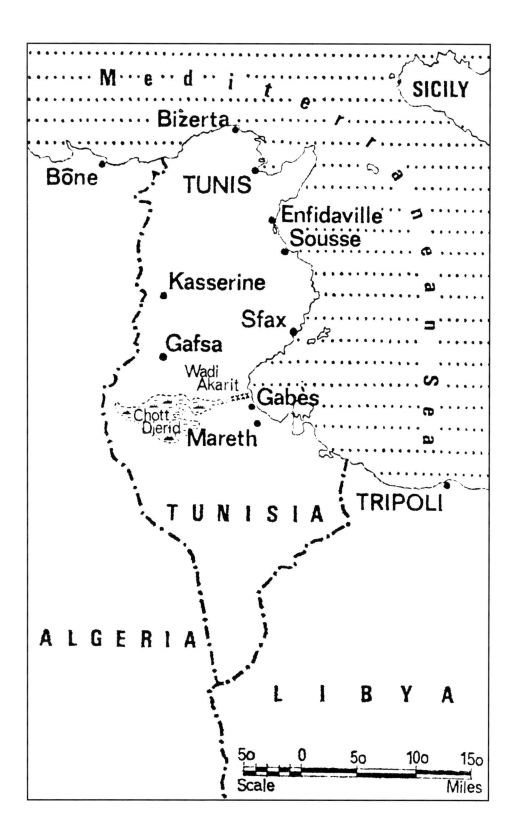

THE 8TH ARMY AT:

The battle of the Wadi-Akarit – 6th April 1943

KEY

VC's:
Subedar Lalbahadur Thapa. VC. OBI ❶
Pte Eric Anderson. VC. ❷
Lt Col Lorne M Campbell. VC. DSO and BAR. ❸

Positions of mine-fields

Anti-tank ditches

Tracks

N · E · S · W

Map by Adkins Design
www.adkinsdesign.co.uk

SFAX.

GABES

VII

YOUNG FASCISTS

XI

II

I

WADI AKARIT

blown

201ST GUARD'S BDE.

51ST HIGHLAND DIV. HQ.

90TH LIGHT DIVISION

II/155

1/55 ❸

7TH ARGYLLS

1ST BL. WATCH

7TH BLACK WATCH

154TH BDE.

1/65

20TH PANZER DIVISION GRENADIER RGT.

15TH PANZER DIVISION

FOLGORE

GRAN

TRIESTE DIVISION

2ND SEAFORTH

5TH BLACK WATCH

5TH SEAFORTH

5TH CAMERONS

152ND BDE.

153RD BDE.

ROUMANA RIDGE

112

11/136

11/126

85

1 COY. 7TH GHs

6TH GHs

7TH GHs

5TH E. YORKS.

1/4TH ESSEX

1ST ROYAL SUSSEX

❷

7TH BDE.

5TH AND 6TH BDE.

EL GUADA

TOBRUK

SPEZIA DIVISION

152

EL HACHANA

EL MEIDA

II/125

A/16TH RAJPUTANA

1/9TH GURKHAS

1/2ND GURKHAS

7/16TH PUNJAB

blown

EL ALIG.

ZOUAI.

275

❶

II/36.

FATNASSA

36° PANZER RGT. GR GRENADIER RGT.

PISTOIA DIVISION

II/35

GABES

50TH (N) DIV. HQ.

4TH INDIAN DIV. HQ.

DJEBEL ZEMLET EL BEIDA

A DETACHMENT OF THE FIGHTING DIVISION

15TH PANZER DIVISION

164TH LIGHT DIVISION

GAFSA

I/35.

I/125.

II/36°.

285

DJEBEL HADOUDI

Abbreviations

Nullah or Wadi	:	Dried Up River-Bed
FDL	:	Forward Defensive Line
DF	:	Defensive Fire
HQ	:	Head Quarters
FOO	:	Forward Observation Officer
BDE	:	Brigade
DIV	:	Division
PLN	:	Platoon
MG	:	Machine Gun
COY	:	Company
A/TK	:	Anti Tank
BN	:	Battalion
LO	:	Liaison Officer
OP	:	Observation Post
ARTY	:	Artillery
POW	:	Prisoner of War
PT	:	Point (high point on a map)
RECCE	:	Reconnaissance
TKS	:	Tanks
CO	:	Commanding Officer
CRE	:	Commander Royal Engineers
LAA	:	Light Anti-Aircraft
BRIG	:	Brigadier
GR	:	Gurkha Rifles
FUP	:	Forming Up Point
ADJT	:	Adjutant
TAC	:	Tactical
IO	:	Intelligence Officer
RAP	:	Regimental Aid Post
DJ	:	Djebel (which means hill)
CRA	:	Commander Royal Artillery
GO	:	Gurkha Officer
BO	:	British Officer
IOR	:	Indian Other Ranks
OR	:	Other Ranks
NCO	:	Non-Commissioned Officer
CSM	:	Company Sergeant Major
RSM	:	Regimental Sergeant Major
STONK	:	Artillery Barrage
RTR	:	Royal Tank Regiment
CLY	:	County of London Yeomanry
SA	:	Small Arms
BC	:	Battery or Battalion – Commander
OPPO	:	Operator
Brewed Up	:	Making tea or a tank that is burning fiercely with its crew still inside
AOV	:	Armoured Observation Vehicle
RHQ	:	Regimental Head Quarters
Sangar	:	Emplacement made of rocks
MMG	:	Medium Machine-Gun
MO	:	Medical Officer
Flimsy	:	Petrol Can
Up The Blue	:	Being out in the desert
LO	:	Liaison Officer
Tattie Masher	:	German Stick Grenade

FOREWORD

It is with much pleasure but with a distinct sense of unworthiness that I write these few lines. There are so many people who have had a much better claim than I have to write this foreword.

But the March of Time is inexorable and there are now few survivors of this epic encounter.

"Epic" is no overstatement. Wadi Akarit was the German's last major stand against the victorious advance of the 8th Army; their position, dominated by the two features of the Djebel Tebega Fatnassa and the Djebel Roumana was a daunting target; no wonder that General Montgomery classified the battle that followed as the hardest he had fought while in command of the 8th Army.

Barrie Barnes has produced a remarkable account; it ranges from his admirably clear setting of the scene, through the terse and laconic entries in unit War Diaries to the vivid and usually confused first hand accounts of those in the front line who could only see what was immediately visible to them in the fog of war.

The accounts of the Victoria Crosses awarded to members of each of the Divisions involved highlight the bravery of the British and Indian soldiers that fought at Akarit. These men were giants in their day; I have been lucky enough to know quite a few of them. Most of them returned after the war to a humdrum peacetime existence; they did not boast of their exploits and many of them showed the marks of a life that had been less than easy; many looked old and tired and sometimes a little shabby; but they were true heroes.

Perhaps the spirit of what took place can be summed up by the story of Major John Lindsay MacDougall of Lunga of the 7th Argylls who, wounded as he was, charged the approaching enemy masses with the five surviving members of his company headquarters shouting "No surrender, 'C' Company! Charge!" as he hobbled after them on his improvised crutch. My father put him up for the Victoria Cross but he received instead the Distinguished Service Order. Known as "No Surrender John" to his men, he was later wounded again in Sicily and died of his wounds as a Prisoner of War.

At a time when any self-pride in Britain's past is unfashionable, when the famous regiments mentioned in these pages have virtually all disappeared, and when most of the figures in this story have passed on, it is all the more important that such events as the Battle of Wadi Akarit should be remembered.

Barrie Barnes has produced an outstanding book and we are all much in his debt.

Alistair Campbell of Airds
Unicorn Pursuivant of Arms

PREFACE

THE 8th ARMY: FROM OCTOBER 1942 TO APRIL 1943

Between the dates of 23 October and 4 November 1942 Montgomery led the 8th Army to a great victory at the Battle of El-Alamein. This famous event did not end the war in Africa, but it was the beginning of the end, and set in motion a series of events that led to an allied victory on that continent. After days of pounding by the 8th Army, the Panzer Army Africa was at last pulling back. During succeeding days and weeks there would be land battles of startling ferocity but the Axis Forces, with the exception of a few local offensives in Tunisia, would never again regain the military initiative.

Within the 8th Army there was a feeling of exhilaration as the defeated enemy was pursued, but on 6 and 7 November the pursuit was hampered by a heavy rain storm. Rommel took full advantage of the situation and although his forces were constantly under air attack – brought out his German units in relatively good order. For the 8th Army the Battle of El-Alamein marked the start of a journey which was to last more than two and a half years.

After El-Alamein the 8th Army's progress to the Egyptian-Libyan frontier was to be swift, the first major objective was Mersa Matruh which possessed a small harbour; it fell to the 8th Armoured Brigade on 8 November. Sollum and Bardia fell shortly afterwards and by 11 November Egypt was at last cleared of all enemy troops.

As the victorious 8th Army advanced into Tunisia the first place of importance to fall was Tobruk, important stores were captured here as the retreating enemy had had little time to carry out demolitions. This town had changed hands more than once and its harbour had been made temporarily unusable by the Desert Air Force. On 12 November South African troops entered Tobruk, the first 8th Army units to do so.

Benghazi fell within a week and its port was found to be in better condition than had been anticipated, other parts of the town had been wrecked by ariel bombardment and there was no electricity, sewerage or piped water.

As the bulk of the 8th Army's transport proceeded up the old Roman road towards El- Agheila, the soldiers were astonished to see in this fertile land carpets of brightly coloured flowers. Not only were there flowers to be seen but in the red earth grew olive groves and trees covered the hills. The surrounding farms looked prosperous and on the walls was daubed in high letters the word 'DUCE', it was not long before the tommies added their own irreverent comments.

As the 8th Army pressed on through Libya major changes were made to the units that composed it as a result of political pressures; the Australian 9th Division was withdrawn to Palestine and soon afterwards returned to Australia; the 1st South African Division returned home to be refitted as an armoured division and was to later rejoin 8th Army in Italy; the bulk of the Greek Brigade returned to Egypt.

Rommel, quite correctly, made no attempt to defend either Tobruk or Benghazi, but what was not immediately clear was where the Panzer army would make its next stand. El-Agheila, where there was a strong naturally defensive position, was a possibility but the withdrawal continued. Rommel was shortening his supply lines and stood next on a line running south from Buerat.

As Rommel's supply lines became ever shorter so inevitably those of the 8th Army became longer, even with this handicap the advance continued with spectacular speed. Ports were opened, sappers improved the roads and railways and American Douglas aircraft ferried supplies to the advanced areas from Egypt. But logisticians always had, at the backs of their minds, the ever present danger of the army outrunning supplies.

As the advance rumbled on into December troops of the 8th Army were confronted with a strange sight rising out of the landscape; a gigantic stone arch stood before them in splendid isolation. Its correct name was 'the Arco dei Fileni' and it had been erected in the late 1930's on Mussolini's orders to commemorate the completion of a new highway joining Benghazi and Tripoli. It was located near the border of the provinces of Cyrenaica and Tripolitania and was known to all 8th Army personnel as 'Marble Arch'.

Montgomery issued orders that this fine monument was not to be defaced or destroyed and as the 8th Army left it behind them the conquest of Cyrenaica was completed, all that was left now of Mussolini's crumbling overseas empire was Tripolitania.

Marble Arch as viewed from the back of a lorry.
(Provided by Mr Mountford, ex 7th Green Howards)

When entering Mersa Matruh on 8 November, the 8th Army had received encouraging news from the outside world of the allied landing in French North Africa near Casablanca, Oran and Algiers. With little prospect of an invasion of France via the English Channel, this seemed to be the swiftest way of bringing other allied units into action in order to affect the war in Europe. As troops in command of North Africa could exercise control of the Mediterranean and at the same time pose a threat to Southern France and Italy, the freshly landed forces were still many miles from Libya but a meeting with the 8th Army in Africa – wherever that may be – was a logical outcome of present operations.

When Montgomery heard of the allied landings he was of the opinion that the meeting point should be somewhere east of Tripoli. At the start of 1943 the reports he received of what was happening in French North Africa led him to the conclusion that it would be the 8th Army, not the Anglo American Forces, which would have the task of taking Tripoli. He set to work laying his plans for the future.

On 3 and 4 January 1943 a violent storm did extensive damage to the port of Benghazi and, for a time, the supplies that would have been landed at this port had to be sent by road. But regardless of this misfortune, by the middle of January the 8th Army was ready to give battle in the Buerat area where Rommel had established a defensive line.

The 8th Army had by this time been organised into two corps, 10th and 30th, commanded respectively by Horrocks and Leese. The terrain over which the British advanced made the going hard; on either side of the coast road salt marshes barred the way and added to these natural barriers were the German demolitions of roads over several wadis. Montgomery decided to launch an offensive at Buerat on 15 January with the intention of entering Tripoli ten days later. If he did not, he knew it would be difficult to maintain his army indefinitely so far west of Benghazi without having control of another port. However, Rommel decided the issue by withdrawing – he was not yet ready to fight a major defensive battle.

The slow pace of 8th Army's advance was a constant anxiety to Montgomery but, on 19 January, the coastal town of Homs fell to the British and marked an important stage in the advance to Tripoli. Inland from Homs is the Plateau of Mizola, the far end of which climbs steadily upward to a massive escarpment – this escarpment dominates the final plains leading to Tripoli.

As the British pressed inexorably on towards Tripoli, no major actions were fought but effective enemy rear guards were continually encountered and took a steady toll in lives. Montgomery's hope of being in Tripoli, within ten days of giving battle at Buerat, was achieved and at 5am on 22 January a patrol of the 11th Hussars entered the town and found the streets deserted. Not long after came the advanced units of the 51st Highland Division with pipes playing.

Montgomery formally entered Tripoli on 23 January at noon and accepted the surrender of the city from the Vice-Governor of Tripolitania. The 8th Army had advanced a distance of 1,400 miles in three months since its victory at El-Alamein. Montgomery described this as being 'probably without parallel in history' in his personal message to his troops and paid tribute to the work of the Desert Air Force in the great feats that had been performed.

The port in Tripoli was in a sorry state, the retreating axis forces had been meticulous in their demolition work and had left it blocked by eight sunken ships; great craters had been blown into the quay and all the moles had been badly damaged. Work began immediately on re-opening the harbour and within two days landing craft were operating in it. A headquarters was quickly established in the Commando Peazza building and the defence and policing of the city was taken in hand, on a more ominous note a camp was found that contained 2,500 Jews - a foretaste of things to come in Europe.

At the end of the 8th Army's long trek across Libya its troops were in peak condition, the sick rate was only one man in one thousand per day. Montgomery commented 'you cannot want anything better than this', morale was as high as it could possibly be in any army – the troops of the desert army knew they were fine soldiers and with their unconventional eccentricity of dress they looked it.

This was the final stage in the liberation of Libya, from foreign colonial rule, by the 8th Army and the naval and Air Forces that supported it, Tripoli was now only a staging post in the North African campaign. The Germans had seen allied troops invade French North Africa and had responded by landing their own troops unopposed in the French protectorate of Tunisia. It now became very apparent that the task of ejecting them would be every bit as much the responsibility of Montgomery's 8th Army as of the force which had landed in North Africa in November.

The land of Tunisia, through which the 8th Army must now travel, is just a bit bigger than England and Wales. Evidence of former occupations are abundant, over the centuries the Romans, Normans, Moroccans, Spanish and Turks have left their mark on this land as they passed through. The most recent invaders were the French who arrived in 1881, of the numerous works which they undertook in Tunisia one was of particular concern to the 8th Army. This was the defensive line at Mareth, it was originally built to prevent any invasion of Tunisia from Italian occupied Libya and presented a formidable obstacle.

The allied force, consisting of the United States 2nd Corps and the British 1st Army, which had landed in French North Africa in November had at first made rapid progress, reaching the northern coastal area of Tunisia by mid November 1942 and occupying the town of Tebourba. The Germans launched heavy counter attacks, which drove them out of the town and checked the advance, heavy rains in December hampered further operations and it soon became clear the campaign was not going according to plan – much worse was to follow.

In mid February 1943 the 7th Armoured Division led the 8th Army into Tunisia. Few villages were encountered in this semi desert country but by 20 February Tataouine and Medenine had been taken by the victorious tommies. From the latter Montgomery planned his attack on the Mareth Line, during the initial advance no serious opposition had been offered by the axis forces as Rommel's attention was focused elsewhere, and on 14 February his forces launched a major offensive against the US 2nd Corps in western Tunisia at Kasserine. Rommel's armoured forces swept through the American units and the lines of communications of the forces advancing from the west were threatened.

This major reverse was serious enough to bring about a major change in the structure of command that had allowed it to happen. General Alexander was placed in command of all the allied forces in North Africa, this united force was known as the 18th Army Group and included the 8th Army, American forces and the British First Army. Alexander quickly sent a message to Montgomery urging him to put pressure on the enemy and so force him to withdraw troops and armour from the Kasserine area. This was quickly done and it was not long before Rommel was ordered to break out of the Kasserine area and to turn and face the 8th Army. As February drew to a close the Panzer Army Africa was withdrawing in the face of attacks from the 1st Army in the west and the 8th Army in the South.

However, Rommel's withdrawal on the Southern front was only temporary and he launched a new attack on the 8th Army's positions at Medenine on 6 March, the assault was headed by some one hundred and sixty tanks and went in under a convenient cover of fog. The units of the 8th Army could hear the rumble of the enemy armour long before they could see them but, when the sun broke through, the anti tank gunners found themselves faced with numerous targets moving across the open ground. A devastating fire was opened up on Rommel's forces as tank after tank was knocked out. Three times the badly mauled Panzers withdrew, re-grouped and came on again only to be met by a storm of steel from the anti tank guns. More than fifty of Rommel's precious tanks had been lost by the afternoon and the British had lost none, only one squadron being involved.

This action was the last to be fought by Rommel in Africa, as some days later he flew back to Germany because of poor health, in his diary he commented 'it was suicide to keep the German forces in Africa.' The command of the German forces in Tunisia now came to Juergen Von Arnim, he was an experienced soldier but his name was not shrouded in the particular mystique associated with that of Rommel.

Extending from the sea to a point twelve miles inland in the Matmata Hills was the Mareth Line, before these defensive positions there was a deep wide wadi that acted as a natural anti tank ditch. The line itself consisted of a system of deep trenches and concrete blockhouses, each designed to give covering fire to the next should it be attacked. Axis engineers, who had laid fields of mines and barbed wire entanglements in front of the forward positions, had worked on these formidable obstacles for many weeks.

Men of the Green Howards, in captured enemy slit trenches at Mareth, await the inevitable counter attack.   (Courtesy of the Imperial War Musum)

The Battle of Mareth began on 20 March 1943, heavy rain and cloud during the days before the battle had prevented any aerial reconnaissance but on 20 March the weather was fine. Following a massive barrage the troops of the 50th Northumbrian Division went into the attack on the main line, the men of the Green Howards, East Yorkshires and Durham Light Infantry pressed on across the wadi and into the trenches and emplacements to fight one of their most viscous battles of the desert campaign. A narrow bridgehead was forced on the enemy side, but this provoked an even more violent assault from German armoured and infantry units, more men pressed forward into this maelstrom of fire and steel and a few tanks crossed the wadi until the crossing point was blocked. No anti tank guns arrived for the hard pressed 50th, and one by one the British tanks in the bridgehead fell prey to their heavier German counterparts. To compound this tragic situation, radio contact was lost and the small numbers of men left in the bridgehead were forced back to the wadi, until after more than two days fighting, the order was given to withdraw leaving the ground littered with their dead and the dead of their enemies.

Montgomery had failed in his attempt to force a decision by a frontal assault at Mareth; this was a serious set back. He now regrouped his forces and whilst holding the enemies' attention at Mareth with the 51st and 50th Divisions, sent the 10th Corps under Horrocks in a long arc to outflank the Axis positions by driving in a north and then north westerly direction, south of Djebel Tebaga in the direction of El-Hamma.

The 90th Light Division took the full force of this left hook as the 2nd Armoured Brigade struck deep into the German lines. The German units fell back, regrouped and counter attacked, but the position soon became untenable and Monty's left hook had torn a great hole in the German flank. Then came a deadly night attack by the New Zealanders who's units swept in rear of the 90th Light and threatened to drive to the sea. The British advance then halted and before it could roll forward again an Africa Corps Assault Group attacked with two Panzer Divisions driving into the New Zealanders flank, bringing the advance to a halt. While this had been going on, Axis forces from Mareth had been withdrawing to the next defensive position along the coast.

By the end of March the noose was being tightened around the Axis forces in Tunisia, while the 8th Army had been battling its way through the Mareth Line, Pattons 2nd US Corps was not idle and had greatly assisted Montgomery by drawing away the 10th Panzer Division from the battle. By 17 March 2nd US Corps had occupied Gafsa. El-Guetar, some fifteen miles further east, was entered the next day and Maknassy on 22 March. Towards the end of that month Alexander directed 2nd Corps to make for the Gabes Road and on 30 March the attack began, the American armoured units ran head long into the well organised German defensive screen and did not get very far. Well sited and mobile artillery, anti tank guns and mine fields took a heavy toll of the advancing tanks, the skilled German defenders offered such determined resistance that the American forces were reduced to a bit by bit advance. The fact that Patton's Corps made little headway was less important than the threat which they offered to General Messe's 1st Panzer Army, a threat which brought about the move of 21st Panzer Division to reinforce 10th Panzer Division opposite Patton and so lighten the forces opposite 8th Army. From the probing attacks on the western and south western sectors of the front the emphasis then fell upon the southern flank where the 8th Army, now having regrouped after the fight at Mareth, was pressing the Axis forces into a killing ground where the campaign could be brought to a speedy conclusion.

The position chosen by the Axis Forces to make their next stand, was the last natural barrier barring the way to the coastal plain of Tunisia from the south. It stretched 18 miles inland from the sea to Djebel Haidoudi in the west, the position was known to the British as the Akarit line because of the wide and deep Wadi Akarit that stretched some four miles inland from the coast. The Germans knew it as the Chott line because the western flank rested on the great salt marshes of the Chott El-Fedjadj. In winter these marshes could not be crossed in vehicles, but in April were drying out quickly and were not such a complete obstacle; this fact does not appear to have been known to the British – but the Axis forces were fully aware of it.

The coastal sector of this formidable position was dominated by two features; to the east and nearest to the coast was Djebel Roumana, a bare ridge that ran nearly parallel to the coast road. This feature was steep sided and 500 feet high, making it impassable to tracked and wheeled vehicles. To the west of Roumana lies reasonably level country which then becomes rolling. At the western end of this open ground springs up the Djebel Tebaga Fatnassa, this feature was a horrible looking labyrinth of steep sided hills, tangled escarpments, gullies and peaks. Dominating the whole feature was a conical hill, some 900 feet high, called Zouai. In between all of these crags and crests was woven a maze of corridors twisting this way and that. To the west of Fatnassa what remained of the position was protected by a range of hills named the Djebel Zemlet El-Beida, these were 500 feet high and ran in a south westerly direction to where Djebel Haidoudi stood sentinel over the metalled road linking Gabes with El-Guettar and Gafsa. Rommel had always favoured making a stand at Akarit rather than at Mareth because of its natural advantages, however it lacked defence in depth and its field works were not elaborate.

Priority had been given to the Mareth position before 27 March and it was not until after this date that work began to organise the Akarit defences, responsibility for this work was given to 20th Corps to construct mine fields and other obstacles. Near the coast the Wadi Akarit had been scarped (sides made steeper) making a formidable barrier, it was then extended to Roumana by an anti tank ditch. From Roumana's western end another deep ditch ran all the way to Fatnassa, wire obstacles were not in any great quantities and approximately 4,000 mines had been sown, mostly between the coastal road and Roumana and in patches along the rolling down land between Roumana and Fatnassa.

On 31 March Montgomery conferred with his Corps Commanders and laid out his plan for forcing the Akarit position, the enemy appeared to be holding the entire front with the 21st Corps and two weak Panzer Divisions – 15th and 21st. As the terrain was not suitable for manoeuvre, Monty decided to attack the front with a division of 30th Corps and when they had made a breach send 10th Corps through it – New Zealand Division leading and 1st Armoured Division following. Reconnaissance of the whole area began at all levels and it soon became evident that the

B.G.S. of 30 Corps (Leese) briefing troops before the battle.
(Courtesy of the Imperial War Museum)

enemy was present in greater numbers than was at first thought. The 20th and 21st Corps were detected and their component parts identified correctly. General Leese took the decision to use two infantry divisions for the attack with the intention of seizing Roumana and the line west of it including Zouai.

The 51st Highland Division and the 4th Indian Division was to break in with the latter seizing Roumana. However, General Tucker of the 4th Indian Division dissented claiming that any attack between Roumana and Fatnassa would be overlooked from the high ground to the west and caught in a cross fire. He reasoned that the Fatnassa Massif was the key to the whole position and that if it was taken, the enemy's flank would be pierced, so rendering the whole of the Akarit position untenable. 10th Corps could then advance around the western end of these obstacles and cut the enemy forces off before they could disengage. Neither Tucker nor Wimberley of the 51st Highland Division liked the proposed plan, but Tucker was now guaranteeing to take the whole of the Fatnassa Massif at night – before the attack in the Roumana sector began, he reasoned that the enemy would be of the opinion that an attack on Fatnassa would be impossible.

However, his troops had sent out patrols in the area and believed that for troops trained in mountain warfare, such as both Tucker's brigades, this position could be taken. To hold such a tangle of hills and crests would, in Tucker's opinion, require a mass of infantry which the enemy did not have, and so what appeared at first sight to be the strongest part of the enemy line was in fact the weakest. These views were put before Leese by the two Divisional Commanders, both Leese and Montgomery agreed and a new plan was draughted.

On 3 April the final plan was revealed. 4th Indian Division was to take Fatnassa on the night of 5/6 April and bridge the anti tank ditch at its foot. On 6 April the 50th Division would force the anti tank ditch in the centre, while the 51st Highland Division stormed Djebel Roumana and the defences south west of it, building crossings over the Wadi Akarit.

The 1st Armoured Division, on the evening of 5 April, would divert the enemy by demonstrating against the 164th Light Division at the Haidoudi Pass – much to the understandable annoyance of the 4th Indian Division who relied on surprise for their attack. While in the coastal sector 201st Guards Brigade would do the same on the morning of 6 April. 10th Corps would press through gaps forced at the eastern or western end of Roumana.

The timing of 8th Army's attack was to be governed solely by the shortest time required for preparations. Monty could not afford to wait for the next full moon and it was possible that changing from his usual tactic of assault by moonlight he could gain surprise. The enemy expected 8th Army's main attack to fall on Roumana and were confident of a few days grace before the blow fell. The three divisional thrust and especially the inclusion of Fatnassa was to be a great shock. The Axis forces at the start of April could muster 178 operational aircraft out of 324, plus 65 from the Italian Air Force. The British Desert Air Force at that time consisted of 5 squadrons of bombers (Boston's and Baltimore's), 8 squadrons of fighter bombers (Kittyhawks), 5 squadrons of fighters (spitfires and hurricanes), a tank busting squadron (Hurricanes IID) and three squadrons of reconnaissance aircraft. The American section consisted of 2 squadrons of bombers (Mitchells) and 4 of fighter-bombers and 4 fighters (all Kittyhawks).

These brave air crews flew above the battlefield swaying the fortunes of the men who fought on it, added to their numerical superiority there was also the powerful strategic bomber and coastal forces of Northwest Africa, Malta and Middle East Air Forces.

Air operations between 29 March and 5 April had a direct effect on the battle at the Wadi Akarit. Long and short distance reconnaissance flights were in the air constantly, any enemy aircraft in flight and on the ground fell prey to the widely sweeping formations of fighters and any enemy that lived or moved on the ground was blasted by the marauding fighter bombers who kept up a relentless barrage from the air.

Between 29 March and 1 April the Germans lost 51 aircraft in Tunisia, consequently the 8th Army enjoyed the benefits in almost complete freedom from aerial observation and attack. Between the above dates the Desert Air Force flew 2,630 sorties for a total loss of 5 RAF and 8 US aircraft. Max Perkins was a young fighter pilot at the time with 601 Squadron RAF:

"During the retreat from Mareth by the German Army our wing was flying from Gabes aerodrome, air activity was high as ground attack Kittyhawks were busy strafing and harassing the retreating forces. Near dusk one evening our Engineering Officer (Mr Jack Keeble. F/LT) requested air and gun tests on two aircraft in order to put them on morning serviceability. F/LT Jerry Westrana (a New Zealander) and myself were the only pilots left in operations.

Normally these were quick flights whereby we would test fire into the sea, Jerry, noting the retreating transports along the desert road, decided we should have a go and test on live targets. These retreating forces were continually being subjected to air attacks – and as we began to fire on them the whole shoreline seemed to open up on us, we were caught in heavy 20mm and 40mm ground fire. As we broke away Jerry was trying to stay under the firing and clipped his wing on some ground object. My flight path was somewhat higher as we made our turn for home and I received a hit from ground fire, this led me to climb in case a bale out became necessary and in heading for more open and less active ground I noted a flat alkaline area with some marshes. As I checked my gauges for possible engine problems the sky lit up with tracer in a pattern I will

Max Perkins, Spitfire pilot 601 Squadron Royal Air Force.

visualise to my dying day – as I looked down I saw 60 plus Tiger tanks in a staggered semi circle.

My aircraft was then struck head on by a tracer round which took out part of my propeller. I continued over this area and noted that ground personnel stopped in their tracks and did not look up. By now the aircraft was shuddering quite violently, yet a check on my instruments showed all to be normal (perhaps part of the problem was me shaking).

The spitfire was nursed back to base at reduced power and with constant severe vibrations. My debriefing with the Intelligence Officer put the Western Air Force and the 8th Army into panic when the locations and numbers of tanks were disclosed. That night the search was on by the light of flares and by day the Tactical Reconnaissance; no tanks were to be located.

After my debriefing I was having a late supper in the mess when Jack Keebles – our Engineering Officer – reappeared to tell me two engine bolts had been broken through, another thick bolt was ready to go and only one had been left in reasonable condition. He indicated that if I had been in the air for many more minutes the engine would have fallen out.

When the tanks could not be located after two or three days of searching I was called before the Air Commodore at Command for further consultation – perhaps my map references were incorrect or they were dummy tanks etc. I stuck with my story and observations and took some ragging from my fellow pilots. A few days passed before the CO came to me in the mess and said 'Perkins – the tanks you saw were real and attacked at Wadi Akarit today.'

I did not fight at Wadi Akarit, but well do I recall my pre-battle experience."

At the start of April, Messe and Bayerlein predicted that the assault on Akarit would come at full moon during the third week. The troops on the ground however expected it daily. The Axis High Command, judging by the activity of the British artillery, deduced that the sector between Djebel Roumana and the coast road was where the main assault would be delivered. Von Sponeck, Messe and Bayerlein all agreed that the key to the whole position was Roumana – a view in direct opposition to Tuckers'. Even so, no more than three small detachments of 200th Panzer Grenadier Regiment were used to reinforce this position.

The battle plan was now agreed upon, commanders had briefed their troops and the 8th Army squared up to the enemy for what would be their last great set piece battle against the old enemy – Panzer Army Africa. The stage was set, all that remained was to give battle, with the promise of an opportunity to finish off once and for all the now badly battered, but far from finished, Axis forces - the 'Battle of the Wadi Akarit' was about to begin.

'If I had the money, old man, I'd buy up these wadis and put 'em out of bounds
to all troops.'

The Two Types by Jon. A Contemporary Cartoon

CHAPTER ONE

THE LEFT FLANK
THE 4th INDIAN DIVISION ATTACKS

GENERAL TUCKER. KCIE. CB. DSO. OBE.
COMMANDER: 4th INDIAN DIVISION

"LOOK BEFORE YOU LEAP,

BUT IF YOU MEAN LEAPING - DON'T
LOOK LONG.

FOR THE WEAKEST FENCE WILL THEN
GROW STIFF AND THE STIFFEST DOUBLY
STRONG."

On 1 April 1943, the 7th and 5th Brigades concentrated in the area around Gabes and found themselves placed at four hours notice for the move forward for the coming battle. Late on 2 April they were transported up the coast road to the village of Oudref, a little village situated amid palm plantations.

Patrols from both brigades probed the enemy defences and gained valuable intelligence about the enemy dispositions in the days before the attack. In the rear area a large sand map, that carefully reproduced the Fatnassa Massif, had been constructed under the watchful eye of Colonel Showers and Captain Hawkes of the Royal Sussex. Gurkha officers and non commissioned officers, under the supervision of Subadar Major Narbahadur Gurung, spent many hours studying and familiarising themselves with the exact lie of the land, for it was upon these men that this whole desperate enterprise would depend. Captain Donald Ramsay-Brown, MC, (later Lt Colonel) 1/2nd King Edward's VII's Own Gurkha Rifles 'B' Company, was responsible for much of the patrolling on 7th Brigades front:

> "We were able to do our patrolling and planning with very detailed preparation, right down to having lines of advance for each rifle company. The 2nd Gurkhas had achieved a very high standard in patrolling and we dominated no-man's land. We performed one or two notable raids where we took prisoners and this was done by this 'B' Company of mine. There was one particular platoon that was very highly trained.
>
> The first task was to get out on patrol and see where the junction between the Germans and Italians was. This was achieved quite accurately as we later discovered; while this was happening we built a large sand model on a reverse slope about nine or ten miles away from Akarit, visibility was pretty good so you couldn't be too close. This sand model was made to represent not only the lateral but also the vertical height, so people would be able, by lying down looking at the model from certain points, to say well that will be the outline for the next move. Everyone down to the Junior NCO's were taken there for sessions where they got to know the feature.
>
> Whilst this was happening, for something like ten days before the attack was due, I had patrols out every night. We marked and got to know all the approaches and because of our domination of no-man's land our patrols moved very freely, and night after night they got up to within 50 or 70 yards of the forward defending line. If any extra wire was being put up we were able to spot it. Finally when the day came we felt we really knew what was to happen, on this occasion we felt we knew what we were doing and what was expected of us."

Gurkhas preparing a meal, 5th April. (Courtesy of the Imperial War Museum)

Captain Ronald Perkin, MC, patrolled in no-man's land in an attempt to gather information on the enemy with men of 'A' Company 4/16th Punjab Regiment:

"On or about 1 April 1943 we, the Brigade, were settled down just South of the Wadi Akarit awaiting the next phase of the campaign. I and Captain W G Popple MC (commanding 'A' Company) were sent for by our CO (Lt Col H A Hughes) and told to carry out a reconnaissance patrol to the hills immediately to the west of the road that runs north to south and at the point where the road enters the hills. The object was to ascertain whether there were any enemy positions to the west of the road. The patrol was to be carried out that night. At about midnight we set off with two sepoys. When we got to within 100 or so yards of the hill we decided to leave the sepoys there and go on by ourselves, as two people would make less noise.

We went on very slowly for about a hundred yards and then heard voices to our front. We had reached a point where there was a small valley running northwards, so we inched our way up this valley and could hear Italians talking amongst themselves. It was very dark and we could not see anything and, without walking into the Italians, we could not get much further so we turned back and returned to the sepoys and then our lines. All we had established was that the enemy were in positions just west of the road. A few days later, probably on 3 or 4 April, we were called to Bn HQ and given the orders/plans for our Division/Brigade's part in the forthcoming 8th Army attack on the Wadi Akarit defensive position."

Captain Cyril Mount, Royal Artillery, was an official war artist and made several studies during the Tunisian campaign. Positions for his unit, 11th Field Regiment, had been found and the guns had to be in position by first light on 6 April. The move forward was not without incident:

"Sitting at the side of the road on a jerry-can that had been well and truly holed, I was making a drawing of the 'road back'. It wound a long way back until it was lost in the shimmering heat haze; back to Gabes to Medinine, Mareth, Tripoli, Sirte, Benghazi, and Alamein, one hell of a long way since October last. Now it's the beginning of April and it's still a sort of desert - barren, dusty, rocky - except there are now patches of tough grass and tiny undernourished poppies and other flowers, and most amazingly, no flies! My desert sores are almost healed.

This morning I had been at the O.P. since early light, told to draw a

panorama of the Fatnassa range ahead of us. God knows why, we're on the move again tomorrow and a panorama is only valid for where it's drawn from! Also did a drawing of the O.P. itself with El-Oudref in the hollow below, a small town with a lot of palm trees 'liberated' by the New Zealanders the day before, but they've moved on.

The grave of a tank crew next to their knocked out Sherman.

They must have been up here on this ridge, the O.P. sanger is facing north, the German ones are facing down the road I've been drawing and apart from some Jerry garbage there are also empty British ration and petrol tins around.

Lower down the road is a brewed up tank in which some poor sods must have roasted and, on the crest opposite, three piles of stones with helmets hanging from their wooden crosses.

The drawing finished, I wander down towards Battery HQ, easy to find because the guns are firing concentrations again. I was greeted by Ernie K my wireless oppo, lying reading Huxley's 'Along the Road'!! with his back propped against his bedding roll. Where the fuck have you been? they've been looking for you, the O.P. party has been back ages?" The connah wagon had been and gone, but he'd saved me a mess tin of cold stew.

I'd barely finished when the Stukas came screaming out of the setting sun making us grab the dirt, but as usual didn't hit anything, later we heard the Bofor boys had got two of them.

When it was dark we moved out and along the road through Oudref to the north of the town, to positions much nearer the now menacing range I'd drawn twice this day and in front of which was the wadi itself. Word had already got around that this was going to be a much tougher do' than Mareth. Was Montgomery going to try another WW1 full frontal attack like Mareth? Just after first light we were stonked, it must have been an Italian battery, not very accurate and no airbursts! Obviously they can see us but we are not the only mob on this plain, there are plenty of other targets. We crawl out sheepishly and squat around with the Battery HQ gang to brew up and fry some bully and bacon rissoles, made with mashed up biscuit and eggs. Feeling much better, until I'm told that tomorrow I am to drive the (Battery Commander) BC in BHQ jeep to do a recce of an even further forward position. Spend the rest of the day with strange forebodings. The BC has been with us for nearly a month now, but I still haven't got to know him despite being his wireless operator in X AOV (armoured observation vehicle called Tatanagars because the thin steel body and wooden floor was built in India at Tatanagar around an American engine and chassis).

The next day, 5 April we set off mid morning with two jeeps, two other officers and their GPAs (gun position assistants) up the road towards Fatnassa for about a mile then turn off across some very rocky ground, marking the turn off point with a dannaert spike and empty 'flimsy' petrol can marked with the battery no (71). The troop positions had no sooner been plotted and marked then a salvo of 88 airbursts blackened the sky behind us. I drove like a mad thing back towards the road, the BC clinging on and cursing. Back onto the road and another burst ahead of us.

This is it, I thought, we're bracketed, but miracle - no more came and we hightailed it down the road back to the battery as fast as the jeep would go. I slept through that afternoon and missed two meals but I don't think many people were in the mood to eat, I just scooped some pilchards out of their tin with a couple of biscuits and brewed up a strong sweet brew of char (O.P. vehicles always have a good stash of 'extras'). I would have preferred to ride in X but am ordered to drive behind in the jeep with a young officer who cannot drive. Keep thinking about this morning and how close we seemed to the enemy and now here we have the whole battery moving up to be in full view when it gets light. We are told that the Gurkhas, Essex and Punjabis are to go in at 4.30am to take Fatnassa and surrounding high points and O.Ps. Let's hope they are successful then it won't be too bad. Capt. Dickson is going up with the Essex as F.O.O. and Bob Mitchell with an 18 set.

So here we are trundling along this starlit road, amazing how bright the stars become and how much can be seen, not a good road, barely two vehicles width and full of pot holes. Suddenly X in front comes to a halt and as I brake, see something else looming in front, a huge tank is slewed half across the road. I hadn't been looking out for the marker but I have a very strong feeling we had gone past it, the BC was still standing up in front of X glaring at the tank when I went over and said as sweetly as I could "Sir, I've got a feeling we have come too far, I don't remember seeing this thing this morning" I was unprepared for his answer, "Bloody nonsense Mount, right hand down Walker" (they were his last intelligible words).

Tommy Walker revved up and turned to bypass the tank, there was an almighty flash and roar and X went over on it's off side front like a huge shot elephant. All hell then seemed to break loose, The BC screaming

Absolution before battle. 5th April (Courtesy of the Imperial War Museum)

about his legs, Walker shouting he couldn't see, people running up from vehicles behind, including Bdr. Courtney, Medical Orderly, and on top of it all, my passenger shouting for me to "get back in the jeep to go and fetch the M.O. !"

By then I had already climbed into X and put my arm round the BC's shoulder to ease him from where he is hanging over the side, but he slides to the floor. Courtney tells me to lift his legs from the hole in the floor whilst he lifts his shoulders but … there are no legs, just warm wet strings and slime. BC is quiet now, maybe he's passed out … or died, or maybe Courtney has given him a jab … I was feeling sick with the smell of warm blood and petrol, and others were there now to help, apart from which, my passenger Lieut is becoming more agitated. I unhook my back pack from the side of X and run back to him, he makes me turn the jeep around so that we can "go and fetch the M.O." He is petrified that I should go too near the sandy edges of the tarmac and so I do a careful ten point turn.

As we drive back down the column I get a non stop verbal barrage "keep away from the edge", "drive faster", "don't slow down" of course I slow at each vehicle to tell them to 'turn round, the verges are mined, we have come too far'. He becomes increasingly angry, especially when I remind him that the BC isn't likely to need the M.O. and that as an officer it is his job to get the vehicles and guns back to where they should be. This was obviously the final straw, he unclipped his webbing holster pulled out his 38, waved it in my face saying he will shoot me if I spoke or slowed down again! I replied that he had better get out first because if he shot me whilst I was driving we would both go into the minefield!

We had already passed about 20 or more vehicles well strung out, and in a gap I thought I spotted the marker, so at the risk of being shot, I pulled over and saw that is was in fact the turn off marker. At that moment a GB 15cwt wireless truck came along with the gun position officer standing up in front, I explained quickly what had happened. He was one of the officers on that morning's recce and so was able to lead his guns and vehicles down to their position.

When I got back to the jeep my passenger had disappeared. I never saw him again. In retrospect I felt that it was he personally who needed the M.O., particularly after the incident with the revolver. 'A' Troop and other vehicles eventually appeared and duly turned off, only to discover the 69th Brigade HQ had occupied their recce'd position, and a fresh position had to be found and prepared."

7th INFANTRY BRIGADE
COMMANDING OFFICER:
BRIGADIER O.D.E.T. LOVETT CBE, DSO

As darkness fell on the night of 5 April, the 5th and 7th Brigades began their approach march - a distance of some six miles - which brought each company column to within three thousand yards of the first line of the Fatnassa escarpments.

A new moon hung in a perfect sky as the troops filed forward shouldering their heavy loads. Standing outside Divisional Headquarters General Tucker watched the silent heavily laden men trudge along star track as it crossed the main road. This must have been a heart searching moment for Tucker, he had refused the original plan of battle proposed by the Corps Commander and had committed his troops to an unorthodox operation upon which his career now depended. Disengagement in this terrain was nigh impossible and for the men of the lead brigade, the 7th, it was to be victory or destruction. The night was cool and a ground mist clung to the earth as the troops disappeared from Tucker's sight over the rolling crests to their assembly areas, he commented to a friend "It is now in the lap of the gods, only one thing worries me, perhaps I have asked too much of them and have set them a task beyond human accomplishment."

Star track was full of vehicles belonging to the 50th Division as they moved up the line in preparation for the coming battle. However, by 2015 hours the first battalion of 7th Brigade had reached its forward deployment position, the battalion signallers were well in advance of the main body and were flashing back directional signals to the companies still moving forward, the last signaller was within five hundred yards of the enemy's forward defensive line. To the north could be seen the great arc, in silhouette, of the Wadi Akarit front. To 7th Brigade's front was the black wall of the frontal escarpment with the high peak of Point 275 serving as a direction post. The whole scene was occasionally lit up as enemy planes dropped chandelier flares in the area searching for signs as to when the expected attack would begin.

Cpt Donald Ramsey-Brown. MC. was at the head of his men of 'B' Company as the 1/2nd Gurkhas pressed on into the darkness:

"When the night for the attack came I had my forward patrols laying out almost continuous lines of tape, this guided each of the formations forward. Our role was to get in and deliver our attack before the 50th or 51st Highland Divisions started because then all the noise would start. My patrols were well forward in small groups from the start, conditions were ideal. One of the things one quickly realised was that with the whole brigade moving, with the best will in the world, it seemed so noisy. I was forward with the leading platoon

22

making for the start line and I could hear this noise behind even though they were moving silently."

At 2330 hours on 5 April the word was received from the Brigade Major that the attack was to go in, 'D' Company, 1/2nd Gurkhas, moved off at once making for the rocky chimney between the escarpments. The remainder of the battalion, 'A', 'B' and 'C' Companies advanced to the left in arrowhead formation - battalion HQ at the centre. The tall foreboding peak of Point 275 served as a direction finder, until the troops closed with the objective and it disappeared behind the black wall of the frontal escarpment which stretched out like a curtain around the main massif. The leading sections of 'C' Company moved forward as silent as ghosts until they stood under this feature, followed by 'A' and 'B' Companies who took cover in a narrow wadi.

1/2nd GURKHA RIFLES
COMMANDING OFFICER: LT. COL. L. J. SHOWERS. DSO

'C' Company began to pick their way silently up the slope and the night claimed its first victim as the cat eyed Gurkhas detected the first enemy post. Drawing their kukris they moved in without a sound finding the first sentry fast asleep, there was a throaty gurgle as the knife struck home and the Gurkhas surged up the escarpment killing all who dare stand. Screams broke the still night air to be answered by shouts from above. All along the escarpment crest enemy outposts, in stone sangars, opened fire over the heads of the attackers, pelting the slopes with Italian grenades.

The assailants of 'C' Company quickly scrambled to the top of the escarpment to close with the enemy who were firing wildly into the night.

An eerie sound now filled the air, this was the men chattering in their high pitched voices that blended into an excited whimper as they guided each other to the kill - the need for concealment now over. 'C' Company burst over the crest cutting down the enemy where they found them.

Without warning red tracer streaked over the heads of 'C' Company. Fortunately, the men were in dead ground over the crest and the fire passed over them, this burst had come from the rear as the 4/16th Punjab's rushed forward to enter the battle on the left of the Rass El-Zouai feature. 'A' and 'B' Companies now moved up the boulder strewn slopes and as they did so, enemy aircraft dropped chandelier flares in the area in order to ascertain the direction and strength of the attack. The whole place was lit up giving the attackers a clear view of their objectives, one officer commented "The Guy Fawkes show was grand for it showed us exactly where we wanted to go."

'A' and 'B' Companies plunged downward into a bowl shaped hollow below the main Rass El-Zouai feature, the enemy were fought at close quarters, 'B' Company veered to the right sweeping over a small amphitheatre enclosed by a number of ridges.

Jemadar Bhimbahadur Rana led 8 Platoon against an anti tank gun position that covered a narrow path. Havildar Bibahadur Pun ran forward and leapt into the enemy position killing three with his Kukri and wounding others, the way was now open. Within an hour 'B' Company had advanced nearly a mile along the escarpment into the enemy's defences, the going might have been much slower had not the enemy been good enough to cast light on the situation. 'B' Company now stood well in the rear of Point 275 and at 0130 hours its success signal went up.

At the same time, 'A' Company made for the tall tower of Point 275 and ran into a well manned outpost line on high ground, Captain Stubbs led his men into the attack overrunning the position and killing the defenders. They approached the eastern slopes of Point 275 and found them to be unscalable. 'A' Company worked around the foot of the pinnacle as enemy machine gunners blazed wildly into the night from the crests above and groped their way up the western slopes.

The going here was easier and the ascent made simple: the leading platoons reached the crest and mopped up an artillery observation post that gave little trouble - the first objective had been won.

The success signal flares sent up by 'A' and 'B' Companies of the 1/2nd Gurkhas was the first contact 7th Brigade HQ had made with the attacking troops. The enemy had laid down a curtain of fire upon the approaches of Rass El-Zouai in which the Gurkha signallers had been badly hit. 7th Brigade HQ had received a direct hit from a salvo of mortar bombs destroying the infantry radio sets and those of the artillery observation groups who were in the process of arranging supporting fire. In this attack, Brigadier Lovett was hit but remained at his post, Lt. Colonel Showers of the Gurkhas went forward in the hope of getting news about the situation. For an hour no news was received from 'A' and 'B' Companies who had gone off the map, and from the all important corridor between the escarpments into which 'D' Company had entered, came the crack of grenades and the chatter of heavy exchanges of fire.

Meanwhile, 'D' Company pressed forward up the corridor between the escarpments into the heart of the enemies defensive system, if the break in was to be exploited this passage must be cleared in the first hours of the battle. Two battalions of the 5th Brigade had closed up and waited impatiently for the signal to follow through, the fate of the whole attack depended on a swift and favourable decision in this passage.

Only a narrow cleft gave access to the corridor which widened into an arena five hundred yards across bounded by cliffs two hundred feet high.

At the far end of this arena a steep and narrow path led up to the crest of the main escarpment. Machine guns, mortar teams and anti tank guns covered every yard of ground on this approach, undeterred 'D' Company closed with the entrance of the corridor, Subedar Lalbahadur Thapa with two sections of 16 Platoon led the way. The first enemy outpost, sangar, was approached without challenge, the Italian sentries were taken by surprise as fearsome figures leapt out of the darkness at them - not a man was left alive. Immediately every defensive position swept the area with machine gun and mortar fire as the Gurkhas raced up the widening passage, grenades rained down from the escarpments and the night reverberated to their blasts.

Many men fell in the first rush but, without pause and with little room for manoeuvre, the dauntless Subedar led the charge overwhelming the next machine gun nest. He killed two men with his Kukri and two more with his pistol. By now the majority of his men had fallen in the hail of continuous fire that was flying everywhere, only rifleman Harakbahadur Gurung and Rifleman Inrabahadur Gurung followed as the Subedar gained the winding track leading to the crest of the escarpment. The top was guarded by a machine gun nest which covered the approach, quickly the three men closed with this position, Lalbahadur Thapa leapt in among the enemy killing two with his Kukri, two more fell before the weapons of the riflemen and those that were able fled screaming from this terrible foe.

The corridor was now cleared and a great victory won - the way was now open. Lalbahadur Thapa and the two riflemen stood guard at the top of the path as 'D' Company passed through, fanning out along the top of the escarpment. The Gurkhas silently moved in on the remaining sangars and machine gun nests, using bayonets and Kukris they quickly eliminated any resistance.

While Lalbahadur Thapa had been clearing the corridor Havildar Manilal Thapa had led 17 Platoon against an enemy position on high ground that covered the extreme right flank of 7th Brigade. The enemy was dispatched in a silent attack using only bayonets and Kukries, this done Captain Nichol ordered the same platoon to clear the right hand escarpment of the corridor. 17 Platoon swept along the crest in fine style destroying many machine gun nests and killing squads of bombers that had been raining down grenades on Lalbahadur Thapa's men. The little Gurkhas leapt through the darkness at their enemies and struck them down with the Kukri - those that survived were hurled down the cliff face.

And so it was, that a full two hours before 8th Army's main assault began, the key objectives on high ground had all been seized, the attacking companies now waited for the dawn as they busied themselves with consolidating their gains. Enemy artillery batteries and mortar teams reacted vigorously and in the deluge of fire - many, if not all, wireless sets were destroyed, at the same time lamp signallers and runners were wounded or killed one after the other. In an attack that was built around such a tight timetable in which the prime ingredient of success was speed, this disruption of communications could have proved disastrous.

From the black forms of the escarpments came screams and yells as the flames from musketry fire and the crack of bombs lit up the darkness; at Divisional and Corps Head Quarters officers waited tensely for news of the battle that was going on up the blue. At 0215 hours news of the successful outcome of the struggle around Rass El-Zouai was transmitted to Divisional, Corps and 8th Army Head Quarters.

As daylight broke the darkness, two thousand yards beyond the high peak of point 275, the long dark finger of the Mesreb El-Alig loomed to the north, 'B' Company crossed the intervening broken ground and before the sun had risen stood at the base of this feature. Three platoons dug in while the fourth was sent by Captain Marley-Clarke, under the command of Jemadar Bishanbahadur Gurung, to clear the narrow crest.

From Fatnassa a hail of machine gun fire descended upon the attacking Gurkhas and from the right, from the rolling ridges of Oudane El-Hachana, came a deadly stream of enemy artillery shells and mortar bombs. Many of the advancing Gurkhas were cut down in this withering fire until only nine were left to continue the advance and on the flanks the enemy were closing in. Jemedar Gurung stood up in full view of his own men and the enemy and rallied his troops to follow him, as he led his men forward at the trot the enemy broke before them and were driven back as the brave group turned to flank. With only a few of his men left standing Jemedar Gurung swept the remaining enemy from El-Alig.

As 'B' Company cleared El-Alig, 'C' Company had come up on their right with the intention of striking at Fatnassa, the last high ground to the north. However, strong counter attack forces were now mustering in the valley through which the military road ran and the long crescent of escarpment between Point 275 and El-Alig was virtually undefended. The slopes littered with boulders and scrub made perfect cover and should the enemy gain the crest, both forward companies would be in danger. Leaving one platoon to maintain contact with 1/9th Gurkha Rifles, the commanders of 'B' and 'C' Companies spread their men in small groups along the threatened crest.

1st BATTALION ROYAL SUSSEX REGIMENT

COMMANDING OFFICER: LT. COL. C. E. A. FIRTH. DSO

Deploying immediately behind the 1/2nd Gurkhas came the 1st Royal Sussex. Shortly after 2100 hours on 5 April the South Countrymen moved forward across the plain on a bearing parallel to the Gurkhas but some way to their right. The troops passed the entrance to the corridor as they advanced, moving into a re-entrant of low ground which progressed upward to the lower slopes of the El-Meida feature.

As the Gurkhas launched their attack at the enemy, the forward Royal Sussex companies suffered many casualties as enemy mortar and artillery defensive fire rained upon them. As with the Gurkhas, the battalion's radio sets were destroyed, the adjutant was wounded and companies operated independently: but by 0130 hours they were just one thousand yards short of their objective. In the prevailing confusion, the attack lost direction and began to fall behind timing, Lt. Colonel Firth put in a request for a directional crash shoot on El-Meida at 0230 hours.

No sooner had the request been heard when the divisional artillery sent lines of tracer streaking through the air toward the objective, accompanied by heavy concentrations of artillery fire. At 0400 hours a second barrage pounded the crest and slopes of El-Meida and under its cover 'D', 'B' and 'C' Companies worked their way up the slopes and along the rugged and broken lip of the crest. It took only thirty minutes to clear the crest of El-Meida and six hundred yards of the western end of the anti tank ditch - three hundred prisoners were taken from the Spezia Division.

A reconnaissance party was led forward to Oudane El-Hachana by Lt. Colonel Firth, only to find enemy light armour in the area. By dawn 1st Royal Sussex were busy consolidating their new positions that had been won at a cost of 8 killed and 59 wounded.

On the right of the 4th Indian Division the 50th Division's assault on the anti tank ditch was thundering on. The 5th Battalion East Yorkshire

Regiment, on the 50th's left, had been pinned down by a storm of enemy fire. One platoon of 1st Royal Sussex moved behind the anti tank ditch and attacked the forces in that area that were firing upon the Yorkshiremen; a number of prisoners were taken and four 65 mm guns captured, these artillery pieces were immediately turned about and used to great effect on enemy batteries and mortar teams that were in action.

4/16th PUNJAB REGIMENT
COMMANDING OFFICER: LT. COL. H. A. HUGHES. MBE. DSO

The 4/16th Punjab Regiment had watched and listened to the fire fight raging on and around Rass El-Zouai with eager anticipation. As heavy enemy defensive fire came down Lt. Colonel Hughes was ordered to take his troops forward and clear the escarpment on the left of the military road. The forward company, under the command of Cpt. W. G. Popple, at last received the order to attack and in their eagerness gave up all thoughts of a silent assault. As they rushed forward with fixed bayonets a heavy barrage burst on the crests before them and above all this din could be heard the age old battle cry of the Punjabi Mussalmans: "Allah Mo Akbar." One officer wrote later of this sight: "I don't know how the enemy felt about it, but they certainly scared me" - there was no stopping the Punjabis as they swept across the military road and over the far escarpment.

This was too much for the men of the Pistoia Division holding this sector, many of them were cut down in their positions but most chose life and captivity. When dawn broke, the Punjabis had a good view of the military road and surrounding area but their positions were still dominated by a tall feature to the south of the military road. This high buttress was attacked by 'D' Company who found the Italians easy prey. Throughout the morning mopping up continued, by noon eight hundred prisoners had been rounded up and a large number of mortars captured which were soon in service against their former owners.

5th BRIGADE
COMMANDING OFFICER:
BRIGADIER D. R. E. R. BATEMAN. DSO. OBE

1/9th GURKHA RIFLES
COMMANDING OFFICER: LT. COL. ROCHE

When dawn broke, the battle was in full swing along the entire front of twelve miles. On the 8th Army's right at Roumana, the 51st Highland

Division had stormed the eastern slopes and were fighting to hold on to their gains against furious counter attacks. The 50th Northumbrian Division in the centre advanced over open rolling ground to be met by curtains of fire from the line of, and beyond, the anti tank ditch. On the left, the advance continued according to plan, 1/9th Gurkhas moved through the corridor cleared by Lalbahadur Thapas men and along the crests making for the rear of the Fatnassa feature and the open plains in the distance. One after another the ridges fell before the victorious Gurkhas despite heavy machine gun and mortar fire from enemy positions.

As they reached the top of a low ridge between El-Alig and Fatnassa they looked down upon a host of Italians in a state of confusion. Any resistance was soon quelled and the Gurkhas found themselves in possession of a large number of prisoners. At a cost of one killed and nineteen wounded, the 1/9th Gurkhas had carried their attack three thousand yards into the heart of the enemy's defences and taken over two thousand prisoners.

4/6th RAJPUTANA RIFLES
COMMANDING OFFICER: LT. COL. R. B. SCOTT. DSO.

Close behind came the 4/6th Rajputana Rifles, as they did so, heavy concentrations of defensive fire came down upon their approach route causing many casualties. Three companies passed through the corridor lined on either side with escarpments, rounded the Royal Sussex positions on El-Meida and broke into the rolling ridge complex named Oudane El-Hachana, thus enabling them to follow the low valley behind the anti tank ditch. 'D' Company led the way as the battalion swept into the enemy's rear and after a brief fight, white flags began to appear from the Italian positions. With their hands above their heads prisoners came streaming in. Before noon the battalion had penetrated half way to Roumana, bringing the plain and rear of the anti tank ditch under observation - here large enemy formations could be seen on the move. This advance, deep into the enemy's rear, was achieved at a cost of three killed and forty wounded, over one thousand prisoners were sent to the rear.

1/4th BATTALION ESSEX REGIMENT

COMMANDING OFFICER: LT. COL. A. NOBLE. DSO

Behind the centre of 50th Division's front the 1/4th Essex had waited patiently for their moment to come, their task was to bridge the anti tank ditch and escort the anti tank guns across the rolling ground, meeting the other units of 5th Brigade as they wheeled round in the direction of Roumana. By 0700 hours the entire battalion front was under heavy shell fire. Lt. Colonel Noble made his way forward to 'A' Company to find the 50th Division held up and under heavy fire from enemy positions, undaunted he began to make preparations for a battalion bridgehead operation when orders from divisional HQ came over the R/T telling the 1/4th Essex to deploy to the left and follow up behind 5th Brigade.

The troops pressed forward along their new axis under heavy fire, contact was made with 5th Brigade tactical HQ by the commanding officer while 'D', 'B', and 'C' Companies followed up. Lt. Colonel Noble received orders that his men were to press on and help secure the Brigade objective. On the high ground before them, the men of the Royal Sussex and the Gurkhas watched as the Essex men moved over open ground with shells bursting among them, one senior NCO of the Royal Sussex commented: "They moved over the plain in near perfect formation, I watched their progress with the most profound admiration." Reaching the western end of the anti tank ditch the Essex men were put to work consolidating the El-Meida feature and rounding up Italian prisoners who were employed filling in the ditch before a crossing was made.

A Nebelwerfer captured on 1/4th Essex Front.

LATE MORNING AND AFTERNOON

The commander of X Corps arrived at 4th Indian Division HQ at 0845 hours. General Tucker explained the situation and pointed out that a swift armoured thrust could reach the open plains only five miles distant - thus preventing the enemy disengaging the bulk of their forces. The office minutes made of this conversation reflected the urgency of Tucker's request:

"Commander X Corps then spoke to Army Commander on the telephone requesting permission to put in X Corps to maintain the momentum of the attack. After this conversation, Commander X Corps said his armour was going through at once, using both 4th Indian Divisions crossing over the anti tank ditch and one on the boundary between 50th and 51st Division, south west of Roumana. Commander X Corps did not give any indication that his advance forward was restricted by bounds on timings laid down by High Command nor that there were any administrative difficulties."

However, and for whatever reason, delays ensued and the armour would not be launched for another twenty-four hours. The enemy was reeling as the battle rumbled on all along the twelve mile front; on the left the 4th Indian Division had made great gains, on the right 51st Highland

Left to right: Lt. J.R.S. Baldwin, 4th Field Coy. Royal Engineers, Lt. C.A. Allan, American 9th Air Force HQ, Major J.A. Murray, MC. 4th Field Coy. Royal Engineers, Lt. Colonel J. Blundell OBE, Commander Royal Engineers. All four were killed by an 88 direct hit on the Wadi crossing, 4th Indian Division front.

Division had taken Roumana, while in the centre the 50th Division had been held up as they advanced over open ground into the teeth of the enemy gun positions, but even here all was not lost as the Yorkshiremen probed constantly for a way through: until on the right, the Green Howards finally crossed the anti tank ditch.

A magnificent opportunity of trapping the enemy passed and, as ever, the Africa Corps were quick to take advantage of any delays. German reserve elements were rushed forward to stiffen the badly shaken Italians and throughout the later morning the situation on the western approaches to Fatnassa grew steadily more menacing. The enemy artillery stuck to their task in tenacious fashion, one group of 88s situated in the rear of Roumana fired obliquely into the west covering every yard of the anti tank ditch, these gunners kept up a steady and lethal harassing fire throughout the day.

In the late morning, 4 Field Company, R.E. had begun work on the crossing over the anti tank ditch started by the 1/4th Essex earlier. The Indian engineers busily worked to complete their task regardless of the incoming fire falling upon them. At 1600 hours Lt. Colonel John Blundell was briefing his officers when a salvo from the 88s behind Roumana - some miles distant - struck them killing Major W.J.A. Murray. MC. (Commander 4th Field Coy), Captain Baldwin and Lt Allan, an American Liaison officer.

Lt. Colonel Blundell was seriously wounded and died in the dressing station. The guns which caused this tragedy may have been partly responsible for the inability of the armour to break through across the ridges.

By midday on 6 April the battle was all but over, except for 1/2nd Gurkhas who found the enemy resisting vigorously. On Point 275 'A' Company was being pounded by heavy harassing fire. There was little shelter for the men and the air was thick with splinters and rock fragments, because of enemy infiltration to the north the troops dare not take shelter behind the south face of the feature. Running at right angles to Rass El-Zouai the long finger of El-Alig stretched out one thousand yards long and three hundred yards wide, dominating this feature were the heights of Fatnassa across a steep sided and rugged canyon.

On the crests of El-Alig the scattered sections of 'B' and 'C' Companies came under heavy fire, throughout the day enemy gun teams sought to regain the lost heights and Gurkha snipers fought individual stalking matches with the infiltrating enemy. Lance Naik Nare Thapa was wounded on El-Alig and was in the process of having his wound dressed when he saw behind his comrade two enemy heads appear over the edge of the cliff, he at once sprung to his feet and shot them both dead. Lance Naik Dalbir Ghale had been exchanging shots repeatedly with one persistent attacker - to flush him out into the open he rolled down some sizeable boulders which the enemy soldier leapt to avoid and in doing so was killed by the artful Gurkha. Rifleman Lalbahadur Pun, upon finding one enemy group infiltrating between his position and the 1/9th Gurkhas on the right, at once leapt into the open and blazed away at his assailants - the enemy returning the compliment. After a sharp fight in which he was wounded in the head, Lalbahadur Pun killed two men with his last five rounds and silenced a light machine gun.

By early afternoon large enemy forces were gathering along the western edge of the feature. One daring gun team, led by a young German officer, gained access to the crest of Rass El-Zouai. The Gurkhas at once rushed to the attack hurling the gun team down the sloped and killing the officer.

A counter attack by strong forces was now imminent, 'D' Company crossed over and spread out amongst the scattered groups of defenders. On a front of more than two miles, and with little ammunition and no reserves, ten platoons faced an enemy that was growing stronger with every minute that passed.

The wireless sets that had been destroyed could not be replaced and the signalling lamps were all out of action. Brigade communications could not be extended beyond 'C' Company's first objective because of guns and snipers firing very accurately from the rear of Oudane El-Hachana.

Clambering from company to company Cpt. Ramsay-Brown, Colonel Showers and Cpt. Ormsby kept abreast of the situation, Major Galletti (31st Field Reg. RA.) had advanced at first light, with the guns of his unit, across open ground to give close support to the infantry - though wounded in the head he roamed all day from one forward position to another seeking new targets for his guns.

Throughout the afternoon guerrilla warfare and tactics of stealth reigned among the gullies and boulders of Point 275, one Gurkha section ran out of ammunition and rolled boulders down upon the enemy to keep them at bay. On Point 275 'A' Company had suffered a constant barrage of high explosive - during the afternoon the barrage increased in intensity and the men knew this was the signal, a counter attack in strength was coming.

It was indeed fortunate that at this very moment a line arrived from the gunners at Battalion HQ - at last communications were established, a call for defensive fire at 1610 hours drew an immediate and accurate response from 31st Field Regiment - a shoot crashed down on El-Alig and dispersed the enemy in disorder. Fresh supplies of ammunition were also brought up by a platoon of 'A' Company and the Gurkhas refilled their empty magazines. Darkness fell with the men in good heart. Over the rest of the front, the battle had now ended which meant that the full strength of the divisional artillery could now be arrayed in support of 1/2nd Gurkhas.

Not long after midnight enemy movement was detected on the northern face of El-Alig, by 0100 hours enemy troops pressed forward along the slender crest towards 'B' Company. A shoot was called for and heavy concentrations of shell fire swept the valley between El-Alig and Fatnassa isolating any groups that had gained the heights, the remaining attackers were now silhouetted against the night sky and were shot down by the Gurkhas of 'B' Company.

At 0300 hours the enemy gathered once more along the military road, only to be met by heavy concentrations of defensive fire that raked the area with deadly accuracy - the attack melted away. Silence now fell upon Fatnassa - leaving the 1/2nd Gurkhas in possession of the key to the whole battlefield, at the cost of 52 casualties.

Back Row standing: Subedar Bishau Bahadurguring IDSM, OIM; Subedar Lalbhadur Thapa VC, OBI; Cpt. Donald Ramsay-Brown MC; Subedar Major Narbahadur Gursung OBI. All served with 1/2nd Gurkha Rifles.
(Courtesy of Donald Ramsay-Brown).

FIRST HAND ACCOUNTS

4th INDIAN DIVISION

CPT DONALD RAMSAY-BROWN. MC AND BAR
1/2nd KING EDWARD VII'S OWN GURKHA RIFLES
'B' COMPANY

"We got up to the start line, one of the enemy sentries was smoking and we saw the glow of his cigarette. We then deployed on our start line to make the attack, we got confirmation from brigade that it was time to go so moved off and rushed the forward defences - it was straight into a hand to hand fight - but we had surprise on our side. The immediate forward line was over run, 'D' Company went off to the right and we went down into point 275 and the rest of the feature.

We infiltrated right and left and got onto the feature. From then on we had lots of small operations where you ran into a company, a platoon or a machine gun post and had to deal with it; all this happened at night but the enemy very conveniently put up lots of flares, initially this was something we would not have welcomed but their flares gave us the extra visibility to see what was happening and to see where the tracer was emanating from. So well before dawn we had overrun the complete position.

When morning came the German 90th Light Division that was on our front started to muster for quite a large assault, our forward positions were relatively lightly held but we held the high ground, there was quite a lot of exchanges and we sent patrols forward to stall them. Eventually they did come in with quite a big attack and we were at that stage literally so short of ammunition that Gurkhas were rolling boulders down, a couple of shots then roll down a rock - it was very exciting.

Up to that time our communications with the gunners had been interrupted. The large wireless sets, that were fine operating under cool conditions, were being carried up a hill side, dropped when the chap was wounded and they just all went off the air. The detailed planning we had done very thoroughly earlier had involved a whole series of defensive curtains of fire that could be called on, the artillery was all ready but we couldn't get through.

At this particular moment one of the wireless sets got through and the gunner officer was there. We said 'could we have a curtain of fire - X Y Z' and literally the whole of the corp's artillery came down. Looking down the slope which the German 90th Light were fighting up I've never seen anything like it. As the artillery came down, rows and rows of Germans just collapsed, it was like one of these pretend things you see nowadays - a bit of firing and a chap collapses. They were all falling down like that and were cut down within a few yards of getting to the top where our chaps were waiting. We just sat back and said 'Gosh - nice to have gunners on your side.

When daylight came, we were reporting back there was nothing between us and the rear positions of the enemy so could they please send a few tanks along and we could get going, but they didn't. There was an air of considerable caution, we'd been up and down the desert many times. When things had gone well people had pressed on, sometimes without the right support and I think General Montgomery erred on caution there and you can see why. It was a pity because an opportunity was lost, had we gone then it would have made the next stages of the German position less strong in that we would have cut off many more of their foremost combat troops.

When the main battle started, we saw the fireworks going off but it was not as heavy a concentration as we saw at El-Alamein. It was a smaller version of that, you could see the small arms and tracer going on the way it does, it sort of wanders about making it very difficult to tell where its coming from. The barrage moved forward before the concentrations of troops and you could see those concentrations. By that time all hell was let loose, we had a grandstand view of what was happening with enemy tanks moving and was able to put down suitable fire, our own gunners were reporting what they could see on the enemy front."

GUNNER/SIGNALLER JAMES CURRAN
31st FIELD REGIMENT. ROYAL ARTILLERY

"As we approached Akarit, there seemed to be many meetings and conferences of Officers and eventually it seeped through that the Gurkhas, 1/2, were going to attack these hills which could be seen in the distance. It was to be a silent night attack and we were to go with them to set up a forward O.P. The means of communication was to be by wireless. Now how on earth the heavy sets, with their accumulators, were to be carried along in a night attack up rocky mountains was beyond my comprehension, we had never done such a thing before. However, it seemed the 57 L.A.A. were to act as porters; 105 Battery's 'Tiffy' Thain was to make back packs out of a steel rod, webbing and leather.

Here I was, about to be a member of a F.O.O. party on a vital mission and I knew nothing of Wadi Akarit, beyond knowing it was the hills I could see in the distance about 5 miles away. I never saw a map, which was usual. All I knew was that the O.P. party was to be led through by the Gurkhas. The back packs were eventually made and there was great "trying on" excitement. My load was to be two big tins of water, about four gallons I think, my field telephone and a pair of flags - what on earth the water was for I don't know, I usually carried my own bottle and some biscuits and bully beef. The back packs were real amateur contraptions and as uncomfortable as hell.

Eventually we lined up in the darkness on the evening of the 5 April waiting for the work to start. I don't know what time we started, it was very dark. It must have been three of four miles to the foothills. The journey was hell with this heavy uncomfortable weight bounding about on my back and it seemed to take hours. Then the climbing and scrambling began. It was inevitable that this damned pack would break and it did, and down I went. By the time I struggled free with the help of 'Happy' the others had disappeared in the darkness. There was nothing else to do but carry on climbing with 'Happy' and his mates, and what a night that was, a story on its own suffice to say.

First light found me with kukri in my hand, unblooded I am glad to say, with a group of about 12 wounded Gurkhas. When I met Major Galetti, the B.C., at the bottom there were some sharp exchanges of words.

It appeared that there was no communication with the O.P. and he seemed to think it was all my fault. He was quite anxious and agitated. The guns had only been able to fire on some prearranged targets and were anxious for orders from the O.P. It appeared that there was an almost complete breakdown in wireless communication. Not surprising when you consider the huge cumbersome sets we had, fit only for vehicle use. After further argument, I said that if I knew where the O.P. was supposed to be and could be provided with enough cable, I should do my best to reach them. So began the climb back up.

We eventually reached the top crest at a point where there was a gap about 20ft wide and walls about the same height. Through this gap could be seen a valley, about a mile across to another peak and to the left of the open mouth could be seen a road on the opposite side of which were enemy guns. At the slightest movement shells thundered into the peak on the other side of the gap. Reels of cable appeared and another signaller. So there we crouched with the cable on the rod ready to go, came a lull in the shelling and off we shot through the gap, down the other side and across the valley.

We eventually reached the other side and began the climb to the top and came on to a long narrow plateau. At the opposite edge the Gurkhas were lined up repelling a German counter attack, to the left of the plateau at the end was Captain Steele with his O.P. The line was quickly connected and contact made with the guns which were soon in action. The time would be about mid afternoon on 6 April, I then went over to the Gurkhas and joined in with them throwing and rolling rocks down on the Germans who were attempting to climb up, I think there was a shortage of ammo. Things eventually quietened down and I spent the night there. Next morning 7 April, made my way back, eventually arriving worn out and hungry."

CPT RONALD PERKIN. MC
4/16th PUNJAB REGIMENT. 'B' COMPANY

"The following account concerning the Battle of Wadi Akarit (in Tunisia during the last War - 5/6 April 1943) is based on my personal experience and the views expressed are those of a junior officer with limited knowledge of the overall plan.

I was a Captain (aged 24 years) commanding 'B' Company of the 4th Bn 16th Punjab Regiment, in the 7th Indian Infantry Brigade of the 4th Indian Division. I had served with this battalion from January 1941 when they were in the Eritrean campaign, through the second desert offensive (under Auchinleck) - to and then back from Benghazi, then through the Battle of Alamein, up to Tunis and then in the Battles of the Mareth Line and on to Wadi Akarit and the subsequent battles at Enfidaville, Garci and Medjez El-Bab to the fall of Tunis itself.

The main Army attack was scheduled for the morning of 6 April but the 4th Indian Division were given the task of putting in a night attack, into the hills leading to the Fatnassa feature - hopefully to capture the high points and denying these to the enemy artillery O.Ps - as the main offensive was being carried out in the open plain below …

The plan was for the Brigade to form up just after dark. The whole Brigade was packed very tight with every man being just able to see the others to the front, left and right of himself. So, with certain ancillary troops, such as Sappers, Medics, Gunners O.Ps and Machine Gunners this large body must have exceeded 2000 men, all advancing to a silent attack.

After some time we were aware that the 1/2nd Gurkhas had been sent off on to their objective, then the Royal Sussex went off and our Bn waited with Bde HQ until Brigadier 'Oz' Lovett was ready to use us. It was still very quiet until we started to hear a certain amount of noise, it was not overmuch considering what was going on.

Then, in the darkness, a runner came to me from the C.O. and I went up to get my orders. Although it was very dark, one could see a silhouette line of hills to the front and left but, for all I knew, they could have been a mile or a 100 yards away. Anyway, my orders were to advance with my company and take the silhouette hill line to the front and left.

I went back to my company and gathered my platoon commanders and gave them similar orders. I told them to go back to their platoons and, when they saw me stand up, to move forward. Having given them time to inform their men, I stood up and the whole company rose up and we started to move forward but then something I was not prepared for happened. Instead of advancing slowly and in silence, the men started to charge and at the same time yelling their traditional war chant 'Maro maro hadri - maro maro hadri'. There was nothing I could do then to stop the onrush, even though I was at the front and tried to slow them down, so I decided to go along with the movement. In fact, after a couple of hundred yards, I felt the terrain rising upwards until I reached the top of what I thought was the ridge I was required to capture. There was a certain amount of small arms fire but we had not come across any enemy and I don't think we had any casualties at this point. In the darkness I spread out the men of my company along this ridge and waited for the dawn.

As the early dawn light came up I soon realised there was another ridge in front and the enemy were on that in some force, so I called the platoon commanders and told them that we would be putting in an attack as soon as possible. The enemy position on the facing ridge was about 150 yards away with a shallow valley in between. My orders were quite simple: when I got up we would all rise up and charge forward - shouting with fixed bayonets. It was all over quite soon. I charged forward, with my signaller running along beside me - he had a wireless set on his back, about half way across the intervening space he was hit and fell. However, I went on and reached the top of the ridge where the enemy were positioned and firing away at our advance. As soon as I got to the top of the ridge they, the Italians, put their hands up and surrendered.

The nearest one to me was a tall officer and I was so cross they had shot my signaller one minute and the next put their hands up, that I was really sorely tempted to shoot this officer there and then. The other side of this ridge they were defending was a very steep drop of about 50 feet. I told this officer to turn round and then gave him a great kick up the backside which sent him flying down head over heels.

When he reached the bottom, I shouted to him to run back up to me again. About 100 or so prisoners surrendered and I collected them on to our side of the ridge. Enemy gunner O.Ps must have seen that we had taken the ridge as they started to shell it regardless of the fact that there were probably more of their troops on it than ours.

Meanwhile, I was receiving a certain amount of small arms fire from a high hill to my front and left and which was on the other side of the north south road. I then sent a platoon under Havildar Mohd Aslam to circle to the north of the hill and then to come back up behind the defenders. While he was doing this we fired everything we had at their position, some three hundred yards away, hoping to frighten them and also to make them keep their heads down while the platoon was coming up behind them. By the time he got to the foot of the hill and started to advance up it, the enemy had had enough and they waved white flags as they came over to my position to surrender.

An extra bonus was that many more of the enemy who were situated further to the west also surrendered. They were probably those Italians that we had heard when on our reconnaissance patrol before the battle started. In all over 500 prisoners were taken.

From where I was standing, by the gap through the hills, the road was now clear up to at least Pt 275, I reported this to Bn HQ in the hope that this would encourage the higher command to exploit this advantage.

In retrospect, and bearing in mind that it was still very early in the morning and the main battle had hardly begun over to the right, I still hold the view that had the armour been pushed through and so round behind the enemy main defensive line, it could have decimated their gun positions and enabled a lot more prisoners to be taken with much less casualties to the 50th and 51st Divisions who had to hammer away for the rest of the day. I was awarded the MC for this action and, on my recommendation, Havildar Mohd Aslam was awarded the IDSM.

The only recollection I have of the aftermath of the action was this: As all the Italians were surrendering, I collected them on our side of the ridge and a very frightened crowd they were too. On the other side of the ridge, under the crest, there must have been some sort of Aid Post. An Italian doctor came up to me and asked if I would send some of my men to collect the wounded from there, as that side of the ridge was more vulnerable to the enemy shell fire which was being brought to bear on their erstwhile position. I refused, but told him that I was quite happy for him to take some of his own men to carry out this somewhat risky job. He could find no volunteers! - and I lost interest in the matter.

While all the shelling was going on, all the enemy were grovelling about on the ground trying to get shelter - all but one, and he turned out to be a German, probably a gunner O.P., he was a Feldwebel who spoke a little English and we were standing up talking while all this shellfire was dropping about us. I was not going to let him see that I was afraid and he, obviously, had the same thoughts about me so we continued to chat as if nothing was happening. Fortunately, much to my relief, the shelling eventually stopped and I then sent all the POWs back with about three men to 'guard' them. In passing, I would mention that my signaller, who was wounded in the attack, survived. A bullet had passed right through him and through the wireless set strapped to his back."

CPT. A. G. BARON
4/6th RAJPUTANA RIFLES

"On the night of 5 April, 5 Brigade of which my unit was part, launched a silent night attack on the right hand end of this mountainous area, with 1st/9th Gurkhas leading. By first light, they had reached all their objectives and it was my battalion's task to push on and take the extreme right hand height, called Oudane El-Hachana, overlooking the anti tank ditch and the plain north of Roumana. My company was given the job of taking Oudane and shortly after first light we were on top of our objective, without much resistance , as the defenders had apparently no stomach for a real fight. As soon as we had reached it however, we were subjected to a heavy mortar barrage, the range being clearly known to a foot. As the ground was more or less bare rock, I ordered my men to retire a few score yards to just below the skyline where there were some softer spots where protective slit trenches or at least sangars i.e. stone walls, could be made.

The company suffered a few casualties from this mortaring. Shortly afterwards, when the mortar barrage had ceased, I went forward on my own and had a good look at the scene. On Roumana, I saw that the 51st Highland Division had taken quite a bit thereof, although I saw an enemy counter attack being launched by the troops who had arrived in trucks down the coast road from the north. I noticed also that, north of the ditch, was an orchard like area, probably of olive trees within cactus hedges and in this was a battery of enemy 88mm anti aircraft guns, at that time firing at some of our medium bombers. It appeared that some of our tanks had in fact crossed the anti tank ditch, but seemed to be static in hull down positions.

One tank was burning and had, I think, been on the receiving end of a solid round from an 88mm gun, for I had some time previously heard the horrible screeching sound of a solid anti tank round hitting a tank. It was clear that the 88s had a field of fire over the ditch, hence the disinclination of our tanks to advance further.

Unfortunately, our own artillery, left behind by our quick advance, were on the move and could not therefore be brought to bear on the battery of 88s.

I passed all the information I had back to battalion HQ and for most of the remaining daylight hours sent back situation reports. One of our other companies made a good haul of Italian prisoners down towards the ditch.

On the subject of tanks, the attitude of the average infantryman was to give our own tanks as wide a berth as possible because they tended to draw the fire of enemy anti tank weapons, especially the dreaded 88mm gun. He would not have got into a tank 'for a pension' and would rather take his chance out in the open or in a slit trench. Conversely, a tank crew man would not have got out of his vehicle, assuming it were not crippled, 'for a pension' and would not, as a rule, take his chance out in the open like an infantryman.

On the subject of the 88mm gun, I recollect seeing some of our Sherman tanks hit on the battlefield of Alamein, with an 88mm hole right through the 9 inch thick steel cupolas of their gun turrets. The solid shell had pierced through 9 inches of steel going in and a further 9 inches of steel going out again. In fact, not one of our tanks was capable of withstanding a hit by a solid shot from an 88, hence their tactic of keeping a hull down position and trying to knock out the 88 and its crew by high explosive shells from their own 75mm guns.

We were still in these positions when night fell and during the night I heard the distinctive noise of tanks and/or half tracked vehicles moving in the enemy positions to the north of me. All at once a Varey light pattern illuminated the darkness and was, I saw, the call for defensive artillery fire. We heard our guns firing away behind us but were extremely irritated to find that all the 25 pounder shells were falling on our positions and at least 500 yards short of any enemy positions in the plain beyond. I did not fancy this one bit and got out of my slit trench to go to that of the signallers, about 10 yards away down the slope, with a view to telephoning the battalion HQ to ask them to tell the gunners to raise their sights a bit.

Try as I might, I simply could not raise HQ on the telephone and felt very exposed, sitting on the open ground outside the small slit trench of the two signallers. I thought that it was reasonable enough to be killed or wounded by enemy fire, but a major disaster if our own guns were responsible. I had to endure about 3 salvos before the adjutant came through on the telephone to say that the gunners had been told.

Apparently, they had not had time to range the area before nightfall and had been using maps which were inaccurate. Furthermore, their largesse had been distributed over the whole battalion area and every company commander had been on the telephone to complain. As luck would have it, neither myself nor anyone in my company were hit in this contretemps.

The next morning revealed that the enemy had pulled back his artillery and anti aircraft guns, and that our tank units could have advanced. Unfortunately, for some unknown reason, they did not and a lot of the Afrika Korps got away to fight another day."

CPT. BEN DALTON. DSO. OBE
1st BATTALION ROYAL SUSSEX REGIMENT. HQ COMPANY

"I had recently taken over HQ Coy and did not expect to be taking part in the coming battle, when the C.O. had completed his orders he suddenly turned to me: 'Ben you would not wish to miss a good battle - come along with headquarters.' As I recall it, the approach march was about five miles; conducted in near silence. The leading companies crossed the start line on time but the enemy concentrated D.F. (DEFENSIVE FIRE) hit Battalion Headquarters as it approached the feature. The radio sets were destroyed and among the casualties was the adjutant, then the C.O. said in stentorian tones 'Captain Dalton I appoint you Adjutant 1st Battalion Royal Sussex Regiment', accompanied by sundry shot and shell.

Battalion HQ had lost contact with the companies but fortunately the gunners set was still working, in the confusion the following companies were held up and direction was going astray. Through the gunners set, the C.O. called for tracer directional fire on the correct axis which was promptly delivered. As the remaining companies moved forward I was ordered to accompany them and report progress by runner. By first light we had secured the objectives beyond El-Meida. A platoon exploited and captured a 65mm gun position, the artillery O.P. officer was with them and the guns were turned round and used on the enemy with devastating effect. At this point I could clearly see the whole of the 50th and 51st Divisions moving across the plain behind the artillery supporting fire. I turned to retrace my steps when a sniper rose up - hitting me in the face, but a marksman nearby spotted him and made the kill. I wended my way back to the R.A.P. and said goodbye to Wadi Akarit."

RIFLEMAN LALBAHADUR PUN. IOM
1/2nd GURKHA RIFLES. 'C' COY. 14 PLTN

"During the day the enemy launched counter attacks on our positions and we were ordered forward to fill the gap between 'B' Company and the 1/9th Gurkhas on the right, the feature we occupied had steep cliffs on either side and the enemy gun teams had gained the crest and were moving about firing at us from cover.

We stalked the enemy among the rocks even though we were very short of ammunition; every round had to count. Myself (on the Bren Gun) and my N°2 approached one particular gun team that had been giving a lot of trouble when they saw us and with one burst killed my comrade next to me: a bullet struck my helmet under the rim and gauged a deep wound in my head, after I regained my senses I tried to look for their position again and as I rose was again hit in the head, blood was now pouring from my wounds and it was difficult to see. I knew it was now them or me so I rose with my gun and fired my last rounds at the enemy killing them both, as I did so bullets flew all around me and I was hit again in the hand. Unable now to carry on the fight because of my condition and my lack of ammunition I moved to the rear and reported the situation as I had seen it."

HAVILDAR MANILAL THAPA. IDSM
1/2nd GURKHA RIFLES. 'D' COY. 17 PLTN

"As we advanced in the dark we moved forward so swiftly that we began to pass the men laying tapes and were ordered to halt. Before us we could see the dark outline of the hills we were to attack, there was a ground mist and the air smelt fresh. Flares were dropped by enemy fliers which hung in the air for a while - but soon the order came to move out and we headed for the rocky feature which was our objective on the night of the attack. We rushed the enemy killing many of them with our

Kukris and bayonets and the feature fell after a brief fierce fight.

I reported back to my Platoon Commander and was in turn ordered to clear the forward crest of enemy positions; the ground we had to cross on the way to our next objective was boulder strewn and rough and we were harassed by machine gun fire and grenades all the way up. Once on the crest we soon were organised and steadily advanced along it, we rushed each post in turn and were soon in among the enemy, killing them with blows from our Kukris and thrusts from our bayonets. The screaming, small arms fire and explosions echoed from the hills around, many of the enemy who could not break away were hurled over the cliff side and those that tried to run were shot down. It was not long before the entire crest was clear."

CPT CYRIL MOUNT. (OFFICIAL WAR ARTIST) ROYAL ARTILLERY

"The attack went in at 4am, the hills ahead ablaze with small arms fire and flares while the gun crews worked like fury to build some sort of protection round the guns. The ground was so hard and rocky it was impossible to do any digging, just camouflage nets up and a few gravel filled sandbags and rocks levered out of the ground. We ran telephone lines down to the troop positions and someone came on foot with a line from RHQ.

We just prayed the enemy O.Ps would be captured before it got too light. Our prayers were answered, it was light and no one seemed to be shooting at us intentionally, our guns were blazing away. We were through on the wireless to our Forward Observation Officer up on the hills with the Essex, they were taking quite a hammering but seemed jubilant. We heard from RHQ that the Gurkhas and Essex had taken all their objectives but fierce counter attacks were happening, and a lot of stuff was coming over in our direction but it was random. 8am I did a quick drawing of the guns in action and the general scene in front of the hills/wadi. I had forgotten about the night's events but was reminded when I realised my hands and shorts were covered in dried blood. The next few days are a blur, Jerry sneaked away that night 6/7 April and the day was peaceful. The following day, after a semi sleepless night in the jeep with a borrowed blanket, (my bedding roll was on X) we go to sea in 3 tonners for a bathe and welcome clean up.

46

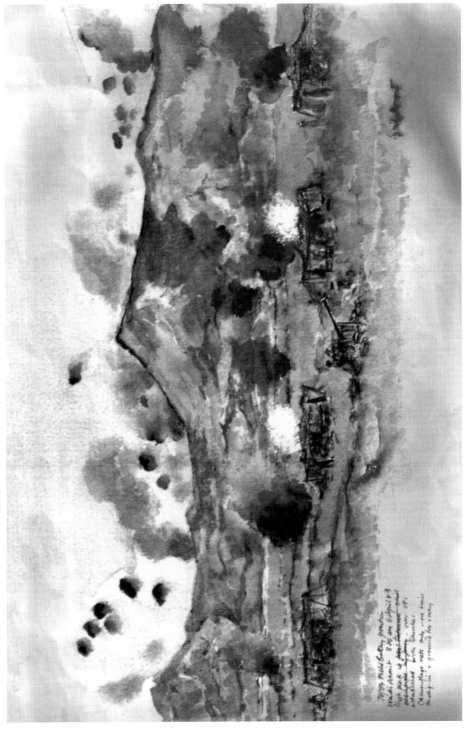

Painting by captain Cyril Mount, who sat behind a gun emplacement and painted the scene as they pounded enemy positions on 4th Indian Divisions Front.

On the move again through increasingly luscious landscape … a riot of wild flowers, whole hillsides ablaze with vermilion poppies and lots of cactus everywhere, little Arab houses surrounded by piled high camel thorn. We leaguered for the night and discover we are amongst the Kiwis - their vehicles dotted around in the flowers and grass and cactus, they share their booze and grub with us, (they are pretty smart at the looting game.) Tinned Jerry luxuries and even WINE! We talked together for hours but the next morning they were gone."

MAJOR JEPHSON. MC. TD
11th FIELD REGIMENT.
ROYAL ARTILLERY

"I have clear memories of our gun positions on the forward slope in full view of the Djebels. I am not certain whether I actually visited them in this position. My clearest memory is of lying on my back in the anti tank ditch (shown on most maps) with the Essex and watching a shower of mortar bombs descending not too far away - looking like cricket balls. I don't think we had casualties though a nasty little hole appeared in the skirt of my great coat, yes great-coat, that little hole was there for the rest of the war though I do not remember the Tunisian dawns as cool enough for great coats.

I also remember a spent small armour piercing shell turning slowly in the air making a whirring sound - before it clanked against the front of my Tatanagar O.P. truck at about waist height as I stood near it. Later in the day I remember being with our 2 i/c (probably deputising for Major O' Hallran who had been killed on a mine - the Tatanagar, though it had an excellent armoured framework, had a wooden floor - just under the last ridge before the plain). We were at the 1/4th Essex Regimental HQ, (i.e. their C.O. and perhaps a couple of trucks) at a point where several fissures met the main track which was our axis of advance. I think the Gurkhas were ahead of us, clearing the last enemy troops from the ridge.

We were certainly not in action as I have a clear memory of listening to the BBC that night, presumable the Forces Programme from England. The announcer, who was often on at that time of night, was a lady with a name something like Marjorie M……….. Her voice was not sexy but it was womanly, friendly and mature, I remember it not as a girl but as a mother with an ample bosom on which to rest one's weary head.

The hills had looked almost impregnable, but, thanks to Gertie Tuker, 4th Indian Division's Targets had been reached with fewer casualties than expected and I had had little to do but wait. Djebel Garci, Enfidaville and Medjez-El-Bab were still to come."

SGT LYONS. 149th ANTI TANK REGIMENT ROYAL ARTILLERY

"Get some sleep," said our troop commander, "because tomorrow morning the Essex lads are 'going in' and our troop is going to keep them company". With this comforting thought ringing in my ears I pulled a blanket over my head and tried to take his advice, only to be awakened almost immediately (or so it seemed) by the arrival of the infantry moving up to the start line. It was still dark, and the last section, moving like wraiths, had barely slipped through our lines when up front the thud of mortar bombs and the 'up and down' rattle of a Spandau told us that the infantry patrol up front had made contact with the enemy and it was, indeed, time to 'keep them company'. It was now 'first light' and I could see across the open ground our objective, the anti tank ditch across the dry river bed and the engineers working frantically to make a passage over it for us and our six pounder anti tank guns, and I thought to myself so this is 'Wadi Akarit'. At 1100 hrs a young Engineer Officer came across and said, 'We've done all the ***** hard work, get yourself across'. This we did, with some alacrity.

A short time later, an 88mm shell landed in the ditch, killing or wounding a whole company of engineers including, I think, our friend the young officer. All afternoon fierce fighting went on, until the enemy was finally pushed off the high ground overlooking the wadi and the way was clear for the armour to go through, (which it didn't) but that's for the historians and 'armchair generals' to argue about.

At 1600 hrs the wadi fell quiet and then, what must have been the last shell to fall in the Battle of Wadi Akarit, fell on our N°1 gun killing a sergeant, a bombardier, a driver, two gunners, and severely wounding another gunner, all my comrades since 16 October 1939."

GUNNER D. R. CORNFORD.
116 BATTERY 31st FIELD REGIMENT.
ROYAL ARTILLERY

"Our battery was to give support fire when requested, vary lights appeared about midnight which meant the hills had been captured. Our forward observation position was hit by enemy mortar fire and the wireless sets put out of action, this meant no contact could be made with our Forward Observation Officer to our guns until early next morning, then a land line was finally connected and we could lay down concentrations to clear the hills of the enemy pockets still left.

We were unable to dig our gun pits until after dark on the night of the attack because we were overlooked by the enemy positions; we were fired on the following morning but escaped any injuries.

Our Forward Observation Officer was a Cpt. Calvert and his signaller was L/BDR Bonney. Cpt. Calvert was awarded the MC and Bonney the MM."

SIGNALLER W. A. BEECH. 52 BATTERY
1st FIELD REGIMENT. ROYAL ARTILLERY

"I was a signaller with 52 Battery and during the battle I was a wireless/telegraphy operator, using a N°18 set, accompanying a Forward Observation Officer - we were in support of the 4/16th Rajputana Rifles who we advanced with. We assembled at the jumping off point at dusk. We moved off at nightfall and, as it was moonless, it was pitch-black. To keep us on course, a Bofors gun fired a round of tracer at fixed intervals. Daybreak found us halfway up the forward slope of the first of three ridges, which was very steep and rocky, and appeared to be several hundred feet high.

At the foot of the escarpment a defensive anti tank ditch had been dug. During the night the Engineers had managed to bridge the ditch, but unfortunately the first tank attempting to cross was knocked out on the bridge, thus preventing the use of the bridge which meant we would not receive any support from the tanks for the time being.

The 4th Indian Division infantry included two British Regiments - the Essex and the Sussex, and I believe it was the Sussex Regiment which achieved the initial breakthrough. A sigh of relief went up at the news, as we had been subjected to a sustained mortar attack which inflicted a number of casualties among the infantry around us.

As the attack moved forward, I can remember seeing our battery of 25 pounders (52 Field Battery RA) swing into action on the plain immediately below us, giving us close supporting fire in a matter of seconds, a stirring sight indeed. Shortly afterwards, the guns were attacked by a lone German aircraft which dropped two bombs, both missing their target. The Bofors Ack Ack guns quickly drove the plane away.

At Wadi Akarit there were three ridges and our objective was the second ridge, with defensive fire (D.F.) concentrated on the third ridge in case of a counter attack. It appears that for some unknown reason we occupied the third ridge, and, when the counter attack came, and D.F. called for, the shells fell among we troops occupying the third ridge.

Unfortunately, my wireless set became a casualty so I was unable to contact the guns to halt the bombardment. However, someone made contact and the shelling ceased. Fortunately, our casualties were very light. When dawn broke we discovered the enemy had disappeared."

ANTI TANK GUNNER. V. HUNWICKS
2nd BATTALION KING'S ROYAL RIFLE CORPS
7th (INDEPENDANT) MOTOR BRIGADE

"I was on the 6 pounder anti tank gun. The 1/2nd Gurkhas past through us which was a bit scary, we were all dotted about on the side of the hill and were told they were coming. Now these Gurkhas like to be quiet and went in without a barrage so they could do what they liked doing best - use their knives.
We were standing around talking when all of a sudden these shadows appeared and walked through us. One of 'em tapped one of the chaps on the shoulder with his kukri and said 'Johnny's not looking', it put the wind up him. It was a quiet night with the odd machine gun going off now and again, but more often than not this was fixed line firing. The Gurkhas went in and we could hear screaming from the valley where they were, then a burst of machine gun fire - all hell broke loose down there."

BOMBARDIER TED (TAFF) JONES.
105 BATTERY
31st FIELD REGIMENT. ROYAL ARTILLERY.
'C' TROOP

"I was a gunner with Sgt Dick Bowery, Ralph Haywood, Roy Pearce, Nick Carter and Shackleton.

The Column was stopped by Sergeant Major Dickie Carr and all Sergeants were called forward for orders, when Sgt Bowery came back we were all pretty shaken up by what he told us.

The wadi in front of the Wadi Akarit was being heavily shelled by the Germans, Dickie said to me outside the Quad - 'See where those shells are landing' - I said yes - 'Well that's our new gun positions.' I thought for a moment he was leg pulling but no, he said 'Get in we have to start moving.'

We started down the road to the pass through the Wadi Akarit - a gentle slope. When we were opposite the shelling we turned right into the wadi, I thought at the time we've had it this time. They say someone up there loves you because when we had the guns ready to fire the shelling from Jerry stopped - we could hardly believe our luck. Some of our signallers went in with the Gurkhas, also Major Galletti and another O.P. Officer, the Gurkhas moved through our guns as they went forward for a silent night attack, when they attacked we could hear the noise as we waited in our positions.

One of the saddest things to me and most of Charlie Troop was that we lost a fine chap in Bombardier Smudge Smith, he was the only man to get killed and not to be found to bury. We searched for him for days, it was a sad day for 105 Battery.

The day after the attack a column of Sherman tanks passed through our guns to give chase to the Italians and Germans. The night of the attack I met a little Gurkha who I had known in Cyprus - he called me Taffy Sahib. I also knew two of his mates and met them again a couple of years later in Greece, they told me little Johnny Gurkha had been killed that same night at Akarit - I felt really sad, he was such a cheery chap.

But all I can say is the 1/2nd Gurkhas and the 31st Field Regiment thought a hell of a lot of each other - we trusted each other to the limit."

PTE JACK HYDE.
ROYAL ARMY-SERVICE CORPS
522 COMPANY

"Our Sergeant came and asked me if I would drive the C.O. of the 4th Indian Division about. I was driving him around when he said to me 'do you know what happened to my other driver?', we was short of drivers then - I said 'no I didn't', he said 'he was sniped'. I got worried a bit then but kept driving, as we got near to the entrance to the wadi the C.O. called a halt and he told all the machine gunners to get mounted and to be alert. As he was looking through his glass he said to me 'look through these glasses driver' and I could see our tanks and Jerry tanks for just a brief moment as there was so much sand blowing about.

All of a sudden he shouted 'Childi - Childi', I knew what that meant - hurry. All the infantrymen were jumping out of their lorries - 'aircraft' - he shouted, we crouched down side of the wagon and lay down. We could hear the bombs coming down so I crouched low. There was machine gunners only about fifty yards from us, the bombs screamed down and exploded - sand was thrown all over us and when we looked there was no machine gunners, they'd just gone, just like that. I said to the C.O., 'The good lord was with us', he said 'I don't know about the good lord, I think it was the sand that saved us.' I said 'Aye but the good lord provided it' and he laughed."

CPL DENIS GILMER. MIDDLESEX YEOMANRY SIGNALS
ATTACHED TO 4th COUNTY OF LONDON YEOMANRY

"My recollection of Wadi Akarit is of moving up in our tanks the night before - then having a regiment of Gurkhas passing through us sharpening their Kukris with broad grins on their faces. They looked as though they were relishing going into battle, as they smiled I could see their eyes and teeth in the dark - they passed us in silence.

By dawn we were in a wadi - concealed to await the infantry attack and the signal for us to move through. We sat there for several hours being very unpleasantly pattern shelled.

Jerry knew the reserves were waiting in the wadi and shelled us all day, nowhere to move - just wait - it was most unpleasant, those who suffered from claustrophobia had a rotten time of it. I was cold but my driver was stripped to the waist and sweating profusely. While we were being shelled I was kept busy listening to reports from our scout cars ahead as they relayed information back to HQ. The enemy shells would fall on us in a line - each crump getting louder as they came closer - this was very nerve racking when you didn't know if the next one would drop on you or pass you by, occasionally a tank would be hit, it was most unpleasant."

PTE WILLIAM JUBB. MM
ROYAL ENGINEERS.
42nd FIELD COMPANY

"We arrived at Gabes and the approaches to Wadi Akarit. We had a short rest and then started to probe at the area around the wadi, patrols were sent off to scout for mines. Then on 5 April 1943, we went to the assembly points at Wadi Akarit and that night the Gurkhas went in to take the high ground, the same night the Germans came over dropping parachute flares to see what ground forces was in the area. The next morning 50 Div put an attack in, the Highland Div put an attack in and we saw the Gurkhas coming out.

All day we lay this track for the armour to leapfrog through and about five in the afternoon they withdrew so many of us because we'd been there a long time under very heavy fire. Our platoon officer was wounded, the M.T. Corporal was wounded and numerous other sappers had small wounds. Lance Corporal Morgan was killed.

At night I took an armoured scout car with four other sappers and drove to the track we'd made through the mine field, we had to light up the lamps so the tanks coming through could see the gap, it was all lit up with green flash lamps on either side and was a wonderful sight to see. An infantry officer of the Green Howards came rushing towards me from the forward areas and was in a really bad way. He said he needed help as his unit had just been mortared and he had 90 casualties to get away. I explained I couldn't leave my post as the armour was about to arrive, but showed him were the C.C.S was, he thanked me and ran off into the night. When the tanks arrived they went straight through the gap, unfortunately the leading tank was hit with an 88mm gun, I knew one

of the chaps on that tank, his name was Bowering.
   (Bowering - features in Appendix 'A').

   When the Italians was surrendering, the Germans shelled them. I remember one Italian, they carried him in a blanket - he had no arms or legs. I believe they shot him, he had no chance of living."

CPT. JACK WATT. DSO. MC
1/4th BATTALION ESSEX REGIMENT. 'D' COMPANY

"My Company ('D' Coy) was in reserve and only got involved in a minor way and I have no clear recollection of the course of the battle."
   "When the C.O's 'O' Group broke up, the senior ex regular officer commanding 'B' Company turned to me - embarking on my second action in command of 'D' Company - and offered his help and advice, I thanked him and then did my own planning. As 'B' and 'D' Companies were to be in the rear of the battalion, and as we were a considerable distance away from the enemy, each company had a three ton supply truck alongside.

   Consequently, the last message I gave to my 'O' Group was 'The company truck will be with us - the cooking gear will be loaded right at the back and the cooks know what they have to do after day break, and if I think we can get away with it, I will order a brew up. We've trained for this, the men know not to bunch, good luck to all of you.' Sure enough there was a long delay, the battle started in darkness and after sunrise the battalion HQ gave no warning of an early advance. When I thought it prudent I gave the order, the cooks had already unloaded and prepared quietly all that was needed for a brew up, so we were away to a flying start. It was not until then that 'B' Company took the same decision, starting from scratch. When the order came to advance we had all drunk our tea, while 'D' Company were unlucky, it was only a small triumph but it was a boost to my confidence.

   Later on as we trudged across the flat desert we came under shell fire, it was never intense, occasionally and briefly heavy enough to go down and take what cover we could - which was very little. But both companies moved forward when the shelling eased and kept going as only the occasional shell landed. I can remember the thought that came to me - 'I'm glad I'm in the front because there is no way I can let down those behind me.' Had I not had that responsibility I might have been less keen to get on.

When the battalion did get into action 'D' Company was the last to take part, we got down to fire our weapons with some cover behind a low ridge with flak flying around us. My runner went off with a message and I then needed to send another message, the soldier nearest to me had been transferred to 'D' Company a couple of months earlier because he was in constant trouble with the NCO's of his old company, as we both had some cover and I wanted him to move, I thought he might be rude to me.

However, I called him over, he came, I gave him the message and away he ran through the flak. He was back in less than ten minutes looking quite pleased with himself - pleased no doubt to get behind cover again and I was pleased because he had done well - bringing back a clear and useful message from one of the platoon commanders."

SGT EDWARD CHAPMAN.
CARRIER PLATOON
1/4th BATTALION ESSEX REGIMENT.
SUPPORT COMPANY

'D' Company of the 4th Essex were in front of us and we followed up in case of any interference by the enemy. We came under a very heavy bombardment that was quite accurate. We began to wonder, as we looked into the distance before us, how far we were going to get, there seemed to be a never ending flat expanse of ground with these huge mountains in front. We were fortunate in having quarter inch armour plate round us, but to see the infantry plodding through it all was something to marvel at. We were in full view of artillery and O.P.'s who were dug in in the mountains ahead and it seemed as if we were never going to get there. However, the accuracy of the barrage made it more urgent we got to the mountains. Having got there we were ordered to make ourselves scarce with as little movement as possible because darkness was falling. In my area the Gurkhas from 7 Brigade came through us chanting steadily in low voices, the officer in charge was just carrying his pistol whereas all the Gurkhas had rifles. When they proceeded to the mountains rather a clatter came back to us, we found later they had dropped their rifles in favour of their Kukris because they had seen what was happening with the artillery fire.

When we were ordered to clear up the battlefield afterwards, all the enemy guns had been taken in tact, even with their sights and there was headless bodies up there - we understood the Gurkhas had been told to be very tidy, the heads were put into empty petrol cans - flimsies. This was something that made us understand how frightened the Italians and Germans must have been.

There was an awful lot of coming and going as units passed through us and, until dawn came, we were told to sit still and be quiet in case there were mines around.

At daylight we rounded up what prisoners were left and collected any arms about."

SGT F NETHERCOAT.
15 PLATOON COMMANDER
1/4th BATTALION ESSEX REGIMENT.
'C' COMPANY

"As we stood on the starting line I thought everything seemed like an exercise, I repeated the orders to the platoon in strict military sequence and we were well briefed and prepared. The Gurkhas had passed through our positions at night moving silently like ghosts. 50th Division to our right and the Highland Division to our far right seemed to be getting a lot of stick.

'B' Company had moved in the direction of point 275 and now it was our turn. The field regiment and the anti tank regiment were sending shells over in a screaming barrage that seemed very low above our heads, every so often a badly packed shell seemed to have the wobbles and you hoped it kept going.

We crossed our starting line and soon came under heavy fire - mainly small arms and mortar. I remember, like most sergeants, I was shouting 'keep spread out - don't bunch - one shell one man', and it was surprising how few casualties we had, I firmly believe our excellent training limited casualties because we simply wouldn't let men bunch. Once we'd crossed the open ground the going was easier, by mid-day prisoners started to come in and later this became a stream of POW's.

At the end, we searched the enemy positions and I became the possessor of the most capital pair of Italian boots that I put on and wore for the rest of the North African campaign, I also acquired a Baretta which I liberated from an Italian POW."

CQMS. LEN WYNNE
1/4th BATTALION ESSEX REGIMENT.
'C' COMPANY

"At that time it was my job to get food, water and ammunition up to the platoons. In Italy we did all the carrying with mules - in the desert we didn't have any, we had carriers. Initially there was a waiting period when we were barraged continuously by these Nebelwefers, six barrelled mortars that Jerry had introduced. They were horrific and could do a lot of damage, coming over six at a time they howled similar to a Stukas whine, Wadi Akarit was the first time we'd experienced them - later on we did capture some. On one occasion going up the line to deliver food, we were stopped by a barrage from the 88s, it meant I had to stay up there for a while and during that period of time I recall laying down talking to the gunner O.P., he then asked me to look through his binoculars and I saw this Gurkha attack going in. That was most interesting, it was like being in a theatre looking down on a stage, I could see the Gurkhas in their sections moving to a position were Jerry was. What impressed me was the Kukris that they were using, the flashes of sunlight on the kukri blades was quite a spectacle, it impressed me and has stayed with me ever since."

CPL J. E. O'DONOGHUE. MM. 9 PLATOON
1/4th BATTALION ESSEX REGIMENT.
'A' COMPANY

"I remember we were operating with a squadron of tanks, we'd never come across them before, and there was some quite long grass we were advancing through. The order was that if anybody went down - stick their rifle in the ground by the bayonet so they could be seen and the Shermans wouldn't run over them.

The concentrated fire came down, we were 'A' Company and first in the attack. Visibility wasn't terribly good and by the time it improved they started shooting at the follow up troops, we were ever so relieved as concentrated gun fire is always better when its falling on somebody else. It wasn't until we got up a precipitous slope past the anti tank ditch where the enemy were holding the rim of a plateau that we found progress very difficult. We tried to get up and they just rolled grenades down at us, the law of gravity being what it is we couldn't reply in kind as our grenades simply came back at us.

After the main battle we were pulled back and we were thinking 'well that was that' when one shell came over, killed 5 and wounded 15, it virtually accounted for two thirds of the platoon. It was just one of those unlucky bloodynessess of the war, as a matter of fact our best medium pace bowler was killed that day. The following day we went up onto the ridge where we met Col Showers, the C.O. of the 1/9th Gurkhas, and we found the gun that fired this shot. It was the last shot it fired in the battle, but the ironic thing about it was it was manufactured by Metropolitan Vickers in 1916, it was a 155mm gun, it had an enormous barrel - must have been 20-22 foot long and a tremendous range. Well we all thought that after sending these guns to bolster up the Ities in 1916, and they were shooting up our blokes with it, it struck me as being a tragic and ironic time."

SGT. G. BACON. 1/4th BATTALION ESSEX REGIMENT 'B' COMPANY

"We had to advance over a large open plain - mortar shells fell like rain all around us. There was a deafening bang and one exploded so close to me I thought the blast was like someone's hot breath on me; the next thing I knew I was sitting on the edge of a crater, there was no damage to me but I was tingling all over.

The plain looked an awful long way to our objective with no smoke or cover - it was the most daunting part but we continued in open order until we reached the anti tank ditch, there was a lot of 50 Div. casualties laid about."

BRIGADE AND BATTALION
WAR DIARIES
4th INDIAN DIVISION

Burying the dead, 4th Indian Division, 7th April.

7th INFANTRY BRIGADE HEADQUARTERS
COMMANDING OFFICER BRIGADIER O DE T LOVETT. CBE. DSO
DATE: TIME:

6 April 0100 We are now creeping forward into the foothills where we know the enemy FDL's are. Suddenly an Italian sentry challenges, immediately a yell of 'Pungaroo' goes up and the gurkhas charge, a fiendish uproar takes place. These posns are held by Italians of Pistoia Div., some fight as the clatter of exploding grenades and Tommy guns show, others run screaming away from their posns. The three fwd Coys arrive at their first objectives almost simultaneously and the confusion and uproar is terrific. The 1st Royal Sussex, who were following closely on the Gurkhas heels, now wheel right and head for their objective - the DJ El-Meida feature. Intense mortar and DF comes down, it is very effective and unpleasant causing many casualties - especially to the 1st R Sussex whose route to the DJ El-Meida is very effectively covered by DF. It is about this time that Brigadier Lovett gets his wrist smashed by fragments from a mortar bomb.

6 April 0200 Bde HQ is now established just back from the foot-hills and a little information begins to filter back. The 1/2 G.R. have taken their first objectives and are pressing on to the further ones - which lie high up on the Rass O El-Zouai and DJ Mesreb El-Alig features. They have such a vast area to cover that they ask for assistance from the 4/16 Punjab (Reserve Bn). 'A' Coy of the 4/16 Punjab has already been launched against a flank pos'n and more Coys are moved up as well. Communications are difficult as most wireless sets, including those of RA F.O.O.'s, seem to be put out of action by mortar fire.

Virtual communication by lamps is established with 1/2 G.R., the 4/16 Punjab HQ is very close to Bde HQ so we can communicate with them easily enough. The 1/R Sussex moved off under a storm of fire and we cannot get any news of them. The battle rages on all night, isolated positions of enemy on the rocky hillsides continue fighting with MG's and mortars until mopped up individually.

6 April 0415 The barrage for the rest of the 8th Army attack begins about this time. The intense, almost hysterical, enemy shelling which goes on throughout the day begins. As the dawn breaks Bde HQ finds itself in a very exposed position covered by MG fire - but there is nowhere else we can go. So far, one signaller has been killed and the Jemadar and three men of the defence platoon wounded by mortar bombs.

At this time we call on 5 Bde for protection to our left flank as we have no reserves of our own, two companies of 1/9 G.R. given to us for this.

6 April 0500 As it slowly gets light 5 Bde Comd'r comes to our HQ and moves his troops through us to advance on 5 Bde objectives, the two Coys of 1/9 G.R. rejoin 5 Bde.

6 April 0630 4/16 Punjab attack a ridge on the left which is troubling us with MG fire and also holds enemy art'y O.P.'s, this they take successfully. From now onwards a steady stream of Italian POW stream back - all Pistoia.

6 April 0830 Cpt Hawkes, LO 1/R Sussex, returns from the Bn with the news that they had taken all their objectives - including the west end of the A/tk ditch. An attempt at exploitation towards Pt 152 had been forced back by arm'd cars and by flanking MG fire. Sapper recce's report that with a little work tks can be passed across the ditch, this is immediately passed back to higher authority and work begins. We are still under constant and heavy ar'ty fire, in the afternoon the NZ Corps begin to pass through our gap. The sappers have done magnificent work although they suffer grievous losses.

The CRE dies of wounds, OC 4th F'ld Coy and 2 i/c are also killed - all by shell fire working in the 'Gap'.

Major Cameron OC, our own 12 F'ld Coy, for whose help and magnificent work 7 Bde has so much to be grateful, is ordered to Div' HQ to do CRE.

Throughout the day the steady streams of POW pour back and we suffer casualties from the intense art'y fire, but not so many as should be expected considering the mass of steel continuously in the air. During the afternoon we see a grand display of flying and guts by JU 88s (stukas) - but also a grand display of shooting by 57 Lt AA Reg't, only two out of six planes get away by flying 20ft off the ground.

6 April 1530 A counter attack is launched against 1/2 G.R. but is beaten off by art'y and MG fire, masses of our own bombers zoom in perfect formation over our heads despite heavy and accurate enemy AA fire.

6 April 1800 Having twice received direct orders from Div' Comd'r to go to hospital Brig' Lovett, who's smashed wrist had caused him considerable pain all day long, leaves. Lt. Col. Firth of 1/R Sussex takes over the Bde temporarily. During the night several counter attacks are launched against 1/2 G.R. and 4/16 Punjab - but all are beaten off.

1/2nd GURKHA RIFLES
COMMANDING OFFICER LT. COLONEL L.J. SHOWERS. DSO
PLACE: FIELD. DATE: 5, 6, 7 APRIL 1943

The Bn was in position on the FUP by 2015. The formation, adopted for the approach march, was square with Bn HQ group on the axis - 'D' Coy right, 'C' Coy left forward, 'B' Coy right and 'A' Coy left rear. Coys with two Pls up in section files, Pls at visibility distance (about 20 yards interval).

At zero 2045 there was no sign of 1/R Sussex in rear. The Bde Comd. came up and the advance started. The pace laid down was 100 yds in 2 mins, and was in fact slower as the Bn had to wait for a tape reeling party to keep up with it. After some 6500 yds a cross track was reached where a change of direction had to be made. A long halt was made here to allow the rest of the Bde coln to close up.

The word was received from the B.M for the advance to continue and 'D' Coy with a Pl of Bde MMG Coy set off direct for their objective which was the double row of jagged cliffs of the outer ridge which showed up clearly on the sky line.

The Bn swung slightly left with 'C' Coy leading, 'A' and 'B' in rear in rough arrowhead, Bn HQ in the centre. Bn HQ was divided into Recce of C.O., Adjt, Lamp Sig and 2 runners; and main under the 2nd in command with Art'y O.P. Party, Bn 11 set, stretcher bearer etc. in rear. The ground rose slightly and several minor ridges were crossed. The precipitous summit of the Pt 275 feature had been used as a direction mark, but this was lost as the Bn approached under the steep outer ridge.

'C' Coy crept silently up the outer ridge, and 'A' and 'B' Coys closed up under it in a narrow wadi.

The enemy then opened heavy fire with automatics and flak guns, and threw grenades liberally. Most of the fire passed harmlessly over the heads of 'A' and 'B' Coys. The firing and shouting spread to right and left and 'C' Coy mopped up along the ridge.

There was an awkward moment as heavy fire was opened on 'C' Coy on the ridge from the plains in rear by automatics firing red tracer, which turned out to be a coy of 4/16 whose enthusiasm to take part in the battle outran their discretion.

The order was then given for 'A' and 'B' Coys to cross the ridge and press on to their respective objectives; 'A' Coy the highest point of Pt 275, and 'B' Coy the head of the gorge where the outer ridge joined the main massif.

Both these Coys engaged in hand to hand fighting before they were able to cross the outer ridge and descend the cliffs to the bowl below the main feature. 'B' Coy kept right handed, and although protected to some extent by 'D' Coy on the ridge above them, there were several pockets of enemy that had to be dealt with as they advanced. 'A' Coy also had a fair amount of opposition as they advanced and killed a number of enemy. Many tried to surrender but 'A' Coy quite rightly had no time to collect prisoners and pressed on to the foot of the cliffs.

'A' Coy made several attempts to scale the cliffs before a practicable route was found. The enemy kept up continuous fire from his fixed lines automatics but this was fairly easily avoided. On reaching the top of the cliffs 'A' Coy swung left handed and gained the crest of the Pt 275 feature with little further trouble. An Art'y O.P. was mopped up on the summit. 'B' Coy also reached their objective and reorganised and had a cold wait for the dawn.

Meanwhile, 'D' Coy had made contact at the foot of their outer ridge. A pathway led between the two ridges up a narrow gully. This was defended by a flak gun at the foot, and two M.G. posts at the top and half way up the gully. This route was most skilfully and gallantly cleared by Subedar 915 LALBAHADUR THAPA and two Sections, all three enemy posts being wiped out. 915 himself killed four enemy with his kukri and two with his pistol.

Once this route was secured Coy deployed along the ridge and did great execution with the bayonet, kukri, and by pushing enemy over the cliffs.

Main Bn HQ meanwhile, had been subjected to very heavy mortar fire and had suffered considerable loss. One bomb landed on the 11 set and severely wounded the Signal Officer, Lieut. HARLEY. Another bomb landed amongst the signal and Art'y O.P. group and severely wounded the 2nd in command, Major EDWARDS. This loss of signallers and all means of communication was a severe blow and made command and control of the Bn extremely difficult the following day.

'C' Coy had by now cleared the outer ridge and had re-organised, Lieut. GIRARDOT having been wounded early on. It was then ordered to move up across the bowl and up the cliffs to the area of 'B' Coy. This advance was helped by enemy aircraft dropping parachute flares which cast an eerie light over the cliffs surrounding the bowl. A route up the cliffs was found without difficulty and 'B' Coy was found to be firmly settled on the top.

No word had been had from 'A' Coy and as Pt 275 was the essential commanding feature of the whole area, 'C' Coy was ordered to move up and secure it. This was accomplished without incident, and 'A' Coy was found to be securely in position on the crest. Both 'A' and 'C' Coys got into position, to shoot up the enemy gun positions known to be in the valley below, as soon as it was light enough to see.

The operation so far had gone almost entirely as planned and all Coys were on their objectives as ordered. The first glimmering of daylight now started to appear, and the long finger of the El-ALIG feature could dimly be seen to the North. 'B' Coy was ordered to move up and secure the eastern end of the El-ALIG finger, and 'C' Coy to be ready to move up and support them. 'B' Coy moved out across the broken slopes of the plateau and by sunrise had secured the eastern end or base of the El-ALIG promontory. Here contact was made with 1-9 G.R. who were covering the advance of 5 Bde down the long spur to Pt 152.

'B' Coy by now consisted of only two Pls and one sec, as two secs had joined with 'C' and 'D' Coys in the confused fighting as the outer ridge was crossed. One Pl therefore, took up a position at the East end of the ridge and one Pl started to advance down the ridge to the West. They at once came under fire from enemy M.G's on the FATNASSA ridge, and also shelling and mortar fire. They pressed on however, and managed to reach the Western tip of the feature. Here they were extremely isolated and were beginning to find themselves short of ammunition. They were accordingly ordered to withdraw to a more compact Coy position at the Eastern end of the ridge.

By now 'C' Coy had moved up and was covering the gap between 'B' Coy and the 1-9 G.R. The enemy however, taking advantage of his elements on the West end of the El-ALIG finger which gave good covering fire, had started to infiltrate more automatics up the deep re-entrant between the El-ALIG and Pt 275 features. One Pl of 'C' Coy was left to cover the gap between 'B' Coy and 9 G.R., and the rest of 'C' Coy was moved over to cover the Southern face of the deep re-entrant.

Positions were extremely wide and Pls were isolated. 'A' Coy had to be left holding the vital Pt 275 feature and 'D' Coy had been moved further North but it was not possible to withdraw 'D' Coy as their position covered the whole advance of 1 R Sussex, 5 Bde, and the construction of the crossing over the A/Tk ditch.

Throughout the day the enemy tried to infiltrate up onto the ridges. Individual stalking matches between snipers and L.M.G. teams was the main feature of this phase. 'B' and 'C' Coys were beginning to get short of ammunition and one Sec even rolled rocks down onto enemy in dead ground to flush them into more open ground where they could be killed. One Sec of M.Gs was moved over from 'D' Coy area to 'B' Coy and was invaluable in repelling later counter attacks.

Throughout the day 'A' Coy on Pt 275 had been subjected to continuous shelling and mortar fire which at times was intense. 75s, some 105s and even an 88 firing direct at the cliffs swept the bare rocky slopes with splinters and flying fragments of rocks. Men had to be left in position watching the possible routes for infiltration, with no cover or means of retaliation. It was an extremely trying period for 'A' Coy who stood the strain magnificently.

During the afternoon the enemy was seen to be collecting for a counter attack, and 'D' Coy was moved up to fill the wide gap between 'C' Coy and 'A' Coy, with two pls up and one in reserve. By now the Bn was spread in one long line with ten Pls up on a front of some 3000 yds, with only one Pl of 'D' Coy in any depth, but with 'A' Coy strongly in position on Pt 275.

The lack of communications on such a wide front made control extremely difficult. 'B' and 'C' Coys had a lamp, but both other Coys had had theirs destroyed. Bn HQ only consisted of Tac HQ, and passage of orders meant long walks by the C.O., Adjt, or runners. All Art'y O.Ps had had no communication with their batteries all day. All 13 sets had been given to the Art'y O.Ps but had failed to work. No L.O. was sent from Bde.

However, at about 1600 hrs an Art'y line reached Bn HQ and it was possible to put down some D.F. 31 Fd Regt did a most effective shoot on the West end of El-ALIG which certainly prevented a counter attack being staged along the crest.

One Pl of 'A' Coy had been sent down to carry up ammunition, at dusk this had arrived and was sent out to the sorely tried 'B' and 'C' Coys.

During the afternoon 'B' Coy Commander and the Adjutant had been wounded and evacuated down the hill.

Darkness came with the Bn widely spaced but all men in position standing to and ready for the counter attacks that were known to be coming. At 0100 hrs the first of these was staged against 'B' Coy on the Northern face on El-ALIG. The enemy were clearly silhouetted against the skyline as they advanced and 'B' Coy took heavy toll of them. At the same time the D.F. fire was put down by the whole of the Div Art'y in the wadi between El-ALIG and FATNASSA with great effect.

The second counter attack was staged against 'C' and 'D' Coys at about 0300 hrs. Again the enemy gave good targets for our men and the D.G. fire, though wider out from our positions, must have caught many enemy moving up to the attack.

The enemies' effort ceased with these attacks and patrols sent out before daylight found that he had evacuated his positions on the end of the El-ALIG feature, and at first light his lorries could be seen in clouds of dust far across the plain to the North. During the early hours of daylight on 7 April the Armoured formations formed up North of the Bn position and set off in their pursuit. That evening the Bn concentrated in the Plains South of the hills and had a well earned rest.

Total casualties during the operation were :- 5 B.Os wounded. 3 G.Os wounded.

12 G.O.Rs killed and 2 died of wounds later.

32 G.O.Rs wounded.

1st BN ROYAL SUSSEX REGIMENT

COMMANDING OFFICER LT. COLONEL C.E.A. FIRTH. DSO

DATE: TIME: 5 April 1930 Hrs

Bn Moves to assembly area and forms up. 2210 Bn starts approach march.

6 April 0100 1/2nd Gurkhas are discovered by the enemy and heavy DF is brought down, nearly all of which falls on Bn, I.O. gives orders for Bn to push on to its objective.

0130 Bn has advanced to within 1,000 yds of its final objective and has suffered heavy casualties, especially in .... wadi 106528 was Cpt W.A.S. Clark - commanding 'A' Coy and Lt. R.N. Symonds (this part is difficult to make sense of but I assume these two officers became casualties in the wadi). The R.A.P. was established in this wadi and worked magnificently under continuous and heavy mortar and shell fire.

0200 Control extremely difficult as the Adj' has been wounded, the rear link set to Bde and control set within the Bn have been smashed by fire. Coys are operating more or less independently in the confusion of the night.

6 April 0230 On C.O's request a concentration of Art'y fire is put on DJ El-Meida to assist direction.

0315 Bn HQ has lost touch with 'D' Coy who have actually reached a point 300X from DJ El-Meida. 'B' and 'C' Coys rest in wadi at 101538 whilst an enemy plane drops flares overhead to assist ground forces to see the Bn.

0400 Another RA concentration is called for and under it 'D' Coy attack and capture DJ El-Meida, taking 300 POW but have the misfortune to lose their Coy Comd' Cpt. D.W. Gaylord. MC.

'B' and 'C' Coys have also advanced taking many prisoners and eventually forming up with 'D' Coy.

0415 I.O., NCO and two men from 'B' Coy go forward on a recce and reach 152 where they saw arm'd cars. C.O. decides to consolidate gains. (600X of the western edge of the anti tank ditch had been cleared on both sides by this time.)

0530 Bn has consolidated on its objectives, Tac HQ is established on the top of DJ El-Meida, many hundreds of Italian POW have been sent back.

0600 5 Bde start to pass through and take up positions without very much interference from the enemy. Snipers and M.G. posts are being mopped up by the Bn.

6 April 0900 Carriers and A/Tk guns begin to arrive as part of the A/Tk ditch has been filled in by this time.

0930 A/Tk screen is in position.

1000 R.A.P. moves up to bottom of DJ El-Meida, mortar and Art'y fire is directed upon the Bn but there are few casualties.

1300 Mortaring has ceased, but as the first tanks roll over the A/Tk ditch some very heavy guns begin to shell the area. This continued throughout the afternoon.

1600 Bn is placed under command of 5 Bde for operations, and Lt. Col. C.E.A. Firth assumes com'd of Bde, Major J.B. Glennie assumes com'd of Bn.

1700 C.Os Conference; when consolidation details were fixed: companies re-organising around DJ El-Meida, special attention being paid to the left flank. 'A' Coy took up position round 095546, 'B' Coy at 099548, 'C' Coy 098547 and 'D' Coy 098544.

1800 Rations and blankets arrive.

1830 Bn stands to, until 1930 hours.

7 April 0210 1/9th Gurkhas, established on Mesrib El-Alig, report suspected enemy forming up for counter attack and call for D.F. Bn stand to.

0330 Bn ordered to stand down, remaining hours of darkness are peaceful.

4/16th PUNJAB REGIMENT
COMMANDING OFFICER LT. COLONEL. H.A. HUGHES. MBE. DSO
DATE: TIME:

6 April 0015 Arrived at cross tracks and proceeded towards gap.

0030 Arrived in the foothills of the main range and squatted: After a few minutes the 1/2nd Gurkhas, having commenced their attack, surprised the enemy who brought down their small arms and mortar DF largely in the Bde area.

0045 'B' Coy sent off to positions (as on sketch), they started off with a great deal of shouting and spirit which infected 'D' Coy and 'C' Coy behind them who also started to follow. 'C' Coy was stopped but 'D' Coy got 'carried' into the attack and only got back after an hour.

0050 'A' Coy sent off to position (as on sketch).

0100 Bn HQ moved up into position in a Nullah, which became too'hot' due to mortar fire and it moved 50 yds into a re-entrant and dug in as quickly as possible. Eventually mortar fire came down heavily in this area too; this area being crowded with the RAP: just below our HQ. Many casualties coming in and being attended to.

0130 'C' Coy sent forward into position (as in sketch), 'D' Coy took up reserve position in Nullah behind Bn HQ.

Mortared throughout the hours of darkness, sustaining casualties in Bn HQ as well as Coys. 6 signallers and 3 being wounded besides others. Aeroplane flares helped enemy locate our positions, these were dropped for a period of about an hour.

0500 'D' Coy ordered to capture a large feature south of main road, on which enemy had an O.P. and guns. Art'y barrage to assist in approach.

0530 to Art'y barrage onto feature.

0545 'D' Coy south of road held up by M.G. and mortar fire.

0600 'B' Coy exploited position in the light and commenced rounding up prisoners: reported 570 and 8 officers (all Italian) by 0830 hrs.

0700 One Platoon of 'B' Coy under Hav' Mohammed Aslam proceeded round and up the rear right of 'D' Coy's objective, so cutting off and eliminating the enemy here, and assisting 'D' Coy who then took over the objective, (as in the sketch).

Bn remained in this lay out, mopping up and rounding up further prisoners throughout the day. Enemy fire continued sporadically and inaccurately due to lack of O.Ps.

1100 Mortars, carriers and anti tank guns arrive in area. One mortar in carrier allocated to 'D' Coy, A/Tk guns placed to cover the road and

Bde HQ area.

1630 Food, blankets etc., mess and other stores arrive in area and distributed to Coys. 'D' Coy reported enemy to the south west as if preparing for a counter attack. F.O.O. asked for from Bde and reported to 'D' Coy. D.F. fire tasks allotted.

5th INFANTRY BRIGADE HEAD QUARTERS
COMMANDING OFFICER BRIGADIER D.R.E.R. BATEMAN. CIE. DSO. OBE

Tac Bde HQ moved up behind 7 Bde and halted at X tracks 130508 at 0200 hrs. C.Os of 1/9 G.R. and 4 Raj Rif were sent for. Intercepts from 7 Bde revealed that they were progressing but rather slowly.

At 0245 hrs 7 Bde were heard asking Div if one Bn of 5 Bde could be sent forward. Div ordered the whole Bde to move up, this they did arriving 7 Bde HQ area at 0315 hrs.

The situation at 7 Bde was not clear and there was no touch with the Royal Sussex who had been sent to El-MEIDA.

Comd 7 Bde said he did not want the Bde to go through but did want 1/9 G.R. There was heavy and continuous mortar fire the whole time.

Comd 5 Bde left 1/9 G.R. with 7 Bde and moved back about 1/2 a mile down the track and halted with 4 Raj Rif.

At 0500 hrs it became apparent that unless the Bde moved at once they would be caught in the open, in daylight, in full view of the enemy. Tac Bde HQ and 4 Raj Rif again moved up to 7 Bde HQ. 1/9 G.R. had not been committed so Comd 5 Bde left two coys with 7 Bde and ordered the Bn, less two coys, round the right where it was possible to move wheels, they were guided by Major Cameron, Comd 12 Fd Coy, and found the Royal Sussex axis. There was considerable congestion while moving off from 7 Bde HQ and several casualties from shell fire including the Signal Officer Capt. Currie.

1/9 G.R. (less two coys) followed by Tac Bde HQ moved up the Nullah at 103430. Italians were met coming off the hills to surrender.

At about 0600 hrs L.O. was sent to order one Coy 4 Raj Rif to come up and move ahead of Tac Bde HQ. They arrived about 0630 hrs.

At 0645 hrs Bde Comd and C.O. 4 Raj Rif went to 1/9 G.R. HQ at 098537 and saw that the leading coy was moving on towards X tracks 087545. It was decided to send 4 Raj Rif after the 1/9 G.R.

On return to the wadi an L.O. from R. Sussex, on his way to 7 Bde, told Bde Comd his Bn had been counter attacked by armd cars and that the posn there was not secure. Bde Comd therefore, decided to send 4

Raj Rif, less one coy, to El-MEIDA - these orders were given forthwith.

By 0700 hrs 'C' Coy 1/9 G.R. were in posn overlooking the enemy posns at 86557.

At 1000 hrs a message came from 4 Div to say that 1/4 Essex were being sent round by 7 Bde axis as the 50 Div bridgehead had not been established. A message from 7 Bde that the two coys of 1/9 G.R. were being sent to rejoin 5 Bde.

1/4 Essex arrived about 1300 hrs and were sent on behind 4 Raj Rif who had, by this time, reached Oudane 0955 and had reported that the R. Sussex were firmly established and had got some A Tk guns through.

At 1230 hrs the two coys of 1/9 G.R. arrived from 7 Bde and were sent on to join the remainder of the Bn which had by this time captured their final objective at 0856.

By 1400 hrs the situation was as follows; 1/9 G.R. were established on their final objective and 'C' Coy was being persistently counter attacked from the direction of BATEUN DJEDARA
The road over the A Tk ditch at 102547 was open and wheels had been through.

The 4 Raj Rif were on the Pt 152 ridge and the 1/4 Essex had passed through the Royal Sussex and were on OUDANE El-HACHANA.

At 1430 hrs Tac Bde HQ moved by this route and established Tac Bde HQ at 104330. This posn and road were heavily shelled until last light.

At 1500 hrs the Comd 7 Bde arrived and said that the R. Sussex were to come under comd 5 Bde for re-organisation of the posn. The verbal orders for the re-organisation of the posn were given out by Bde Comd.

By 1800 hrs an A Tk screen had been established and defensive fire tasks fixed.

At 1830 hrs it was decided to change the location of Tac Bde HQ as the nala in which they were situated was very crowded and under accurate enemy shell fire.

Bde Comd and L.O. recced a site at 103542 and Tac Bde, less signal exchange, moved at 1900 hrs.

At 1900 hrs O.C. 4 Raj Rif telephoned to say that he thought there was a counter attack forming up and he wanted Hawkins mines and A Tk guns, also an ambulance. 500 Hawkins mines were sent up from 7 Bde with a sapper who had brought the message, he also took an ambulance but this went astray in the dark.

B.M. visited O.C. 1/4 Essex and told him to ensure that he had established contact with R. Sussex on his right and that he was to be prepared to support 4 Raj Rif in case a counter attack developed. D.F. fire was called for by 4 Raj Rif during the night but the counter attack did not develop and turned out to be a screen put out by the enemy to cover a withdrawal.

By first light the armour had not passed through and 4 Raj Rif sent out carrier patrols as the armour reported that there was still 88 mm's about. Co-operation between the artillery and carriers resulted in the rounding up of a considerable number of prisoners. The armour then moved into the plain. Patrols were also sent out by 1/9 G.R.

The enemy had withdrawn from the posn during the night.

At 0900 hrs orders came from Div that the Div was to concentrate in an area SOUTH of the A Tk ditch. Unit recce parties were sent for at 1000 hrs.

The total Bde casualties were about 120 killed and wounded. Lt. Col. J.H. Blundell, C.R.E., and Major W.J.A. Murray, Capt. J. Baldwin of 4 Fd Coy were killed near the A Tk ditch on 50 Div front.

1/4th BN THE ESSEX REGIMENT
COMMANDING OFFICER LT. COLONEL A. NOBLE. DSO
DATE TIME

5 April 1/4 Essex with the following supporting arms were alone 1943 responsible for attacking frontally and securing the approaches to the bridgehead made by 69 Bde:- 11 Field Regt. R.A., 513 Bty. A/TK Regt. S Bty 149 A/Tk regt., 'D' Coy MMGs RAJ. RIF., 4 Field Coy. I.E. On securing the approaches a local bridgehead over enemy anti tank ditch was to be made. The C.O. then gave the order and times of Bn advance.

1915 Bn left for assembly area and on arrival the C.O. called an 'O' G.P conference at 2015 hrs to issue final orders and timings for the attack.

6 April 0230 The C.O. held an 'O' G.P. conference to give final check on co-ordination of advance.

0300 'A' Coy went fwd to Pt 51, map ref. 123518, and at 0400 hrs the arty laid preliminary barrage on Pt 85, a previously selected target.

0440 Bn HQ with 'C', 'D' and 'B' Coys proceeded to Pt. 51, map ref. 123518.

0600 'A' Coy succeeded in reaching first objective and linking up in rear of 7 Bde, they were however, at once subjected to enemy arty fire. Bn HQ advanced to a point 500 yds NW of Pt. 51, at this posn 'C' and 'D' Coys followed by 'B' Coy in reserve passed through Bn HQ at 0645 hrs.

0700 The entire Bn axis came under heavy shell fire from the enemy. During the morning the Bn continued to advance, but progress was slow, though 7 Bde appeared to have captured the enemy psns on the left, resulting in many POW, and the storming of the ROUMANA feature by the 51 Div appeared to be continuing successfully, the issue fwd appeared to be confused.

On arrival in the 'A' Coy area the C.O. found that 50 Div had failed to secure a bridgehead over the anti tank ditch and decided that the battalion would have to form its own bridgehead to enable a crossing to be made. O.C's 'C' and 'D' Coys were called fwd for orders but before a bridgehead operation could be launched the C.O. received orders from Div by R/T to the effect that the Bn was to switch to the 7 Bde axis and follow up behind 5 Bde. The change of axis was successfully carried out under heavy fire and the C.O. went fwd to contact 5 Bde Tac HQ with 'D', 'B' and 'C' Coys following.

The support group under Major L.W.A. CHAPPELL was left at the foot of the hills with 'A' Coy for protection and to be available for porterage.

6 April   On arrival Tac Bde HQ the B.C. gave orders for the Bn to 1943 secure the OUDANE feature and to exploit fwd. Contacting O.C. 4/6 RAJ. RIF a plan was made for securing OUDANE and for re-organisation of the Bde objective area. This was immediately put into effect. Reorganisation weapons were brought up on the 7 Bde axis over the tank ditch.

1330 The C.O. left to visit 'B', 'C' and 'D' Coys to co-ordinate the defence of the OUDANE feature. 'A' Coy who were still in the area of the crossing proper came under comd 1/9 GURKHAS. The C.O. then issued orders for patrols from each fwd coy to contact flanking units; after which the C.O. liaised with the O.C. 4/6 RAJ. RIF. to discuss measures to block any enemy counter attack and DF tasks were arranged.

At this time the advance elements of the armour began passing through the bridgehead and on to the open country. Supporting arms also arrived and from thence manhandled to appropriate defensive posns.

For the remainder of the day the enemy continued to shell the Bn area, concentrating mainly on the approaches to and from the A Tk crossing.

Bn casualties during this action were 1 officer killed, Lieut. G.R. C. SINGLE, 8 O.Rs killed, 25 O.Rs wounded, 2 of the latter later succumbing to their wounds.

7 April During the night, 90 Light Div formed up to counter attack the posn but the attack was broken up by D.F. fire.

1/9th GURKHA RIFLES
COMMANDING OFFICER: LT. COL. ROCHE
PLACE: FIELD DATE: 6, 7, 8, 9, 10 APRIL, 1943

6 April   At 0400 hrs - 0500 hrs, we were shelled and mortared and casualties occurred. At 0415 hrs, the barrage of 50 and 51 Divs on our

right began. Shortly before first light we contacted 7 Bde HQ and awaited information from them as to the success of their operation.

At first light the Bn, less two coy's, advanced. 'A' and 'D' Coys were put under comd Comdr. 7 Bde. 'C' Coys objective was the gun posns. 0855 and 082561 (74 NE) Pt. 152 to be taken by the 4/6 Raj Rif. The excellent navigation and clear marking of the route by 7 Bde assisted greatly in 'C' Coy making a good start. It was now light and enemy O.Ps still on some of the heights dominating the whole of the remainder of the Division.

By the prompt action of 'D' and 'A' Coys under Capt. M.P.F. Jones and Capt. D.H. Donovan, acting on orders from Comdr 7 Bde, the SW of the GAFSA road were captured, meanwhile 'C' Coy pushed on very quickly and captured its position. We now dominated the enemies' positions but unfortunately R.A. communications broke down and good chances were missed for a space of three hours. The 3" mortars with 'C' Coy did not have sufficient range to make good use of this opportunity. The R.A. W/T was carried by men of a Lt. A/A Regt. and failed to appear until later in the morning.

At 1300 hrs 'A' and 'D' Coys rejoined the Bn and extended 'C' Coys posn to the right to cover the attack on Pt. 152. Shortly before 'A' and 'D' Coys arrival, a counter attack was put in on 'C' Coy's posn. This was pressed home and one Pl had to withdraw slightly, as its own posn was untenable owing to M.G. fire. A Pl of M.Gs from M.G. Bn Raj. Rif. were sent to 'C' Coy. who were now running short of ammunition, having only what they had carried forward. The Bn reserve had not arrived, as the priority over the A/Tk ditch crossing was given to the armour and NZ tps who were to pass through our posn. Some M.G. amn and 3" mortar amn was borrowed from neighbouring units and relieved the situation until our Bn A. Echelon arrived with ammunition.

4/6 Raj. Rif went through to capture Pt. 152 at 1400 hrs.

Heavy shelling was taking place during the afternoon of the only crossing of the A/Tk ditch causing casualties to vehicles and men, but none from the Battalion. At dusk the situation remained unchanged and our position made more secure by a Coy from 1/4 Essex put under comd. for counter attack.

The enemy had reached within 30 yds from 'C' Coy's posn, at one period during the day. During the night a counter attack was put in on the 1/2 G.R. on our left but only machine gunning and mortaring of our posn was experienced. The counter attack on 1/2 G.R. posn was not successful, and after this it became apparent that the enemy was making preparations to withdraw.

7 April At 0830 hrs, the pursuit of enemy began. Our armour and NZ Div went forward of our posn EAST of the TEBAGA Hills (map ref. 1053 (74 NE). This was completed by early afternoon. This was the first real engagement the Bn has been in and the reactions of the men were beyond even our expectations. The oppositions was mainly Italian, but the Germans carried out the counter attack on 'C' Coy being men from 90th Light Division. 'C' Coy killed 5 and captured 4 Germans. The total number of prisoners is hard to assess as Italians were continually coming in and walking to Bde or higher Hqrs without escorts, it being impossible to escort all of them but approximately 500 were taken by the Bn with the majority of their equipment including artillery and M.Gs. A lesson learnt was that the men detailed as porters must be controlled and commanded carefully, especially at night and NCO's told off for this task. Casualties sustained by the Bn were 2 G.O's and 29 G.O.Rs wounded, two of the latter died in the RAP. Five men are missing. A stick of five bombs fell in Bn area in the evening. Jemadar BHUPAL THAPA was seriously wounded and died in the ADS.

8 April Major General F.I.S. TUKER. OBE. Comr 4th Ind Div visited the Bn and spoke to B.Os, G.Os and also selected men brought forward by the Coy Comdrs for good work. This was greatly appreciated by all ranks, many of whom could remember Major General as Commanding Officer of the 1/2nd Gurkha Rifles. The remainder of the day was spent in checking up and field maintenance.

Message from commander 4th Indian Division to 5 Brigade read 'I cannot express my gratefulness and admiration for each one of you.'

9 April The Bde is now salvaging the battlefield. M.O. discovered three of missing men had been wounded and were evacuated. Two are still missing.

10 April Bn still salvaging Battle area. The following were put in for immediate awards as a result of operations:-

Captain D.M. Amoore O.C. 'C' Coy. Jemadar Uttarbahadur Basnet.

2319. MC. BHIAN BAHADUR ICHATHI. 'C' Coy.2470. L KHAR BAHADUR ICHATHI. 'C' Coy. LT. S.H. JAMES.

4/6th RAJPUTANA RIFLES
COMMANDING OFFICER: LT. COL. SCOTT. DSO
HOUR PLACE: FIELD DATE: 6 APRIL 1943

0400 Battalion heavily shelled whilst advancing along STAR track. One V.C.O. and one I.O.R. wounded.

0530 Battalion advancing towards hills in WADIS. Enemy suddenly opens heavy and accurate fire on Battalion with artillery and mortars. We suffer casualties.

0645 Battalion in WADI at 100532.

0800 'A' Company protection Company for 5 Brigade Headquarters.

0830 Receive orders to reinforce the Royal Sussex Regiment (7 Bde) on the El-MEIDA feature (0954). Battalion moved forward under heavy artillery and mortar fire to the Royal Sussex area.

1000 Liaise with C.O. Royal Sussex, who informs C.O. that they had reached point 152 (0956) early but had been forced to withdraw by enemy Armd. cars.

1030 C.O. orders 'D' Company supported by 'C' Company and by 'A' Company M.G. Bn to capture the OUDANE El-HACHANA feature (1055).

1130 After being under heavy fire during the advance 'D' Company captures its objective taking some 700 POW. (SPEZIA & PISTOIA Divisions, and Marco Marino Bns).

1140 Battalion Headquarters moved forward to 'D' Company area. 'C' Company advances through 'D' Company to further objective.

1210 'A' Company rejoins Battalion.

1230 'C' Company capture objective taking some 450 prisoners.

1245 'A' Company advance through 'D' Company and attempt to get round to the right of Pt. 152 but come under very heavy fire. Company Commander changed direction and continues advance to the left.

1400 'A' Company capture Pt. 152.

1430 C.O. orders 'C' Company to take up positions on left of 'A' Company.

1500 Battalion Headquarters moved forward to a position 500 yards in the rear of forward Companies. 3 R.T.R., about eight Shermans and four Crusaders come up.

1530 Battalion reorganises on Pt. 152 feature with 'C' Company left forward, 'A' Company centre and 'D' Company right, protecting our right flank.

1530 1/4 Essex Regt. takes up positions on OUDANE El-HACHANA feature. R.A. O.P. engages large concentration of enemy M.T. and tanks about 5,000 yards forward of our position.

1730 Observe formations of enemy in M.T. with tanks advancing towards Battalion.

Co-ordinate D.F. tasks. 3 R.T.R. take up positions in wadi NE of Pt. 152 to cover the possible approach of any enemy tanks.

1800 Fighting vehicles group arrives.

A/Tk guns and mortars put in position. Battalion prepares to receive expected counter attack.

During 6 April the Battalion suffered 3 I.O.Rs killed, 2 B.Os, 1 V.C.O. and 35 I.O.Rs wounded.

SUBEDAR (LATER HON CPT) LALBAHADUR THAPA. VC. OBI 'D' COMPANY. 1st BATTALION. 2ND KING EDWARDS VII'S OWN GURKHA RIFLES. (SIRMOOR RIFLES)

Subedar Lalbahadur Thapa shows his kukri to photoraphers at Buckingham Palace, 26th September 1943.
(Courtesy of Imperial War Museum)

BIOGRAPHICAL DETAILS

Lalbahadur Thapa was born in 1907 in the village of SOMSA THRUN HUP, GULMI TEHSIL, BAGLUNG PARBAT DISTRICT, NEPAL. The life of his people was hard and a constant battle against hunger, exhaustion and disease. They live on a meagre diet of rice and maize, there is no medical treatment available and children are deemed to have a good chance of survival if they reach their second year. Fighting against the forces of nature is a way of life for the people of Nepal and such natural selection has produced men small in stature - but as hard as nails.

For his magnificent achievement at the 'Battle of the Wadi Akarit' Colonel Showers recommended Lalbahadur Thapa for an immediate Military Cross, the Army Commander read the citation and at once increased the award to the Victoria Cross - the highest award for valour. He was decorated with the ribbon of the Victoria Cross, by His Majesty King George VI at Tripoli on 19 June 1943, and with the Victoria Cross in the quadrangle of Buckingham Palace, 26 September 1943.

'Who's Who' recorded the life and achievements of the dauntless Subedar as follows:

THAPA, Hon. Captain Lalbahadur. V.C., O.B.I.,

Subedar Bahadur (ret) 4th Class Order of the most refulgent order of the star of Napal. Is farming in Nepal. Born 1907. Hurkha, Hindu. Married 1932 Hagti; 4 sons, 2 daughters; rifleman, Indian Army, 1925; Lance-Naik, January 1930; Naik, May, 1930; Havildar 1933; Company Havildar Major 1935. Jemadar 1937, Subadar 1940; Subadar Major, 1944; Retired 1949 (granted hon. rank of Captain), 2nd King Edward VII's Own Gurkha Rifles, The Brigade of Gurkhas, Malaya.

Recreations: Hunting boars and tigers, gardening:

Address: Simsa, Thantap, 4,000 Parbat Baglung, Nepal.

The citation for the award appeared in the London Gazette on 15 June 1943, and is here recorded in full:

WAR OFFICE, 15 JUNE, 1943

The King has been graciously pleased to approve the award of the Victoria Cross to:

Subedar Lalbahadur Thapa (915), 2nd King Edward VII's Own Gurkha Rifles, Indian Army. On the night of 5/6 April, 1943, during the silent attack on the Rass-El-Zouai feature, Subedar Lalbahadur Thapa was second-in-command of 'D' Company. The Commander of N° 16 Platoon was detached with one Section to secure an isolated feature on the left of the Company's objective. Subedar Lalbahadur Thapa took command of the remaining two sections and led them forward towards the main feature on the outer ridge, in order to break through and secure the one and only passage by which the vital commanding feature could be seized to cover the penetration of the Division into the hills. On the capture of these hills the whole success of the Corps plan depended.

First contact with the enemy was made at the foot of a pathway winding up a narrow cleft. This steep cleft was thickly studded with a series of enemy posts, the inner of which contained an anti tank gun and the remainder medium machine guns. After passing through the narrow cleft, one emerges into a small arena with very steep sides, some 200 feet in height, and in places sheer cliff. Into this arena and down its sides numbers of automatic weapons were trained and mortar fire directed.

The garrison of the outer posts were all killed by Subedar Lalbahadur Thapa and his men by kukri or bayonet in the first rush, and the enemy then opened very heavy fire straight down the narrow enclosed pathway and steep arena sides.

Subedar Lalbahadur Thapa led his men on and fought his way up the narrow gully straight through the enemy's fire, with little room to manoeuvre, in the face of intense and sustained machine gun concentrations and the liberal use of grenades by the enemy.

The next machine gun posts were dealt with, Subedar Lalbahadur Thapa personally killing two men with his kukri and two more with his revolver. This Gurkha officer continued to fight his way up the narrow bullet swept approaches to the crest. He and two Riflemen managed to reach the crest, where Subedar Lalbahadur Thapa killed another two men with his kukri, the Riflemen killed two more and the rest fled. Subedar Lalbahadur Thapa then secured the whole feature and covered his Company's advance up the defile.

This pathway was found to be the only practicable route up the precipitous ridge, and by securing it the Company was able to deploy and mop up all enemy opposition on their objective. This objective was an essential feature covering the further advance of the Brigade and the Division, as well as the bridgehead over the anti tank ditch.

There is no doubt that the capture of this objective was entirely due to this act of unsurpassed bravery by Subedar Lalbahadur Thapa and his small party in forcing their way up the steep gully, and up the cliffs of the arena under withering fire. The outstanding leadership, gallantry and complete disregard for his own safety shown by Subedar Lalbahadur Thapa were an example to the whole Company, and the ruthless determination of this Gurkha officer to reach his objective and kill his enemy had a decisive effect on the success of the whole operation.

Lalbahadur Thapa retired from the army in 1949, with the honorary rank of Captain, he returned to his homeland and tended his fields to provide for his family as his forefathers had done before him. In 1956 he returned to England to take part in the 'Victoria Cross Centenary Review' on 26 June held by Her Majesty Queen Elizabeth II in Hyde Park, London.

He died at 11pm on 19 October 1968, at the age of 61 years, from tuberculosis. His place of death was PAKLIHAWA, NEPAL, his obituary appeared in the Daily Telegraph on 2 November 1968; recounting his bravery at the Wadi Akarit.

In his tiny village, his wife was determined his bravery would not be forgotten and pinned his twelve medals to a rough wooden cross, this was then planted in the maize field he had tended since leaving the army. The villagers know the meaning of the medals but few know the details of how Lalbahadur's Victoria Cross was won: when as a young man he and his comrades had stormed the heights of Ras-El-Zouai and earned the respect and admiration of friend and foe alike.

Subedar Lalbahadur Thapa receives the Victoria Cross from the King at Buckingham Palace.
(Courtesy of Imperial War Museum)

CHAPTER TWO

THE CENTRE:
50th NORTHUMBRIAN DIVISION ATTACKS

Major General J.S. Nichols, DSO, MC, Commander,
50th Northumbrian Division.
(Courtesy of the Imperial War Museum)

'Give me a brew-can and let me go far away up in the blue,
Sit in a laager and talk of the days of Benghazi and Mersa-Matruh.
Sand in my teeth – sand in my hair,
Free from all worries - far from all care,
And no red-cap to check me for the clobber I wear,
Far away up in the blue.'

'The Blue': supplied by
Mr William Gleave. (ex Green Howards)

69th BRIGADE
COMMANDING OFFICER: BRIGADIER E. C. COOKE-COLLIS. DSO

On 2 April, General 'Crasher' Nichols returned to his headquarters with orders concerning the Division's part in the coming battle; its various components were scattered over a wide area and most of its transport had been sent to other units and not returned. As it was to be only the 69th Brigade that was to take part in the actual assault at Akarit, transport was taken from the Division's artillery regiments. The artillery support for the attack was to be provided by the gunners of the New Zealand Division.

The men of the 69th Brigade had the unenviable task of making a frontal attack on the centre of the Akarit positions against strongly held defences, before their 'forming up positions' (FUP's) stretched the open rolling downlands that would at first glance seem to give easy access to an army. The hills on either side however, dominated every yard of this sector and enemy engineers had added to the natural barriers artificial ones; deep anti tank ditches made jagged scars across the foothills, one of these lay across the front of the enemy's defences in the centre and the 69th Brigade would have to cross it to get to their objectives. Its approaches were peppered with mines and wire, making very unpleasant traps for infantry and tanks. The brigade would have to advance over several low ridges and only when they reached the last

one, would the anti tank ditch come into view. On the ground that fell away before them, they would come under fire from every enemy gun on the front and as they struggle in the deep mud of the anti tank ditch, would be subjected to terrific enfilade fire from Roumana Ridge and a battery of 88's to its rear.

Standing sentinel to the enemy's main central defences and to the front–

Sappers clear and mark a path through a minefield for the attacking troops.

right of 69th Brigade was a feature known as the 'Pimple'; that rose straight up out of the plain to a height of three hundred feet and allowed the enemy machine-gunners and mortar-teams to dominate the right flank of 69th Brigade and the left flank of the 51st Highland Division.

It's early capture was essential if the main assault was not to be held up, in the brigade war diary this feature was code-named 'cutie' and was marked 'Point 85' on their maps.

On 1 April a warning order was received to the effect that 69th Brigade was to be ready to move at short notice under the command of 30 Corps as from 0800 hours on 2 April. In the early hours of 2 April the 69th Brigade arrived at the area north-west of the village of Oudref and came under the command of the 4th Indian Division. Reconnaissance parties from Brigade HQ and the 6th Battalion Green Howards paid a visit to 4th Indian Divisions HQ and then proceeded to seek out a suitable spot for the 6th Battalion's forward observation post, facing the hills of the Akarit positions.

At 0900 hours on 2 April Brigade HQ and 6th Battalion Green Howards started their move to the forward area, by 1800 hours Brigade HQ was established at z.164475 and by last light the 6th Battalion was moving into their new positions; establishing themselves during the night.

On 3 April at 1045 hours a warning order was sent out by 50 Div' HQ that the Brigade – with 124th Field Regiment RA and New Zealand artillery under command – would take part in the coming attack. The remainder of 69th Brigade was still in the rear and was ordered to move forward at once. At 1100 hours General Nichols gave out details to his brigade and company commanders of their role in the coming battle and 69th Brigade once again came under the command of the 50th Division.

On 4 April enemy activity along the front was quiet except for some shelling of the 6th Green Howards positions. At 0900 hours General Nichols visited 69th Brigade's HQ – to brief it's officers on the forthcoming operations.

Late at night of 5 April the 5th Battalion East Yorkshire Regiment and the 7th Battalion Green Howards moved through the dark towards their assembly areas and were in position by midnight. From here they pressed on to their start line. Enemy aircraft dropped chandelier flares in the area lighting the place up like day and the troops were grounded for some considerable time but were in position on schedule.

The Yorkshiremen of the 69th Brigade stood to arms on their exposed position protected by the darkness, beyond them lay the rolling downland which was their objective, at the foot of which lay an anti tank ditch 8 to 10 feet deep. Cpt C.E. Lucas-Philips was sat beside Brigadier Cooke-Collis at the advanced command post of 69th Brigade and looked on, entranced as the Ghurka's stormed Zouai:

"The sudden outbursts of fire, the long flashes of the Italian Bredas stabbing the night, the streams of tracer shot, the crackle of grenades, the chatter of bren and Tommy gun as the Ghurka's cat footed and cat eyed rapidly fought their way up the steep uprising of the hill. What could not be observed was the swinging of the Ghurka Kukri. Higher and higher rose the flashes and the streaks of coloured tracers, until at last the pinnacle was reached and, for a moment, all was silent."

At 0415 hours in the chill of a desert night, a terrific barrage opened up on the enemy positions, those who witnessed such a barrage will never forget its violence. General Messe described the sight as "an apocalyptic hurricane of steel and fire."

THE 7th BATTALION – GREEN HOWARDS
COMMANDING OFFICER: LT COL A SEAGRIM. VC

At 3.30am 'C' Company of the 7th Green Howards was ready and waiting at their start line. Captain Mansell led them to the attack and the heavily laden troops plodded forward towards Point 85, one hour in advance of the remainder of the battalion. The front face of Point 85 was too steep to attack and so the leading platoon, under the command of Lt

Underlay, made for the left flank of this feature, this gave an easier line of approach. Sappers moved before the infantry laying tapes through the mine field for the men to follow, as they did this, Sergeant Topcliffe directed the fire of his section upon the enemy making them keep their heads down.

As the lead platoon rushed to the attack, they were met by a storm of grenades, rifle and machine gun fire, heavy casualties ensued; Sgt Topcliffe being killed outright and Lt Underlay wounded. Simultaneously, Captain Mansell and Sgt Dixon led another platoon round the rear of the feature and rushed at the enemy firing from the hip and hurling grenades before them. While the battle was in progress, Lt Nosotti had taken his platoon up the front face of Point 85 on their hands and knees. Upon reaching the crest they were very close to the enemy and a grenade thrown at them wounded Lt Nosotti and Pte Brennan, and blew the foot off Pte Priest. Many of the enemy were now caught in a cross fire between Lt Nosotti's and Sgt Dixon's platoons and gave up the fight; the position was then cleared.

'C' Company had suffered heavy losses in this swift and successful action, as dawn broke only two officers and twenty two other ranks were still fit for duty. Approximately eighty prisoners were taken and many more enemy troops were killed or wounded. Point 85 was to prove an invaluable reconnaissance aid during the battle to come and was to remain securely in the hands of the Green Howards.

While this action was being fought, 'A' and 'B' Companies moved up to their start line and began their advance upon the anti tank ditch at 0430 hours. Their final objective being two hundred yards beyond it. As they moved up, the troops walked straight into a minefield, which held up their progress.

By daylight they were in the open, unable to get forward and exposed to extremely heavy fire from enemy positions. Lt Colonel Seagrim went forward to see what was happening and in an effort to get the attack moving again he led his men down towards the anti tank ditch. Seagrim fell at the head of his men, never knowing he had been awarded the Victoria Cross for his brave actions at the Mareth-Line.

'D' Company had by now been led by Captain Roberts up Point 85 to reinforce 'C' Company, taking numerous casualties in the process. 'A' and 'B' Companies could not now, despite valiant efforts, get to their objective because of the terrific volume of fire directed upon them.

THE 5th BATTALION – EAST YORKSHIRE REGIMENT
COMMANDING OFFICER: LT. COL. R. B. JAMES. DSO

The 5th East Yorkshires deployed and advanced towards the anti tank ditch which lay deceptively beyond the dead ground of a reverse slope strewn with mines. Enemy defensive fire was light at first and the troops followed the creeping barrage closely as it rumbled and roared before them. By 0500 hours – judging distance from their maps – the forward troops calculated they should now be at the anti tank ditch: but it was nowhere in sight. The barrage was still coming down to the Yorkshiremen's front, indeed some shells were arriving among them. The advance continued at the pace set by the creeping barrage, that of one hundred yards every three minutes.

The complete absence of small arms fire lulled some men into thinking the enemy had withdrawn. These thoughts however, were soon rudely dispelled when after crossing a small ridge the men where confronted with the anti tank ditch and a storm of machine gun fire from the high ground to the north east. Any forward movement by the Yorkshiremen was met by intense small arms fire and direct fire from mortars, 47mm guns and other close support artillery.
'C' Company advanced on the right under cover of smoke laid down by mortars and artillery. This move met such violent opposition that many men were killed and wounded, only a handful made it to the anti tank ditch but had to be withdrawn, so intense was the volume of fire they came under. Long range guns were now adding to the carnage and the battalion was forced to pull back some two hundred yards behind the crest, bringing many of their wounded with them but inevitably leaving others behind on the exposed slope.

It was now daylight and slowly the sun dispersed the early morning mist. In a forward observation post, manned by an officer and his signallers, the observers were astonished to see a solitary figure crawling down the fire swept slope in front of them, the figure was Pte. Eric Anderson, a stretcher-bearer with the 5th East Yorkshires. He crawled 150 yards down into the deep anti tank ditch, under full observation of the enemy.

There he gave morphine to a wounded soldier, picked him up onto his shoulders and slowly crawled back up the slope to the comparatively safe side of the ridge. As he did so the ground all around him was being ripped up by enemy fire. This was only the start, the observers watched in awe as Anderson went out a second time to bring in another wounded man in the same way. Without thought for himself, he went out for a third time and seemed fated to be unhurt as the enemy machine guns and mortars did their worst. A fourth time he ventured forth and with each gallant exploit the odds of survival were lessened, the shrapnel and flying bullets cannot be defied forever.

Anderson must have been physically worn out by now, but each time he returned other wounded men would call to him 'can you return for me Andy?' and he did. And so he set off with his fourth casualty on his back up the slope, now the only target on this sector, and was hit and mortally wounded.

THE 6th BATTALION – GREEN HOWARDS
COMMANDING OFFICER: LT . COL. G. LANCE. DSO

Following the 7th Battalion came the 6th Battalion Green Howards. When the dawn broke, the men of the 6th were caught in an exposed position on open ground, unable to get further forward because of the opposition encountered by the 7th who were hung up. The enemy spotted the exposed men and at once directed an artillery barrage upon them. Shells exploded with shattering detonations in and around the helpless men and killed and wounded many. When Point 85 had finally been cleared, the companies of the 6th Battalion moved up to a position in the lee of this feature, affording them some small protection. As they arrived, a shower of mortar bombs fell among 'C' Company who took more casualties as they passed through. Many Italians now gave themselves up as the Green Howards advance overran position after position.

'A' Company advanced to the lower slopes of the Jebel Roumana and became pinned down by the terrific rate of fire being directed against them. 'C' Company however, did not meet such strong opposition and pressed on until they too were stopped by the heavy concentration of defensive fire coming from the wadi and ground beyond. Every effort to break the dead lock was met by a ferocious response from the defenders and each effort cost the attackers dearly.

The platoons fought their way forward into this maelstrom, taking many prisoners as they did so. Many of the positions now being taken could have severely impeded the progress of the forward units, especially the high velocity anti tank guns, which had been holding up

Troops of the East Yorkshire Regiment advance over the rolling downlands as mortar fire drops around them. (*Author's collection*)

any vehicles using the only track. L/Sgt Laidler and L/Cpl Bull pressed on up the wadi and were rewarded for their efforts by the capture of four Italian Officers – one of General rank. The General packed a suitcase and asked Laidler if he would take him to his Commanding Officer. The four officers then stepped into the General's car with Sgt Laidler keeping an eye on them.

Laidler was looking forward to taking his captives to the rear when a member of another Company spotted the strange car and shot the General dead, all the other officers then decided it was more prudent, and a lot safer, to walk.

The forward companies now began to take a pounding from enemy high velocity guns and tanks, and casualties were high. 'D' Company had lost all means of communication and many of its officers and men. A decision was made to form a joint defensive position and the troops braved the storm of steel to join up with 'C' Company, losing many good men in the process. Once the two depleted companies joined up, this left them isolated, with the nearest friendly troops some fifteen hundred yards to the rear and no communication with them at all.

Five or six tanks of the County of London Yeomanry moved to the right flank and took up a hull down position, some thousand yards behind the Green Howards companies. No artillery observation officers or anti tank guns were able to get forward because of the intense enemy fire that was now sweeping the entire front. Any major movement brought down a hail of fire and all efforts to break the stalemate proved to be only partially successful.

As dusk approached, the enemy gathered their strength for one last counter attack that would throw back the 69th Brigade from the wadi, on a front five thousand yards wide and one thousand yards in front of the Green Howards. The enemy infantry and tanks pressed forward at a steady pace. In the absence of an Artillery Officer, Major Pullinger of the 6th Battalion spotted for the guns. Fire from the enemy tanks, small arms and artillery fire raked the British front as the enemy force came on for five hundred yards. At this point, the massed firepower of the concentrated British forces opened up on this vulnerable target, now completely in the open. Fire and steel rained down upon them and amid this scene of carnage the attack was halted, just four hundred yards in front of the Green Howards. The terrible sacrifices made by this counter attack were in vain as the battle was already lost.

When darkness finally came, all enemy activity on the Green Howards front ceased; the night air was disturbed only by the continual noise of moving transports behind the enemy lines. Even so, the weary men of the Green Howards remained alert to any possible danger from the enemy forces that were only one thousand yards away.

Later that night the 6th Battalion D.L.I. moved into position on the right flank.

FIRST HAND ACCOUNTS

50th Northumbrian Division

PTE FRANCIS WILLIAM VICKERS. MM
6th BATTALION THE GREEN HOWARDS
'D' COY. 17 PLATOON

"The 6th Green Howards got along the top of the wadi and our platoon was well forward, our section was led by Sgt William Allan Hill who was my best mate - he was later killed on 6 June 1944 on Gold Beach: Rufty was his nick name. We came onto a German Spandau machine gun post and took all the crew prisoner in their slit trench, they were all Africa Corps men and one of the lads took them back the way we had come, the rest of us got into the slit trench. Below us in the wadi was a piece of high ground that could best be described as an island, on it was a 50mm Anti Aircraft gun and an anti tank gun: we opened fire on the crews with the captured German machine gun and my bren gun killing or wounding both crews. The anti tank gun had a clear view of the entrance to the wadi and, I believe, it was this gun that was responsible for the two knocked out tanks standing motionless at the entrance. On one, an officer was hanging out of the turret with his entrails blown out, his sergeant was dead on his hands and knees being killed by blast.

Someone on the island fired at us and I was hit on the left front of my steel helmet by a tracer bullet which dented my helmet. While we were in the slit trench a couple of vehicles came up to the island with ammunition for the guns and was unaware we had got so far into the wadi, the drivers were taken prisoner and the vehicles driven out by our men.

Our section opened fire on the island to give covering fire to our mates as they went into more covered slit trenches taking more prisoners. From our position we could see the 51st Highland Division on the slopes of the high ground to our right - the enemy started to shell and mortar them and they took cover, our fighter bombers roared over us and straffed and bombed the enemy on the open ground beyond the wadi, at the same time 25 pounder shells from our own artillery were flying over us and landing on the open ground.

'D' Company moved forward and out of the protection of the wadi: the enemy must have been waiting for us to come into view as we were shelled, mortared and machine gunned constantly, there was plenty of slit trenches to take cover in, but not before we had taken numerous casualties. The men I saw hit were CSM Jim Oliver. MM - he was an old regular soldier who had served in India with our 2nd Battalion before the war; the company runner who was a reinforcement from Devon and a lad from the signal platoon. When there was a lull in the fighting we buried them where they had been killed.

Before the battle of 'Wadi Akarit' five of my mates and me were sat talking and the topic came up what we would do when the war was over and we got back home; one said he would open a newsagents and general store, another said he hoped to get a lorry and go into the haulage business, the next one said he hoped to buy a mini bus and run bus trips, the next one said he hoped to get his job back at the steelworks. The last one said he hoped to get a job in the building trade because with all the houses destroyed and damaged in the air raids there would be work for years. Then I was asked 'What are you going to do when you get home Bill?' my answer was 'I'm going to wait until I get home', I knew we had a lot more battles to fight and I was right.
Fate decreed that of the six of us, I was the only one to get home; two were killed at Mareth, two killed in Sicily and lastly my best mate Rufty Hill - one of the first killed on the beach on D-Day. None of them were married or had children, fate decreed my wife Gladys and I should have six children - three boys and three girls - one each for my mates and one for me."

LT (LATER MAJOR) G. M. YOUNG. MC
7th BN THE GREEN HOWARDS
'A' COY. 9 PLATOON

"I had been out on patrol on the night of 5 April and found no entanglements or minefields, we actually got so close that we came across some trenches which had just been dug - but luckily were not occupied. Someone however, must have heard us and a patrol was sent out hastily to find us - led by an officer buttoning up his greatcoat against the cold; followed by his sleepy soldiers. We lay quietly on the ground covered a little by the sparse blades of barley, as their patrol passed a little to our right. I had my pistol in my hand and the last man in the single file as it passed looked round and saw us, I pointed by pistol at him and followed him round with it as he passed, he was not a very brave chap I suppose and thought it wiser not to give the alarm immediately.

There were five of us in the patrol and we jumped up as soon as they had vanished and ran sideways away from the direction of their patrol. We then spread out several yards apart and I gave the order to run like hell and hope for the best. By now, I suppose the fearful soldier had concocted some story to alert the officer and as we took to our heels the machine guns on fixed lines began to chatter. Perhaps they feared an attack was about to be launched - but by now we were emulating Linford Christie and after half a mile settled down to get our breath back and then covered the remaining mile or so which separated the contending lines. When we attacked the next morning we were able to move forward swiftly over the undefended territory, until we came under heavy artillery fire as we approached the anti tank ditch. We halted and awaited orders, my platoon and I dived for cover behind a rocky hillock and in order to protect myself as much as I could, I began building a rocky wall to hide behind from shrapnel etc.

Almost immediately the brigadier of 69th Brigade (Brigadier Cooke-Collis) arrived with our colonel (Lt Col Seagrim) and joined my company commander who had chosen our little hillock as Company HQ.

I watched as the Brigadier spoke to the Colonel and the Colonel spoke to my Company Commander (Cpt Honeyman), 'It'll be me next' I said to my platoon Sergeant and sure enough I was right. The Colonel gave me the orders 'Take your Platoon across the open and get into the ditch and cover our approach.' Quite simple really, except for a certain amount of artillery barrage and the odd chatter of automatic weapons. This chatter was more disturbing than the barrage in a way, as the men behind the automatic weapons may have been able to see us clearly enough to aim properly.

As luck would have it, we ran through the bursting shells and found the ditch deserted. No sooner had we lined the ditch to cover the approach of the rest of the Battalion, when the C.O. himself leapt into the ditch and shouted 'Young - your a bloody funk! Don't just hide here do something.' I angrily told him that I had carried out his orders to protect the advance, he shouted again 'You're a bloody funk' and started to march towards the enemy. I told the Sergeant to keep the men undercover and went after the Colonel, after we had gone about a hundred yards he turned and saw me. 'What the hell are you doing - following me' he shouted 'Well' I answered 'As soon as you're killed I'll go back and tell Major Brunton that he is in command of the Battalion.' Logic now began to reign and he lay down and said 'Take your platoon and gain contact with the enemy' - which I did and a few hundred yards further on we came under fire from directly in front and also from the flanks. We could see the enemy quite clearly, Italians judging by their head gear, hats with plumes indicative of the Bersaglieri, and an exchange of fire took place as we crawled towards the opposition.

Just as we neared the trenches, we came under a hail of 'Red Devils', plastic grenades, which landed among us causing more dust and noise than serious damage, though several small pieces of shrapnel hit me in the face and blood began to pour from my cheeks. The rest of the platoon thought I must be badly wounded.

By this time, Private Whelan, a very young lad who didn't look old enough to be in such a maelstrom, had managed to work his way round to the left of the enemy and opened up with his Bren gun - killing several and causing the remainder to give up the attack and make one of three choices: 1) To lie down and hope for the best: 2) To take to their heels: 3) Show the white flag. By this time the rest of the battalion had arrived and the advance continued along a wide front. Still operating in front of the main advance, my platoon reached the top of the wadi and found ourselves with an excellent field of view for quite a distance. I left the sergeant in charge of the platoon and ran back towards my Company HQ where there would be a wireless set and I could tell the C.O. he could see quite a bit of the terrain if he joined us.

As I ran back, some Italians began sniping at me. One bullet kicked up the dust in front of me, that was when I realised the danger because the general din of battle had covered the noise of the rifles. I hit the deck, rolled over and over sideways, paused for a moment, then leapt up and ran a few yards zigzagging and hit the deck again. The manoeuvre seemed successful and I got back to Company HQ to find that Italian resistance was crumbling. The battle passed and we were left to lick - or in my case wash - our wounds, only when I took off my haversack at the end of the day did I discover how lucky I had been, for peeping out of the back of my haversack was the point of an Italian bullet. It had pierced the folded ground sheet held under the flap of the haversack, pierced one side of my mess tin, had gone right through a tin of bully beef and out through the other side of the mess tin; saved by a tin of Bully Beef."

LT H. D. CADEN
7th BN THE GREEN HOWARDS

"Our objective was a rocky feature that we could clearly see from the assembly area in daylight prior to the battle; we made good use of our binoculars. Before we moved off there was considerable artillery fire and I remember seeing two soldiers slapping each other on the back as though approving of the artillery support, there was a great deal of varey light activity from the enemy. One poor fellow ran across our front calling that we ought to go back because we must have been seen and we'd all be killed.

Just before first light I heard the sounds of vehicles followed by shouting and screams, I sent my runner to find out what was happening. He came back and said that armoured cars coming up in support had run over some fellows who had been lying down. I went around to get all of my fellows on their feet and clearly remember saying 'no point in dying if you don't have to', stupid perhaps but it didn't seem so at the time.

It was early light when we were ordered forward. After about 100 yds, spurts of dust from machine gun bullets were being kicked up - for some reason they always seemed to be a few yards in front of us and the gunner never corrected his aim. I saw a few men go down but there was never any hesitation and I felt very proud of our chaps. We advanced into a slight depression and the machine gun fire stopped though the shells were exploding with increasing frequency. Coming out of the depression we pressed on to the low ridge line and was just short of it when six huge black shell bursts exploded along the top of it, I believe we were saved by seconds.

We then charged forward to our objective and I saw two more men bowled over, we scrambled up (no other word for it) to the top without opposition and I looked over the crest - several men were hit at this point.

I was astonished to see a machine gun position firing in infilade across the reverse slope, we grenaded them out of it and from that point on - provided we kept below the summit - we were comparatively free from interference except for the occasional mortar bomb and even these stopped by 0900 hrs.

Looking back over our approach area I could see the wounded being stretchered off - mostly in bren carriers."

REVEREND CANON GERVASE W. MARKHAM. MA
CHAPLAIN: 124th FIELD REGIMENT. ROYAL ARTILLERY

Tuesday 6 April - one of the most exciting days I have known. Our guns opened up at 4am, there was no sleep from then on - as soon as it was light, I got up and walked round to the nearest battery just as they were finishing their barrage. At the same time Jerry began to send some long distance shells back, but no one was hurt. The whole ridge is crammed with artillery, field and medium, they are all blazing away. We hear that the Indians have reached their objective and the Highlanders have got 2 battalions onto Roumana. Our infantry goes in as the barrage stops, at first light.

The mess is in use at Battle HQ, 3 telephones and a wireless, with Poly Bull and Hep going hard at it all the time. The Colonel is up at Brigade HQ with the Battery Commander with the battalions. We get breakfast sitting about at the edge of proceedings, listening to news as it comes through. The Doctor and I, of course, have no part in the operations, but keep silent and listen.

We expect to be moved up at about 8am, but our infantry have been held up at the anti tank ditch. We remain to fire concentrations at the defences, if we move over the ridge we are in full view of the enemy who can still observe from the high ground ahead.

As the morning passes, and the battle went on up at the foot of the hills, I went up on to a nearby point from which the whole operation could be watched through field glasses. Away to the rear are the Matmata Hills, from which we pushed the enemy last week. Then comes 10 miles of rolling ground, with the trees of Gabes by the sea, all this is studded with vehicles of every kind.

All the wagon lines and 'B' echelons and rear Divs Corps HQ and Army HQ itself are dispersed over the open ground; a bomb falling anywhere in all this big area is bound to be within 50 yards of a vehicle, it is the biggest concentration of MT I have seen - in fact it is the 8th Army.

On the slopes just behind me the tanks are leaguering, nestling in folds of the ground, nosing up into wadis and among them are the medium artillery, their long noses point up to the sky, distaining camouflage, their twin horns (compressor springs) making them easy to identify. They are firing pretty constantly, the guns just behind with a sharp crack, those on the flanks with a dull thud like a bass drum.

On a line with myself are the field guns, each troop concealed and camouflaged in some wadi, firing bursts at the targets observed by their F.O.O.s. The shells whirr clearly away through the air, with here and there a badly rammed shell whirring and whistling as it rockets along off its balance.

The ground slopes away in front of me in green folds, for the corn is well grown, this broad valley laughs and sings, it stands so deep with corn. I can see some Indian troops on the left deploying anti tank guns along a ridge, where there little pits can be seen with 6 pounders or 17 pounders poking out to repel a possible break through of enemy tanks.

In front of them, the valley dips out of my sight then rises steeply to the line of hills that we are attacking. Puffs of smoke spring up from the cliffs as our shells land and a few seconds later the noise of the explosion can be heard, though there is usually too much noise to identify any particular shell. Somewhere ahead in a deep ditch protected by cross machine gun and mortar fire, our 69th Brigade Infantry are having a hard time there, 5th East Yorks, 6th and 7th Green Howards. Reports come through to our control room, we can picture the scene as we order new concentrations of fire on some suspected gun position.

I spend my time between watching this amazing battle away from the hill top, listening to the operations in the control room, and sitting with the M.O. in the R.A.P. We have hardly any casualties at the guns, as the enemy does very little counter battery fire, and our air superiority keeps his aeroplanes out of the sky.

One shell-shocked man is brought in from another regiment, he is crying and speechless: all he can do is sit and wring his hands, while big tears fall from his eyes and nose onto a sock with which he wipes his face and his hands. The M.O. tries first, but failed to do any good for him. Then I was given a chance and only succeeded in getting his name etc, and induced him to talk about his family at home, but it was no good. He waited there until two or three fellows came in with bullet wounds, and then was sent back in the ambulance.

At last we heard that the anti tank ditch had been taken and we prepared to move forward. In the afternoon we got stonked, the guns first. (They were only out of action half an hour between leaving their old position and going up to new ones 5 miles away.) By the time we went up, the whole broad valley was a mass of moving vehicles, going up the sandy tracks and through the corn. We had to keep on halting, and could look forward and see our heavy tanks going up a dusty track on the ridge of a hill, while enemy shells landed all around. At last we were shown a place right at the foot of the slopes, in a deep valley 100 yards wide, at the other end of which shells are falling. Down at the bottom is the bed of a stream which has cut a trench 7 feet wide, but is now dry and stoney. Our little Jeep manages to get down inside this and is well protected. The shelling gradually stops as our advancing troops offer fresh targets elsewhere. A column of prisoners struggles into sight unguarded by anyone, 200 or 300 Italians walking along happily but untidily going towards our rear positions. We all stare without fraternising, but as more columns arrive we give up noticing them.

At 5.00am I am asked to go back to old position and bring up the 3 tonners, which did not come at first in case there was no room. It takes half an hour to find them, and then we find the R.S.M. is also there to lead them up, so we go back to the forward position. As we hump along a straight track, we hear a sudden burst of small arms fire and see men diving into slit trenches. I say loftily 'Drive on - only aircraft', and an Indian Major runs across our bows to a hole, so we pull up and I poke my head out to look round. Two enormous stukas are roaring directly down our little track from behind us, at 30 feet high, spitting bullets.

We both leap out, Hawkins gets under the bonnet, I jump into a slit trench that some angel has dug 4 yards away. The Stukas sweep over us and the whole air is full of shot, as every man with a gun in this crowded area lets fly horizontally. We learn later that 7 came over and 4 were brought down, though they killed one of our lads in a gun position.

We drive on, and reach HQ safely. Within half an hour 5 separate flights of 18 bombers go overhead to bomb the Bosche. As dusk falls he counter attacks all along the front. The Indians and Jocks repel this, and in our sector a concentration of five from 124 Field Regt breaks up his attack. When we go to bed we knew that 14,000 prisoners have been taken, all our objectives taken, but that the enemy is still only 5,000 yards away from our guns - too close to be pleasant.

Wednesday 7 April - Up at first light and heard that the enemy had retired. Before washing or shaving I walked up to the nearest rise to see what could be seen, but could find no view point. On my way round the nearest battery I found a dead man by the side of the track. He proved to be of the East Yorks, so I got a sand bag from a passing vehicle and collected his personal effects from his pockets, and cut off his identity disk with his own bayonet. After breakfast we buried him under a nearby fig tree and sent all the necessary papers in, and wrote to his mother. Meanwhile, up at the anti tank ditch, the padre of 5th East Yorks was conducting mass burials, as several score of their men were killed there.

CSM LAURIE WHITTLE
5th BN EAST YORKSHIRE REGIMENT. 'A' COY

"In single file we set off across no-mans-land to the assembly area which we reached quietly and safely. We still had a few hours to Zero hour so I settled down to sleep. It was so cold however, that sleep was right out of the question, and as I sat up I was fortunate enough to see the attack start on our left. I believe it was the Indian Div., and anyway, it was a breathtaking sight with tracer bullets of all colours flying in every direction and the yellow flashes of the bursting shells and mortars were everywhere. Further interest in this show was ended by my having to warn the scattered platoon that they were to be ready to move. An ambulance drove up at this time and would have carried straight on had someone not stopped it. When the driver was told that we were the most forward troops in this sector and that Jerry was only a mile or so in front, he soon turned round and sped away.

At last, we received the order to advance and from here there was to be no undue noise or smoking. I think the enemy must have heard us breathing, for not very much further on we began to receive unwelcome visitors in the shape of mortar bombs. These were not near enough to cause us any worry, but they still made you think a bit. By now we were behind the enemy's positions on the left where the Indians were attacking, it was an eerie feeling, but we were still some distance from the main positions. A very uncomfortable twenty minutes was caused by flares dropped by planes hovering overhead. Because these illuminated the whole ground around as bright as daylight, we were compelled to get down as quick as possible and not move an eyelash. After 10 minutes I had developed violent cramp and was debating whether to stand it as long as possible or get up and take a chance.

My thoughts of the possible results to my comrades caused me to stick it. When it had become sufficiently dark enough we advanced once more, and now those confounded mortar bombs were beginning to get too close. Very luckily for some of us there were plenty of duds amongst them.

On, on, on, still plodding silently through the night, thoughts all over the place, now praying, now wondering what the wife would be doing at this time, wondering what the chances of coming through safely were. Would my luck bring me through once more, or was it my turn to join that band of heroes who have laid down their lives so that England and Home might be spared the horrors that we ourselves had patiently endured without a word of complaint. I was rudely interrupted by the beginning of our barrage, which was later recorded and broadcast. As the barrage increased in strength, the moan of the shells overhead was like the sound of some gigantic orchestra tuning up.

Out in front where they were bursting in and on the German positions, it gave you the impression of a thousand stars twinkling as in the sky above. A grandstand view of a battle is a wonderful sight, and for these few minutes I was one of those privileged few who get the chance to see one. To actually take part in one though is an entirely different matter, it is a thing that you do not feel really like repeating, but the war has to be won so you just have to grin and bear these things.

As the pale rays of dawn stole into the sky we were still not onto our objective. We stumbled onto it quite by accident, as we topped one of a succession of ridges, there was suddenly bared to us the enemy defences. We could tell for some minutes before this that we were getting somewhere near, for some of our own shells had been falling short and a corporal immediately behind me was wounded by the shrapnel from one. There was not a sign of life in the positions before us and most of us thought that the enemy had really pulled out to straighten his line, and would most probably be waiting for us somewhere ahead.

Over on our right a red flare went up, this must have been a signal, for Hell was let loose. We were fired on from all over the wadi and as we were on the exposed or forward slope of the ridge, we only had one alternative and that was to get back on to the other side. This was done with very few casualties, considering the amount of fire power which was being brought to bear on us, I considered it something of a miracle. Except for some few who had taken shelter in a trench on the crown of the ridge and could not get out, (they were right in the middle of a most accurate cross fire), we mustered in comparative safety and reorganised as well as we were able. I lit my first cigarette and how sweet it tasted, as soon as one was smoked I had another one lit. It is surprising what a soothe this is to ragged nerves in the din of a battle.

I have only hazy recollections of this part of the action, but I do remember the MMGs coming up under cover of a smoke screen and putting a deadly barrage into the enemy. It was at this time that one of our stretcher bearers won the VC for bravery on this same ridge. I think that anyone who went onto that fire swept patch of ground deserved the highest of decorations.

A little later my platoon was ordered to get over behind another ridge on the right. This we did, but not without losing the Platoon Officer and a few other ranks, as we crossed an open fire-swept gap between the two ridges. It was impossible to do anything without being badly cut up, so we just had to take what cover there was and lay there until something happened. All this time we were being heavily mortared and shelled, the machine guns had a bit of a go too. Most of us were so exhausted that we were continually dozing off and being rudely awakened when something came unpleasantly close. Sometime after midday, one or two of the early-wounded managed to crawl back to us.

Two Ities also came back, being afraid of them drawing the enemy's fire on to us, we motioned them to get out of it as quickly as possible. They just waved cheerily back and shouted 'Finito', it certainly was because we saw another formation with tank support routing out the last of the enemy shortly after. What a relief to stand up again after almost 8 hours of crouching on the ground. Just as I stood up though, the enemy's rear guard gave us a few parting shots and as these almost parted my hair, I quickly resumed my lying position. Now our aircraft came over to harass the fleeing enemy, they gave us a nasty moment when they circled overhead before going on after the foe. It didn't take long to scale the anti tank defences and push on through the minefield which the R.E.s were clearing even then.

No time for loot or anything else, we left that to those coming up behind, our job was to get through as quickly as possible to the high ground behind. Here we took up defensive positions ready for the enemy's counter attack. This, when it did come, fell onto another unit who repulsed it with very heavy casualties. For the rest of the day we were still under shell fire from the rear guard who were concentrating on the gap in the minefield and so delaying immediate pursuit.

Unfortunately every so often one would fall short in the wadi we were holding, there were no casualties as luck would have it. At dusk, as the shelling began to ease up, we began to move about more freely. We were soon in our trenches again as we became the target for a 'stuka' who hit The Bn HQ with one of his bombs, killing some officers and men, and so ended that day. We had our first meal since leaving for the attack, sometime in the early hours of the morning, I could not tell you the time because I had only just awakened from a deep sleep of exhaustion. How well that meal tasted, although it was only bully, and cold at that.

Daylight next morning, we could go up on the top of the ridge for the first time. I did so and was immediately detailed to bury the numerous dead which were scattered about in profusion. This grisly job took up an hour or two until we heard a shout to 'come and get it'. With breakfast, we received about a pint of water each, to wash and shave with. I felt a different man when I had at last removed the last traces of a bristly beard."

PTE LEONARD WHITE
7th BN GREEN HOWARDS
HQ COY - RADIO OPERATOR

"When the attack went in we were in one line going across, Peter Fox and another signaller went on first and we had the number 18 sets carried on our backs. The battle hadn't been on very long when they were killed. Me, another signaller and a Corporal were in reserve. The other signaller was carrying the 18 set and I was carrying a bakerlite case with four 60-volt batteries in, it had a lead from it so if the set's batteries failed you just plugged it in to it.

We were ordered forward but things got bloody bad, we made our way to Colonel Seagrim who was wandering all over the place, he told us to fall back 'cos things were getting a bit hot. The corporal and the other lad did, but I said 'I'll stop with you sir', so I took the wireless and never saw them no more.

I had the set and the bakerlite case, and was laid down on my stomach when I got a message from brigade to tell Colonel Seagrim that the 51st Highland Division had achieved their objective, he said 'Oh good' and went off. Then there was a bloody big bang and that's all I remember.

What had happened was the set and batteries in front of me had taken all the shrapnel and blast, and saved me but I was concussed, when I came round all about me was dead soldiers. I've never forgotten one poor lad who was laid there, his pack was behind his head like a pillow and his teeth were showing as if he was smiling.

The next day I volunteered to help the army chaplain to bury the dead. We had to dig a trench and bury about three, and have a bit of a service over them. I always remember he found a leg, he put this leg in with one of the fellas we was burying. War is a funny thing you know - you had to laugh - I thought they'll think he comes from the Isle of Man."

L/CPL S. C. PENTON
42nd FIELD COY. ROYAL ENGINEERS
ATTACHED TO THE GREEN HOWARDS

"We were given the task of following the assault infantry to make a crossing of an anti tank ditch which, as far as I can remember, was 12' wide and 8' deep. Given the time factor, it had to be in double quick

time. On a given time we advanced and as we approached the ditch we could see that the assault troops had quite a mauling, as we saw scores of bodies on the ground.

However, they had completed their job and had secured the high ground across the ditch, now it was up to us to do our job: we inspected the ditch and realised that, in view of the time factor, it would take too long to do it by hand. So it was quickly decided that in order to meet the time table we would have to use explosive charges, they were placed in both banks of the ditch hoping that both sides would cave in, and we then could level it off by hand. Up to that time it had been fairly quiet, apart from the occasional mortar shell.

However, we realised that as soon as the charges were fired, it would bring a hail of artillery fire on us. The charges were fired and the result was a complete success and we soon completed the job by hand, and within the time allotted. As I have said, within 10 mins of the explosion we were subjected to about 15 mins of intense fire from 88s and mortars, but I am glad to say we had no fatalities. We then stayed until vehicles and tanks were safely across, as soon as the tanks were across this again brought heavy fire on us. At this point the orders came for all engineers to withdraw, we did not want telling twice."

PTE R. E. YOUNG
7th BN GREEN HOWARDS

Just before the battle I happened to be an M.T. Driver without a truck and got pushed into a Rifle Company. Their Company Clerk was a bit ageing and battle weary, so I took his place for the event.

I recall being sent to Battalion Headquarters to collect the Varey Light cartridges together with instructions, as it happened, from the Commanding Officer's own hands, which was very gratifying to me at the time (being a 'nobody' in an unfamiliar Company).

The C.O., Lt Colonel Seagrim, was a soldier much liked and respected by all and was about to be awarded the Victoria Cross for action in the Mareth Battle, but was to lose his life in an anti tank ditch at Wadi Akarit the next day, along with so many others of the Battalion.

We moved up after nightfall, heavily laden as is usual. The 2nd Cheshires (Heavy Machine Gun Battalion) who were seconded to us, seemed to have the worst loads, so I carried a couple of two gallon cans of water for them - better than a Vickers gun barrel all the same.

After four miles we arrived at our start line area, where we dug in silently and rather close, it seemed, to the enemy held hills in front of us - looking rather like a succession of smallish pit mounds. The quietness was interrupted by one of 'our' armoured cars which blundered into our area and dropped its wheels into a trench, crushing the lads who were in it.

Thereafter, quietness reigned until the artillery bombardment started; a bit like being in the orchestra pit with the explosions happening on stage - real theatre of war stuff - the exploding shells lit up the night sky and we could see great lumps of rock hurled into the air off the escarpment.

We assembled for a 4am start - my company had the job of taking and holding the hill on the right. To get there we had to cross a nasty stretch of open ground, it was light by then. The bloke beside me got shot through the leg but help was at hand - the lads from the motor transport were weaving around in the smaller trucks, picking up the fallen and getting them off the battlefield without delay.

Occupation of the hill didn't seem too difficult - what we had was a rocky reverse slope, exposed mostly to enemy mortar bombs.

At one stage I had to get a message off - the Signal Unit was a bit of a way round the bottom of the hill. As I approached them there was an explosion, the Signallers and the wireless set got put out of action. I was knocked off my feet in the blast and a bit dazed. Anyhow, I reported back as to what had happened.

The next thing was that I got earmarked for a trip across the 'Gap' and thence across open ground, for god knows how far, to reach the anti tank ditch and confirm that we had taken our objective. Just then an armoured car drew up at the bottom of the hill; a Liaison Officer jumped out and clambered up to speak to our Company Commander - it was explained to him about our communications problem and that someone was to be despatched to say 'objective taken'. The Liaison Officer strongly advised against this and said that anybody they sent on foot wouldn't get through - he said that he would get a message off for us - that was truly a life saver for me and in the nick of time!

At one stage of the battle, several of our tanks moved up to try and exploit a narrow gap at the right hand side of the hill. Just then, a

German twin engine plane, flying low, came battling towards us, parallel to the range of hills and attracting a lot of small arms fire. With diabolical accuracy they dropped bombs on the lead tanks, knocking them out.

Later on in the proceedings, whilst down in this right hand gap area, I spotted two figures creeping from enemy territory. I hid behind a boulder and waited for them to get nearer - then I heard 'all right Johnny we see you' - they were a couple of Gurkhas who had been out scouting and landed back in the wrong sector. I took them back to Company HQ and they stayed with us for the rest of the battle - (useful to have two cheerful chappies with us who knew from first hand just what the enemy was doing on the other side of the hill and beyond).

PTE HARRY FORTH
5th BN EAST YORKSHIRE REGIMENT:
'B' COY

"We were given orders to advance in extended order. I was in the leading company (B company). As I started to move forward, the enemy was putting up flares at a pretty regular rate. This slowed us down considerably. The enemy must have known that something was happening! We then heard that the 4th Indians had put in a silent night attack and had reached their objective, still going forward, but slow. An order was given to fall in single file and keep following the next man in front, also to keep inside the white tapes which were noticeable in the dark.

It was slow going. What with the flares and having to drop flat on the ground. I was up and down like a jack in a box! It made me realise we had walked into a minefield and I was carrying the bouys anti tank rifle that night. It was no joke dropping down every ten minutes or so with that thing on my back.

By now it was getting daylight and we had only just got through the minefield and was in open ground. The last hundred yards or so we had to run for what looked like a bit of a ridge. By the time I got there, I had a bit of a sweat on and had to start digging a hole using my steel helmet, as I had lost my entrenching tool during the night.

I set the anti tank rifle on top of the ridge, then dug a bit more until I had a hole large enough to lay in behind the rifle. I then settled down to what I thought was going to be a long day's fighting. The enemy started to fire mortar shells quite quickly, there also seemed to be, in the distance, two 88s sending high velocity shells over.

While waiting on watch for something to happen (ducking in between shellings) a German truck pulled up about two hundred yards away in front of the wadi. It looked as though it was carrying up ammunition for another mortar team!

I was given the order by the sergeant to try and knock it out. I had only fired the anti tank rifle once before and that was back in England, and I had not much confidence in doing this. Anyway luck was with me and the first round of armour piercing went through the radiator giving off a lot of steam. The next round went into the side of the bonnet and it started to smoke, then burst into flames. Out jumped three or four men and then our Bren gunners opened out.

It was a long day but towards the evening things started to be quiet. The enemy had begun to withdraw and just before dusk the Green Howards and the Durham Light Infantry were passing through our lines."

PTE. THOMAS R. ATKINSON
233 FIELD COY. ROYAL ENGINEERS
ATTACHED TO GREEN HOWARDS

"The attack on Wadi Akarit was a night raid. I was one of a sub-section of sappers attached to a company of Green Howards and our job was to lead them through the minefield. Our area of penetration was covered by a knoll which contained an observation post and this we noted as we crawled up to the minefield. Leading was the sapper with a short arm detector, followed by me to warn against trip wires and to mark the mine for clearance by two sappers following in single file who unrolled a white tape as we progressed.

We reached the base of the knoll without any difficulty. As we continued to the left, to circle the hill, I noticed that we were being watched by an Italian soldier. At that point I stopped the leading man and as my mind raced to keep time with my heartbeat - should I shoot him and raise the alarm? Because everything had been quiet so far. Fortunately the Iti made the decision for me because he ducked down below the skyline. So I went back to inform the infantry escort and they went dashing up the rise and then all hell broke loose with small arms fire both ways and Iti 'money-box' grenades coming our way.

Obviously the O.P. had a mine free path to the enemy lines, so we concentrated on widening our track to enable our carriers and trucks to bring in support. This took time so it was daylight when we managed to clear a track. While this was going on we were under fire from mortars and 88s which eased off as the sun rose."

LT HAROLD LIMER
40th RTR 23rd INDEPENDENT BRIGADE
NO. 2 TROOP. 'A' SQUADRON

"At Wadi Akarit I was commanding No. 2 Troop, 'A' Squadron, 40th Royal Tank Regiment and Major W. R. Hughs DSO was the squadron commander. Strangely enough, in a conversation with Cpt Mason-Fisher - 2 i/c 'A' Squadron two days before the battle, when we knew what we were going to do, he said 'We can go to the well once too often Hal', he was sadly prophetically correct as he was killed and I was wounded in the battle.

We formed up in darkness in a not very good area, with enemy small arms fire zipping overhead which was somewhat unusual, as such areas were usually secure. As we were moving up, the Commanding Officer Lt Colonel Jim Finnegan DSO, was watching 'A' Squadron go past and shouted: 'Hal! Put your bloody tin hat on', which I promptly did, and as it happened it saved me later.

The squadron fanned out on the enemy side of the wadi behind our infantry and I took up position with my troops on the extreme right, squadron HQ was in the middle with two troops on either side. Unusually all tanks had to fire their Besa machine guns at a set elevation for a certain length of time, over the heads of our own infantry. This was to augment the fire power available, great care had to be exercised when doing this as it attracted enemy fire within a short time.

We continued to fire into the distance - when I heard on the air 2 i/c 'A' Squadron had been killed. I learned later he had received several bullets in the forehead although his head, with his tin hat on, was only out of the turret enough to let him see, an enemy machine gun had raked the top of the turret.

About five minutes later, just after I had been out on foot to visit my other two tanks, I was back in the turret when a shell landed near the front right track and I was hit in the right forehead by a small piece of shrapnel which went through my helmet and through the tough fibre headband.

I collapsed into the bottom of the tank for a few moments, then informed O.C. Squadron I had been hit but not seriously.

My driver rose to the occasion, bandaged my head and drove the tank back to the regimental aid post. I told the officer that apart from a headache I was alright and could go back, he refused to allow it, informing me that if the shrapnel had penetrated the skull I had a problem and must go back to have it x-rayed. I was transported to the casualty clearing station and was waiting to go back, when my Troop Sergeant, Steve Harrison MM, appeared having been shot through the jaw, he could hardly talk but seemed quite well. He died in hospital in Tripoli, he was a very fine NCO from the pre-war regular army - sadly I never saw him again.

I was then transported to a field hospital with other walking wounded in the back of a three ton truck sitting on the floor. It was a very uncomfortable ride over rough ground and was of three hours duration, it did not do the headache any good. There the shrapnel and fibres from the helmet band were removed and an x-ray showed no penetration of the skull and I was sent to the base hospital in Tripoli."

L/SGT KEN RUTHERFORD. 'A' COY 5th BATTALION EAST YORKSHIRE REGIMENT

"The mortar fire was very heavy in our sector, we picked up one chap who had been hit low down with shrapnel, it cut straight across his stomach. All his intestines were hanging out - we got them back in and put two shell dressings on the wound.

We got him back to a 15 cwt truck, sat him in the passenger seat and sent him to the rear - poor devil. It turned out that when he got back to the R.A.P. everything had fallen back into place as a result of being laid on the stretcher, the M.O. put in some stitches and sent him to hospital - within three months he was back with us."

CPL ALLAN DRAYCOTT
5th BN EAST YORKSHIRE REGIMENT

"The distance between us and the Wadi Akarit was quite a way, during the night R.E.s had marked a path with white tapes for us to move along. As we moved forward a plane was circling over us and dropping flares - every time one burst we had to halt, this was a let down and made us late to our start line. When we finally went in, it was light and we were sitting ducks and shells were exploding amongst us. One 19 year old, who had just come into my section and had not been in action before, was crying his eyes out and kept saying how frightened he was. I took him under my wing saying: 'Stick with me kid, you'll by alright'. It was not long before he became much calmer and more settled: he had regained his confidence.

As we neared the anti tank ditch we moved up some rising ground to a crest. When we crossed it and descended the far slope, there was all hell let loose and it wasn't long before there were bodies laid everywhere. Our colonel was just walking about shouting orders, but the fire was so fierce he was hit more than once and someone managed to get him out of the action - a very brave act.

At this point they were throwing everything at us, one thing they used was a small cannon with only slight elevation - the shells bounced about five times before exploding. Anyway it came to my turn, along with my good section, to try and make it to the anti tank ditch. When we were ready I gave the order 'let's go' and we moved forward over a mound in front of us before going down into the ditch, we passed some wooden box mines but none of them exploded.

We had been told not to move forward in a straight line but to zig-zag making a harder target to hit, I carried a Tommy gun against my hip at the ready. The gun flew out of my hands, a bullet had passed through the space between my body and upper right arm just grazing my arm and making me drop the gun. Someone had been aiming at my chest but with me zig zagging had missed, I picked up my Tommy gun quickly and moved forward into the ditch.

I spread the section out along the ditch and ordered the bren gunner onto the parapet in front of the ditch, this turned out to be a mistake as he went up in pieces from either a mine or a mortar bomb. Before we could do any more, mortar bombs were dropping all along the ditch - we had to withdraw. On getting back, the sergeant ordered me to go and get my wounded arm seen to."

PTE ALBERT HALL
25th LIGHT ANTI AIRCRAFT REGIMENT
ROYAL ARTILLERY

"On 5 April we started our approach, we were about five miles away from Akarit. All the tanks were lined up right across the desert - with infantry and bren carriers in between. You could imagine what happened when that lot started to move - it was just like being in a heavy fog. This mass of troops and armour carried on until we reached the hills that was shielding Wadi Akarit, everyone soon sorted themselves out when we stopped at our destination: the tanks moved into position, the infantry dug in and we moved up between them with the 25 pounder field guns just to the rear.

Everyone was more or less dispersed for the attack when, out of the clear blue sky, eight Junkers 88s appeared and all hell let loose - just to our rear there must have been a concentration of guns because six of the aircraft were blasted out of the sky. I have never witnessed such shooting, the remaining two were hit as they flew over us trailing smoke.

The night before the attack the Gurkhas went into the hills, no barrage assisted them but we heard a great deal of small arms fire; next morning all was quiet. Our Officer, Captain Wharton, who was a school teacher in civvy street, decided to go to the top of the hill we were behind. As he popped his head over the top there was a great puff of sand and one of the lads says 'He's had it.' At that moment he comes strolling down the hill covered in sand - he was quite a sight, even his glasses were that covered in sand he could hardly see. As he passed by us he shouted 'wrong again', the lads shouted back 'that was the last thing we were expecting', we all thought he'd been blown up. He shouted back at us 'Just a little bit of excitement but they are still there.'

When the attack finally went in, some of the infantry lads passed us and were very casual about it; with cigarettes hanging out of their mouths, tin hats on the backs of their heads and bayonets fixed. They said to us 'Are you coming', we said 'We'll catch you up', the barrage then opened up and they disappeared over the hill. The machine guns and small arms were banging away and we heard some terrific explosions, there was loud swishing noises overhead and I'll swear we could see some of the shells. Our officer came over and said this noise was made by six inch shells being fired by monitors out at sea.

We could actually see the 51st Highland Division picking their way up the hills on the right. Later in the morning we were told to move over the hill and down into the wadi itself. On the other slope of the hill there was our dead all over the ground and we came under heavy mortar fire. As we crossed the anti tank ditch we could see the knockout machine gun posts that had been placed in such a way as to catch any attackers in a cross fire, I looked into the bottom of the ditch and I have never seen so many officers killed in one place - all the lads commenting on this.

Once across the ditch we began digging in and things seemed to quieten down except for some small arms fire. The thing we had to be most careful about was mines - they were laid everywhere. There was a little dug out nearby and one of the lads decided to have a look in, there was quite a few dead Italians in there - the officer had his head blown off.

That night the bren gun carriers came up with some wagons. In the moon light we could see them lifting the bodies onto the wagons, it was an eerie sight as some of the corpses had rigarmortis and were being lifted with their knees bent: what an experience, but there are some things you try to forget."

PTE F. BLACK
ROYAL ARTILLERY

"One incident happened at Wadi Akarit I will never forget - two German fighters came over at very low level and straffed us, as they roared over our position we were put on full alert. Minutes later six low flying bombers approached and we cheered thinking they were ours. My mate Corporal O' Toole, standing behind his gun in his carrier, screamed 'Jerries' and immediately pumped bullets into this sitting duck. Flames engulfed the plane and soon every gun large and small was in action - five planes were destroyed, we thought the sixth had got away but this was not to be.

He was badly hit and the crew bailed out too low for their chutes to open; they plummeted into the ground: The sight of this quietened down our cheers, it was ironic that the German fighters were responsible for us being on the alert to kill their mates."

GPO J. OVERMONT
74th (N) FIELD REGIMENT. 452 BATTERY. 'E' TROOP
ROYAL ARTILLERY: ATTACHED 7th GREEN HOWARDS

"As our guns were not directly involved in the attack, I was ordered to go forward with a w/t truck - a thin skinned Dodge delivery van - to provide an additional w/t link, reporting on the progress of the hard pressed engineers who were labouring to bridge the wadi so the armour could get across. I found myself with a forward Coy of the 7th Bn Green Howards, here I met the Coy Q.M.S. who I knew from school days. I can't remember which net we were on - probably our Divisional HQ.

We could see the Gurkhas on the left of the gap winkling out the remaining few Italians from their fox holes, but the poor sappers were having a rough time of it and progress was slow. During the day we had our fair share of harassment from dive bombers and mortar fire. Fortunately, it was not very accurate.

LT LYMBERLEY: TROOP COMMANDER
40th BN ROYAL TANK REGIMENT.
'B' SQUADRON

On 6 April at about day break, we halted on the approach march and I left my tank for a while to speak to my Squadron Commander who was about 150 yds away. A stray shell (believed to be a 210 mm) came over and landed near my tank where my driver was standing, he was killed instantly by a splinter which went through his steel helmet, through his head and out of the other side of his helmet: his name was George Bentley, he was from Nottingham and we had a particular affinity because I too had been brought up there. A very nice man, single and aged about 29.

It was about midday that we approached a cleared gap in the mine field, I had my same gunner Donald Austin - Aged 21: Charterhouse and undergraduate of Leeds University - and a fresh driver. Going through the gap was, for me, a chilling experience. Among the litter of our knocked out tanks and other debris was one which had half of one of its crew sitting on the turret - all one could see was the bottom half up to the exposed ribs: Where the top half was I do not know. I was almost sure I recognised who it was from his desert boots, unfortunately I was right - it was Trevor Wykes who came from Ilkeston and with whom I had become very friendly back at base on sick leave: I believe he was a troop leader with 50th RTR.

Having got through the gap, the rest of the day was a tense waiting for an infantry counter attack which never materialised, although we were subjected to shelling."

SGT ARNOLD GREEN. MM
40th BN ROYAL TANK REGIMENT

Sgt. Arnold Green (left).

"The night of 5 April I think everyone felt jittery. We had instructions to write what we once again thought would be our last letter, and crept through the night to our assembly positions. It was a black night, no moon but Jerry planes had altered that with chandelier flares illuminating us. I thought, as we rumbled forward in eerie shadows - curtains this time!

6 April (my brother's birthday.) I shall never forget it. Our barrage started at 4am and we stood around waiting our time to go in - something went wrong - then there were eerie silent spells. Then we received an avalanche of shells. I think we all counted our lucky stars, except one. George Bentley, wearing his steel helmet, sitting beside his tank was hit. I noticed the ambulance take him to an R.A.P. nearby - not more than 30 minutes later, looking through my glasses, I saw two graves having crosses affixed .... G. Bentley 40th R.T.R., killed in action 6.4.43. The other grave a Capt. R. A. Wilson. Apparently George had a piece of shrapnel penetrate his helmet and his skull. He was a nice, quiet likeable chap to everyone. The amazing thing to me was that I was less than 50 yards away from George, guiding my tank on foot, to disperse more and without a steel hat on!

Long columns of prisoners came out of the hills. Our time to go in had come and gone. Occasionally we had shells to duck from. We did not know what to expect. I learnt afterwards that the 5th East Yorks were carved up badly on their wave (first in line), the 6th and 7th Green Howards who followed at intervals were also thinned out badly. There were to be four lines of penetration in the attack. A - Adeline, B - Bertha, C - Carol, D - Daisy. Whereas we were to take C or D, owing to the terrific odds and sniping everyone went in on A and B, hence our lateness!

Hurriedly, we received orders that our squadron would go in without the A/T guns and off we went some hours behind schedule.

What a shocking sight this track through the minefield was. It was overlooked by the mountains known as Roumana, and was riddled with machine gun posts and snipers who could not be dealt with from the front. There were tanks blown up and crews lying in various positions dead, on or off the tanks, in an attempt to escape, sometimes burnt to death. There were lorries, bren carriers, an ambulance or two. Quite 15 vehicles, all much the same. Shells were falling, gun fire came down on us from above. It was unhealthy to have the turret open and we crossed our fingers when we pulled around crippled vehicles, hoping not to run over a mine.

Out of the corner of my eye, I noticed a few brave R.E.'s fixing tapes of direction, joggling along on their stomachs. Coming the other way, three wounded chaps locked together, helping each other to make it through this terrible death-trap.

We lost 6 fine chaps that day, officers and sergeants, all tank commanders, with bullets through the head. Names I remember are Capt. Mason Fisher and Sgt Steve Hamson.

I got through this lot with my only remaining troop tank. I was still stunned with the sight of dead soldiers all around me when Harry Monkey, the nickname for the O.C., came on the air asking for all miners to report to him immediately. Well, I cursed myself for being a miner that day, 'miner' being the code for officer.

I had to cover a vacant piece of ground to reach his tank and a blasted sniper nearly had me - I cursed the officer for making us come out of our tanks in such a dangerous position. He then detailed my troop to find and destroy a certain machine gun that was being a nuisance. This meant going away into the hills. On my way I saw some 22nd Armed Brigade tanks hustling away from the direction I was going. They had Shermans and Crusaders with 6 pounders. I had a 2 pounder Valentine! For once I used my loaf. I knew I could not find a sniper by going after him.

I decided to take cover and watch - I found a nook and got in there, kept watch and nibbled a couple of biscuits and corned beef onto a sick stomach.

We did not stay here long. Orders came through to move into a new position. It was very tricky going, picking our way in single file trying to keep our hulls below the skyline and avoiding many bodies. We passed a couple of Shermans that earlier had been hit by an 88mm A/T gun, before this gun crew gave themselves up. So fiercely did these tanks burn, that the crews went up in smoke - it was eerie.

We now held an awkward position, certainly not useful for tank manoeuvring and during the remainder of the day came under heavy shell fire, causing some casualties.

The Green Howards were being fiercely counter attacked. We stayed with them until dusk. Around us, in the cave like dugouts, were loads of Jerry kit and loot. Several of our lads collected vests, Luger revolvers and rations. I remember holding my fire when three M. E.'s came over so low that I was afraid we may hit our own chaps.

When we moved back that night beyond the A/T ditch and minefields, we passed on 'Clara Track' and the sight around us was terrible. Dead soldiers laid around as close as trees in a forest. I felt silently sick, some vehicles were smouldering and a plane blazed away nearby.

We stayed for the night just behind the line and, as acting Troop Officer, I had to attend the evening conference regarding orders for the next day. I remember saying to the O.C. that I thought our many losses and casualties were not worth the costly advance. His reply was what must we have inflicted on the Hun! I learnt that it was impossible to bury the majority of the bodies and recover vehicles because of more casualties suffered by the recovery sections, and the ground was abandoned for three weeks owing to mines and booby traps. Late that night we dug a shallow trench to sleep in.

We were dead beat. When I awoke I found that we were sleeping near the late George Bentley's grave and felt he was best out of this terrible state of affairs. Two columns were now formed and this morning we all had to pass through a clear track of the bottle-neck while all the hundreds of vehicles were moving through, it was very congested and a couple of dive bombers surprised us all by unloading on the leading vehicles to make matters worse.

Captain Strange took over today, as J. B. was slightly wounded yesterday and we hit the open desert again after passing through Wadi Akarit, which I have often thought was the scene of the bloodiest action I knew - I felt too sick of it all to collect dead men's booty."

MAJOR C. MACDONALD. MC
6th BN GREEN HOWARDS

"First light found us just behind the bridgehead, at point 85, receiving all the fire the enemy could direct at us. The bridgehead at this time had not definitely been established, so the C.O. (Lt. Col. G. Lance DSO) decided to get round on the right. This we did, and before the enemy knew where he was, the leading company were right in among them.

We had taken them completely by surprise by this daylight attack, and the move was very definitely a bold one. After several sharp exchanges of small arms fire, the first enemy prisoners were extracted and then the rot began, and they came out in swarms. Sections of our troops attacked on their own, and although in some cases there was heavy opposition, they went in with their bayonets, rifles and Tommy guns, and soon overran the enemy.

My own company collected between three and four hundred prisoners. We did not escort them, but simply directed them back. There were many acts of heroism. One Lance Sergeant was opened fire at by an enemy strong point. With three men he went into the assault with the bayonet and captured the position. He took sixty prisoners. He killed a number of them and the rest gave themselves up, despite the fact they had eight machine guns.

A Lance Corporal was attacked with his section from two directions, he sent his section to deal with one strong point, and tackled the other, single handed; with his Tommy gun; they collected about fifteen prisoners.

Platoon Commanders tackled positions which would normally have necessitated Company attacks. We reached our final objective, a point 1600 yards beyond the anti tank ditch and consolidated there. In the evening, the Bosche counter attacked with tanks and infantry, but, with the support of artillery and the Cheshire's (machine gunners), we drove them off.

My Sergeant Major passed an enemy pit, not knowing it was there, and after he had done so one of the occupants opened fire on him. He turned round and with his machine pistol killed the lot.

Our C.O., Lt. Col. G. Lance DSO, played a magnificent part, as also did Brigadier Cooke-Collis DSO, who was with the forward elements at first light and stayed with us so that he could see what was going on and formulate his plan.

Major R. J. L. Jackson, of Guisborough, Yorks., commanding HQ Company, and whose duty it was to remain at Bn HQ, said 'We knew that the forward elements had met with success when we saw the steams of prisoners coming out' and Sgt. John Clayton said 'Some of the prisoners were laughing, others crying and some were in hysterics.' 'We owe a lot to the other two battalions' he added."

CPL WILLIAM CHEALL
6th BN GREEN HOWARDS. 'C' COY

"During the night of 4 April we were taken by three tonners to a place that was sheltered from the hills we were going to attack. When we were told about the way the assault would go in the battalions parted, I do not know what the private thoughts of the lads were, none of us expressed any fear of battle or it's consequences, we had been trained, knew what had to be done and just got on with it.

We left the start line at 0400 hours during the morning of 6 April, it was a dark night, the approach was over flat ground and very open, we advanced steadily four yards apart. We could hear the shells from our 25 pounders screaming over our heads, nothing entered our thoughts except the job we had to do. Suddenly the enemy put up flares which made the night eerie and as light as day, some of our boys began to fall because 88s had opened up, of course we kept moving forward at the same steady pace. Machine gun fire was now directed towards us causing more casualties: but not for long because we were soon below their line of fire.

It was now becoming light and I saw the anti tank ditch which spanned the full length of the attack. Part of the ditch had been filled in and one of our tanks, that must have approached in the hours of darkness, had been knocked out. I passed within six feet of that tank and a dreadful sight confronted me; the tank commander must had been observing from the turret when he had been killed, his intestines were hanging over the side of the turret and blood still flowed freely. Seeing such things did not affect me at the time because whatever we say the attack had to go in. We had all been told what our sections had to do and our section made its way along the wadi and into the hills where we soon came under machine gun fire and were pinned down.

One of our tanks must have seen our predicament and came to our assistance by blasting the machine gun position. We then carried on attacking isolated positions and taking Italian prisoners - never German. Our section was about to attack a position that had been set up on the forward slope of the hill, when suddenly our section leader fell dead right beside me from a single shot. The reaction to this was so swift - I grabbed a Tommy gun and shouted: 'Come on lads let's get the bastards, let's kill em!' - firing as we ran, we reached the slit trench with five cowering Ities in it and we killed them.

During the afternoon the enemy made a counter attack, but our blood was up and we gave them a hot reception causing them to withdraw. The noise of battle had almost petered out at 1700 hours and a meal of hot bully stew was brought forward to us.

I was now told, with another lad, to bury a body about 150 yards away, the body was blown to pieces, we could not find the head. We buried the remains and then I found the bottom half of a cap badge, it was all twisted and nearby I found the identity discs: I could hardly believe it was Arthur Oxley - one of my pals. I have the badge as a souvenir, I was deeply affected for a while.

The battle was over and we made our way forward past the battery of 88mm guns on top of a hill, the same guns which had been firing at us."

LT COL F. M. H. HANSON. DSO. OBE. MM
COMMANDING OFFICER: NEW ZEALAND ENGINEERS
(MINE-FIELD TASK FORCE)

"We advanced as a Coy in desert formation and, though the shells and mortars were coming in thick and fast, no one got hit. We halted out there and took what cover we could behind small slopes and hillocks while the O.C. and 2 I/C made a quick reconnaissance. Then N°s 2 and 3 platoons got busy on the job. Mines were easily seen and detectors hardly necessary, except for checking suspicious looking places - not a sure guarantee anyway as there were a good many wooden box mines about.

My lane ran right up the main track and I had just given the lads a starting point when Jerry began to plaster it with mortars, so we waited a few minutes until he switched a bit and then got cracking. Shells and mortars were still whistling in all round the place so, believe me, we lost no time.. . . . It was a long lane and had quite a variety of mines-tellers, wooden box, A/P, N5, and B2. At one point where it crossed over a slight rise, a sniper with a machine gun let go a burst or two every time he saw anyone but either he was a good distance back or not a very good shot as none of his bullets found a home. The zip zip overhead was rather disconcerting though.

The whole enemy position was a strong one and why they allowed us to gap the minefield after the barrage had passed over them I do not understand. Our 'D' Coy Inf. and our Crusader Squadron were certainly alert and were determined to shoot up any signs of the enemy so that the sappers could get on with the job, but at the same time a really aggressive enemy would never have allowed us to gap the minefield as we did. Luck was certainly with us this day. 50 Div Inf. and Sappers had fairly heavy casualties when they were first halted on the minefield and they were unlucky again when they eventually pushed ahead. . . . We were fortunate that from the late morning onwards much of the fire, which was still heavy, was directed on the track a little to the east of our right."

PTE ARCHIE NEWMARCH
5th BN EAST YORKSHIRE REGIMENT

"Later we found out 50 Div was to be used at Wadi Akarit, there wasn't a great deal of time since Mareth. Reinforcements started to come in, we got rearmed and reinforced and proceeded to a point about 10 miles from Akarit and went to our assembly points.

In the early morning the New Zealanders put down a barrage on the German positions, we went in and Jerry sent over star shells and lit up the area. As we went forward and got into this huge wadi we came to a standstill - the valley was full of exploding shells from the German guns. We lost 3 bren gunners, my mate had his fingers blown off and I was hit on my shins. We were all just stuck in that position, the sky was full of stars and we could see our officers waving to us to come up the hill. We got onto a narrow track and edged forward to the right and down into another wadi were we dug in and got shelled until daylight. Capt Harrison took a section out to find a way forward, there was machine guns firing at us and no way was found through the minefield. We stayed there while later that afternoon.

Cpl Church ran up the wadi side, he'd heard bagpipes. Sgt Edwards and me went up, we could hear the Highland Division in the distance but couldn't see anything.

Two tanks appeared over a distant ridge, two shots hit them. One crew was killed and three men escaped from the other into Italian positions, the Ities came out with their hands up - the gun crews were unarmed.

We then saw the Highland Div and more tanks coming over the forward ridge, to our right was an escarpment and as the Italians got to this Jerry shelled them.

4754532. PTE RON. L. RICKWOOD
7th BN GREEN HOWARDS

"17 Platoon is detailed to provide 8 men and an N.C.O. to protect our Intelligence Officer who is taking some Royal Engineers to lift a pathway through the mine field, and to report to HQ at 2300 hours. Now the usual routine to deal with this kind of situation is to call for volunteers. I am intent on staying mum – not so Pete Donaghue – "Come on Rick, we've got to go sometime, it's better than being detailed anyway". Why people have to open their BIG GOBS is beyond me, and I say "If I buy it on this patrol, I shall haunt you for the rest of your days!" So he and I volunteer and six others do the same, and a Corporal is detailed.

Now this guy is a Motor Transport Corporal from HQ, not used to leading a patrol, has been posted from the HQ company in rear to "fill in" until a replacement comes up the line. He has been in the desert for 2 years, been up to Tobruk and back, and up to Benghasi and back yet again, and has come up this time from Alamein – oh! by the by, he is, what is termed out here as 'Bomb happy!' 11pm arrives and we report to HQ and find the Intelligence Officer – I nearly collapse with laughter, my elder readers will perhaps remember a pre-war music hall turn called 'Claude Dampier' who did a piano tuning sketch.

This character has a long pointed nose, protruding upper teeth, thick pebbled spectacles, and looks as 'Goofy as hell!'.

He starts "Good evening Corporal, Good evening men. Do we all know what we have to do?" "Yes Sir!" "Right then, I'll go and draw the rum ration". I say to Pete "This must be some job, they're intent on getting us fighting mad!" Back he comes with a bottle of rum, but someone has been at it before us – it is only 1/3rd full!

He uncorks the bottle and like 'Merlin the Magician' produces a dessert spoon from his pocket and we line up for the only rum ration I have ever had before, or after, an attack. We get one dessert spoon each, and it's an insult to our mouths.

Ok, it's 11.30pm and we are off. There are two R.E.'s crawling in front and after testing for land mines, are laying out 1" white tape on pegs, showing those that follow a safe passage, also they are marking the safe path with lamps similar to a bike lamp but the front glass blacked over to leave a letter V showing. These lamps also had a hood over the front, so that no light is reflected upwards. I think it must be midnight now, and out of nowhere comes a German spotter plane which is dropping huge candelabra flares, turning pitch black night into daylight almost – this illumination shows up all the Ghurkas moving forward in front of us, and on looking to the rear, Bren gun carriers and tanks are moving forward.

The pilot, having seen what he was sent for, does an about turn and flies off and I say to Pete "Now the Jerries know where we are we can expect 88mm shells bursting around us any minute" and darkness returns. We hear screams and shouting going on up in these hills, and we know that the Ghurka's and their kukris are 'doing the business!' As we lay there we hear a bren carrier start its engines, move forward and run over riflemen laying on the ground waiting to move forward. Their screams even drown out the sounds of battle up in the hills.

We go forward each time the Sappers declare "it's safe" – about an hour later we see a figure coming out of the darkness towards us and is saying "Don't shoot it's Johnny Ghurka, don't shoot, it's me Johnny Ghurka!" Safety catches were off ready in case of need, but true enough it is a Ghurka, only a young boy – I couldn't see any wound, he was scared, and became adrift from his unit – we allowed him to pass through our lines! The Intelligence Officer says "the job is completed, stay where you are. I'll get back to you" and just went. We stayed there looking to our front the whole time and as the dawn begins to break all hell breaks loose!

There is 88mm shells bursting all around bracketing a New Zealand Tank unit, heavy machine guns firing, mortar bombs, all with their distinct warning of approach one gets used to in action, and a whistling sound our Corporal identifies as an old Italian 2" solid shot anti tank gun.

To our left there pulls up a 'Heath Robinson contraption' in the shape of an open 3 ton army lorry loaded with 50 gallon oil drums filled with sand, loaded back to the cabin on a ramp, and some armour plated sheets welded around the cabin for crew protection.

The whole thing is motivated by the driver reversing the lorry at top speed towards this 8ft wide anti tank ditch, and he and his mate running to the rear with sledge hammers knocking away the chocks, so letting all these sand filled drums roll down into the tank trap. Following this up is an old sand coloured bull-dozer with armour plate around the front of the cabin who is already pushing sand on top of all these drums to provide a crossing for vehicles. How this 'Itie' solid shot anti tank weapon misses this I don't know, but the bloody rounds are still whistling overhead. We now are pinned down, out in the open with no cover at all, and mortaring getting heavier all the time.

One of our party, a Private Mather had left England 9 months before and hadn't received any mail from home at all. He, believe it or not, is laying next door but one to me about 8-9ft away on his back sun bathing almost, when 'swoosh' came from out of nowhere, and bang an explosion. I hear shrapnel whine over my head, look around and Mather has received a mortar bomb blast in the stomach. He is screaming and has lost most of his intestines in the blast, and we all clench fists expecting another amongst us. As we lay there a New Zealand tank stopped, the top opened, and up popped the Officer in charge. We had spotted two 'Ities', carrying a stretcher with a wounded comrade on it, come across the now bridged tank trap and walk towards us supposedly to surrender.

On seeing the tank moving towards them they had dumped the stretcher and the wounded man, who is also screaming, and were running back towards their own lines. The Officer shouted to them, and started to beckon them back-they stopped running and started to come towards us again, and got to within 6-8ft of the tank and the officer shot them both dead. Just like that! Bang! Bang!

He says "I'd have let those 'Itie' bastards through with their wounded mate, but dropping him and running, that decided me. What's that man like Corporal?" "He's done for" says the Corporal who is as white as a sheet, and glassy eyed to be honest. "He has received a direct hit with a mortar bomb"- the Officer says. "Well you better put him out of his misery Corporal!" to which the Desert Rat replies "No Sir I cannot do that to one of my own, and I only have a rifle".

"All right Corporal I'll attend to it, and you better retreat from here, there is a counter attack coming by the sound of it – leave here two at a time and go about 400 yards, that should take you out of range of small arms fire and mortar shells!" I for one didn't need any second bidding, but allowed four others to go before Donaghue and I started off. "Ready Pete?" "Yes mate" – I say, "Don't run in a straight line, keep away from me and zig-zag all the time. No one can get their sights lined up on us then!"

We both run as we never ran before, I suppose around 300 yards, to some small scrub bushes, only inches high really. Donaghue beats me to the spot, and I witnessed something superhuman that morning. He has run 300 yards at the speed of Jesse Owens, flung himself onto the ground, and with tongue almost licking his boots, has extracted his entrenching tool from his pack and is digging in! The ground is rock hard, and the most we are able to do is to scratch about 6" deep, and pile it around our faces. I observe "we must look like a couple of ostriches with heads buried in the sand".

More tanks and motorised infantry pass over this makeshift road across the tank trap, and by afternoon we are able to go forward and climb these hills. The Company Commander, fresh from another unit, wants to know 'where we had been' and after the Corporal's explanation, Donaghue and myself went 'walk about' on the other side of the hill and examined the dugouts there.

Firstly, all the dead lying about are Italian, most having been killed by kukri blows. Secondly, I am amazed – in these dug outs are hundreds of condoms all strewn about all over, side by side with coloured postcards of the Virgin Mary and the Crucifix – a very queer mixture you may think.

And thirdly, most of the dead bodies had the Italian Red Devil hand grenades booby trapped to them, we left them all with a million flies having a birthday! Another queer detail (there's a pun there somewhere) is that many of the fallen Italians have extra long hair and are wearing women's hair nets?

Later, we were ordered to gather up their rifles and old-fashioned bayonets. . . (all of which were rusty) and make them unfit for use. This was easily carried out by holding the barrel end of the rifle and giving the butt end just one sharp blow on a nearby rock, which would detach the butt end completely from the weapon.

We are told this afternoon that our Commanding Officer has been seriously wounded, attacking a German machine gun post firing along the tank trap in which 'A' Company were lodged. Two Germans had surrendered with hands held aloft and then had thrown a 'potato masher hand grenade' at him. Another heartbreaking twist to this chapter is that next day on Post Call, when letters are delivered from home, as the names were being called out there was 'MATHER', someone else 'MATHER', 'MATHER' someone else then 'MATHER'. A whole pile had been held up somewhere in the system, and arrived just a day too late.

That evening we are given a Bren gun and told "train it on the gap in the road down there, we have been informed by field telephone that the German 90th Lt Division is counter attacking and are making progress, so you will open fire on anything that moves along that road". I try to make the point, "If the Jerries are advancing, surely our troops will be coming through that gap first?" "Are you questioning my orders Rickwood?" "No Sir!" "Well then, do as you are told!"

I let him get out of earshot, called him by a name not in the dictionary and said to Pete "I'll fire on our own – I don't think!" We never had to make that choice as the counter attack was beaten back. The next day they call for volunteers to bury the dead – just wrapped in an army blanket about 6" below ground, wooden cross made by the pioneers at HQ company, and a steel helmet and one identification disc left fixed to the steel helmet. We are told today that our Hero C.O. has passed away due to wounds received in his defence of 'A' Company. I for one am sorry!

LT (LATER COLONEL) FENNER
6th BN DURHAM LIGHT INFANTRY

"We were now in the gun line and it was very noisy .... We set off in the dark to find our defensive positions which neither of us had seen, the platoon and I moved in bounds - checking with Peter (Walton) from time to time. There was a certain amount of artillery noise except where we were, where it was quiet. Then we heard a vehicle noise to our front and we could see vehicle movement on the sky line.

Down a track towards me came a motorcyclist, he drove up to us and stopped to say something, then we grabbed him - one very surprised Panzer Grenadier. By first light we had made contact with 'B' Company on our left and they were in contact with 'A' Company. Bobby Pringle took the Carrier Platoon through and rounded up about 300 Italians."

COLONEL W. I. WATSON. OBE. TD. DL
6th BN DURHAM LIGHT INFANTRY

"The 6th Battalion had moved up in readiness, to the earlier position of 69th Brigade Headquarters which by now had moved forward into the Wadi Akarit. At 3.30pm General Nichols told the C.O. that although the attack had been a success there was a perilously large gap on eleven hundred yards astride the track over Hachana Ridge, between the Highlanders on Jebel Roumana and the 6th Green Howards. He explained that he now wanted the 6th Battalion to fill that gap in case of a possible counter attack. The C.O. who had himself been on a reconnaissance as far forward as possible along the track, drew the Divisional Commander's attention to the fact that to move in during daylight would probably mean very heavy casualties, since the whole route up from the anti tank ditch to the top of the ridge was receiving a continual heavy shelling, so it was agreed that the move should take place at last light or as soon a possible thereafter.

By 4pm the C.O. and his Company Commanders, after being badly shelled on the way, were in the Headquarters of Lieut. Colonel G.C.P. Lance who was commanding the 6th Green Howards. From this not very healthy place it was possible to look down on the gap and on to the slopes of Jebel Romana beyond, but there was no time to make a further more detailed reconnaissance; it was a question now for each company to move into its selected position as best it could.

At dusk the shelling died down and the air cleared and, as the sun went down behind the Ridge, the Battalion started to move forward. 'B' and 'D' Companies went first and it was almost dark as they passed the Pimple and crossed the anti tank ditch to start the slight climb into their positions, which they reached by 6 o'clock. The rest of the battalion soon followed and eventually everyone was more or less in the chosen localities. The task would appear to have been quite simple but it was, in fact, just the opposite.

To add to the difficulty of finding a chosen piece of ground on a dark night after only a quick and distant peep under difficult conditions, the area proved very rough with slit trenches and emplacements everywhere.

It was a question of each Company feeling its way in, with the added hazard of not knowing what the Germans would do next. Any moment the customary counter attack might well have been flung against the battalion, now very much balanced on one leg.

At times, too, much motor transport could be heard rumbling not far away, which might well have indicated the arrival of fresh enemy forces; as can be imagined everyone had their fingers crossed as they gradually got into their positions, ever hoping and praying on the other hand that the noise of the turning engines meant that the foe was pulling out. The prayer, fortunately, did not remain unanswered for long; a German despatch rider, from the renowned 90th Light Division, drove straight down the track into the Headquarters of 'C' Company as it moved in and was taken prisoner by Captain Walton. The rider obligingly declared that he had lost his way and his friends had gone. Gone they had, and it must have been very speedily too, for Captain Kirby found a Lancia Car all ready to drive away.

No opposition of any kind was forthcoming, except for four flights of mortar bombs from a six barrelled Nebel-Werfer which went whining harmlessly overhead, which was about the first time the Germans had used these disconcerting weapons in the Campaign. Some quite unasked for Defensive Fire, in and around Battalion Headquarters from our own artillery, thumped down from nowhere.

Communications were difficult as most of the wireless sets failed to work at the critical moment and the bren carrier, with the set linking the Brigade Headquarters, overturned - fortunately without damage to it or the signallers on board. At very first light the adjustments necessary in the Company positions were made and the anti tank defence was organised.

In front, all was very quiet and it was not long before patrols were probing forward with the news that the foe had gone, except for many hundreds of ill-kept and war-weary Italians, mostly from the Spezia and Pistoia Divisions and Independent Bersaglieri Companies together with a few Germans from the 90th Light Division and 15 Panzer Grenadier Regiment, who were waiting to be rounded up.

The mental state, to which some of these Italians had reached, was typified by the pathetic corpse which we buried later in the day. He had cut his own throat with one of the large daggers the Italians had issued to them.

Meanwhile, the armour of X Corps was coming forward and pushing its way out in front of the infantry positions. It was slow at first, but by 9 o'clock the New Zealand Division was streaming up the track over the ridge and down into the plains beyond - tanks, lorries and guns rumbled onwards raising clouds of dust as they went by. What a relief it all was, and what a joy to see yet another advance.

In the other direction rolled a great tide of prisoners quickly swelling to huge proportions, first in hundreds and then in thousands. Throughout the day the flood poured through the Battalion positions, bedraggled and weary, carrying a few worldly possessions, they were herded continually backwards to the cages.

During the morning the patrols from the Battalion ranged far and wide. The M.O. - Captain Runmey - working like a black on the wounded prisoners, was able to set up his own Regimental Aid Post in that of a well stocked Italian unit, which he himself first cleared of the Italians lying in it."

WAR DIARIES

50th NORTHUMBRIAN DIVISION

The grave of a tank crew next to their knocked out Sherman.

5th BN EAST YORKSHIRE REGIMENT
COMMANDING OFFICER: LT COL R. B. JAMES. DSO
(LT COL JAMES WAS KILLED IN 1944)
DATE: TIME:PLACE: GABES.

1 April. Bn re-organised on a four rifle company basis in area 1844 approx 5 miles North of GABES. Working parties and training.

2 April. Working parties and training.

3 April. Working parties and training.

4 April. Bn moves to concentration area 1844 approx 1 mile north of village of OUDREF so as to carry out preliminary recce of WADI AKARIT posns.

5 April. Detailed recce and orders for attack on A.Tk ditch from 110550 to 121555. 7 Green Howards on our right to make preliminary attack on Pt 85 129549 with one coy and the remainder of the Bn to attack A. Tk ditch and ground beyond on our immediate right. 4th Indian Div to take high ground on our left this attack to be silent and to be put in earlier in the night.

Plan of our own attack as follows - Attack on a two coy front - 'A' Coy on right, 'B' Coy on left, two coys to split 400 yds apart at the assembly area and proceed forward to start line and objective in column of threes - each coy preceded by sappers with mine detecting equipment covered by well armed protection party. Start line to be laid and lighted by I.O. in conjunction with 7 G.H. This to be ready by 0330 hrs.

Bn left concentration area at 1200 hrs and arrived at assembly area without incident just before midnight.

6 April 0330. Start line completed by 0330 hrs and Bn advanced from assembly area to start line. During this advance many flares were dropped over axis of advance by enemy aircraft and the Bn was 'grounded' for a considerable time.

However, this did not prevent us crossing the S.L. on time - 0415 hrs. Our artillery had already opened up at 0400 hrs on Pt 85 so silence was no longer necessary.

0445. At 0445 hrs arty commenced creeping barrage in front of us and lifted at the rate of 100 yds in 3 mins. Enemy D.F. was almost negligible and we proceeded quite happily close to our own barrage. Our troubles began at 0500 hrs. We had already advanced the distance calculated from the map to bring us to the A.Tk ditch and as yet there was no sign of the ditch.

Confirming this, our own arty, which at this time was calculated to be firing beyond the ditch, was still coming down close to our front - in fact several loose shots were arriving amongst our forward troops. The advance continued at the maximum pace permitted by the arty barrage, i.e. 100 yds in 3 mins with complete absence of S.A. fire from the enemy - just the usual mortar and artillery DF which was almost completely ineffective.

We began to think that the enemy had withdrawn but these ideas were somewhat rudely dispelled when, after crossing a small ridge, we were suddenly confronted with the anti tank ditch and a few seconds later, with a perfect hail of M.G. fire from the high ground to the N.E. of the ditch. Our forward troops were quickly disposed on the reverse slope of the ridge we were then on, and we waited for the artillery barrage to move forward on to the opposing enemy M.G.s and so enable us to continue the advance to our final objective - the high ground beyond the ditch. This however, was not to be.

According to the timed programme, the artillery should at this time have been firing well beyond the ditch in its final phase, whereas in fact it was still concentrated on the area of the ditch. The situation was difficult - the troops on our right seemed to be having a hard time and any movement forward by ourselves was met by intense S.A. fire and direct fire from many 47mm and other close support artillery. Enemy mortar and long range artillery fire was now intense and casualties were frequent.

Lt. Col Seagrim paid us a visit to acquaint us with the position on our right. Lt. Col James decided to put an attack in by 'C' Coy on our right under cover of smoke from our own mortars and artillery. 'C' and 'D' Coys which had, up to the present, been fairly well back were moved up and 'C' Coy commenced the advance round the right - over the ridge and down the re- entrant to the ditch.

This was bitterly opposed by the enemy who seemed to concentrate every weapon on 'C' Coy. Only a few men with Major Wallace succeeded in reaching the ditch at all. Capt Wood and Lt Beaty being killed on the way there and Lt Smurthwaite killed on arrival at the ditch. The position was covered by many weapons and was definitely untenable - as was any advance beyond the ditch also out of the question at this stage, 'C' Coy was therefore extricated and pulled back to its former position.

Courageous work was being done by the stretcher bearers - dressing and evacuating casualties under extremely heavy fire, particularly Pte Anderson who, after carrying three casualties over an exposed forward slope, was himself killed in his fourth attempt. Lt Col James was wounded in the thigh whilst endeavouring to observe the situation but remained on duty.

Meanwhile, there was an obvious improvement in the situation on our right.

6 G.H. accompanied by tanks had succeeded in pushing on through

the 7th and this, in conjunction with the forward movement of the Ind Div on our left, caused the enemy to our immediate front extreme discomfort. Doubtless they would have pulled out sooner had they dared to do so - this however, was an extremely hazardous operation for them owing to the stout work by the Cheshire machine gunners both on our front and Pt 85, ably assisted by the Bren gunners of 'A' and 'B' Coys who had continuously engaged the enemy at every opportunity.

About midday the rot had definitely set in the enemy's lines and we prepared to move forward to bridge the ditch. This was done without difficulty except for heavy mortar and artillery fire which now came down on the ditch itself. By 1430 hrs the Rifle Coys had crossed the ditch and took up positions on our objective, followed quickly by the Northumberland Hussars and our own A.Tk guns.

Signs of the hurried enemy evacuation were abundant - everything, guns, ammunition and equipment had been left behind. Our tanks were by now well forward on our right engaging targets further ahead of us.

A counter attack by German tanks and infantry in the evening was repulsed by the 51 (H) Div and 6 G.H. The day closed with a grievous loss - food arrived and was being sent out to Coys when three bombs were dropped on Bn HQ by an enemy plane, resulting in the death of Major H. N. Wallace, Cpt A. A. Blackwell, Lt (QM), A. S. James and Lt J. A. Atkinson, together with 3 O.R.s.

WAR DIARY
69th INFANTRY BRIGADE HEADQUARTERS
COMMANDING OFFICER: BRIGADIER E. C. COOKE-COLLIS. DSO
DATE: TIME: PLACE: FIELD.

6 April, 0525. 7 Green Howards capture Pt 85 (CUTIE). 0700 5 East Yorks and 7 Green Howards held up by mortars and MG fire on line of A/Tk ditch.

0730. O.C. 7 Green Howards evacuate. (Lt Col SEAGRIM).

59 Italian P.W. of Spezia Div brought back from Pt 85.

0800. 37 Italian P.W. also of Spezia came back.

0810. Brig went forward to Pt 85 to see the situation.

0905. Orders received that 6 Green Howards were to be passed through on the right.

1015. 6 Green Howards carried out this operation preceded by a Sqn of Sherman tanks of 4 C.L.Y. This manoeuvre virtually crumbled the enemy opposition and many of the enemy, about 400 in number, gave themselves up.

During this period the 5 East Yorks were unable to get across the anti tank ditch. However, at about 1200 hrs enemy resistance grew less on this front also. 8 Armd Bde and 2 NZ Div passed through the gap beyond Pt 85. However, they did not get far beyond the gap as the presence of 88mm guns were reported on the high ground to the North.

1500. 6 D.L.I. came under comd 69 Bde. The 6 Green Howards established themselves on the line of their original objective but were in a fairly precarious posn. The 6 D.L.I. were therefore sent up to reinforce them at 1800 hrs.

2359. Warning was received of the N.Z. plan for breaking through the remaining

7th BN THE GREEN HOWARDS
COMMANDING OFFICER: LT COLONEL D. SEAGRIM. VC
(LT COL SEAGRIM DIED OF WOUNDS AT WADI AKARIT)
DATE: TIME: PLACE: AKARIT.

6 April 0200. Intelligence Officer and 3 O.Rs, with covering party from 'D' Coy, move forward to lay start line.

0300. 'C' Coy move to start line.

0330. Zero hour for 'C' Coy to advance to objective Pt 85, art'y barrage for Coy lasting 10 minutes.

0400. 'A' and 'B' Coys reach start line with 'D' Coy following in reserve.

0430. Zero hour for 'A' and 'B' Coys, 'D' Coy remain on S.L.

0515. 'D' Coy move forward to support 'C' Coy on Pt 85.

0520. Positions on Pt 85 captured and consolidation in progress.

0600. Own art'y barrage lifts, 'A' and 'B' Coys take up positions in A/Tk ditch.

0700. Lt. Col. Seagrim and Intelligence Officer wounded.

0800. 'A' and 'B' Coys withdrawn to re-organise after being relieved by 6th Bn Green Howards.

1500. Lt Depoix appointed Intelligence Officer.

1730. Bn less 'C' and 'D' Coys, move forward to take up contd. positions forward of A/Tk ditch.

1740. Orders received to return to area of F.U.P. less 'C' and 'D' Coys, Major Edgar takes over command of Bn.

6th BN THE GREEN HOWARDS
COMMANDING OFFICER: LT COLONEL G. LANCE. DSO
DATE: TIME: PLACE: AKARIT.

1 April. Bn re-organised to consist of 4 rifle Coys and HQ Coy. Coy commanders are now; HQ Coy Capt Jackson, 'A' Coy Capt Honeyman, 'B' Coy Capt Fairclough, 'C' Coy Maj. Hull, and 'D' Coy Capt Lofthouse. Capt Hull was promoted.

Major and Lt. Morgan Capt. Bn ordered to stand by for move at 0800 hrs next day.

2 April, 0900. Bn moved out and passed through Gabes to Metouai. Advance parties went forward to Wadi Akarit area.

2000. Bn marched into positions south of Wadi Akarit facing Italian Spezia Div.

3 April. Bn dug in and remained under cover during day. Sporadic enemy shell fire during day.

4 April. Carrier patrol encountered heavy enemy fire from Pt 85.

2000. Patrols report Pt 85 occupied by enemy.

5 April. Bn makes preparations for attack. Intention:- 5 E.Y. and 7 G.H. to breach minefield and force bridgehead over A/T ditch, 6 G.H. to pass through 7 G.H. bridgehead and occupy objectives one mile to West, and consolidate with tank support.

6 April, 0345. Zero hour - barrage started.

0415. Bd. attack went in and Bn started moving slowly up to Pt 85.

0545. First light. Bn now lying in open ground behind enemy minefield, under heavy shellfire. Lt. Levine, R.S.M. and several others wounded. 7 G.H. were having great difficulty in breaching A/T ditch, but many prisoners were coming back.

0730. 'A' and 'C' Coys pushed through minefield and A/T ditch and advanced under heavy fire taking prisoners as they went.

0800. Bn HQ, 'B' and 'D' Coys move up through minefield on to Pt 85.

0900. Forward Coys held up half way to objective by very heavy fire. Very heavy shellfire was also directed on to gaps.

1030. 'D' Coy moved up and with 'C' Coy pushed forward another 600 yds on to final objective, meeting heavy opposition but taking many prisoners.

Support weapons started moving up immediately.

1230. 'A' and 'B' Coys and main Bn HQ moved up to positions 400 yds in rear of forward Coys.

'D' Coy were heavily shelled by 88mm guns and suffered casualties.

1506. D.L.I. advance party recced forward positions; enemy shellfire had now slackened off considerably.

1830 Enemy tanks and infantry seen approaching forward positions -

counter attack expected.

2000 2130 hrs. Heavy enemy shellfire but counter attack did not materialise. 6 D.L.I. moved into position on right flank.

7 April. At first light. 8 Armd Bde tanks went through and by 0800 hrs it was clear that the enemy were withdrawing. Many prisoners were taken.

4347754 - PTE ERIC ANDERSON VC
'A' COY. 5th BN EAST YORKSHIRE REGIMENT

BIOGRAPHICAL DETAILS

Eric Anderson was born at Fagley, Eccleshill, Bradford, on 15 September 1916 and was educated at Thornbury Boys School, Bradford. He enlisted into the East Yorkshire Regiment in June 1940 and was killed at the battle of the Wadi Akarit, 6 April 1943, while serving as a stretcher bearer with 'A' Company at the age of 27 years. For his bravery under intense fire, he was awarded the Victoria Cross posthumously, the following citation appeared in the London Gazette on 29 July 1943:

"On 6 April, 1943, a battalion of the East Yorkshire Regiment was making a dawn attack on a strong enemy locality on the Wadi Akarit with 'A' Company leading. After some progress had been made, and 'A' Company was advancing over an exposed forward slope, it suddenly came under most intense and accurate machine gun and mortar fire, from well concealed enemy strong points not more than two hundred yards away. Further advance in that direction was impossible, and 'A' Company was able to withdraw behind the crest of a hill with the exception of a few men who were wounded and pinned to the ground by heavy fire.

Private Anderson, a stretcher bearer attached to 'A' Company, seeing these men lying wounded in No Man's Land, quite regardless of his personal safety, went forward alone through intense fire and single-handed carried back a wounded soldier to a place of safety where medical attention could be given.

Knowing that more men were lying wounded in the open, he again went out to the bullet swept slope, located a second wounded man and carried him to safety. Private Anderson went forward once again and safely evacuated a third casualty.

Without any hesitation or consideration for himself, he went out for a fourth time but by now he was the only target the enemy had to shoot at and, when he reached the fourth wounded man and was administering such first aid as he could to prepare for the return journey, he was himself hit and mortally wounded.

Private Anderson by his valour, complete disregard for his personal safety and courage under fire, probably saved the lives of three of his comrades and his example was an inspiration to all who witnessed his gallant acts."

Pte Anderson was buried at Wadi Akarit and later moved to SFAX War Cemetery, Plot II, Row 'C', Grave 14.

His widow, Mrs I Anderson, was presented with his award at Buckingham Palace on 28 October 1943, by His Majesty King George VI.

A memorial plaque to the memory of Eric Anderson VC, was unveiled at Thornbury Boys School Bradford on 3 April 1944. His heroic deed would also be commemorated by the presentation of an annual book prize at his old school which would be awarded on 6 April every year, the first recipient of the prize was Derek Harris.

OTHER MEMORIALS

BEVERLEY MINSTER

ST JOHN'S UNITED REFORM CHURCH, BRADFORD

At the annual reunion of the East Yorkshire Regimental Association, on Sunday 10 October 1954 at Victoria Barracks, Beverley, his widow Mrs I Pilling (Nee Anderson) of Intake Road, Fagley, Bradford, presented his Victoria Cross to the Regimental Museum.

CHAPTER THREE

THE RIGHT FLANK
THE 51ST HIGHLAND DIVISION ATTACKS

General Wimberley, Commander 51st Highland Division, and Montgomery. *(Courtesy of the Imperial War Museum)*

'To Those dear houses with chimneys reeking
In Angus or in Fife,
No Spirit came its words of omen speaking
To Mother or to wife,
Yet in the homeless desert to the southward
Before the sun was high,
The husbands whom they loved, the sons they mothered
Stood up and went to die.'

143

THE 51st HIGHLAND DIVISION
COMMANDING OFFICER: MAJOR GENERAL D. N. WIMBERLEY

The 51st Highland Division had been given the task of taking the Roumana feature on the right of the 8th Army's front. The 152nd Brigade would attack Roumana Ridge while on their right 154th Brigade would attack the wadi, and on their right (under command of 51st Highland Div) the 201st Guards Brigade would perform a holding role from the coast road to the sea. The Divisional Reserve was to consist of the 5th Battalion Black Watch – the rest of 153rd Brigade had moved forward early to gain contact with the enemy and consolidate a line 2,000 yards short of the Wadi Akarit.

If the attack by the Highlanders was a success, the enemy would have to be pushed back far enough to allow the 8th Army to dominate the northern plain: once this had been achieved the Axis forces would find their positions across the whole of the plain untenable and be forced to withdraw – leaving open the routes to the important ports of Sfax and Sousse – and take up a new defensive line at Enfidaville.

In the coming battle – on the front to be attacked by 154th Brigade – the 7th Argylls were to move through the mine-fields and attack the anti tank ditch and the Wadi Akarit thus forming a bridge head. The 7th Black Watch would then pass through them – wheel left in the wadi and clear the area before the Roumana feature. The 1st Black Watch would be held in brigade reserve.

Simultaneously, on 152nd Brigade's front the 5th Camerons on the left and 5th Seaforths on the right, were to assault and capture the left of the ridge, moving up on the right of the 5th Seaforths, the 2nd Seaforths were then to advance and clear the top of the Roumana feature – turn right and make contact with the 7th Black Watch on the plain below.

154th BRIGADE
COMMANDING OFFICER: BRIGADIER J. E. STERLING. DSO. MC

At 0415 hours on 6 April the barrage opened up along the Highland Division's front and, under its protection, Scorpion tanks rumbled forward with flails churning up great clouds of dust as they passed through the holding Gordon Battalions of 153rd Brigade. The tanks forced their way forward clearing gaps in the minefield, to be followed by units of the 40 R.T.R. – towing the guns of the 241st Anti Tank Battery. Parties of divisional engineers also advanced and, under heavy concentrations of enemy artillery and machine gun fire, managed to gap the minefield and bridge the anti tank ditch by midday.

THE 7th BATTALION ARGYLL AND SUTHERLAND HIGHLANDERS
COMMANDING OFFICER. LT. COL. LORNE CAMPBELL. DSO. TD

At 0515 hrs the battalion attack began supported by strong artillery fire. The plan was to advance in two lines, 'B' and 'A' Companies leading, and 'C' and 'D' Companies, with Bn HQ between them, following some seven hundred yards in rear. Rear Bn HQ followed by bounds approximately another seven hundred yards back. 'B' Coy was to capture the long sandhill on the right and 'A' Coy was to seize the ditch and the nearer of the two posts beyond it, pause fifteen minutes and then push on to the further post and reorganise six hundred yards beyond the ditch. During the fifteen minutes pause 'C' Company was to pass through 'B', who appeared likely to have their hands full in capturing the sandhill, and to take the position beyond. 'D' Company, as reserve Coy, was to move behind 'A' and give depth to the reorganisation in their rear.

Bn HQ would, if possible, be established at the junction of the wadi and the anti tank ditch and rear Bn HQ in the neighbourhood of the Causeway Crossing of the OGLET EL SMALA. At the very last moment fresh air photographs arrived which showed the enemy positions almost doubled. In front of the sandhill there was now a similar position of equal or even greater strength right on the lip of the wadi, whose banks were reported to be anything up to twenty four feet high, and a few machine gun posts had also appeared on our side of the AKARIT. It was too late, however radically, to alter the plan so arrangements were made that if 'B' Coy were held up as now seemed very possible, 'C' Coy would give covering fire from the south of the AKARIT while 'D' Coy attacked the sandhill from the west.

The advance began quietly, but after it had gone about five hundred yards the enemy guns opened and machine gun fire came in from both flanks. This fire steadily increased and caused a fair number of casualties, but the advance continued quite steadily and in good formation.

The navigator, Capt. CAMERON, was hit very soon after the start and although his reserve took over almost immediately: either owing to this or more probably to the line of the OGLET ES SMALA, which ran at an angle to the advance, the whole battalion swung too much to the left, and the right instead of the left flank of 'B' Coy, hit the junction of the wadi and the ditch.

As it turned out this was a lucky mistake as the troops were able, by helping each other, to swarm across the ditch but the wadi bank which had been artificially cut, and which they would probably have had to scale, would have been a serious obstacle. The minefield was no worse than expected and though only 'A' Coy were able to use the gaps made by the Scorpions the rest of the battalion walked straight through the mines, the casualties from mines were few.

'A' Company and 'B' Company both captured their objectives after some rather half-hearted opposition and started the stream of prisoners which began to flow to the rear. Capt. MEIKLEJOHN, Commanding 'B' Coy, quickly realised that he was too far to his left and turning his reserve platoon to the right, took both the wadi and the sandhill lines from the flank and started to reorganise as planned. 'C' Company were held back for two or three minutes to see the result of 'B's attack, but it became clear that rapidly 'B' Coy were succeeding, so 'C' was ordered to push straight through them to their objective, which they secured. 'D' Company had little fighting to do and reached their pre-arranged position without much difficulty.

The bridgehead had now been formed and the job was to hold it for the rest of the day. 'A', 'B' and 'C' Coys were much weakened by casualties and very thin on the ground and the enemy shelling and small arms fire increased steadily. The first threat came from the right flank where 'B' Coy reported that the Germans from the neighbourhood of the road were becoming very active with L.M.G. fire and sniping and were trying to work round their right rear. To counter this move a platoon of 'D' Coy was detached to support 'B' and a section of the M.Gs of the 1/7 Middlesex, which had just arrived, were put into action south of the AKARIT to cover the right flank.

No further advance was made from this direction but the small arms fire, though subdued from time to time by mortar fire and once by an effective artillery concentration, continued and was a nuisance all day. Meanwhile, the two left hand companies and both Bn HQs and the whole area between the two wadis was subjected to very heavy artillery fire by guns of all calibres. This fire continued with intensity and accuracy all day and was almost incessant. Machine gun fire from the hills north of ROUMANA later added to the annoyance.

At 0800 hrs, the 7th Bn B.W. attacked on the left of the Bn and enlarged the bridgehead on that side, thereby greatly improving the position.

The next three counter attacks, all by infantry and all in the morning, were made on 'A' Coy on the left front, but they were half hearted affairs and each was broken up by accurate artillery fire. At 1200 hrs the first gap was completed and valentines of 40 R.T.R. came through it and supported the battalion from the cover of the sandhill. Later they withdrew and their place was taken by Shermans of the City of London Yeomanry who remained in support until dark but were subjected to very heavy shelling and suffered considerable losses. At 1400 hrs Valentines crossed the gap towing the 6 pounders of two troops of 241 A.Tk Bty. These guns were dropped approximately on their sites and were manned, but could not be dug in owing to the heavy shelling in which one was knocked out. At about 1600 hours eight enemy tanks appeared on 'A' Coy's front about 2500 yards away, men were seen climbing on to them and small bodies of infantry began to advance, but again our artillery engaged them and this attack also petered out.

At 1800 hrs the most serious counter attack developed from a force estimated as two battalions with tanks in support. 'A' Coy, who had gone rather further than their objective, and were isolated from the support of the other companies, had been ordered to draw back two or three hundred yards at dark; so when he saw this attack coming in and realised his weak strength (30 all told) and isolated position, Capt. ROBERTSON decided he should make the move.

Unfortunately, Capt. Bate who was sent back to reconnoitre the new position and get the Coy into it, was wounded and consequently the Company having no guide came back further than was intended; but it withdrew in good order under its officers and took up new positions in line with the forward platoon of 'D' Coy.

From here fire was opened with L.M.Gs and rifles to such good effect that the attack on this front was completely halted. On the right flank the attack was pushed in to within three hundred yards of 'C' Company, where it too was halted within fifty yards of Coy. HQ. Major LINDSAY MACDOUGALL, the Company Commander, thereupon climbed out of his trench and standing on top shouted "No surrender, 'C' Company. Charge". The only five men he had, charged with the bayonet and the enemy fled and twelve surrendered as prisoners. The remainder came on no further before dark fell. Major MACDOUGALL, who had been twice wounded, was unable to lead the charge, but hobbled out after his men as quickly as he could and was never far behind them.

Just before dark 'B' Coy, 1st B.W. were sent to reinforce the position and joined 'B' Coy and later 'C' Coy 1st B.W. also came in and the situation became much more comfortable. There was active patrolling by both sides during the night and a few prisoners were lost and taken, but before dawn the whole of the enemy had withdrawn. A carrier patrol pushed forward to the wadi and was just in time to see the last of his guns and transport pulling out.

Little use of wheeled transport could be made during the day owing to the heavy shelling, but the Ambulance made several journeys and the carriers did excellent work bringing up ammunition etc to rear Bn HQ, whence it was carried forward by hand.

THE 7th BATTALION BLACK WATCH
COMMANDING OFFICER: LT COL J.A.OLIVER. DSO. MBE

The 7th Black Watch advanced at 0625 hours, the gap they had to pass through had by now been registered by the enemy artillery and mortar crews and a deluge of fire descended upon them as they moved through the minefield. Once over the anti tank ditch the battalion reformed on the far side and looked on in amazement as hordes of Italian prisoners passed over to the British lines.

As they advanced towards Roumana heavy machine gun fire took a steady toll in lives as the troops pressed on, but by 0930 hours they had gained their objectives though as yet no contact had been made with 2nd Seaforths on the ridge. The Seaforths were now having difficulties in their advance on point 112 and this affected adversely the activities of the 7th Black Watch who were trying to clear the wadi of enemy troops, they were under direct observation from the northern end of the ridge and came under heavy fire making their task impossible.

Heavy shelling of the battalion positions and sniping carried on all day, at 1700 hours tanks and German infantry counter attacked the battalion front over-running some of the forward positions and penetrating between them and the 7th Argylls on the right. However, Lt Col Roger Caldbeck of the 1st Black Watch sent up reinforcements and the situation was restored and at 2300 hours the battalion retired 1,000 yards – closing up with the Argylls.

THE 152nd BRIGADE
COMMANDING OFFICER: BRIGADIER G. MURRAY. DSO. MC

On the left of 154th Brigade Brigadier Murray's 152nd Brigade had launched their attack on the ridge; at 0330 hours the 5th Seaforths – with the 5th Camerons on their left – began their assault on Roumana and its highest point known as point 198. The advance was over a rocky grassy landscape with the barrage crashing and roaring before them, the troops moved forward at the rate laid down in the plan, one hundred yards every four minutes and as dawn broke they arrived at the base of the slopes of Roumana.

THE 5th BATTALION SEAFORTH HIGHLANDERS
COMMANDING OFFICER: LT. COL. J. H. WALFORD.
DSO AND BAR

The barrage was now creeping up the slopes before them as the men began to scramble up the craggy hill side, at 0545 hours they disappeared from view and over the crest of Roumana. The numerous Italians they had come across gave up without a fight and the 5th Seaforths found themselves upon their objective without having to fight for it, the thundering barrage halted on the reverse slope of the hill forming a protective wall of high explosive and smoke.

Quickly the troops reorganised in preparation for the counter attack and extra ammunition was brought up from the foot of Roumana, the ground was too hard for digging so the Jocks found themselves any nook or cranny that might give them some protection. On the right 'A' and 'B' Companies had a wide front to cover that was completely overlooked by point 198 and point 112, to their left was 'C' and 'D' Companies and left again across a wide gap was the 5th Camerons. The 2nd Seaforths on the right now occupied point 112 and so long as this and point 198 were held the front was sound, this fact was also obvious to the Germans who now began to put steadily mounting pressure upon these positions: it started at 0700 hours when mortar bombs rained down upon the Scots, spandaus joined in and the din was deafening.

Under cover of this barrage the Germans moved up machine gun teams in great numbers and opened up on the attacking companies from concealed positions among the rocks. Colonel Walford, now up with the leading platoons and observing for himself the precarious situation the battalion was now in, came to the conclusion that if the enemy reached point 198 the whole of the ridge would become untenable and so long as a counter attack was a possibility, any forward movement was impossible with the small numbers of men left at his disposal. Walford left to get reinforcements and it was not long before 'D' Company returned to the rocky crest to hold on until help arrived.

At 0910 hours a heavy infantry counter attack was delivered from the north east end of Roumana, all over the hillside shooting broke out as the Germans closed in. 'A', 'B' and 'C' Companies were forced from their positions in this ferocious assault but soon reorganised below the crest, 25 pounders of the Highland Division now joined in aided by a lone Honey tank from the New Zealanders.

The battle raged in a most confusing way and amid the crash of exploding shells, that sent showers of rock fragments hurtling through the air, stick grenades exploded and there was a constant rattle of machine guns and small arms. The numbers of the 5th Seaforths slowly dwindled amid this maelstrom, companies were down to twenty men and by the afternoon the situation was desperate.

Waiting in reserve the 5th Black Watch had been watching the battle from the plain below and were ordered forward to reinforce the Seaforths- they arrived at 1800 hours and two of their companies relieved 'D' Company on Point 198. For eight hours 'D' Company – consisting of less than twenty men – had held off one hundred and fifty Germans in close quarter fighting, these were the only men on the crest and should they have failed to hold their ground the whole of the brigade front would have been at risk. Major Davidson – assisted by Cpt Willock – and the remnants of 'D' Company can, along with the rest of the battalion, be justly proud of this feat of arms.

THE 2nd BATTALION SEAFORTH HIGHLANDERS
COMMANDING OFFICER: LT COL R. D. HORNE DSO.

The Bn left its rest area at 1930 hrs on 5 April to move forward to its forming up position for the attack on the ROUMANA Ridge.

The plan was briefly that the Bde would attack with two Bns foreward, 5th Seaforth right and 5 Camerons left. These Bns were to secure the ROUMANA Ridge itself, while 2nd Seaforth would follow 5th Seaforth, turn right when astride the ridge, and finally secure the feature at the N.E. end of the Roumana Ridge, marked by pt 112 on the map.

The Bn had breakfast in the FUP at 0200 hrs and were issued with a mess tin ration for the day. The Bn crossed the start line at 0350 hrs in rear of 5th Seaforth, as follows:

Two Coys forward 'C' Coy right and 'B' Coy left, with Bn Tac HQ between them, followed by 'A' Coy right and 'D' Coy left with main Bn HQ between them. The mortar pl and the carrier pl (carrying ammunition and water) and the M.G. platoon of 1/7 Middlesex (under comd) were left one mile behind the FUP and bounded forward as soon as the barrage opened.

The A/Tk platoon was left under Bde control ready to come forward when called. The plan was to call them up as soon as the objective was taken, by means of the track through the re-entrant, when reported clear by the Sappers. Although the Sappers completed their task, the objective was never held for long enough, so the A/Tk platoon never came into the battle.

The ground between the start line and the ridge was flat and open, and it was crossed in darkness without meeting anything very much in the way of enemy defensive fire. The barrage opened at 0415 hrs.

As first light came the Bn was climbing the steep, rocky slopes of Roumana Ridge having passed through the HQ elements of 5th Seaforth which were left at the foot of the ridge.

At this time certain factors caused slight confusion in the darkness, resulting in a few of each Coy losing touch and becoming attached to the wrong Coy. Firstly, there was the darkness and the difficulty of distinguishing 2nd from 5th Seaforth men. Secondly, the unexpected steepness and rocky slopes broke formations and loosened control. Thirdly, the mass of Italians surrendering in the half light caused a check to parts of the Bn. Consequently 'B' and 'C' Coys were not at full strength when they arrived on the far side of the ridge, prior to forming up for the advance to the right along the ridge.

Meantime, 'A' Coy had suffered some accurate mortar fire as soon as they arrived at the foot of the ridge and the Coy Comd, Capt. S.J.S. Lee and the Coy 2nd i/c., Capt. D.B. Law, were both hit. However, the Adjutant, Capt. W.G. McHardy, collected that Coy and the remainder of 'C' Coy which had become separated, and took them along the lower slopes towards the 112 feature.

As already stated, scores of Italians were surrendering all along the ridge. Disposal of these delayed the advance slightly and depleted the ranks of each Coy. Certain isolated Italian posts held out however and caused a number of casualties in the ranks. The evacuation of these was extremely difficult and slow over the steep rocky slopes, and the available stretchers were soon used up.

The left wing of the Bn, under Capt. D. W. Hudson, 'C' Coy, and W. L. Givens, 'B' Coy had, meantime, made considerable progress along the far side of the ridge, sending back more prisoners, including 4 Germans. They drove off a party of Germans, inflicting some casualties, when they endeavoured to attack them from the North. Automatic and Mortar fire, however, from German positions in depth, became heavier, and they suffered casualties including both officers. When they had got about half way to the objective further advance became impossible and the remnants were forced back onto the near side of the ridge and joined up with 'D' Coy.

Two sections did manage to hold out on the ridge for the rest of the day and later joined up, one with 5th Seaforth on the left, and the other with 5th Black Watch, who were sent up to fill the gap in the afternoon.

Meanwhile, the right wing, 'A' Coy and part of 'C' Coy, under Capt. McHardy, had no difficulty in gaining the 112 feature by 0645 hrs, although they arrived on the objective somewhat depleted in strength and ammunition. The Germans were then seen to be approaching up the wadis on the N.W. side of the ridge and working round the eastern flank of 112. This would not have mattered if the left wing had been able to make good the tops of the ridge overlooking 112. As it was, the troops on 112 were subjected to a counter attack at short range from their front and right. The result was that they lost the feature and suffered heavily. In this attack all Officers and Sergeants of 'A' and 'C' Coys were wounded. The remnants hung on to the lower slopes, from where they could cover the top of the ridge, and later joined up with 'D' Coy. The C.O. could see from the main ridge the loss of 112, so, having two platoons of 'D' Coy under his command, and Capt. J.A.G. Corrie (O.C. 'B' Coy) with one platoon 'B' Coy, he ordered Capt. Corrie to retake the hill with this party, while Capt. J.M. Anderson (2nd i/c 'B' Coy) with two sections was ordered to protect the left flank.

The 3" mortars, under Lt. J.F. Flugel, had been in action in a wadi 800 yds to the South and had engaged the enemy as they appeared on 112. The enemy had the advantage of observation, necessitating frequent change of position by the Mortars to avoid counter mortar fire. At the time of Capt. Corrie's attack on the 112 feature, a concentration of mortar fire was arranged in support. One of the features of this battle was the handling of the mortar platoon centrally under the platoon commander, necessitated by the nature of the ground. Detachments were unable to move with Coys in close support. As it turned out far better effect was obtained by this centralised control.

This second attack on the 112 feature went in at about 1000 hrs and reached the first ridge successfully, but as soon as they began to advance further they met overpowering M.G. and Mortar fire from Armoured cars and positions on the reverse slopes and tops of the Roumana Ridge.

Capt. Corrie was hit and there were so many other casualties that the position proved untenable. Nevertheless, more Italians surrendered during this attack. A few of the wounded were again seen to fall into German hands who worked round the right flank. The remnants again took up positions on the lower slopes.

By 1200 hrs it appeared to the C.O. that the Germans had thinned out the positions they had re-occupied, so a fresh attack was ordered supported by a 10 minute concentration from 308 Bty. This went in at 1300 hrs, under Lt BH Blyth. A reserve was collected from oddments round Bn HQ and sent up as a second wave under the Bn 2nd i/c, Major A.M. Gilmour, MC, who was instructed to organise the consolidation of the feature after capture.

The attack was again successful as far as the first ridge, and about 25 more Italian prisoners were taken. However, the Germans had only thinned out their forward positions to thicken up those in depth, and the same withering M.G. and Mortar fire as was previously experienced, was again met, killing Lt. Blyth and wounding Major Gilmour, Lt. J. Douglas and many O.Rs. Major Gilmour decided it was too costly to try and hold the position and ordered them back under the near slopes of the feature from which they had started. A fire fight ensued for the remaining hours of daylight, small parties of each Coy holding on to what they had gained, but, nowhere were they in possession of the crest.

The carrier platoon was used for bringing up reserve ammunition and water. Some of the crews fought dismounted in support of the Coys, while the carriers themselves did valuable work in evacuating wounded from the bottom of the slopes to the RAP, which had set up near 5th Seaforth HQ, where the Bn first started to climb. The carrying of wounded down the slopes, once all the stretchers had gone, presented great difficulties and at times prisoners with captured blankets were used for this task. Carriers always drew heavy automatic fire and some very courageous work was done in lifting casualties on to the carriers, this was not always respected by the enemy.

Communications were almost non-existent, N°18 sets were carried with each Coy HQ, but none of them ever passed a message. A cable was laid by signallers forward of 5th Seaforth HQ with the intention of maintaining communication with Bde, but this was soon broken in many places by constant shell and mortar fire. The N°11 set was carried in the C.Os carrier which reached the A/Tk ditch.

The carrier received a direct hit from an enemy mortar on its wing, breaking the track, but fortunately, neither the driver, W/T set nor operators, who were all inside the carrier, were touched. The same bomb killed Capt. W.H. Spreull (O.C. 'D' Coy) and Sgt. Scott of the Mortars, but the Adjutant, who was on the opposite side had a lucky escape.

The W/T set was taken off and set up in the wadi and communication was established with Bde by 0715 hrs. The Adjutant actually reported having gained the objective, but he had left 112 just before the counter attack. Bde were later informed of the situation regarding this feature and of the growing number of casualties. At about 1100 hrs two Germans worked their way down the wadi to Bn HQ and were only seen just in time. A grenade duel ensued at which, miraculously neither side suffered. One German was shot but the other escaped. The 11 set was damaged by the grenades and from then on messages to Bde were passed through 128 Fd Regt by means of 308 Bty W/T truck.

THE 5th BN QUEEN'S OWN CAMERON HIGHLANDERS
COMMANDING OFFICER: LT COL R.D.M.C. MIERS. DSO

On the extreme left of the divisional attack were the troops of the 5th Camerons – who's job it was to link up with the right flank of the 50th Division's infantry. At 0330 hours they crossed the start line, led by Lt

Col Ronnie Miers, with 'A' Company on the right followed by battalion HQ and 'D' Company on the left followed by 'C' Company. They made their way forward without incident for the first few hundred yards: the battalion advancing in silence. Their own barrage now rumbled before them, creeping steadily towards the slopes of Roumana, enemy artillery fire opened up on the lines of men and vehicles advancing across the open plain. Undaunted the troops pressed on, making their way up the slopes of the lower end of Roumana Ridge and into the wadis around it, the men worked feverishly consolidating their new positions; by 0530 hours the objective was firmly in the hands of the Camerons and over three hundred prisoners had been taken.

On the left, the infantry of the 50th Division had not yet arrived, while on the right the 5th Seaforths were in position, however, it was obvious that the enemy was regrouping for a counter attack to be delivered by troops of the 90th Light Division. As this attack fell, mainly upon the 2nd and 5th Seaforths, the Camerons held their ground against these seasoned veterans of the Afrika Corps: all the time watching their open left flank. In the dust and smoke the enemy pressed forward into the Camerons, only to be met by troops who refused to give ground.

When the enemy did break in, gallant groups of individuals fixed bayonets and made charges across the rocky terrain, with each action the groups holding out became smaller. CSM Macrae of 'D' Company led three bayonet charges and killed nine Germans in the melee, only to be shot dead defending his position. Many such acts of gallantry were performed that day – the majority going unnoticed in the general confusion.

Later in the day tanks were seen going through the mine field gap and the troops of the 50th Division arrived on the left flank. As night fell the badly depleted ranks of the 5th Camerons settled down to await events.

THE 5th BATTALION BLACK WATCH
COMMANDING OFFICER: LT COL THOMSON

On 6 April the 5th Black Watch were held in divisional reserve and moved up at first light to a position to the rear of TAC Div HQ. The battalion was ready to form part of 'Spearforce' under the command of 23rd Armoured Brigade and carriers of the Camerons were already employed by that brigade to cover a gapping operation.

At 0900 hours the battalion was ordered to move forward and Lt Col Thomson met with the Divisional Commander at advanced Tac Div HQ, he was told to be prepared to relieve the 5th Seaforths on Point 198 and to fill the gap between them and the 2nd Seaforths on point 112. At midday the battalion was ordered forward onto point 198 itself to come under the command of 152 Brigade, as the troops moved in formation over the open ground it soon became apparent that the situation on Roumana was not as good as it had been thought to be, as British gunners were shelling an area to the left of point 112 and small arms fire was coming from point 198. It was now a question of who would reach point 198 in force first – the Germans or the 5th Black Watch.

From 1400 hours the enemy were in possession of the high ground of point 198 and as the 5th Black Watch scrambled up the slopes sections of German infantry could be seen infiltrating on the left of 5th Seaforths HQ, fire was now coming from both flanks and grenades were being hurled down the slopes to the Seaforth companies below.

The leading company of the Black Watch arrived at the Seaforth's HQ at 1430 hours as mortar bombs thudded continuously along the ridge, after having marched over five miles over open country and having suffered casualties from shell and small arms fire, 'C' Company were ordered to occupy point 198 immediately.

Major Owen directed the 128th Field Regiment to put down a stonk on the highground and at once a very heavy concentration descended upon the target, this allowed 15 platoon, led by Lt H.R. Crichton-Melville, to reach the enemy observation post which they stormed – killing all the Germans occupying it. By 1530 hours point 198 was secured by the Black Watch.

Meanwhile, 'B' Company had moved up the hill to the right in an effort to secure the ridge, but suffered severe casualties from small arms fire coming from the direction of Point 112 and south east of it. Mortar fire falling on point 198 and on 'B' Company was now intense and to deal with the sniper and machine gun fire on the right flank a platoon of 'D' Company (the Bn consisted of three Coys only) advanced under a smoke screen on to the feature next to point 112; this had the effect of making the enemy withdraw.

Throughout the evening repeated attempts were made by the enemy to shell the troops off the ridge which was bare and stoney and afforded no cover, at one point a platoon of 'B' Company was forced to withdraw temporarily but was soon back in position.

'C' Company dealt with three machine gun posts beyond point 198 and by 1800 hours the position was reasonably secure. At last light a platoon of 'C' Company advanced two hundred yards beyond point 198 and collected three Italian officers and twenty 'other ranks', shell and mortar fire continued until midnight and eventually died down altogether.

FIRST HAND ACCOUNTS

THE 51ST HIGHLAND DIVISION

PTE STANLEY HAILWOOD
5th BN SEAFORTH HIGHLANDERS

"We advanced to the start-line at about 3am, it was quite cold and very dark, after a tot of rum we were spread out in long single straight lines and compasses and watches were set by our leaders. Our attack on the Roumana feature began with a long slow walk for quite some distance, I carried my bren gun and all the others had fixed bayonets. When the barrage started the noise was deafening with the screaming of the shells overhead sounding like express trains, from what seemed like hundreds of our 25 pounders; it was eerie! Finally we reached the end of our advance behind the now static barrage, we stopped to wait for it to lift or we would be killed by our own covering fire: we were now at the foot of Roumana.

At first light we went straight in to take the first line of trenches manned by Italians who were very scared of our bayonets. We took them all prisoner then moved up the slope gradually to the second leg, higher up we found a stiffer mixture of Ities and Germans. Third and last came the real opposition on the top high up, we could advance no further as we were pinned down by concentrated enemy fire.

We were firing nearly the whole time, I can't remember a time when it was quiet. The ground was all covered with rocks and we couldn't dig in. Neither could the Germans. We just lay behind what we could find and moved about a bit if they got our positions taped. I was maybe thirty or forty yards away from the hill and then you'd be shot at from three hundred yards away, or from the next hill. I'll never forget the sound the bullets made smacking off the rocks. The Boche were in little groups all over the place and there was bags of cover. You never knew what was going to happen next. Look at that bunch that got round behind us – we chased them all right, but they'd shot one of our lads in the back before we nailed them.

We'd plenty of food but I don't think any of us ate at all. I know I didn't. I had nothing to eat for twenty-four hours and I didn't feel hungry. I was thirsty though. There was a bit of a panic when the tattie-mashers came over. We weren't expecting them. The lad beside me had the back of his head blown in and I was half stupid with the blast. Then I heard Major Davidson shouting: "Over here, over here!", and we went back a hundred yards or so and then he stopped us and we managed to hold them again. Not many officers could have stopped that move back once it had started. We thought a lot of the Major.

I don't know how word got up to us that the Black Watch were on their way but I remember someone telling me. I didn't believe it. I said "Ay, they'll be up here next week, maybe. It didn't seem possible that they could arrive in time to do any good, because we were just hanging on by the skin of our teeth and there only seemed to be about half-a-dozen of us left. There were more, or course, but you couldn't see who was there and who wasn't among the rocks. About five minutes later the lad next to me said: "Look at that!", and I looked round, it was the most wonderful sight I ever saw. The Black Watch were coming across the plain behind us, stretched out in two lines, all neat and tidy, like an exercise. You could even see how they were split up into platoons and sections. I knew then that we'd made it. I can't tell you what a wonderful sight it was."

MAJOR DAVIDSON. DSO
5th BN SEAFORTH HIGHLANDERS

"I ordered a defensive position on Point 198 which was occupied about 0930 hours by the remnants of the Company – about a dozen men in all, just enough to man the flanks and watch the front. Ian Mackenzie had disappeared. He was afterwards found well forward. He must have been cut off but had fought to the last. There were three dead Germans lying near him.

Shortly after occupying this position I became aware that the enemy had penetrated right forward and had at least two positions within forty yards of us, immediately above our heads. We tried to climb the last few yards of the crest to get at them but were at once machine gunned from the right. From then on it was a case of hanging on and being as offensive as possible. Magazine after magazine was fired from our brens. Private Smith from Caithness and myself watched the crest above our heads. Sergeant Mackenzie moved about from place to place and was a tower of strength. About 1230 hours a determined German attempt was made to get round our left flank and a party of nine was seen getting into position behind us. We gave them all we had and they withdrew in disorder, leaving three dead and assisting two wounded. We got one or two reinforcements from Battalion HQ, who were immediately below and could see every move that both we and the Germans were making. The New Zealand Honey on the plain, directed from Battalion HQ, did invaluable work pumping solid shot into the German positions above us. I reckon it made all the difference.

About 1500 hours the situation was getting desperate. I could hear

German voices above me, and I knew my right was vulnerable. Just then George Willock from Battalion HQ appeared with a bren and helped a lot; but the Germans above had crawled forward silently and started to let us have a shower of stick grenades. I gradually moved the Company back about a hundred and fifty yards to another position and succeeded in re-establishing ourselves there, and managed to prevent the enemy getting Point 198. The 5th Black Watch arrived about 1800 hours and took over. We relaxed and heaved a sigh of relief…"

SIR PATRICK (PADDY) NAIRNE. MC
INTELLIGENCE OFFICER.
5th BN SEAFORTH HIGHLANDERS

"It was pleasant April weather: Tripoli lay behind us; Tunisia ahead. As Intelligence Officer I went with the Second-in-Command, Maj Geordie Andrews, at 0600 hrs on 5 April, to recce the route to the Forming Up Place. The fields below the high ridge of Djebel Roumana were glistening yellow with daisies and silver with dew. I remember we passed two rough stone shacks standing in casual unripened corn.

"Its like the Hebrides," I said. "And the birds are singing, as in a Disney film."

"The dew's made the barley damn wet," said Major A. Certainly it looked idyllic; but, after walking another 2,000 yards, we were personally shelled by a German mortar.

It was a busy day of route recces by platoon commanders and orders to 'O' Groups. Inessential kit had to be packed. On our way to Brigade HQ in the morning the Divisional Commander, General Wimberley, passed us – not straight past, however. He saw us and his jeep stopped. He jumped out and reached for his map board.

"You 5th Seaforths, aren't you? Now you've an important job …" And he gave us a quick exposition of the Divisional plan as we stood on the dusty track.

At 1900 hrs we left our rest area. It was nearly dark. Anti aircraft fire against German planes over Gabes airfield sent up red sparks in the sky behind us. We had to wait at a track junction for half an hour because the Camerons were delayed in moving; and later it must have been for over an hour that we shivered in our shorts and pullovers while the track to the FUP was changed. But, except for the irritating noise of our carriers and the Scorpions of 154 Brigade, all remained quiet until by 0130 hrs we were settled behind the start line.

At 0330 hrs we crossed the tape. 'A' and 'C' were leading companies; Bn HQ moved 300 yards behind between 'B' and 'D'. As we began to move forward, very slowly at a hundred yards in four minutes, enemy planes droned overhead and dropped flares. We felt naked, like a criminal caught red-handed. But Roumana ridge remained as silent as the Sphinx. Only on the left, where the Indians were already attacking the Fatnassa feature, could the familiar stage effects of an attack be seen and heard. We tramped slowly - so slowly - through the grass. At 0415 hrs a volcano of flashing flames opened up behind us; the sing of shells over our head, the smell of cordite in our nostrils. The artillery barrage had begun.

It was beginning to get light when we reached the foot of Roumana's Point 198. We had reckoned that the highest feature would be clearly visible to us throughout the advance, as it had been to our patrols on the nights previous. But we had forgotten the fog of war. At 0520 hrs the small wadis at the foot of Roumana, massed with our companies, closely followed by the 2nd Seaforth along the same axis, resembled a faded lithograph of the Fighting round Rorke's Drift variety. My batman, Bremner, and I moved over to the right to get a view of the 2nd Seaforth starting on their advance eastward along the slopes of Roumana towards Point 112. We crouched in an Italian slit trench in front of which German mortar shells were falling at rapid rate. At about 0545 hrs we saw our companies move over the crest of Roumana. It cheered us and the leading companies of the 2nd Bn who were just starting to move forward.

"Have a piece of chocolate, Sir?" said Bremner.

"Good idea."

Bn HQ was established in a wadi a hundred and fifty yards further west. Here I found Sgt Macleod, the Int Sergeant, grappling mentally rather than physically, with the problem of two to three hundred Italians of the Spezia Division who had emerged, half dressed and hands-up, from their holes, when we appeared on the heels of the barrage. Taking Jones of the Int Section with me, I climbed towards Point 198 where 'D' Company was consolidating. I met Bill Gray of the Mortars coming down from a recce.

"Likely place for an O.P. up there Bill?"

"Should doubt it." He smiled, "It's pretty hot already."

Mortar shells were falling all over the slope. We moved as quickly as we could to the crest and scrambled into an evacuated Italian O.P. Capt. Ian Mackenzie was supervising the loading of a stretcher, 20 yards to our left. We looked over the top – bad observation. 'D' Company explained that there was a flat ridge beyond them, too rocky for digging and covered by fire. We slithered down to Bn HQ. Must try elsewhere. This time I took Harrison, from the Section, and climbed the hill further to the right. Under the lee of the top crest we discovered 'C' Company or, more accurately, Sgt Carnduff and seventeen men. Douglas Gordon, the Company Commander, had been killed and the other two officers wounded. Cross of the Middlesex was here too, trying to get his machine guns into action. The position was under observation and severe mortar fire from the enemy on the western slopes of Point 112. I spoke to the C.O., Colonel Jack Walford, on the 18 set and he outlined his plan for the move forward to the Corps' objective at 0900 hrs. I sent Harrison off with a wounded man to the Regimental Aid Post. After explaining the Battalion plan to Carnduff I moved back.

Bn HQ had moved round the corner of the wadi. An accurate spasm of mortar fire had wounded Grant Murray and some signallers. The Adjutant, Douglas Findlay-Shirras, was wearing a shell dressing round his head. The time was 0815 hrs and Gordie Begg reckoned it was the moment for breakfast. He shared mine as we waited for the artillery and air bombardment scheduled for 0830 hrs along the line of the Corps' objective. I don't remember noticing it. At 0845 hrs I went with the C.O. up to 'D' Company. Sitting at Maj Jack Davidson's headquarters we saw a fascinating sight. Away in the sunlight on Point 112 a group of men appeared.

"2nd Seaforth's prisoners?" I said.

"Can't see their hands up," said Maj D looking through his glasses. Our ideas soon changed. Behind the group appeared a party of men in close formation, a party of men in grey uniforms who deployed and began moving along a ridge towards us. It was the start of the German counter-attack.

'D' Company organised themselves for defence. It was a pity the enemy were still out of L.M.G. range; for we had no Vickers or 3" mortars on this ridge. I explained the situation to the Adjutant at Bn HQ. The positions of 'A', 'B' and 'C' Companies were obscure.

Gordie took a party up the high ridge on 'D's right. I took nine men on to the foothills 200 yards east so that at least we could control the eastern slopes of Roumana, for it was clear that the 2nd Seaforth had lost the Point 112 feature. For the next three hours we fired at the enemy and the enemy fired at us.

I remember learning in school OTC days about the Approach, the Fire Fight and the Assault. These expressions always sounded so stilted; but here indeed was the Fire Fight, whose fire was going to control the Roumana crest. In answer to the enemy 105s whirring majestically over, to his 3.16" mortars crashing like a charwoman beating carpets, and to his Spandaus irritating as an electric drill, we fired our Brens, rifles and mortars, though target location was very difficult. We got support from our 25 pounders and an independent NZ Honey tank, though we could not always be sure of the positions of our own forward platoons. It was hot dusty work. Twice I fell asleep for a few seconds with my binoculars to my eyes.

But, meanwhile the story told by the C.O. over the field telephone jittered Brigade. 5th Black Watch was dispatched out of Divisional Reserve to reinforce our position. And around 1500 hrs, soon after some daring enemy infantry had been wiped out only a few yards over the heads of 'D' Company, they arrived. Immediately two companies were sent up the crest; with the result that the Spandau fire died down and Maj D could be relieved, though the German mortars recommenced. News was coming through of tanks passing through the Cameron gap on our left. Our job was simply to hang on. Never mind the mortars, never mind the Spandaus, let the 90 Light Division counter attack … our job was to hang on. I found a trench near the Adjutant's beck and call and went to sleep.

An hour and a half later the situation was much the same. A hot shallow dusty wadi with dusty Jocks sitting on the ground and a group of dusty officers standing round a dusty 'Dunrobin Castle' carrier. A composite company was being organised under Patrick Agnew, to fill the gap between the 5th Black Watch and the Camerons. The C.O. and I selected a new Bn HQ in a wadi further west. We moved and I joined the Int Section in a supper of biscuits and Sardines. Black smoke crumps still descended on Point 198.

Gordie had been wounded in the afternoon and Bill Gray killed in the morning. It was a beautiful twilight with a young moon. Eight shells made us duck on their way to the Cameron minefield gap. To our delight a hot meal arrived at 2030 hrs; tepid tinned stew, as we sat by the C.O's jeep.

I was duty officer from 2230 to 0100 hrs. Relays from the force on the hill were still collecting their evening meal. But the atmosphere was cool and quiet. Suddenly in the distance came a loud angry chatter of machine guns from the coast – as enraged as a wasps' nest disturbed. Were Germans still there? But when I climbed the hill after stand down next morning the birds were singing again. I stood unmolested in the clear April sunshine on the highest peak of Roumana and watched our armoured cars a few miles away probing the green and yellow Tunisian plain. Two or three yards to my left a gunner Forward Observation Officer sat in a small sangar smoking an Italian cigar.

"Seems to have gone all right," I said.

"Yes, and left me a cigar as a present for my breakfast."

BRIGADIER G. L. W. ANDREWS
2 I/C 5th BN SEAFORTH HIGHLANDERS

"Our short rest was over, we moved forward some twenty-five miles to relieve the New Zealanders in the bottleneck where the Wadi Akarit crosses the plain between the mountains and the sea. Beyond rose a rocky ridge perhaps six hundred feet high called the Djebel Roumana; and here the Germans were likely to make their next stand.

We reached our new area after dark and when morning came we found that the Spring rains had performed their annual miracle and before us lay a carpet of wild flowers, stretching away to where Roumana stood in a blue haze, quivering in the heat. The ridge apparently overlooked our every movement, but at such a range that we soon learnt to live with it as the next few days passed in patrolling forward and other preparations for the attack.

This was fixed for the early hours of 6 April and it was to be a 'silent' attack – that is, without artillery preparation, in the hope of gaining surprise. 152 Brigade objective was the Roumana ridge, whist 154 Brigade on our right were directed up the main road. 5 Seaforth were to take the centre of the ridge, which was the commanding feature, whilst 5 Camerons on our left attacked the west end. 2 Seaforth, initially in reserve, were to pass through us and swing right to take the east end. This turned out to be a hard-fought engagement which well merited the Battle Honour 'Wadi Akarit' awarded the three battalions after the War.

My own part in it was undistinguished but I shall describe it in some detail because it exemplifies the kind of silly things which can go wrong on such occasions, with potentially serious results.

It was common for a Second-in-Command to be left out of an attack in case the C.O. should be hit, and it occurred to me later that this was probable in my case; but at the time I sourly felt that I was just becoming the brigade odd-job man.

I was given two tasks; the first to find and mark a route across country for the battalions to reach their forming-up positions, and the second to marshal the anti tank guns and fighting echelon vehicles of the brigade and pass them through a gap in the enemy minefield which the divisional engineers would make once the battle had started.

To provide a firm base for the attack, 1st Gordons had filtered forward by night into the Wadi Akarit itself, which cut a six-foot-deep gash across the plain to our front. Our forming up position was to be beyond this, in full view from Roumana by day, so I met the three Battalion I.Os in the wadi before dawn in order to reconnoitre our route in the half light. The air was fresh, the flowers covered in dew and the birds just starting their dawn chorus. It was an idyllic scene until we were brought rudely back to earth by the arrival of a shell a hundred yards in front of us.

Seconds later another dropped fifty yards behind us and we knew we were bracketed, so flattened ourselves while they loosed off a few more – none very close. The gun was a small one, and really it was all in the nature of a gentle reproof to the five of us for walking about in a group once it was light enough to be seen. We retired one by one and were not troubled further. On later occasions, I found that a lone figure in the middle distance was seldom regarded as worth a shell; and this was a handy thing to know. As we retraced our steps the Provost Corporal and I brought up the rear, knocking in pegs every hundred yards on which he was to fix screened lamps that evening.

The rest of the day passed in making arrangements for my second task and in finding a suitable spot to do it from. This done, I left Hamilton and Fulton digging doovers there for the three of us and returned to Brigade towards dusk to meet the section of military police who were to mark the route we had pegged.

There followed an exasperating delay when half of them got lost coming up on their great flat feet, and when they had at last begun to fix up their lamps word reached me that the Brigadier was talking of altering the route. With darkness falling and the battalions already on the move I hurried back to find out what was up.

George Murray had become increasingly irritable and indecisive of recent weeks, and this cannot have made things any easier for Ian Robertson, who had taken over from Harry Cumming-Bruce as Brigade Major only the previous day. After a lot of talk, George finally made up his mind to abandon the route he had laid down in his orders and to follow instead a telephone cable which his signallers had laid the previous night. He then retired, saying he did not wish to be disturbed until the Battalions were formed up.

In a night attack it is vital that the units should keep proper direction and formation. There was an established battle drill to assist this whereby they were formed up on previously laid white tapes, so as to cross the Start Line in good order. This may seem a bit of military mumbo-jumbo, but when you consider that in forming up a brigade attack you are dealing with numbers comparable with the Queen's Birthday parade on The Horseguards, but on strange ground in the dark and in silence, you can appreciate the problem. Furthermore, the units are in tactical formation rather than in nice straight ranks.

John Thornton, the Brigade I.O., had been made responsible for laying out the tapes and for directing the battalions onto them as each arrived up the approach route. Now that this route had been changed, we agreed he should set off at once up the new one with his guides whilst I rushed off to intercept the leading battalion, 5 Camerons, who had already started up the original one.

Ronnie Miers their C.O., was not normally noted for his patience, but he took this change of plan without exploding and, more by good luck than anything else, we found our way across to the new route, up which I led the way running the telephone wire through my fingers and praying that it would not suddenly come to an end in my hand.

In later night attacks, I found that a cable if correctly laid, was in fact the best way of marking such a route. Not only was it something tangible but also it could be laid one night, left in position by day without the enemy seeing it, and then be supplemented with white tape the next. On this occasion, the cable seemed endless and sometimes I could have sworn it was leading in quite the wrong direction, but eventually it ended in roughly the right place. To our dismay, however, there was no sign of John Thornton or his guides. I had visions of the Brigade being caught disorganized on the open plain at H-Hour and I began to sweat. To make matters worse, our tanks had started moving somewhere in the rear and were making so much noise that we felt the enemy could not fail to realize that something was on.

Eventually John did turn up, having lost his way on the featureless ground in the dark – a thing that could happen to anybody, but which nearly had serious consequences this time. By then battalions had more or less sorted themselves out on their own and all was ready, although it was now 1 am – two hours later than planned – and the troops had that much less rest before H-Hour at 3.30am. Not that they were likely to get much sleep, lying on the ground in fighting order, and with battle looming.

Having reported progress to Brigade I made my weary way across country to the scene of my next task, a mile or two away. This was on a low ridge which overlooked the whole battlefield from a respectful distance and I lay huddled in my doover there for an hour or so, watching anxiously to see if the battalions got across the open plain without being spotted. Miraculously, in spite of flares dropped by enemy aircraft they seemed to manage it and there was not a sound from Roumana until, with an almighty crash, our barrage opened on the ridge at 4.30am.

Until dawn came there was little to be seen up there beyond the flashes of bursting shells, but in the meantime I made contact with the Sappers and found that they had managed to clear two gaps in the minefield; which was a very good effort under the heavy fire which came down on them.

Once daylight came, I lay with my glasses fixed on Roumana, but not a man could I see amongst the clouds of slate grey smoke and chestnut dust which cloaked the entire ridge as the German guns and mortars hit back. Beneath this, as I afterwards learned, there was hard fighting amongst the rocks as first one side then the other gained the crest.

This continued all day, and for eight hours of it the main objective was held, against repeated counter attack, by Jack Davidson, a Caithness sheep farmer of sterling character, and just twenty men of his company. His well deserved DSO was among several decorations won that day; a day which cost the battalion ten officers and over a hundred men killed or wounded. 2 Seaforth suffered even more heavily and, apart from Battalion Headquarters, had only four officers left by evening.

During the morning I got a message calling reserve ammunition trucks forward and when I went to collect them I was surprised to find one of the Company Commanders hanging about by the transport, when he should have been up on Roumana in action with his men. It was another distressing example of a character unequal to the situation but, remembering the unfortunate D.R. I had had to try back in Tripoli, I think he was lucky to escape a Court Martial. He should have been removed at once but, inexplicably, both Jack and George Murray stalled over it and it was a week or two before he left.

Having delivered the ammunition forward I spent the rest of the day feeling rather useless, whilst the New Zealand Divisional Cavalry, as they liked to be called – actually they were mounted in 'Honey' light tanks – formed up beside me ready for the breakout. One of their tanks got mixed up in the 5 Seaforth battle when Jack Walford grabbed it and got the commander to fire his gun at a troublesome spot on the ridge. Seven years later, on a battlefield tour with the 1st Camerons from

Tripoli, I found one of its 37mm solid shot up there; a memento which is sitting on my desk now.

During the afternoon there was a sudden stir when five Ju 88s came roaring up from behind us at low level. Everything in sight opened up at them and one was hit before they reached us, diving away to crash in flames a mile or so off with one parachute floating down after it. Then another started smoking right overhead, shot vertically upwards like a towering partridge and turned over in a huge burst of flame. My natural horror at this sight was dispelled by the NCO in charge of a nearby Bofors, who came running up to ask me to sign a chit to certify that it was his gun that brought it down.

The Germans withdrew that night, pursued at dawn by the New Zealanders and 7th Armoured, and it looked as if they would soon be driven into a corner between First Army's advance from the west and our own. Most of the Italian defenders, having nothing left in Africa but their own skins, had handed themselves in quite early in the battle.

I spent most of the following day up on the ridge, where there were still a good many dead of both sides to be brought down for burial and a mass of abandoned arms and equipment to be collected. The task was hindered by a profusion of unexploded Italian percussion grenades. About the size of an egg and painted scarlet, they were a well known hazard on many a battlefield, being apt to go off at the slightest shock; so one had to move carefully. Once the sadder business up there was over Douglas and I had a glorious scrounge set up the mess with lentils, lemons and a huge circular cheese from Italy. I picked up a Schmeisser – which I carried in my jeep for the rest of the war – and rode happily back to our lines on an Italian motorbike with two flat tyres.

Next day George Murray moved me to 2 Seaforth, who were reduced by their casualties to two companies and were very short of officers. I was sorry to leave my friends in the 5th, but it seemed it might be only a temporary move and I felt Rory was probably glad to have some help."

COMPANY QUARTERMASTER SERGEANT
(LATER LT) GEORGE LISSLE. MC
2nd BN SEAFORTH HIGHLANDERS

"Unlike a lot of actions we crossed the start-line and advanced in complete silence for over a mile, initially we were behind the 5th Seaforths before swinging right to capture the right-hand sector of Roumana Ridge to link up with 153 Brigade. The 5th Seaforths had a very hard fight before they achieved their objective but we met very little opposition as the Italians seemed to have very little heart, and our barrage had knocked the stuffing out of them. However this was only the lull before the storm and soon mortar bombs came raining down as we were digging in, these gave us no notice of their arrival as they were quiet until the explosion – unlike the 'moaning minnies'. The counter attack was so ferocious that we were pushed back some way down the hill but managed to stabilise our position and ultimately held fast throughout the day, we finally fought our way back to the crest on top of the ridge and had a

commanding view of the land to the north. This time we dug in very effectively and Jerry could not move us – try as he may. During the night of 6/7 April the Germans pulled out but unfortunately for us our casualties – both killed and wounded, had been heavy and we were glad of the respite to re-group and recover."

LT COLONEL CHARLES PIERCE
4 TROOP. 'C' SQUADRON
COUNTY OF LONDON YEOMANRY

4 April 1943 We sat at this place Oudref all day, the Mediums were in front of us and they got some nasty shelling. The gunners had one or two random guns which roamed around the place. For instance they'd put over about a dozen rounds from 4.5" or 5.5" and then limber up and clear out; peace for some five minutes and then absolute hell – shelling – very unfortunate if the gun comes near you. You immediately get inside the tank or in slit trench.

That day, we had orders to attack the day after next across the Wadi Akarit (6 April). The two Sherman Squadrons were to do the job. The Crusaders for once were not to be employed – it was 'I' Tank work and would just consist of sitting and taking it.

This Wadi Akarit consisted of a wadi and anti tank ditch running from the sea to the salt lake, which was impassable, some six miles in length. Overlooking this wadi was a ridge of hills, several hundred feet high called Roumana on which the Germans had excellent observation posts. On our side the ground rose gradually for about a mile from the wadi and then there was a reverse slope. No troops were in front of this crest.

The attack was to consist of 51st Highland Division against the salt lakes – this latter to be a silent attack with a barrage. The line was known to be held by Italians with possibly Germans in support. About midnight the orders were changed, the 'B' Squadron Leader was not considered capable to command well enough – there being no regimental control – so a composite squadron was formed with 'C' Squadron Leader in command. This was Peter Scott, MC – a very fine soldier and only an acting Major.

The composite squadron consisted of two troops of 'B' Squadron, 3 troops of 'C' Squadron plus Squadron HQ of two Grants with Tony Jarvis and 3 Crusaders. Our troops were Ken Hiscock's, Sam Pennington's and mine – always Ken's and mine. 'A' Squadron to attack with 50th Division under Major Cameron, MC and bar; we to attack with 51st Highland Division. At first light next morning we moved – not feeling very well after celebrating not being in the battle. At the last minute Mike Richie – a very keen soldier – persuaded Sam Pennington to drop out so he came too.

We moved over to the area of 51st Division near the sea, and arrived quite early in the morning. We were on our own link with a rear link to RHQ. We all went up to recce the route and have a look at the wadi from the forward positions. Guns everywhere, all dug in even in the front line, this to get maximum range: the wadi looked almost sinister, not a movement or a shell burst anywhere, these enormous hills over-looking everything. Everybody made up their own minds but did not tell anybody else: I'm sure everybody thought we'd never break through or – if we did – at enormous losses.

We went back to our leaguer and we were given a position to go to when we moved, prior to the attack. A most complicated procedure and it had to be done in the dark. We eventually moved when it got dark – absolutely pitch black and we followed little lights somehow – dust everywhere – and eventually arrived at this area after about a couple of hours: a fine feat and not ours. Orders were to dig in; as usual the ground was like rock and we got down about 3 inches and had to give it up. This was in case of shelling whilst sleeping. We were to support 154 Brigade with Lt. Colonel Lorne Campbell commanding the Argylls, the other battalions being the Gordons and Seaforths.

I had a wireless watch about 3.30–4.30am in a Sherman: everybody had to take turns at something – guard etc. The guns started a barrage about 4am and the Scorpions – flail tanks – started clearing the minefields followed by the R.Es to blow up the anti tank ditch. The German shelling started shortly after that but not near us. Shermans are fairly thick and when the watch finished practically everybody was up and in their tanks. Shelling now was everywhere, in fact no object is moving except to disperse.

At first light, in a light mist and clouds of dust, we moved forward to the edge of the wadi and waited: the shelling was getting really heavy and several tanks were hit but not put out of action. About every five minutes four 88 airburst would crack straight over us. These never seem to do much damage but are very demoralising. You can't hear them coming to start with. We had some terribly near ones, shells practically falling in the tank, but just could not move. During the whole of this time only one man in my crew got out and he was the gunner, to give a wounded Highlander a drink.

Thousands of prisoners were pouring in and the Germans kept shelling them as they passed behind us, leaving a trail of dead: A normal German habit. Many of these Ities were in pyjamas etc, an amazing sight considering they were in the front line. They had enormously deep slit trenches and almost caves, making them impossible to defend. There seemed to be hundreds of wounded or dead Highlanders everywhere but is was impossible to do anything. We were on a link to the Infantry Brigadier who wanted some tanks across; some Valentines had already gone over and they came back to fetch 6 pounders, he wanted some more support.

Major Scott agreed to send the two Sherman troops plus the two Grants with Tony Jarvis to control. A number of Valentines had been blown up on mines but our chaps got through the minefield and pushed out a bit the other side. Shelling was just as heavy all the time, especially on the minefield gap. This was probably about 12 or 1pm – I don't know – anyhow about 2pm the Brigadier wanted more support so we went through: Peter Scott led, then my troop, followed by the others.

I turned right the other side and halted. The shelling, mortaring and small arms fire here was even worse. It was impossible even to put your head out, except for an occasional glimpse: we had to use the periscopes.

6 Pounders for anti tank were facing the wrong way, the crews quite unable to dig them in due to the small arms mainly. As usual the order came, a counter attack expected, could we push forward. Ok we'd try. The Shermans went forward, I went right, Mike left.

Suddenly all six Shermans blew up, direct hits – a few people got out but they were mostly killed. The order came to pull back but too late, my tank was hit in the engine with a hell of a crash. Actually we had already had a track shot away but did not know – my troop Corporal told me afterwards. I told them to get out, fortunately we had not moved the turret so the driver was OK. We were immediately hit 3 times more, one hit somewhere round the starter-motor, one by the operator and the other hit the engine: it then began to catch fire.

This was all before we could get out and we'd all been in tanks that had been hit before so did not delay; obviously several guns were firing at us. We got out and knelt to the right side waiting for the driver. They began to mortar us like hell so we had to move. The driver appeared and just as we were going to move another shell hit the tank. We shifted remarkably quickly and ran to the troop Sergeant's tank behind – Tommy Marshall – he waited for us and picked us up. We sat on the back and slowly reversed, shells falling everywhere and small arms whizzing over us.

Normally a Troop Leader takes over Troop Sergeant's tank but I considered it was more dangerous here than inside so told the Squadron Leader that we'd get into the wadi, he said good luck and we ran for it.

We reached the anti tank ditch first, about 100 yds. I don't know how we made it but if I'd been asked personally, I'd have said that it was not worth bothering and we were bound to be killed anyway. Myself, I would have stayed with the tanks, no more dangerous if you could say as much. However, with the others it was different, Tony Jarvis waved to us as we passed him. In the anti tank ditch there was an absolute shambles: Italians and Highlanders all together. The Italians cowering at the bottom and the Highlanders were not taking the slightest notice of them. Firing was coming from all directions, including from behind, apparently Germans were now behind us. We learnt afterwards that the 90th Light Division had infiltrated down our right flank.

I told some platoon leader what was happening, but he did not seem fully to appreciate what I said. The Germans had this ditch absolutely registered with mortars; it was only some 12ft wide and shells were actually falling in it.

We had 600 yards to walk along to get to the gap but behind us was a minefield, only about 30 yards wide. I thought for a while whether to risk the minefield or walk along the ditch and through the gap 100 yards along. The minefield was permanent so I therefore decided to walk along the ditch. 2 others joined us here from the Shermans and they said that all their own crew was killed. We set off; the others seemed fed up but followed. I think they thought it was hopeless too. We only had revolvers and had the Italians done anything we would have been absolutely finished because there were no British troops for 200 yards of the sector.

An anti tank Captain appeared from nowhere with a Sergeant and asked where Brigade HQ was, I told him I'd show him and he followed the column some 8 persons long. Twice the sides of the ditch fell on us, caused by shells bursting on top but nobody was hurt. Eventually the entrance to the minefield gap was reached; still the wrong side and we saw Ken Hiscock and his troop just going across. To go through the gap was a serious matter, 8 people are a lot and bound to be seen. Further more we knew it had been very badly cleared but there were several knocked out tanks about and I reckoned that we'd just have to risk mines. I said we'd all run together and halt at each tank to have a rest and make sure everybody was there. We set off well and passed from one tank to another, shelling was continuing all the time but I think it was just normal shelling from the gap.

At one stage we lost the Captain and the Sergeant and looked back but could not see them, I think they must have been hit direct by a shell as one burst very close behind us. At last we reached the other side and I walked them, the shelling seemed nothing, yet I suppose people there thought it was terrific. That often happens and you can get an entirely wrong impression by moving from one shelled area over to a lesser one. We reached the other side and stopped in the wadi.

I knew roughly where RHQ was and was going to set off there later. A few minutes later Tony Jarvis' Grant appeared with the front of the turret knocked in, hit by a high explosive shell. He seemed in a very bad way and the gunner had his jaw broken. Tony had no injuries as far as I could see but he could not speak, I reckoned that the gunner's head or something had hit him a very sharp blow in his stomach.

There were a number of wounded Jocks about, some seriously, and most of my crew found they had wounds all in the legs from mortars, yet they never realised it until now. One chap, the driver, when he saw his leg wound found he could barely walk, yet I think he'd moved better than anybody, always encouraging the others. Ryan, the gunner, also had a wound in the leg yet on the last stage through the minefield gap he picked up a bedroll as we'd lost all ours – saying we might need it – another Scot.

Whilst getting people on to the tank six M.E. 109s came down this wadi and let us really have it, there was nowhere to go so we just had to stay there: Cannon and machine gun fire. Some chaps got in the tank but there was not much time, some of us got behind and when the last one passed, nipped round the front in case they came back. Nothing happened for a couple of minutes so I decided to move. Nothing is worse I think than to see wounded being shot up, particularly on stretchers as they have no means of escaping. We had no ambulances near us so of course these planes were entirely in the right. None of our chaps were hit.

We moved off sitting all over the tank, Jocks, our own chaps etc: Tony told me he'd show me where RHQ was so that was OK. The doctor would be there, but he collapsed after a few minutes so I continued roughly in the direction. It was now about 6pm, quite light yet of course. Shelling was practically nil and it was quite a relief, everybody relaxed and started talking. I went to where I thought the RHQ was but as I could not find it, decided to cut away to the nearest Dressing Station, which was quite near. We halted and I went to see the M.O. who was a New Zealander. He said bring them in so we did. They quickly fixed everybody up and I said goodbye to Tony who said he'd soon be back: I made the good old comment "don't rush back, you've had enough".

Nobody ever takes the slightest notice, he gave me his map case to look after – I nearly lost it a few days later – and I returned to the tank. Tea was just on the boil and the driver of the tank and wireless operator plus my own crew who would not go to hospital were only patched up – all had a drink. First since yesterday evening, over 24 hours. Everybody was already cheering up and making the usual remarks. Unfortunately, the wireless set was smashed so the tank was useless and I decided to go back to Oudref where we left the remainder of 'B' and 'C' Squadrons yesterday morning.

We got back in good time – about 3 miles – but not a soul. Some New Zealanders who were very kind gave us chocolate, tea and whisky. I still decided to go on and knew that if we went down the road we'd come to the A Echelon with Dick Sutton.

The others all agreed with this, so off we went and strange to relate it was only 100 yards down the road. We could actually see it from the other place but did not know. Luck was in; it was now about 8.30pm, getting very dark. The crew began cooking an enormous meal – very wise – and I went off to see Dick Sutton.

Dick said that he was just going up to the regiment so I said I'd come, but he forbade it and being junior rank I'd had it. He knew a little and said that 'A' Squadron had lighter casualties than ours. Off he went with the petrol and ammunition lorries and I went back to the tank to have an enormous meal of stewed bully beef and M & V (meat and veg). We thoroughly enjoyed it and went to bed.

About 1am an air raid started, the first of which we knew was when a bomb dropped in the Echelon. We were all opened out but at night it is very difficult to assess what is happening. Nothing happened after that fortunately. Next morning about 5.30am when it was getting light I set off to find the fitters – our own fitters – a wonderful gang – but could not find them, but M.Q.M's Brazendale MM said that he was going up to the regiment and said that there'd be room for another one. I saw Sergeant Moore MM, one of 'B' Squadon Troop Sergeants in the M.O's truck. He had a nasty wound in the arm, the piece of metal from the turret ring was almost the size of a cricket ball.

He was a hefty chap and had been given a few drinks. He was very cheerful and said he'd be back soon. I rather doubted it. I'd know n him since early 1939, always seems to be the old ones that get killed and wounded, but I think it only seems so because we knew them better and won't listen to figures anyway.

However, I left my crew and set off with the M.Q.Ms picking up John Simmonds MM Officer in charge of the forward lorries, just a few. He was amazed to see me and told the others on the air. He was then waiting to go through the minefield gap, not the one on the right but 'A' Squadron's gap. The tanks were just going through – apparently the battle had been won – hard to believe but to the front line soldier victory and defeat are almost similar, sometimes one is better than the other, but not often".

PTE DONALD KENNEDY. MM.
5th BN SEAFORTH HIGHLANDERS

"I would not say Akarit was any different from any of the battles before it en-route through Africa, prior to any battle one is well aware of the dangers that may lie ahead so everything has got to be prepared meticulously and hopefully at the end you will be a survivor. Despite what you hear and read most soldiers go into battle with a certain amount of fear, the adrenalin is working overtime during an action but a sense of humour always helps to relieve tension.

I do remember vividly the Wadi Akarit scenery – unusual in terrain to previous engagements, most of my time during the battle was spent moving and darting about around rocks and boulders – for ever dependant on which direction the enemy fire was coming from. It was an experience I shall never forget as long as mind and memory last".

GUNNER F.W. AUGUST
'B' ECHELON,
50th ROYAL TANK REGIMENT

"Due to the grievous losses suffered by the regiment at Mareth, it was a much reduced party that got together for the Akarit do. I was gunner/operator to Lt sam Nixon on one of the six pounder Vallies (VALANTINE TANKS) cobbled up for Mareth. The original crews had tested and fired them, but although I had received instructions on them, I cannot recall testing them and I was eager to try out the unusual way of getting over the problem of the Coax M.G. – the Besa Coax had to be discarded as the mount of the 6 pounder anti tank gun was too large to give it room. A Browning machine gun (AMERICAN) had been welded into a 6 pounder shell case, and in use it was loaded into the breech of the 6 pounder and wedged into place by the breech block, resting up against the end of the Browning. Another place also had to be found for the smoke discharger, in the 2 pounder vally this was loaded from inside the turret when a 2" projectile was dropped into the open discharger, it was then closed and, being fitted into the turret roof, would fire on pulling the trigger – it was about as much use as an indoor firework.

The answer to this was a 4" diameter cylinder welded on the outside of the turret – this took a 4" mortar bomb which fired from an ordinary firing mechanism consisting of the trigger parts of a Lee Enfield Rifle, the trigger being operated by pulling a wire from inside the tank. Having noticed that the open mortar gathered a lot of sand churned up by traffic, I sought to remedy this by wrapping an old piece of gas cape over the mouth of the mortar, wedging the protective material round the back of the mortar. I had forgotten the rifle mechanism and by accident must have activated it as – with a loud bang – the mortar bomb went sailing through the air and landed two or three hundred yards down the line of the wadi, where our six tanks had moved up with the Jocks of the 51st Highland Division: our infantry for the attack.

Seizing the tank shovel, I hared off down towards where the mortar had landed – now emitting a quite enormous column of smoke – and started piling on shovels of sand, of which there was thankfully plenty.

I was soon joined by a gang of Jocks who by now had got over their astonishment and joined in with their entrenching tools, soon a pile of sand was formed and the smoke dwindled and eventually died away. We were only a short distance from the Roumana feature where no doubt the Jerries had their observation posts. Luckily we were in dead ground on the way back to my tank and I thanked my lucky stars there was no injury to man or vehicles, also that I was standing beside the mortar and not in front – at least I knew now that the mortar worked.

We set off in line ahead on the next morning while it was still pitch dark, the infantry had already gone, Lt Nixon would have liked to lead as this was always where he liked to be – but he had been warned by the Squadron Leader Dickie Garret that he was not to risk losing his 6 pounder tank. At the last laager, as we moved up from Mareth, he had gone off the road to cut a corner and had lost his 2 pounder vally on a mine after being warned of uncleared verges. Sgt Ken Jones was now the lead tank and as we approached the anti tank ditch there was one almighty bang! The tank stopped and dust and dirt filled the air, when our hearing recovered and the dust settled Sam Nixon found that his sergeant's tank was alright, but that we alas were the one that had copped it. There was nothing for it but for Sam to take over his sergeant's tank, worse was to come as two other tanks immediately ran onto mines and all this in a space of fifty yards or so: there had been no mine clearance along this track at all.

As it got lighter enemy infantry could be seen on our left on the flattish stretch between Roumana Ridge and the next feature were the Indians were busy clearing out the enemy, wanting to try the machine gun I suggested shooting up the enemy with a few bursts. This was ok so I let rip a few short bursts, towards the end of the second belt I became aware that all was not functioning well, the shots were emerging in a fan shape – visible by the tracer in every third round.

I jerked down the breach actuating lever, hoping to trip the ejector levers and pull out the shell case carrying the M.G., nothing I could do would shift it. I then realised the cause of my problem – the Browning is an air cooled weapon and gets red hot when confined in a 6 pounder gun barrel and so we had no armament at all: just our personal weapons and a Tommy Gun.

I was just about to screw together the gun clearing rod to shove down the barrel from the muzzle, when there was a cry of 'enemy approaching'. Looking up I could see three soldiers – Ities – approaching. As I drew my revolver, the only time during my service, I could see it would not be needed as one was wounded and was being assisted by two of his mates. By signs and broken English we were made to understand that the Jocks were not taking prisoners and they had come to give themselves up and ask for assistance – this we readily gave.

At this moment our three remaining tanks came racing back past us with their guns pointing backwards over their engine louvers, now I don't know if anyone had contacted Sam Nixon or not but I noticed everyone started trucking back to our lines. Not wishing to be left out I started tagging along until I remembered our driver who had remained in his seat all this time and was no doubt enjoying a pipeful – he was a stolid type. I told him we were evacuating and he reluctantly joined in, on our way back we were chased along by shell fire and that was the end of my part in the 'Battle of the Wadi Akarit'. Lt Nixon went forward again with the remaining tanks to tow anti tank guns across the ditch and help fend off a powerful counter attack – for this he was awarded the Military Cross, sad to say he lost his life in Sicily taking prisoners."

L/BOMBARDIER H. J. JENNER
'D' TROOP 230th BATTERY. 58th FIELD REG'
ROYAL ARTILLERY. 5 AGRA

"The 58th Field Regiment was in support of the 51st Highland Division at Akarit and our gun positions were not far from the road north, my memory of much of that action has faded, but I do remember in our case it was very hard work. The normal expenditure at that time for a 25 pounder was up to six hundred rounds per gun, gun pits were shallow but quads were dug in at an angle to protect engine and radiators from possible air attacks. From our point of view it was quite routine, we fired a 'stonk' mainly to break up armour: this was a line of fire six hundred yards long and two hundred yards deep with about twenty rounds from each gun. We sent over a 'ball of fire' and this was a devilish thing as all guns were concentrated on one point – imagine being on the receiving end. When a call came for something that was not such a pin-point as to require a 'ball of fire', we sent over a 'murder'; this was a line of fire sixty yards long. Yes Akarit was a full day of very hard work."

SGT GUNNER ROLENT YEOMAN
241/61st A T REGIMENT. 'C' TROOP
ROYAL ARTILLERY

"We were scheduled to begin moving between three or four in the morning, but it didn't happen like that, the engineers were supposed to blow the anti tank ditch to make possible our crossing. We were on the backs of valentine tanks with our guns.

There were two mine fields across the anti tank ditch and we got on the open ground on the other side, it was full of deep trenches occupied by the Italians. Our Major was killed, the officer who was with him was put on our tank with shrapnel wounds in both legs, we were told that if we left any wounded we should leave a rifle stuck in the ground beside them so they could be found later.

Our tank was hit by shellfire, I was blown off and when I looked up the tank was ablaze with the six pounder ammunition and the bren magazines spiralling round like Catherine wheels as they exploded. I looked around and I was alone, my detachment had vanished and I was on the edge of this huge anti tank ditch watching the tank and ammunition blazing, one man was dying, another was badly hit in the shoulder and the other two had vanished. So I got back into the ditch and the Germans were putting in a counter attack. Well I had nothing but a revolver which wasn't much good. I got back on the tank and knocked on the cover and shouted that the tank was on fire and he came out, the tanks ammunition didn't explode but it was on fire.

At the point where the anti tank ditch had blown in, I came across Lt Col Lorne Campbell of the Argylls, he was controlling the battle from there, the Argylls were getting it pretty hot. I went back with this chap with the smashed shoulder."

BATTERY SERGEANT MAJOR McPHAIL. MM
241/61st ANTI TANK REGIMENT
ROYAL ARTILLERY

"I was at this time the Battery Sergeant Major of 241 A/T BTY operating with 154 Brigade – I was 25 years old – probably one of the youngest BSMs in the army.

We had been chasing the enemy from El-Alamein and had been in various actions at Mersa brega, Mareth etc. and now Akarit. Our Battery

Commander (Major Reginald Maunders) had, at a lecture the day previous to the action, impressed on us the necessity of getting our guns across the wadi in support of the infantry, the enemy were well 'dug in' and supported by 'Tiger' tanks. The aim on our part was to assemble on our side of the enemy mine field and have our guns towed across by valentine tanks.

At 4am on 6 April we took up our position at the assembly area, and, one troop was also moved out – the battery captain went across with the men riding on the tanks and were subjected to shell fire in the process. On the return of the tanks I had to get the Battery Captain (Capt. Rude) off the tank and into an ambulance as he was badly wounded. He told me, our Battery commander had been killed whilst helping to make up a road across the anti tank ditch. This now left me in command of the assembly area!

The Major in Command of the valentine tanks then came to me and told me the operation was suicide, and asked me to call it off, but I replied that my orders were to get the guns across and I couldn't countermand that order. The Corp of Signals' vehicle was parked by my side and the Tank Major prevailed upon me to wireless our Regt HQ for permission to stop the action – which I knew would not be given – however, the signaller said the message was "get the guns across" and was final. I communicated this to the Tank Major, and he shrugged his shoulders and said he would continue, which he did.

During all this time we were subjected to shellfire and solid shot from the enemy tanks, when suddenly we were targeted by enemy 'nebelwerfer' – 5 barrel rocket launchers, which we hadn't encountered before, and on first hearing were devastating – we thought at first the noise was from 'stukas' but I then realised what they were, however, there was only one salvo! Curiously no aircraft appeared, neither enemy nor ours, but the noise of battle was fierce. There now occurred a diversion which I had never seen before or since.

My attention became focussed on movement to my left flank and this was a battalion of Italian infantry who had decided to leave their positions in the line and surrender. It was amazing, there they were marching out in a long column, their colonel and the officers at the head, batmen staggering under the load of baggage, and 'Jerry' mortaring them, but the shot falling short about 10 yards behind them. So far as I could see they had no casualties. I made a motion to them that I didn't want them near me and they marched away – I presume into captivity.

About 3.00pm or there abouts, the action quietened down, and about 4.00pm or 4.30pm a stillness descended on us, which was so different from the previous clamour. 'Jerry' had fled to fight another day. We had sustained a lot of casualties and damage to guns".

PRIVATE O'NEILL
5/7th BN GORDON HIGHLANDERS

"At Wadi Akarit we didn't actually take part in the fighting as we were in reserve, but that leads me to a little tale I would like you to know about and it is totally true. Lots of prisoners were taken at Akarit – mostly Italians, it was common knowledge that the Germans had no time whatever for the Italians as a fighting force – who did? One of the prisoners captured was a high ranking German officer, he was taken for interrogation by one of our corporals to the officers' quarters. This is the story the corporal told me, he said "That German spoke better English than us", he told me he went to a big college in London before the war. I asked him what he thought about the Italians – his reply was: "Well we have the Italians and you have the Americans – enough said". It really made us all laugh."

LT. JOCK SIMM. Mc 5th BN
CAMERONS HIGHLANDERS
HQ: 152 BRIGADE

"I was a Liaison Officer at the time and was asked to go into the attack with Colonel Walford of the 5th Seaforths. When they reached their first objective which was the top of Roumana Ridge, I was to come back after first light to report to the Brigadier exactly what had been achieved, did they get to their objective, where were the companies, did the machine-guns get there – a normal account of what had happened in the battle and that is what I did. I came back about an hour after first light to say that by and large they had reached their objective, but very few people had reached the top of the hill.

By the time I got back – which was about a mile and a half, after being shot at, it was clear the hill-top battle was still going on, you could see it and hear it because we were in full view of it a mile and a half away. After I reported in, I was sent back to get an update because clearly the fairly optimistic picture I painted in the first instance didn't appear to be quite right, so when I went back, again I was shot at, I got out of the jeep and got up the hill but I couldn't find the C.O. Colonel Walford and I wandered around a bit but couldn't find Pat Nairn or anybody. Quite clearly, the thing was much worse than I originally thought, so I went back to Brigade Head Quarters again and on the way was in full view of the enemy – and was shot at again.

After I had been back an hour or two, I was told to go back again and tell the C.O. of the 5th Seaforths that the 5th Black Watch were coming up to reinforce them.

Again, I went up and passed on this message, on the way back – which was by now in the afternoon – the 5th Black Watch were across the open desert in extended order. I stopped and had a chat with their C.O., told them where to go and the best way to get up and eventually came back to Head Quarters. I'd been awake all day and all night and then went to sleep. I never saw any of the fighting, all I did was to act as a target.

When we were following the barrage at the bottom of the hill, Battalion Head Quarters was up with the leading companies because they weren't getting up the hill very fast. There was an enormous number of prisoners – Italians who were half dressed and goodness knows what, one German with an iron cross popped up along side of me – it was a real mix-up. Battalion Head Quarters had only ten or fifteen people and we had about fifty or so prisoners.

When we were at the top of the hill, before the second phase of the attack, looking out in broad daylight, various shouts went up of 'counter-attack!'

Everybody got ready, a few shots were fired – a few bursts from machine guns and we then realised it was in fact the Italians coming in to surrender on the low ground below us and they were surrendering to the Camerons on the left, we realised they were surrendering because they were all carrying their great-coats. They didn't have any weapons or anything, but one or two of them were shot in the process but we stopped firing. There was an enormous number of prisoners taken.

The plain over which I travelled was devoid of cover, the enemy were mortaring anything that was moving and as I was the only thing that was moving, they spent their time shooting at me and that I didn't particularly like. My driver at the time was a little bit too careful, so I made him stop and said 'for Christ's sake get out of the driving seat' and

I went and drove it myself and zig-zagged back and forwards to try and avoid being hit. There was an enormous amount of dust and if you created enough of it, you could conceal yourself in it."

TALKING TO 5th CAMERONS CO DURING ADVANCE

"I was telling him he had to be careful not to go too far to the right – which was point 112 – because that had been taken by the Seaforths who had then been thrown back and it was now held by the Germans, therefore they could machine-gun the valley down below and shoot up the Seaforths. "Go to the left" I told him and as we looked to the left – where a lot of the tanks were lined up just waiting to go through the mine-field gap, the tanks were being hammered, there was an enormous amount of shell-fire and mortar-fire, it was a thoroughly unpleasant sort of place to be. The C.O. said 'no way am I going to take my battalion through there'. When I had got further back, I sat in my jeep and watched the Camerons fan out and ascend the hill with about ten yards between each man, they spread out covering about half a mile of desert to avoid being hit".

ARCHIE DEANS
ROYAL ELECTRICAL AND MECHANICAL ENGINEERS
ATTACHED TO THE 40th ROYAL TANK REGIMENT

"Before the battle I had been running round frantically getting together 'D' shackles to string across the rear of the tanks in a chain, to carry the towing eye centrally for a six-pounder anti tank gun. If a gun had been hitched to the side towing bolt holes of the tank, a gun wheel might well have touched off a mine to the side of the swept track across the anti tank ditch and the mine-field beyond it. We had to collect a large number of shackles from all the formations in the 8th Army, give them a receipt and promise to return them after the battle. If all the tanks in the 40th R.T.R. were to be fitted with them this meant seven shackles each for thirty-eight tanks. The reason for this was that at Mareth on 20 March, the 50th Division had attacked with 50th R.T.R. in support and had been unable to get anti tank guns across the Wadi-Zigzaoi and lost a lot of tanks as a consequence.

On 6 April, 40th R.T.R. and 23rd Armoured Brigade HQ supported three crossings over the Wadi Akarit by the 51st Highland Division – a squadron of Valentines to a Brigade, 50th R.T.R. did the same with 50th Div'. I followed the progress of one squadron, the Technical Adjutant Captain Strachan followed another and QMS Martin followed the third.

Our tanks towed the anti tank guns and carried crews and ammunition across the anti tank ditch and through the mine-field against the concentrated fire of guns and machine-guns.

When they got through to open space we were facing an amphitheatre of hills well prepared by the Germans as the strongest defence line in Tunisia; our infantry gunners had been knocked off or dropped off the tanks under the intense fire; most did catch up eventually but in some cases the tank crew had to climb out under fire to unhitch the gun and unload the ammunition.

Fortunately, none of the ammunition was hit on the rear louvers of the Valentines; these tanks continued their work all day under a murderous fire in support of the infantry – mostly with only two-pounder armament and a Besa machine-gun in the turret.

A few Panzers appeared over the hill and the low Valentines then looked for the nearest gully. German and Italian gun-fire was concentrated on our five mile front, as far back as the gun-line. From 6.00am until dark, it was worse than anything I had seen at El-Alamein. We lost six tanks but four were easily repaired.

I drove up to the anti tank ditch in my jeep with the hood up as I was still suffering from sandfly fever, but it was rather silly to be so conspicuous. There was no breakdowns causing obstruction as there had been at Mareth and I was tempted to go through the mine-field gap under heavy fire.

However, the wounded survivors from Trooper Green's mined tank wanted a lift back to the M.O. and were absolutely sure that Green was dead. I offered to go back and check but they needed urgent treatment. On the way back the fire was so intense we had to stop the jeep and lie down on the flat plain whenever the German creeping barrage overtook us. It was the only time I wore a tin hat all day in Africa and it didn't do my sandfly headaches any good at all and air-bursts also dropped metal on our heads.

I only have a note of three men killed in the tanks, Captain Strachan was wounded. At the end of the day we were all worn out but on the following morning were amazed to see that the Germans had pulled out leaving large numbers of Italians to surrender with suit-cases packed. Brigadier Richards (23rd Arm'd Bde) with the Brigade E.M.E. Major Robinson and Captain Martin (Bde – Recovery Officer) decided to leave the regimental E.M.Es to clear up the tank casualties on the battlefield while they followed the 40th and 50th R.T.R. break-through, advancing against possible obstructions on the roads to the north.

Mines were still the greatest danger and help from the R.Es around the damaged tanks had to be arranged with Highland Division or South Africans. When another mine was discovered, the men would gather round out of curiosity and I had to shout to make them spread out, so that only one man would be hit should anything be touched off. Dead bodies were everywhere – some in the most lifelike positions, but if the sandy dust was over their eyes you knew that they were not tired infantrymen having a sleep. You had to be very circumspect in moving about even in rubber soled desert boots. Sgt. Campion's tank was completely burnt out and Trooper Green's badly mined under the driver. On the second day we buried them both in a cemetery with a Highland Division Padre".

MAJOR J.P.R. POWER
126th (HIGHLAND) FIELD REGIMENT
ROYAL ARTILLERY

"I WAS BATTERY Captain at Wadi Akarit supporting the 51st Highland Division. In preparation for the battle we were supplied with three first line issues of ammunition: i.e. 115 high explosive shells, 20 smoke and 15 armour piercing shells per gun. These were dumped at each gun position which contained four 25 pounders. Throughout the day it was my job to keep the battery supplied with ammunition from the Ammunition Point some ten miles away. My battery was in direct support of the Argyll and Sutherland Highlanders commanded by Colonel Lorne Campbell VC. Throughout the day, the guns fired a total of 650 shells, starting with the opening barrage and concentrations at 4.15am and finishing at approximately 7.00pm."

PTE. A. G. SHAW
61st ANTI TANK REGIMENT

"My chief memories of Wadi Akarit is being taken to the Akarit gap towed behind tanks, the powers that be thought it would be too dangerous to go into such a heavy cauldron of fire with our usual soft-skinned vehicles, so special hooks were welded onto the rear of each tank for our guns to be attached to which were six pounders at that time.

The five man gun crew sat on top of the tanks with all their ammunition and equipment, all I could see was a long line of tanks towing guns behind them. I was on 84 gun, the last one in the regiment; we were loaded up and ready to move at first light and behind our tanks as far as the eye could see was a line of ambulances, I thought 'Christ!'

Each man was issued with two 36 grenades with seven second fuses in case we had to fight our way off the tanks, which thank God we didn't. I always remember my apprehension at the time – wondering if the intense heat of the tank's engine under my backside would set the grenades off.

Upon arriving in our fighting positions, the tanks remained protectively in front of us warding off the enemy small-arms-fire until we got dug in. The tanks then withdrew leaving us to get on with it. Jerry was putting down a hellish bombardment on us – and there was a lot of air-bursts – these exploded about 25 yards up in the air and rained shrapnel down on us – these were going like hell".

SGT. R. T. MACDONALD
61st ANTI TANK REGIMENT.
ROYAL ARTILLERY

"At Wadi Akarit we were armed with six pounder anti tank guns which were towed forward by tanks under a hail of fire from Jerry. This was the first time I had seen Tiger tanks, but it was obvious that the enemy commanders did not want to risk losing them so they stood off about 1,500 yards and shelled us with their 88s – a nerve wracking experience even if you are not the immediate target. Another troop sergeant told me his Troop Commander asked him to engage the enemy, but he advised the officer that this would be unwise as the fire would be ineffective at such a range and it would reveal his positions to the enemy gunners making them sitting ducks; fortunately he concurred.

The real answer to this – as we all knew – was to use the 3.7" anti-aircraft gun in an anti tank role; there were thousands of these weapons in service and it is comical to think that a 3.7" gun was developed as an anti tank weapon a fortnight before the war ended".

GUNNER ALLAN TURNER 'A' BATTERY
72nd ANTI TANK REGIMENT.
ROYAL ARTILLERY

"We were ordered forward to positions at Wadi Akarit but never actually took part in the battle – we stayed in the rear area. There was quite a lot of shell-fire coming down on us in the rear and so much of the ground was solid rock that when a shell burst, fragments of steel and rock flew in every direction, unlike in the desert where the sand would take most of the blast throwing up spouts of sand.

One event of that day stands out in my mind – it was when Jerry plastered us with a battery of 88s and I took shelter beside a big fellow, both of us lay flat out in the sand with our faces pressed into it. It was only later when I could stand up I realised he was dead – he'd been decapitated".

SGT. H. J. SOWDEN. 'B' SQUADRON
40th BN ROYAL TANK REGIMENT

"At 0300 hours the 40th stood ready to move into the battle in support of the 51st Highland Division, our formation was two squadrons up front – 'A' and 'C', with
'B' Squadron as the second wave.
'A' Squadron Commander: Major R. Hughes
'C' Squadron Commander: Major McLaren
'B' Squadron Commander: Major J. B. Lumby

At first light 'A' and 'C' Squadrons attacked and suffered heavy casualties, Captain Mason-Fisher being the first one killed. As 'B' Squadron waited we came under heavy shell-fire and Trooper George Arthur Bentley was the first killed in our ranks. As 'B' Squadron moved over the wadi crossing, a few tanks were hit and we saw the terrible bashing the 50th R.T.R. had taken – they had put up a good show. Later on the prisoners came staggering in and I noticed they were all Germans and not so cocky now.

We eventually caught up with 'A' and 'C' Squadrons and a terrible sight it was, burning tanks and numerous casualties, it was an awful scene. As we pushed forward, I noticed some portees in the area – in each one was a six pounder anti tank gun manned by Rhodesian troops; we then took up firing position and a big shell exploded very close by and I was knocked out for a few minutes. As I came round I heard my operator shout 'My commander's wounded', it looked a lot worse than it was – my first thought was for the Rhodesians close by but they had all been killed – wiped out. I then cleaned myself up with a shell dressing and reported I was OK.

We then got orders to continue to press home the attack and as we did so, news came over the radio that the stores truck had received a direct hit killing SQMS Bill Jackson and others – they had been the victims of an air attack.

The day was drawing to a close now and the Germans and Italians pulled back as their front was cracking up the numbers of dead Italians strewn about the battlefield told a story of troops who had fought to the last. Night started to fall and we stopped only to continue the move forward the next morning with the 'Spur Column – 154 Brigade".

PTE ANGUS CUMMINGS
175 FIELD AMBULANCE 153 BRIGADE

"I was there at the battle of the Wadi Akarit as a stretcher-bearer with 175 Field Ambulance. During the attack I was with the Seaforth Highlanders. We marched forward in the dark across the desert for about three miles and in the morning we halted for breakfast and a rest. Then round about 0500 hours the artillery barrage opened up on Jerry and we set off – arriving shortly at the foot of the Roumana Ridge. Then the 5th Seaforth's Commander gave the signal and the war cry of the regiment went up as the men charged forward with bayonets fired. It was very eerie to hear all those men shouting and then there was all kinds of pandemonium let loose what with all the gun-fire and shouting.

The battle raged on for quite some time and we stretcher-bearers were kept very busy attending to our wounded troops, we had to keep our heads down when carrying them up the wadi as we were sniped at constantly – the snipers did a lot of damage and we could hear the whine of the bullets as they passed over our heads – it was a big relief when we got out of their range. The sweat was lashing off us and occasionally we had to rest to get our breath back before carrying on. At one point when we had gone back for more wounded, we were carrying a badly wounded lad back down the wadi and some of the walking wounded were told to come back with us – their nerves were very badly shattered and they were carrying their bren-guns and rifles.

The Jerry snipers were shooting at the soldiers carrying weapons and the bullets were flying around us thick and fast; we stretcher-bearers had to run like hell to get out of range. All the time there was this terrific battle going on around us and numbers of our dead and wounded littered the ground. Well the gaps for the tanks were made – but as the first few tried to pass through they received direct hits from German 88s and the break out was held up. General (Big Tom) Wimberley was there at the mine-field gaps with the 5th Camerons urging them on to get the tanks through".

PTE LACHLAN-TAYLOR 'C' COY
7th BN ARGYLL AND SUTHERLAND HIGHLANDERS

"I was a bren-gunner with 'C' Company and we put in an attack just as the light was breaking in the morning. Jerry knew something was going on as we were being shelled and I could plainly see bodies of our comrades lying stiff around the area. We came on and reached an anti tank ditch which was deep and wide, and a party was picked to build a bridge of sorts so our vehicles could cross; i.e. bren-carriers which carried our mortar teams.

When we finally got to the first enemy trenches they had scarpered, we moved forward past their positions to dig our own trenches but found the ground too hard. Shell fire was exploding all around us by now and, judging by the big craters these left, Jerry was using some heavy artillery – so we moved back and settled down in the enemy trenches to get some cover. The head of our operations had arranged with the American Air Force to give us cover if needed and we could see one of their formations coming towards us. Our officers had fired numerous varey lights into the sky – green to say we had taken the position, the sky was ablaze with green flares and the soldiers on the ground were cheering the Americans on. We could see the bomb doors open as the planes were so low and dozens of bombs were then released – on us! I can, to this day, hear the whistling of the wind as they rushed by while at the same time thinking my number was up. They mostly landed among the Black Watch on our left who received a lot of casualties through this.

During the day, Jerry put in a half-hearted counter-attack but we beat them off. Lt. Colonel Campbell won the VC here. When Jerry was shelling us I could hear this one coming straight for me and as I ducked my head it exploded close by and a piece of shrapnel hit my helmet so hard it was left a tangled mess with sharp edges all over it and my brow was bleeding like a stuck pig. My mate got out the bandage we all carried and wrapped it around my head like a turban to stop the bleeding – but he never said how bad it was. I stuck my mangled steel helmet on top of this.

When the battle was over and we knew it was won, the officers paraded us to inspect the walking wounded and have them sent back to the field hospital. When he came to me and saw the mess of my helmet and the thick caked blood on my face – he said he thought I had a bad one. He took my helmet off, unwrapped the turban of bandages and washed the blood from my face with a water bottle – there was nothing to be seen. It had only been a jagged point from the helmet which had only punctured the skin – in other words just a scratch".

SGT KINNON M. RANKIN
BDE HQ. 1st BN BLACK WATCH

"The Brigade HQ of the 1st Black Watch was in reserve on the line of the road; the situation deteriorated rapidly and we were called upon to supply men for 154 and 152 Brigades.
Because of the rapidly changing situation, the information coming to us was very confusing and chaotic. As the Italians left Roumana Ridge to surrender, the Germans shelled them.
During the action Brigade HQ moved forward to the wadi itself, there was no question of tents, we were in the open and just dug a hole - that was it. The whole situation was very fluid and very confused, we received a lot of attention from the enemy artillery and often had to dive for cover. My friend who worked in the orderly room with me was killed. When he was buried his rifle with a bayonet was stuck into the ground – he still had his identity discs around his neck so that when he was picked up later they would know who he was.

The conditions were, for us, the worst since Alamein but when we did finally cross the wadi the north bank was found to be very steep and a mass of mines. When we finally made a gap in its side it wasn't long before Jerry knew we were concentrating here and shelled it heavily. Italian prisoners flooded in and later we took large amounts of German equipment, even 88 millimetre guns were left".

PTE STEVENS
5th BN CAMERON HIGHLANDERS

"We were advancing during the attack and got cut off from our own troops by German Infantry and ended up being taken prisoner; we were marched back most of the day for what seemed like miles before being put into trucks – about 20 of us in each one. After we had gone a couple of miles, I decided to escape and jumped off the truck. My mate Charley McCann did the same, though we had not previously arranged to do so. The Jerry guards opened fire and hit me in the hip while Charley was hit in the hand – he did not seem to be very bad.

We lay there all afternoon and some of the evening – some of the time I was conscious and some of the time I was flat out. Later that evening our tanks must have broken through because they found us – I was more dead than alive. I was lifted onto a tank and taken back to a field hospital. I asked for Charlie and was very upset to learn he had not survived as the bullet had passed through an artery in his hand and he had bled to death. If we had not jumped from that truck we would both have been prisoners of war and my friend would have lived. I met his wife after the war and had to tell her what had happened".

SAPPER G. MACKAY. ATTACHED 152 BDE
275 FIELD COY: ROYAL ENGINEERS

"It was the evening of the 5 April 1943 at approximately 1830 hours when we left for the assembly area, having been briefed previously as to the role we were to play in the forthcoming battle.

After debussing from our vehicles we marched some considerable way before reaching the area were, amongst the grassland, figures of men sitting waiting for the order to move, some were chatting to one another whilst the officers and senior NCO's studied maps. It was almost dark by this time and I well remember that evening. The air was still with a smell of freshness, it was also quiet except for the sound of the crickets and the occasional distant firing. This was the infantry we had come to join, men of the Seaforth

Highlanders waiting to go into battle.

As Engineers it was our task to make a crossing point over an anti tank ditch which stretched the whole length of the front. The chosen site was situated at the approach to a valley at the very western end of a rocky range of hills which ran from the coast. It was called the Roumana Ridge, the right side of this valley rose sharply from the level plain, the opposite side rose less steeply to form yet another range of hills to the north west; consequently, the defending troops both Italian and German had the advantage of being able to observe any movement on the lower levels of the plain.

The defences comprised of a thickly sown mine field of some considerable depth over which an apron of barbed wire had been laid to a height of no more than a foot or so, behind this lay the anti tank ditch which was to be filled simply by manual effort, but prior to this a gap in the mine field had to be made, gladly our party was not detailed for this part of the operation.

After several hours of waiting most of us just dozed off until the time came to move, from my notes, zero hour was around 0330 hours. Then, as we crossed the start line, suddenly all hell was let loose, the artillery barrage had begun and the whole of the sky line behind us was lit up by rapid gun fire.

The noise was deafening making it impossible to hear what the next chap was saying, the only way to make yourself heard was by shouting, it had the effect of making one feel very isolated. We moved forward in no particular order. I remember following one of my pals ahead of me; there were others to the left and right, soon we became spread out.

The air by this time reeked with cordite and it must have been at least an hour or so since we crossed the start line. Eventually, we came to the minefield, here we followed it to our left until we came to a track leading to the right which lead us through the minefield that had been successfully cleared by some of my fellow comrades just before. We had finally reached our allotted task.

Dawn was now breaking and the barrage had lifted, we began with much haste the job of filling in this deep obstacle, we took turns in standing on the parapet working frantically shovelling the stoney soil into the ditch, as we did this so, the infantry clambered over the rocky slopes towards their objectives, there was constant machine gun and rifle fire also mortaring.

It seemed only minutes after starting this task that we found ourselves on the receiving end of one of the most terrifying weapons the Germans had begun to use against its forward enemy, this weapon was nick-named "The Moaning Minnie" by the troops, officially known as the Nebelwerfer Rocket Projector. It was obvious we had become one of the prime targets, for salvo after salvo of these missiles were raining down upon us; fortunately, we were able to hear them coming since they must have been firing at a very high trajectory.

No sooner had we heard the initial distant sound of what one would describe as a barrel organ beginning to play, we quickly jumped back into the ditch to await for the terrifying sound and multi explosions to follow. This continued mortaring delayed our work but somehow between intervals, we managed to carry out our task while our infantry dealt with the opposition coming from close by. While all this was going on a figure on a motorcycle came towards us, it was in fact a German D.R. His reaction upon seeing us resulted in him falling off his machine only to be taken prisoner.

Prisoners were now appearing in ones and twos, coming down from the lower slopes followed by many others. They looked dazed and disarrayed, they had not long before been subjected to a concentrated carpet of shelling laid down by our 25 pounder and 5.5 field guns, not to mention the small arms and 2" mortars which our infantry were also using with great effect.

The odd mortar still continued to fall around us but with less intensity. A Valentine tank I remember arrived on the scene in readiness to cross the ditch, but this made matters worse for this drew yet more fire. A covering of smoke was laid down directly in front, it soon began to drift towards us then finding ourselves enveloped in a white cloud, not being able to see what was happening, gave one the feeling of being isolated from the main supportive group, not being able to see enough of the action going on around us.

I remember, it was early morning around 7 or 8 o'clock after the first tank had crossed, being told to retire from the scene having completed our mission. As we set off in the direction from where we had come earlier that morning, I remember as I glanced back seeing yet more shells falling in the area, but these were from the 88s who had now targeted this narrow entrance to the minefield and the ditch beyond.

I could not help thinking at the time of the men and vehicles who were now travelling towards this gauntlet of fire, in support of their comrades who were encountering some very fierce opposition coming from the steep approaches leading to the upper rocky slopes of the hill.

As my memory has it, there were no more than 15 of us assigned to this part of the operation which took at least 3 hours. The worse 3 hours of my life! Thankfully though, we only had one casualty. Our officer Lieut Tom Duncan was wounded in the buttock by a piece of shrapnel and was hurriedly evacuated from the scene by the infantry stretcher-bearers. It was months before he rejoined the unit. Our O.C. was amazed by such a small casualty figure. It was expected at the outset to be much higher, something like 25% or more.

Fortunately, luck was on our side on that particular day, but some were less fortunate and suffered many casualties, especially the hard pressed infantry whose job it was to clear the enemy out of their well prepared positions which they did some hours later, bravely but not without sacrifice.

No sooner had we arrived back at our company HQ and was about to enjoy a mug of tea, a message was received for a small party to return to the site to rectify the marking tapes which had become disarranged by the constant shelling.

We drew cards and those with low numbers were the unfortunate ones. I remember I qualified since my number was a 2 or 3. So four of us set off once again to this dreaded spot! But this time we were transported some of the way. Having some knowledge of the general lay out it did not take us very long to re-mark the lane, hoping all the while no shells would land, our hopes were soon dashed when the first salvo came crashing down. We were able to take advantage of putting things right during the brief intervals before the next likely salvo arrived. We finally staked out the route for the follow on and hastily returned to finish our promised breakfast without any casualties to report".

PTE PETER HEAD. BDE HQ
7th BN ARGYLL AND SUTHERLAND HIGHLANDERS

"The battle was very intense, it left an impression on your memory equal to Alamein, in every area it was very noisy as we suffered intense shelling all day long – it was a very uncomfortable time. Tactical HQ was always within running distance of the front, wireless was not always reliable. There was a fair concentration of troops visible in the area.

Bde HQ were in a final position, monitoring all the details that were coming in, my officers task was to go from place to place – get information and report back. From the Djebel Roumana we were under direct observation – Jerry knew our positions and made it as uncomfortable as possible for us. But as soon as the attack went in, the enemy directed their fire onto the attacking battalions. The artillery (ours) were firing none stop and had to pause occasionally to let the gun barrels cool down. They admitted that at times their rounds were falling short.

We suffered from so called friendly fire at a point when 18 mitchel bombers came over and bombed us".

PT. WILLIAM McMILLAN
'A' COY: 1st BN BLACK WATCH

"Wadi Akarit is one place I will never forget. I was wounded on 1 April while on a night patrol. Being one of five chosen for a night recce of the wadi, we were stripped of anything that would make the slightest noise, my pay-book was taken from me and I didn't see it again for some months. From what I recall, four of us had rifles and one a bren which we took turns in carrying, we made our way to the railway line which we knew would take us near the Wadi Akarit. It was about 11 o'clock at night when we reached the railway. The officer instructed us to count the steps approx so we would know when we were near the wadi. It is amazing what you hear at night, after a while we came to what I believe was a small station – it was covered with barrel wood.

Then varey lights seemed to appear everywhere, we went to ground expecting to be attacked but nothing happened. We then made our way inland to take us to the wadi. The next thing to happen was when we saw about 15 figures coming toward us, just as well we didn't open fire on them for it was a fighting patrol of Seaforths, they gave us the password and went on their way.

The next few hours were the worst for us, we came up against barbed wire entanglements. I told the officer that I heard faint voices but he just dismissed my comment. I took off my cap comforter – as we were without steel helmets – putting it on the wire to avoid any noise. We had just gone through it about a couple of yards when we were hit by grenades. The last words I recall saying was: 'Christ, I've been hit', and down I went. One of many mates managed to drag me out through the wire and downwards out of sight. The officer disappeared for a while and came back with some Seaforths who got us back to their lines somehow – myself being carried. God Bless the Seaforths".

PTE. HAROLD JOHNSON 7th BN BLACK WATCH
3" MORTAR PLN. HQ. COY

"We set off in daylight at 0530 hours in the morning over a mile of flat desert which was devoid of cover. We'd been assured it would be a walkover more or less but when we got so far all hell let loose. Jerry had an anti tank ditch dug about twelve foot deep and the first tank that tried to get over was blown up at the crossing point that had been made, the result was that no other armour could get through so we had to go on foot. My pal that was carrying the (MORTAR) bi-pod was wounded, I was carrying the base plate which of course was no good to me then so I chucked it away – got my rifle and went up.

It was all like a nightmare, people were getting killed – I threw myself down and as I looked up, four of 'C' Company fifty or sixty yards in front of me, got a direct hit with a big one, as the sand and dust cleared I can vividly remember one gattered boot standing there, the rest of them was all up in the air and then started coming down – it was terrible. Anybody who says they weren't frightened are bloody liars because I was terrified.

I carried on and we got over this anti tank ditch, I joined up with a sergeant Ross – a Platoon Sgt of 'C' Company and there was just us two as he'd lost all his platoon. Major Roller came up and asked who we were, I said 'I'm all that's left of a detachment supporting 'C' Company' and Sergeant Ross told him who he was. He said we've got information the Germans are forming up for a counter-attack about seven hundred strong; he said we've lost an awful lot of men and are very weak. He said 'I've got bad news – they're not taking prisoners, so if you've got anything you don't want to fall into the hands of these people you'd better bury it.'

I remember I had tears in my eyes as I took a photograph of my wife and son I kept in a cigarette case; I buried this in the sand and prepared for the Germans coming.

We'd been there about twenty minutes – I'll admit I was shaking a bit – and I said to the sergeant 'When do we start firing?' He said 'when they get to that little hillock just in front', I said 'I think I'll be firing before that'.

Suddenly, I heard the pipes playing and told the sergeant, he gave me a clout on the shoulder and said 'get a hold of yourself Johnson you're going bomb happy'. I said 'no I'm not, I can hear the bloody pipes going'. He wouldn't have it until he said 'Jesus Christ you're right, I can hear the bloody pipes myself'. I think when the Germans heard the pipes, they turned tail and went.

I was then told to go back to see if I could get my carrier – the 3" mortar bren carrier we was driving. I got the carrier and went up a track the engineers had marked with white tapes where they'd lifted the mines. There was a 15 cwt truck coming with a red-cross flag; I pulled over to let it get by, the next thing I knew there was an enormous bang and the tracks blew off on the driving side and I was blown into the mine-field. They told me to stay where I was but there was a lot of machine-gun fire so I decided I was coming out. I got my bayonet, prodded about in the sand and found a mine or two – skirted round them and got back onto the track. I wasn't feeling too bad until I got onto the track then I couldn't keep a limb still. CSM Fox came up and told myself and David McLelland to go back to the Advanced Dressing Station.

When we got there it was terrible, oh it was really awful; there was men with legs off, one chap I knew very well, he was a big dancing fan from Glasgow – he'd lost both his legs; others were lying about. I said to McLelland, 'I can't stop here'.

A nurse gave us a drink – a sedative; we looked at one another and said 'Let's go back up'. So off we went back up the track, we looked at one another in the moonlight and said 'We must be barmy going back up here when we could be back there'.

We got to the battle area and met CSM Fox, he told us Jerry had pulled out and I want you lot back for a burial party. When it got light we went round pulling them out of the slit- trenches and piling them up on a lorry. They gave us an army mug full of rum before we started and had had nothing to eat for thirty six hours – the effect of the rum was to numb us. I remember CSM Fox coming round a sand dune – he said 'Oh Christ go round there it's awful'. We went round and there was some Green Howards that had been killed some time ago and they were just crawling - crawling with maggots and ants.

We got a couple of entrenching tools – laid a blanket down and shovelled them onto it, took off their identities and put them in a sand-bag. We were all day picking the dead out of slit-trenches; we were covered in blood. It got dark and we didn't have them all buried and had to sleep among them that night. I'll never forget waking up the next morning – the stench was terrible. We buried about thirty or forty of our own Black Watch; these Green Howards, quite a few Germans and some Italians."

THE EARL OF AYLSFORD
INTELLIGENCE OFFICER
1st BATTALION BLACK WATCH

"As we were in reserve we were ordered to recce the start line which I did with Sergeant Pringle, and later, with a large fighting patrol provided by my brother's platoon, laid the start line greatly aided by some Italian prisoners that we took en-route and who were terrified of the 'ladies from hell' they had heard so much about. My brother's throat cutting gestures cannot have done much for them, they had been stripped of their over-coats as they were known to carry grenades (LITTLE RED-DEVILS) in their pockets which they often used after having surrendered. It was bitterly cold and I ordered that they be given back their great-coats – an action which they took to mean they would not be slaughtered, from then on they did all the heavy work, even when a spandau opened up firing on fixed lines. That gun, firing tracer, fired a stream of bullets between my legs and those of my brother, who were – quite against the C.O's orders – face to face having a chat. Though very funny afterwards, it was not so at the time – it was very frightening.

And as so often happens when fearful, one does the most extra-ordinary things. I reminded my brother that spandaus tended to shoot progressively higher and to the left and that we should therefore lift our respective legs over the line of fire and get ourselves progressively lower and to the right.

Sgt Pringle and I had gone into no-mans land in a bren-carrier and at once attracted the attention of a couple of sniping 88s, it seemed to me that the carrier was what was drawing the fire, so I sent it to the rear into dead ground to await us and we would do the recce and walk back to it. However, the gun went on harassing us personally; what they thought we were about I don't know.

I remember saying to Sgt Pringle 'We will have to zig-zag but don't run or move too fast as 88s have an automatic traversing mechanism". Under fire quite sensible – but in retrospect how silly can one get.

As I had been on the original planning for this action, and according to Monty's dictum that those who knew the plan should not take part, I was sent with a Sergeant Major of ours back to the gun-line. I did not actually take part in the battle but heard bits of information over the gunner's radio.

While in exile in the gun-line, some displaced Arabs went past going to the rear out of the fighting – complete with flocks of sheep. The CSM signalled to me and dipped his hand out through the side of the tent and produced a lamb who became 421357. Private Lamb Larry - he was posted to the Cook's truck where he travelled for a few months 'til finally the North African fighting was over and we moved into a rest camp. There I made the suggestion that a celebration would be in order of real sparkling wine and Larry; this produced a near mutiny and some other lamb was brought forward and Larry reprieved".

AN ARTICLE FROM THE 'ROYAL ENGINEERS JOURNAL' APRIL 1993
SIGNED 'NITEBAR' (LATIN: 'I KEPT ON STRIVING')
CONCERNING THE DEATHS OF THE FOLLOWING OFFICERS AT THE WADI AKARIT:
BRIGADIER F.H. KISCH. G.B. GUERRE-AVEC PALMS. RE. AGE 54
MAJOR O.M. BELL MBE. SOUTH AFRICAN RE. AGE 37
CAPTAIN F.C.M. VOIGHT. MC. SOUTH AFRICAN RE. AGE 27
MAJOR D.M. PURSER. RE. AGE 26
WITH A CONCLUSION BY LT. COLONEL G.E.P. MULHERN. OBE. MC

"Late in the evening of 6 April a Liaison Officer came direct from army headquarters and told me to go to the Wadi Akarit, where the main road and railway bridges had been demolished, to clear the area of mines in preparation for work on the crossing by the South Africans (who had a high reputation as military engineers). The order said "clear" and not "check for" mines and I sensed what we were in for. I arrived at the demolished road bridge early on 7 April. All was quiet: the war had moved on.

One South African officer was already there and told me he thought there were mines on the other side. I prodded my way down the steep bank, with an NCO, and up the other side. The area between the road and railway was heavily mined, the wire fence still intact, and I carefully climbed in to have a look. I could see the prongs of several "S" mines and trip wires leading to the fence. This was going to be a snorter even if there were no mines outside! The troop had now arrived and I went back to talk the problem over with Sergeant Lyle and Lance Sergeant Parks.

There were to be no heroics, I said and it did not matter if we took two, four or six days over the job. There was no hurry – the new bridge would not be needed until the autumn – the crossings further up the wadi being good enough in the meantime – and all that mattered was clearing the area thoroughly and safely.

Our tentative plan was to tape the whole area in eight foot strips – the width of a mine detector sweep.

Suddenly a sapper announced that a staff car had arrived "full of senior officers." Out jumped Brigadier Kisch, Colonel Shannon (his South African deputy) and a staff officer (probably Captain Voight, a South African). The Brigadier was in great form, congratulating us on the Hallouf operation and praising all the 8th Army sappers for defeating their opposite numbers in the Afrika Korps. 'The war in North Africa would soon be over', he said.

When I told the Brigadier about the minefield on the other side, he immediately said "Let's have a look," and I had to take all three officers back across the wadi. I warned them twice about the "S" mines but could not stop them climbing up the low bank into the minefield while I turned to speak to my sergeant. What I did not know was that my O.C. had arrived, crossed the wadi further up and entered the minefield near the trip wires. I remember the Brigadier saying "keep spread out" just before a mine exploded. One of them must have set off an "S" mine – there was no other explanation – and all four officers were killed almost immediately. Five of us, including Lance Corporal Shiels, our medical orderly, went in but there was nothing we could do. While we were talking another mine went off, how and why we never found out, wounding everyone in the rescue party but with nothing like the power of an "S" mine. It could have been a booby-trapped Italian hand grenade judging from the smallness of the pieces of shrapnel. We lay there dazed and horrified, not daring to move, until the second rescue party, organised by Lance Sergeant Anderson, got us all out without further trouble.

Once outside the minefield I realised I was more frightened than hurt and, after having a tiny piece of metal removed from my backside by the medical officer at an advanced dressing station, was able to drive to Corp's Headquarters and report to the chief engineer, Brigadier Rae. He had just heard about the mine accident and was furious at 3 Field Squadron being put onto mine-clearance again without his knowledge. He suspended work on the crossing and told me to take the squadron to Sousse where we would be given work on the harbour. This I did with some relief and was glad to hand over to Teddy Hadow, who had been away."

LT. COLONEL G.E.P. MULHERN. OBE. MC

"The life of Brigadier Kisch CB, CBE, DSO, his outstanding courage and distinguished career have been well documented but the timing and circumstances of his tragic demise on 7 April 1943, to me, are particularly poignant.

Firstly, the timing – It was some months earlier (Nov 1942) that Brig

Kisch's South African DCE (Roads), Colonel Shannon and I (Staff Capt. RE with Rear Army HQ) were seated on a wooden box on a flat featureless site at Fort Capuzzo in a sand storm.

He was a tall, slim, gangling figure irreverently known to his fellow South Africans as "Shuffle dem feet" or affectionately, as "Daddy".

We drank from his bottle of Cyprus gin. It was awful stuff – nitric acid and razor blades and he urged that we drink it quickly before it took the enamel off our pint tea mugs. However, it did dissolve the sand in our throats.

He confided his profound admiration for our Chief Engineer and said also that it was their mutual intention to retire at the end of the North African campaign which seemed, and in the event was, not too far distant. And so, when their lives ended on 7 April they were within 35 days of their goal when, on 12 May all enemy resistance ceased. Kisch was 55 and, from his appointment as Chief Engineer, Western Desert Force on 27 February 1941, his service there covered an unbroken two years.

Incidentally, killed also with him and the others mentioned, was Major Bell, the O.C. of a South African Roads Construction Company of which Capt. Voight was the 21C.

It was very sad too that along with other Officer casualties, 3 Sqn lost two fine Sqn Commanders (Majors Clive Tandy and David Purser) who were on Kisch's staff at ALAMEIN. Tandy was his I.O. and it was Kisch who personally made the field appointments in relief of battle or other officer casualties – never sparing his own staff from the chance of earning their spurs.

This was Fred Kisch's day and he rose to the occasion in full sapper majesty. So appropriate to the subject of mines and booby traps and to his Old Testament philosophy, he opened his address with:

"Ponder the path of thy feet and let all thy ways be established – Proverbs, chapter 4,
26th verse".

In the end, either he or one of his tragic party sadly lapsed".

SAPPER B GRAHAM
ROYAL ENGINEERS

"Our job was mainly clearing mines and booby traps, myself and another Sapper was ordered forward with the advanced party which consisted of a corporal and two officers. At daybreak a huge artillery barrage began – the target was two big hills and the areas around them.

We moved forward about a mile until we came to this wadi, our officer (second i/c) was telling us a lot depended on us – he said he knew this was a clear area of land but beyond this, mines were laid at the enemy end of the wadi where it turned right sharply running up to a pass between the two hills.

Our party had almost reached the pass when all hell was let loose, where the wadi turned sharp right the enemy was dug in, the first wave of our infantry was caught in the fire and suffered heavy casualties. The next wave of our infantry knew where the enemy was positioned and attacked over open ground; then the battle became a slaughter house. Of our small party, two were killed and two badly wounded, the lad who came with me was called Buckingham and he got a large hole blown in his chest. I was the lucky one – getting out – with only shrapnel wounds in both arms, all credit to the stretcher-bearers, they were constantly dashing through the fire to get the wounded and bring them out.

Later in the day, we got news that our tanks had got around the hills, for such a short battle it was one of the bloodiest I had seen".

CPT. FINCH KNIGHTLY
1st BN BLACK WATCH

"I was within sight of Lorne Campbell in the action when he got shot by a sniper.

Most battles were very similar, this was our sixth battle since Alamein, battles were terrifying, crossing the wadi was not like crossing a river, it was a waterless hazard to get over. It was darkness when the attack went in but enemy flares lit the place up making us feel very exposed. They had these multiple mortars that would wind up like a siren firing six at a time, you certainly knew when they were coming.

The Italians with their 88s were very good gunners and there were many tanks knocked out and burning, they couldn't get out. I've rode on tanks but you wouldn't get me into one, they were like sardine tins and if you got hit you were in a lot of trouble – not a good place to be."

PTE PATRICK BODNICK. SUPPORT COY CARRIER DRIVER
7th BN ARGYLL AND SUTHERLAND HIGHLANDERS

"We left our carriers behind because we couldn't move them on the escarpment, we were used as part-time infantry then – bren gunners. The first unit I was with was the 13th Battalion, a machine-gun battalion, we were trained on all types of machine-guns, enemy weapons and anti tank guns; you name it we did it.

Early in the morning we were lined up on the start line with a flail tank in front of us. My job was to carry ammunition, a bren-gun and white serum netting to mark the path that had been cut through the mine field. After the path had been cut through, we were faced with this anti tank ditch which we had to climb over onto this ground in front of the wadi.

This is where they had us covered because it was quite an open piece of ground. There was some Italian slit-trenches in front of us, they gave themselves up straight away when the firing started. They came out and we jumped into their fox holes, as we did so we could hear Lorne Campbell roaring and bawling and when he was angry he used to roar and bawl in Gaelic – I could naye understand it. He was some man – some bloody man.

I saw him do the self same thing at Alamein, standing up and lighting his pipe in bloody defiance with his kilt on – sheer defiance of the enemy; they must have been frustrated that they couldn't hit him. The fire was heavy, that was the first time we came across the multi-barrelled mortars that they had – or as we called them 'moanin' minnies'. They gave us a fair old stonkin with these.

I was guarding one of the flanks with a machine gun because of the fear of a counter-attack; the Germans did counter-attack and we beat 'em off but we were beginning to run short of ammunition. This sergeant, Willy Gardner, says to me "do you want to come back to the lines with me and collect some ammunition?" I say "Aye OK Willy" - we ran back and picked up a box of ammunition each, put it on our shoulders and carried another box between us by the handles up the line. We did this twice.

Sgt Willy Garner says to me "I think the Jerries will try to break through down the right hand side of the anti tank ditch, so he took me down this ditch with my bren-gun and said 'I'll send somebody down to give you a hand out'. Well I dug a wee sort of slit-trench to get me under cover. Jerry was stonkin this bloody anti tank ditch with his multi-barrelled mortars and there was some Italian prisoners in it. As the Italians came down the Jerries were actually shooting them and bloody mortaring them as well.

Well, we were sitting in this anti tank ditch and there was this Italian officer there with some of his wounded men who were moaning like hell. Well I was laid down, firing down this anti tank ditch and I looked up and I thought to myself that if these mortar shells hit this escarpment above me, it was about six foot high, then I'm going to get buried. Next minute, I was buried under a pile of bloody sand and I tried to struggle my way out; I felt somebody pulling my leg and it was this Italian Officer, he pulled me out from under this pile of sand. I collected my bren-gun again and some ammunition and I cleaned the bloody gun and started firing down the ditch again.

Willy Garner came running down again and he says to me "Are you alright for ammunition?" I says "Aye". He went back for some mortar ammunition, he ran through the mine-field instead of the gap and finished up in the bloody air; his two legs blown off.

Later I became thirsty and bloody starving, we had a hot meal the night before and a hot sweet cup o' tea. By now it was about 12.30 to 12.45pm. I heard the bag pipes playing and as I looked down I could see two battalions of Black Watch coming up, their pipes were playing "Bonnie Dundee". They came through us, Jerry saw them coming and started to draw back. As he drew back, he had these multi-barrelled mortars on the chassis of an old Chevy and he kept firing these bloody things as he was retreating and then the tanks came through. We was relieved and told to get back and get a cup of tea; when we did we found we'd a lot of the bloody boys killed.

I went looking for my pal Joe Drummond, I was on the right flank, he was on the left, I found him dead in the slit-trench, there wasn't a mark on him, I was mystified. We got his body out and took him back – his tongue was down the back of his throat – that's what killed him, the blast from a shell had caused him to swallow his tongue.

We'd eight casualties, some of the Italian prisoners were told to dig a grave for them, they was terrified, they thought we were going to shoot them into the graves – aye, they were bloody terrified. Anyway, they dug these graves and buried their own, at this point the priest came up, Father MacRory, he gave a service for them. We were really upset, 'cause that was our two officers: we were very, very pally with them because Captain Alison and I were the two forward men at the battle of Alamein – we were very close, we got word his wife had had twins, he was delighted. I was very upset when I lost them two."

"Lorne Campbell was entitled to his VC, a sniper had got him on the neck, he just took his neckerchief out and put it around his bloody neck, tied it tight and carried on, roarin' and bawlin' in Gaelic.

The battalion Padre came up, it was a Lt. Sells, a bit of shrapnel hit him on the bum and I said to him "you know what the good book says sir, if the enemy strike you on the cheek – turn the other". He couldn't stop bloody laughing."

PRIVATE ANGUS REYNOLDS 'A' COY
2nd BN SEAFORTH HIGHLANDERS

"We got no breakfast just a watered down whiskey, at daybreak orders came to stand-to, and when I stood up I looked left and right and there was a straight line of soldiers as far as one can see, it put me in mind of a throw back to the 17th century.

The order came to advance and we moved forward over rising ground 'til we came to the Wadi Akarit, which was at least six feet deep. There was trenches cut on the side of the wadi facing the direction we came from. We crossed over and lay down on the far banks, I was a bren-gunner at that time and engaged incoming machine-gun fire from up the hill. At that time I couldn't see any friends of my own either left or right, I seemed to be on my own. Eventually an officer in highland dress passed carrying a walking stick, he told me to keep firing and disappeared. A sergeant came from the right carrying a bren-gun and said "follow me" which I did. We ran along the banks of the wadi, we saw quite a few enemy soldiers that had surrendered – mostly Italians I think. We didn't see many members of my own company.

The sergeant and I descended into the wadi – up the other side onto the flat ground, we made to move forward and almost immediately, were stopped by machine gun fire. The sergeant dropped to the ground and landed in a shell hole, I went back to the wadi. In the wadi an English soldier spoke to me, I think he was from the London Yeomanry.

My platoon officer saw me and called to me "What's wrong Angus?" I said 'there's a sergeant out there squealing – he's been wounded'. 'I'll try to get him', he said 'I'll go with you'.

A young fella – officer's batman came up to help us. I moved over the flat to where the sergeant was lying. We grabbed his two hands and the young batman got at the back of him and crawled 'til we got to the wadi. The young man was shot and I presume killed. The sergeant received another bullet wound and never squealed again – he collapsed and to my mind he was dead.

The Londoner says to me "We'd better get out of here", so we crossed back over the wadi and I retraced my footsteps, I was wounded and the Londoner was wounded; we arrived at the point where I had crossed the wadi originally, at that time there was bodies lying about, a friend of mine was lying there, his face was covered with blood. I tried to talk to him. Rifle fire and machine gun fire was still going on all around the area.

Just near us, there was a fissure in the rock – a narrow cave, with a number of wounded in it. We called out " Is there any room in there?" we had to squeeze in feet first. We heard voices later that afternoon and a patrol of Black Watch appeared."

MAJOR IAN GLENNIE. 'D' COY COMMANDER 5/7th BN GORDON HIGHLANDERS

"The night before the actual battle 153 Brigade was in reserve and I was sent with 'D' Company to go about a thousand yards in front of the start line to protect it and that's what we did, it was in the evening, quite a nice bright night. The plain between where our lines were – which was sort of slightly hilly – and the Wadi Akarit – were on the opposite side the cliffs rose very abruptly, was flat but covered in big sand-hills – mounds about six foot high.

We ambled off on a lovely moonlit night and travelled about a thousand yards, then I settled the company down, dug into the sand-hills and waited. During the night I remember particularly the machine-gunners, who were for a long time firing off behind us at positions on the enemy side. Then the shelling started, shells flew over our heads and we could see them landing beyond, then the first wave of the attack went in which I think was the Argylls, we watched them go in and could hear the fighting as the foot of the cliffs was about a mile in front of us. We then could do nothing but watch, but couldn't see very much at all. I remember seeing a group of tanks that seemed to be stuck halfway up a valley. I don't know whose tanks they were. I recall prisoners coming back who were nearly all Italians – thirty or forty at a time. One particular sight I shall never forget is one poor man being brought in a blanket, he was quite conscious but both his legs were blown off – I've never forgotten that.

Once the crest had been taken, which was quite a long time after dawn, we followed up behind mopping up the debris, just below the crest I saw two dead privates from the Camerons.

Then the company combed the battle-field on top of the ridge, once the Germans had gone, looking for wounded. We did find three or four of our own people who'd been lying there for quite a long time and managed to get those out. We had a grandstand view of the attack."

SGT. THOMAS JACKSON
SCOTS GUARDS. ANTI TANK GUNNER.

"I was a sergeant on a six pounder anti tank gun; there was two of us on the gun with two in reserve. We was put in front of a big road through the mine-field about 200 yards from it. When the barrage started two Bofors were to be firing tracers, the infantry would attack in between their lines of fire, the Germans were used to this tactic so this time it was used as a decoy and the infantry went in elsewhere.

The Highland Division were away on my left, although I could not see them, with the Scots Guards on my right, who I could see occasionally.

My job was to see that if tanks tried to get through they did not get among the infantry. But no tanks came, it would have been suicide for them as behind me was an 18 pounder gun.

I looked at my watch when the barrage started, it was a quarter past four in the morning. It stopped as the infantry attacked and as they were driven back, started up again.

About 10 o'clock that morning, there was all this smoke and cordite fumes – it was quite hard to see but suddenly a vehicle started to come through a gap in the mine-field, I couldn't recognise it and the other fella with me said "fire at it Tom, fire at it". I said 'no' as I don't think it's a tank, there was somebody in front of it, they must have seen us for they were making straight for us. I said "There's somebody in front of us walking dead slow", that was in no-mans land.

Then I recognised there was a soldier in front carrying this pole with a flag on it and I says "it might be a white flag" so I got up and signalled to him to shake this pole so I could see what it was – he shook it from side to side – it was a red cross. The ambulance then turned right, he must have been loaded with wounded and began making for the first aid area and seemed to know where he was going. I watched him for about 20 minutes and all firing absolutely stopped – the silence was deadly, it was terrible.

He came back the same way he had come in and through the gap in the mine-field, as soon as he was through that gap the barrage started again. Then the officer came to us and said "Don't fire" - the Scots Guards Infantry were going to attack, some of them got caught in the mine-field. Late in the afternoon, all firing stopped and it became quiet, we were taking prisoners and the wagon came up that pulled the gun, we were told to hitch up, we're on the move and went through the gap in the mine-field we had been guarding.

"The Germans had a Nebelwerfer – a six barrelled mortar and a deadly weapon, the Germans brought it up and fired a salvo, very demoralising it was. This officer that was on the 18 pounder gun came over and says "What do you think to that? I've got to get that thing or the battle's lost". After they fired another salvo, we got it, they never laid off until the artillery got it. I can remember it clearly."

SIGNALLER EDWARD COTGREAVE ROYAL SIGNALS: ATTACHED TO 201 GUARDS BRIGADE

Shot and shell was flying about, machine-gunning and so on and I heard a very funny little conversation. I used to do occasional switch-board relief operator and the brigade major (Lord Gilford) came on and asked for the Coldstream Guards, I rang them and a voice said "Hello", I said 'is that the Coalies' – there was a distinct pause and a voice said "This is the 3rd Battalion of the Coldstream Guards to whom do you wish to speak?" I said "Call from Brigade Major" – put him through and the conversation went something like this. "Hello Gilly", he replied "Oh hello how are things with you?" The Coldstream chappie replied "We're being mortared most monotonously". Gilly says "Oh too bad" and Coldstream says "Old so and so has just been killed". "Oh has he – too bad – knew him well – knew his people". It all sounded so funny in this laid back languid voice in the middle of a battle.

WAR DIARIES

51st HIGHLAND DIVISION

A soldier of the Black Watch sits on Roumana Ridge and watches tanks
passing over the anti-tank ditch on 50th Division's front.
In the distance the 4th Indian Division's objective stands out clearly.

War Diaries : 152nd Brigade Head Quarters
Commanding Officer : Brigadier G Murray DSO MC
Date : 6 April

All Bns were in position at the FUP by 0100 hours and the start line taped. Soon after 0300 hours 5 Camerons and 5 Seaforth moved off and passed the start line punctually in accordance with the Operation Order. Their attack went well, there being little opposition during their approach to the feature. Large numbers of Italians were found on the feature and almost immediately large quantities of prisoners began to flow back. At 0440 hours the enemy defensive fire began but though comparatively heavy, Bns' casualties were slight. At soon after 0500 hours Bns were on the lowest slopes and by 0525 hours 5 Seaforth HQ was reported established at 134568. 5 Camerons HQ was established shortly after at 132564. At 0540 hours 5 Seaforth reported their 'A' and 'C' Coys over the top of the ridge which constituted the first objective and at 0545 hours 5 Camerons troops were also seen on top of the ridge. In the meantime, Major Lloyd 275 Fd Coy, with his gapping party, had got on very well in spite of enemy M.G. and small arms fire and at 0600 hours their first gap in the minefield and bridging of the A/Tk ditch was complete. The Cameron Coy in this force captured about 200 Italian prisoners when occupying positions to cover this operation. The gapping was covered by smoke from the tanks and at 0600 hours more smoke was asked for from the arty. At 0605 hours the gappers reported that more smoke had arrived with good effect. Where the smoke came from is a mystery since our gunners, though registered to supply it, had not by then actually fired it. At 0630 hours the second gap and bridge were completed and at 0635 hours four tanks of 50 R.T.R. went through. The R.E. party then withdrew and the Cameron Coy reverted to 5 Camerons.

Phase II of the main operation was due to start at 0545 hours. It was feared at first that 2 Seaforth might be a little late on the barrage, but at 0555 hours 5 Seaforth reported that 2 Seaforth has passed through and had turned North. At 0625 hours 2 Seaforth had reached the wadi at 140582 and had taken a number of prisoners. At this stage communications with 2 Seaforth became very difficult and news was only got from time to time from 128 Fd Regt through the F.O.C. They did however, capture Pt 112 and therefore, achieved their objectives.

Phase III began at 0900 hours and the barrage went down as planned, but by this time the enemy were beginning to counter attack, infiltration and numerous pockets of enemy resistance with heavy and light M.Gs and Mortars still remained amongst our Coys. Our troops were therefore unable to move forward to any appreciable extent towards their final objectives and turned their attention towards dealing with the local situation. 5 Camerons had an uncomfortable time early on but their position improved considerably as 50 Div came forward. They also had the support on the left of 50 R.T.R. and 6 Shermans from 4 CLY. 5 Seaforth had a very hard fight to retain their ground. Their two forward Coys were cut off and touch with them was not made until nightfall. Their F.O.O. was also captured.

The enemy made continuous and determined efforts to recapture the Trig Pt V198 (1356) but 5 Seaforth were able to hold on until support from 5 Black Watch arrived in the afternoon. Though they had considerable casualties 5 Seaforth also inflicted very heavy casualties on the enemy throughout the day. 2 Seaforth had the hardest battle of all. They were counter attacked and driven off Pt 112 but a fresh attack restored the situation. They were then again counter attacked and pushed back once more. In the meantime, the enemy had infiltrated back on to the high ground at about 138583. The Bn had inevitably become very scattered and their reserves had been used up in regaining the feature. At this time it was reported that the C.O. and 60 men were the only collected body and they were on the main Roumana ridge. Gradually they were forced off the hills and finally took up positions in the plain at 146576. Throughout the day, but particularly in the morning, prisoners poured back, over 3000 being counted by 153 Bde who handled most of those coming from our front. These were largely from the Spezia Div, a few from Trieste and a smattering of Germans from 1st and 8th arty Rgts and from 90 Lt Div. The number of prisoners was so great that it was a definite embarrassment to fighting troops since escorts could not be spared immediately to deal with them. It was in fact possible for some of the enemy who had surrendered to take their arms up again after our troops had gone through.

During the afternoon 5 Black Watch were put under command and they were ordered to try and fill the gap between 5 Seaforth and 2 Seaforth. On their arrival they found 5 Seaforth being very hard pressed on Pt V 198. With the help of arty support, they were able to relieve this pressure and took up positions subsequently along the ridge to the North. They then came under the same conditions of M.G. fire and sniping and efforts generally by the enemy to reoccupy the feature. They too inflicted casualties on the enemy and collected a considerable number of prisoners. Late in the afternoon the 5/7 Gordons were also placed under command and moved up to the area of 142578 at last light. During the night they were able to move forward on to the North of the ridge and to occupy Pt 112.

When darkness fell all our Bns were out of touch with some of their troops and patrols were sent out to try and establish contact with them. 5 Camerons and 5 Seaforth were successful in this but 2 Seaforth could do little until daylight. As soon as it became dark the enemy began to withdraw and at daylight practically all had gone except for a few enemy posts who were out of communication and who surrendered.

The enemy having withdrawn, it was possible for the Bns to reorganise and to search the ground for their dead and wounded. The final assessment of casualties in the battle was:-

2 Seaforth = 9 Officers, 118 O.Rs. 5 Seaforth = 13 Officers, 156 O.Rs. 5 Camerons = 6 Officers, 95 O.Rs.

Date : 7 April

Examination of the ground showed that the defences had been much more thoroughly prepared than had been thought. Many of the positions were only slight development of natural cover and fire positions amongst the rocks and gullies. In some places however, elaborate defence posts had been dug for A/Tk, M.G. and L.M.G. posts with mortars in support. There had been many enemy OPs on the feature. The enemy had abandoned large quantities of equipment, rifles and L.M.Gs. Heavy M.Gs, 50mm and 81mm mortars, 20mm and 47/32 A/Tk guns were scattered all over the area. There were also considerable numbers of enemy dead. An escaped 2 Seaforth prisoner reported that the enemy had many casualties and that our arty fire was very accurate and effective, he himself and two of his companions being injured while at an enemy HQ to the West of the hill.

During the day the NZ Div, 7th Arm'd Div and the 51 Div Pursuit Force moved forward. 5 Camerons HQ was established at 132564, 2 Seaforth at 146576 and 5 Seaforth at 134568. 5 Black Watch and 5/7 Gordons moved off under 153 Bde. Bde HQ moved up complete to TAC HQ at 175530.

Date : 8 April

The day was spent in continued reorganisation. A joint burial service was held by 2 Seaforth and 5 Seaforth. The work of clearing the battlefield continued and much enemy equipment and material was collected. Our troops were brought down off the Roumana hill and camped in the plain to the East.

Situation normal.

153rd Infantry Brigade
War Diaries : 153rd Brigade Head Quarters
Commanding Officer : Brigadier D A H Graham
Place Date

South of GABES

1 April. Further plans were made for the formation of an advanced guard to be called Spear Force.

Adm Order N° 15 containing the adm plans for feeding Spear Force A issued and attached as Appx 'A'.

Diagram of W/T comns for Spear Force issued and attached as Appx 'B'.

2 April. The Bde prepared to move fwd to a concentration area North of GABES. Details of the move were given in O.O. N° 50 attached as Appx 'C'. Later in the day the Bde was ordered to take over 152 Bde sector and form a firm base in front of the Wadi AKARIT posns from which attacks by 152 and 154 Bdes would be launched.

Details for the occupation of this sector of the line were given in O.O. N° 51 in readiness to move fwd after the bridgehead had been made.

3 April. During the afternoon the Bde moved fwd, debussing in an 'A' Ech area at Z2046 and moving fwd on foot. It was a wet and dark night but all units reached their posns without incident.

4 April. The Bde dispositions were as follows:
    5 Black Watch in res with Spear Force
    1 Gordons on right in area Z1653
    5/7 Gordons on left in area Z1453
    Bde HQ Z183506
    ADS Z213463

During the night the Bns moved fwd approx 1000 yds and gained closer contact with the enemy. The FDLs ran from Z140540 – Z160546 – Z177553 and linked up with the 201 Guards Bde on the right and a Pl of Green Howards (69 Bde) on the left.

5 April. Bde HQ moved to Z173521. In the afternoon the Bde Comd held a conference to fix final details of supporting fire to assist 152 and 154 Bdes. O.O. N° 52 giving details of the attacks by 152 and 154 Bdes issued and attached as Appx 'E'.

6 April. The dawn attack by 152 and 154 Bdes was successful and objectives were reached in spite of fierce opposition. Many prisoners

were taken and approx 3000 passed through this HQ. There were many counter attacks in the area Pt 198 Z1356 during the day and the enemy recaptured some of the ground. 5 Black Watch came under comd 152 Bde and established themselves on Pt 198 in spite of heavy opposition and held on to it for the remainder of the day. During the night 5/7 Gordons came under comd 152 Bde and were ordered to clear the area on the right of 5 Black Watch. This was done at first light 7 April without opposition as the enemy had withdrawn during the night.

7 April. During the morning units of 7 Armd Div moved fwd through the Bridgehead and plans were made to move Spear Forces A and B during the early afternoon. The crossing of the Wadi AKARIT did not, however, stand up to the traffic using it and Spear Force B did not move until 2000 hrs. O.O. N° 53 outlining the bounds and order of march of Spear Force to SFAX is used and attached as Appx 'F'.

8 April. The move fwd continued at dawn and by last light the Bde was located area Z3287 South of the X rds at HACHICHINA. Here the enemy had blown a crater in the road and was covering this with some Spandaus, 88mm Guns and 1 or 2 field guns.
    The 5/7 Gordons moved fwd to hold the line and attack the enemy at dawn should that be necessary. Comd of the front passed to 153 Bde for the night.
During the night the enemy withdrew and message G112x (att as Appx 'G') gave orders for the move fwd on 9 April.

9 April. The Bde moved fwd with 1 Gordons in Spear Force instead of 5 Black Watch, who had been forced to debuss the previous evening. By nightfall Spear Forces A and B were located at the Wadi CHAFFER North of MAHARES area U6612, where the front was again taken over by 153 Bde for the night. During the night the enemy withdrew. O.O. N° 54 issued and attached as Appx 'H'. This gave orders for the move on 10 April.

10 April. O.O. N° 55 regarding occupation of SFAX is used.
    Forward elements of Spear Force entered SFAX at 0900 hrs and although vehicles were held up by a crater at the edge of the town the marching troops of Spear Force B entered on foot before 1200 hrs. By 1500 hrs all units of the Bde had entered the town and were located as follows:
    Bde HQ Industrial School
    5 Black Watch Area NW of SFAX
    1 Gordons Public Gardens

5/7 Gordons Barracks
ADS Dispensary
The remainder of the day was spent in recceing the town and establishing TCPs to control an unceasing flow of MT.

11 April. The Bde remained in SFAX. General Sir B L Montgomery KCB, DSO received the town of SFAX at 1200 hrs. A Black Watch Guard of Honour and the Bde Pipes and Drums were present at the ceremony. Messages of congratulation received by the Bde are attached.

154th Infantry Brigade
War Diary : 154th Brigade Headquarters
Commanding Officer : Brigadier JE Stirling DSO MC
Place Date Time

Gabes 1 April. The Bde remained in the area just outside Gabes. Everyone benefited from the rest in a pleasant spot by the sea and tps got a chance to clean and smarten themselves. Fwd body sent out patrols from three Bns and useful information was gained, although our FDLs were three to four thousand yards from the enemy. Our night patrols worked right up to the enemy's posns and by day our carriers and 'I' Secs pushed fwd into No Man's Land. The enemy was apparently strengthening and reinforcing his posns and meant to hold them. Bde Movement Order N°5 issued.

2 April. 0800 Bde HQ and the whole Bde moved fwd to a concentration area Z 2426.
1300 The Bde HQ rejoined Main Bde HQ, there no longer being any need for 154 Bde Tac HQ, 152 Bde having taken over the line from the NZ Div on the sector which interested us. Our own Bde having moved up. In the morning C.O.C. visited Tac HQ and personally interrogated the patrol leaders; he also discussed plans with the Bde Comd for the pending attack. In the afternoon Bde Comd attended a conference at 51 Div on the same subject and later himself held a conference for Comds in the Bde G.P.

3 April. Two patrols had been sent out the previous night and had discovered a minefield in front of the enemy posns. They also reported the enemy were active during the night working on their defences.
Another patrol with sappers and a Tk officer from both 40 R.T.R. and Scorpions recced the Wadi Es Smala from the causeway 169563 to Oglet Es Smaler 158555 and places were found which could soon be made

passable for vehicles 700 yds West of the causeway.

The 1 Black Watch also had a party out marking Start Lines for the 7 A&SH and 7 Black Watch. There was a series of conferences throughout the day at Division and Bde regarding the attack which had now been postponed for 24 hrs. The attack was to commence 6 April.

4 April. 7 Black Watch and 7 A&SH did exercises for the attack, otherwise the men had an easy day making full use of the sea which was so close. An Argyll patrol was out at night and found exact location of the minefield in front of the anti-tank ditch between 172568 and 167570. Sappers were also working on the crossing of the Wadi Es Smala and the Start Line was completed by 1 Black Watch. 1154 Inf Bde O.O. N° 33 issued. Adm Instr N° 14.

5 April. 1000. G.O.C. explained to all officers of the Division down to Coy Comds the arrangements for the attack on a Sand Model. Notes 1 and 2 to Bde O.O. N° 33 issued. 154 Bde March Table for 5 Mar issued. Everyone rested as much as possible prior to the attack.

1845. Bde HQ moved fwd to its battle HQ 180528.

1900. 7 A&SH marched fwd to the Assembly area followed by the remainder of the Bde G.P. as laid down in Bde O.O. N° 33.

2330. Everyone was formed up in their Assembly areas.

6 April 0415. Gapping parties moved fwd as arranged under the noise of the barrage. Two Crossings of the Wadi Es Smala had already been completed by 0130 hrs.

0515. 7 A&SH crossed their Start Line.

0605. Four gaps had been made through the minefield in front of the anti tank ditch.

0642. 7 A&SH had captured all their objectives. They had encountered a certain amount of M.G. fire and casualties were light. Approx 500 prisoners had been taken. Meanwhile, the attacks on our left by 152 Bde and 4 Ind Div had been progressing well. 50 Div, who were attacking between these two, had been held up by the anti tank ditch.

0710. 7 A&SH was threatened with a counter-attack from their right flank but this did not materialise. 7 Black Watch on 7 A&SH capturing objective had gone fwd and at 0810 they started their attack North West along the anti tank ditch from the A&SH.

1020. 7 Black Watch had captured all their objectives and also taken approx 400 prisoners. They were however, being fired at from the East, North and West by enemy M.Gs and there was a gap of some 1500 yds between them and the 7 A&SH. Their posn was improved when the 2 Seaforth captured Pt 112 which dominated their area at 1100 hrs. This Pt was disputed throughout the day by our own tps and the enemy and whenever it was in enemy hands 7 Black Watch were pinned to the ground.

1130. Two gaps were completed across the anti tank ditch by Res with the assistance of Italian prisoners and one Sqn of 40 R.T.R. had managed to cross. The whole area between the Causeway Wadi and the anti tank ditch was most unhealthy, being under direct fire from the enemy who kept up a very heavy bombardment. This caused the 7 A&SH considerable casualties and made it very difficult to work on or to get anything over the Gaps which were still only fit for tracks and not wheels.

1230. One tp 4 Cly crossed the A.Tk ditch. Tanks however, were not much use across the ditch as the ground was completely flat providing no cover and tanks were heavily engaged by enemy A.Tk guns. News was received that the Indians were doing well and 50 Div had forced a crossing of the A.Tk ditch and made a gap for the NZ who were waiting to push through.

1300. Eight A.Tk guns from 241 A.Tk Bty towed by Valentines were brought up to the 7 A&SH but could not be properly dug in on account of heavy shelling.

1400. A Bn of German Inf and 6 to 8 tanks were seen forming up North of the 7 Black Watch for a counter-attack. We asked for Air Support and between 1600 and 1700 hrs four sorties of 18 bombers attacked them, one sortie unfortunately bombed the fwd tps of the 7 A&SH.

The enemy counter-attacked the 7 Black Watch and over-ran their two fwd coys. The tanks were the chief trouble because the 7 Black Watch had no A.Tk guns and our own tanks could not engage the enemy effectively. 7 A&SH were also counter-attacked by tks and inf and confused fighting continued till dark but at last light the posn was that all the 7 A&SH Coy posns were held although the Coys had been considerably thinned. 7 Black Watch had only about one Coy strength left which was in the Bn HQ area at 158578. A Sqn of 5 Cly which had crossed the A.Tk ditch had lost all its heavy tanks and had only 6 Crusaders left. Another Sqn of 4 Cly had come to assist them in late afternoon but they did not cross the A.Tk ditch. The Sqn 40 R.T.R. across the A.Tk ditch had only 5 runners left and their other Sqn which was towing A.Tk guns was still fairly well intact and after dark managed to tow another 7 guns across the ditch.

1 Black Watch had been sent down to fill the gap between 7 A&SH and 7 Black Watch at 1600 hrs and two coys had been committed helping the 7 A&SH to beat off their counter-attack.

154 Inf Bde Draft Op. Instr N° for night 6/7 April was issued.

154 Inf Bde Draft Op. Instr N° cancelling above was issued.

It was decided to reorganise our posn and draw in 7 Black Watch just after last light. 1 Black Watch was to strengthen the bridgehead which was to consist of two composite Bn sectors. The Rt under Colonel Campbell and the Left under Colonel Oliver. The bridgehead was to be roughly a 1000 yds semi-circle in front of the gaps which we had made. The Scots Gds linked up with our Rt flank and the gap on the left between 7 Black Watch and 2 Seaforth was to be covered by a Sqn of 4 Cly on the South side of the A.Tk ditch. All 241 A.Tk Bty's guns were to be taken across the A.tk ditch; the A.Tk Pls of 7 A&SH and 7 Black Watch were to go into action South of the A.Tk ditch. All tanks were withdrawn to their rallying points South of the Wadi Es Smala.

At last light the enemy shelling died down and his inf which had come right up to our posns ceased counter-attacking. It appeared that the enemy had counter-attacked to hold us off to last light when he started withdrawing leaving fighting patrols to cover his rear.

2200. Our patrols went out a short distance but the enemy had withdrawn. After a quiet night at first light 7 Black Watch carriers went out to their Bn posns of the previous day but there were only stray parties of enemy about who surrendered at once. 7 A&SH carriers went out to 1662 and reported that the enemy had withdrawn and could be seen moving off in tpt to the North.

Our attack had been successful and it now remained to clear the battlefield and collect prisoners. In all the Bde had captured at least 1000 prisoners, perhaps 1500. Nearly all Italians; but there were also some Germans of 15 Panzer and 90 Lt Divs.

Black Watch and 7 A&SH had both suffered fairly heavy casualties.

War Diary
1st Battalion Black Watch
Commanding Officer: Lt Col WN Roper-Caldbeck DSO
Place Date Time

5 April, 1000. C.O. held conference and discussed Battle Drill for the Bn in 'the attack'. Day spent preparing for future operations. Captain GA Clark evacuated.

1800. R.I.O. assisted by Lieuts. AH Finch-Knightley and WMD Pearson left to lay start line for 7 A.S.H.

2350. Bn arrived in Assembly area.

6 April, 0915. The move forward went without incident for the first few hundred yards, the wadi being easily negotiated. From the wadi on tape was laid in the rear of Bn HQ to guide the transport which was following behind under Major CAB Malden. The advance from 0330 hours was carried out in absolute silence.

At 0400 hours our artillery opened up with a barrage on the enemy FDLs. On the opening of this barrage the transport which had been left in the FUP started up and followed in the rear of the Bn.

War Diary
2nd Battalion Seaforth Highlanders
Commanding Officer : Lt Col R D Horne
Place Date Time

North of Gabes, 5 April, 0530. The three I.Os from Bns of 152 Bde met Major Andrews and proceeded to recce and mark route to Bde FUP at 1654. This group came under slight mortar fire from the enemy and in order not to compromise the plan the recce was curtailed.

0900 .The C.O. attended a final conference at Bde. During the morning Lt HM Black arrived from N° 1 I.T.D.

1430. A conference down to Platoon Comdrs was held by the C.O. when final orders were given out for tomorrow's dawn attack on enemy at Djebel El Roumana.

1930. Bn moved out by march route led by C.O. with Major AM Gilmour, MC as guide to FUP. Cook's trucks followed up Coy groups and before reaching the FUP the column was halted and a hot breakfast was issued.

6 April: The day was full of tragic reverses, and it was extremely disappointing to all that we could not secure the objective. Nevertheless, there is no doubt that the Bn fought hard and did very well to hold on where it did until dark, and to inflict as many casualties as it did.

It is impossible to say how many prisoners were taken, but it was literally hundreds. An immense quantity of enemy weapons, ammunition and equipment was left abandoned on the ground.

7 April: By first light the enemy had evacuated the whole position and the work of clearing the battlefield commenced. A few seriously wounded, which had been in enemy hands all night, were recovered, including Lts Douglas and Payne.

Our casualties were as follows:-

Killed
   (a) Officers
      Capt WH Spreull (O.C. 'D' Coy)
      Lt JF Flugel (O.C. Mortar Pl)
      Lt BH Blyth (Pl Comd 'D' Coy)
      Lt WL Givens (Pl Comd 'B' Coy)
   (b) Other Ranks 41

Died of Wounds
   (a) Officers
      Lt J Douglas(Pl Comd 'D' Coy)
   (b) Other Ranks 6

Wounded
   (a) Officers
      Major AM Gilmour MC (Bn 2nd i/c)
      Capt JAG Corrie (O.C. 'B' Coy) Capt SJS Lee (O.C. 'A' Coy) Capt DB Law (2nd i/c 'A' Coy) Capt DW Hudson (O.C. 'C' Coy) Lt AGM Napier (O.C. Carrier pl) Lt AK Gallie (Pl Comd 'A' Coy) Lt RE Payne (Pl Comd 'A' Coy) Lt JS Cruickshank (Pl Comd 'C' Coy)
   (b) Other Ranks 114

Missing believed POW 5 Other Ranks

7 April: In the absence of the cook's trucks Capt C Perry and the A/Tk Platoon provided a hot breakfast to those at Bn HQ. During the morning men came in in scattered groups from the Ridge and other units to whom they had become attached.

1000. A Echelon transport arrived.

1700. B Echelon arrived in Bn area.

C.O. held a conference at which all officers, W.Os and Platoon Sgts attended, and it was decided to form the Bn into 2 Coys, each about 100 strong - 'A' and 'B' Coys forming one Coy and 'C' and 'D' Coys forming the other.

Rest of day was spent in re-equipping and reorganisation.

1800. Pipers played a Retreat Set.

Mention must be made of our supporting arms. Firstly, the F.O.O. Lt Henderson of 308 Bty advanced with 'C' Coy intending to establish an O.P. on the forward ridge of pt 112. When Capt Hudson was wounded he took charge of that part of 'C' Coy and fought gallantly with them until he was wounded himself. His assistant was killed and he never established his communications with the Bty. Capt Connel of 308 Bty spent the battle with the C.O. and did valuable work in support of the Bn.

A platoon of 275 Fd Coy, R.E., under Lt George was allotted for breaching the A/Tk ditch and clearing any minefield there might be in order to open the track for vehicles through the re-entrant between the main ridge and pt 112. They found the track across the A/Tk ditch was complete, so they only had to clear a small number of mines from the track which they did very quickly, and were working before the objective had been reached in the original instance.

A platoon of 1/7 Mx (M.G.) was under command for the purposes of consolidation, but were never called up from the bottom of the ridge, as we were never in possession of the top for long enough. The situation on the top was too confused to allow them to sit back in the plain and take on targets on the ridge.

War Diary
5th Battalion Black Watch
Commanding Officer: Lt Col Thomson

On 6 April 1943, 5 Black Watch were held in Divisional Reserve and moved up at first light to a position close behind Tac Div. HQ. The Battalion was organised and ready to form part of Spearforce under comd 23rd Armoured Brigade and the Carriers were already employed by that Brigade to cover a gapping operation.

At about 0900 hours the Battalion was ordered to move forward about 4 miles in Troop carrying transport and the C.O. was ordered to meet the Divisional Comdr at Advanced Tac Div. The G.O.C. ordered the C.O. to be prepared to reinforce the 5 Seaforths at Point 198 and to fill a gap which was thought to exist between that battalion and the 2 Seaforths on Point 112. The actual order for the operation was received through Brigadier Graham at about midday and the battalion was directed across country on to Point 198 itself to come under command 152 Brigade.

The C.O. reported to Brigadier Murray at about 1230 hours and after receiving his orders went on to meet the C.O. of the 5 Seaforths. During the journey across the open from 152 Bde HQ it became apparent that the situation on the Roumana Hills was not so good as it had been thought to be, as our own guns were shelling an area to the left of Point 112 and small arms fire from about Point 198 was directed on the Jeep as it approached the high ground. O.C. 5 Seaforths confirmed this and from then on it became a question of time whether the Germans or 5 Black Watch would reach Point 198 in force first. The enemy were from 1400 hours onwards in occupation of the O.P. on the Feature itself, and sections were seen to infiltrate forward on the left of 5 Seaforth's HQ. M.G. and sniping fire were also coming from both flanks and German infantry were seen hurling grenades from Point 198, at the remnants of a 5 Seaforth's Company below them. Mortar fire was also heavy throughout the afternoon. The leading Coy of 5 Black Watch arrived at 5 Seaforth's HQ at about 1430 hours having covered 2 miles across open country and having suffered some casualties from shell and small arms fire. 'C' Coy were immediately ordered to occupy Point 198 and a heavy and very accurate concentration was put down on the Feature by 128 Field Regt, directed by Major Owen. This allowed the leading Platoon 15 Platoon under Lieut HR Crichton-Melville, to reach the O.P. and kill the Germans who were in occupation, and Point 198 itself was secure by about 1530 hours.

Meantime 'B' Coy had moved up the Hill to the right to secure the ridge there, but were suffering heavily from small arms fire coming from the direction of Point 112 and south-east of it, mortar fire by this time was also intense, both on Point 198 and on 'B' Coy area. To deal with the M.Gs and snipers on the right flank a Platoon of 'D' Coy (the Bn consisted of 3 Coys only) advanced under cover of smoke on to the Feature next to Point 112 and this had the effect of making the enemy withdraw. Throughout the evening repeated attempts were made by the enemy to shell the troops off the ridge which was bare and stony, and afforded no cover, but although a Platoon of 'B' Coy was forced to withdraw temporarily, it was soon back in position again.

Meanwhile 'C' Coy dealt with 3 enemy M.G. posted beyond Point 198, and by 1800 hours the position was reasonably secure although no sign of the 2 Seaforths could be seen on the right. The lack of Carriers had been a great handicap but 5 Camerons assisted greatly by lending a section of Carriers which assisted the 'D' Coy platoon on the right to reach its objective, the fact that the south-eastern slopes of Point 198 were under enemy small arms fire from the right flank, also had been a great nuisance. At last light, a Platoon of 'C' Coy moved forward 200 yards beyond Point 198 and collected 3 Italian Officers and 20 O.Rs, and while shelling and mortaring continued till midnight, it soon became obvious that the enemy was moving away as activity gradually ceased and eventually died down altogether.

Casualties: Officers : 6 Wounded
O.Rs : 12 Killed
53 Wounded
5 Missing
Total 76

There is no doubt that the day marked the fiercest fighting that the Division has experienced in this campaign. Our arty and machine gunners were in constant support on a very large number of targets throughout the day. Our Infantry had a gruelling time, and certain units suffered very heavy casualties, but by nightfall our tps had succeeded in driving the enemy off some very difficult ground, holding most if it in the face of very fierce counter-attacks, causing the enemy severe casualties in dead and wounded, and taking over 3,000 POW.

Early on the morning of 7 April 1943, the code word to reform Spearforce was received and soon after 1000 hours the battalion was ready to move again through the 154 Bde gap as part of that force. At about midday the Carriers led Spearforce through the gap and the advance to SFAX began.

War Diary
5th Battalion Cameron Highlanders
Commanding Officer : Lt Col RDMC Miers DSO
Place Date Time
Akarit 6 April, 0300. Tea and sandwiches were issued to all men except Bn HQ who were unlucky in that the truck bringing their food broke

down and never reached the FUP.

0330. Bn started to move forward to the Start Line. The Bn objective was the left hand half of the Roumana feature, a high rocky escarpment about 2000 yards from the Start Line. The 5 Seaforth were taking the right hand half of this feature and the 2 Seaforth were to follow up behind the 5 Seaforth and swing through the latter when they had gained their objective, to attack Pt 112 an isolated feature to the North of the Roumana Hill.

The Bn moved forward with 'A' Coy up on the right, 'D' Coy up on the left, Bn HQ following behind 'A' Coy and 'C' Coy following behind 'D' Coy.

Enemy aircraft were over the forming up area as the advance was due to start and many flares were dropped making the night, which was very dark, uncomfortably like daylight.

The move forward went without incident for the first few hundred yards, the wadi being easily negotiated. From the wadi on tape was laid in the rear of Bn HQ to guide the transport which was following behind under Major CAB Malden. The advance from 0330 hours was carried out in absolute silence.

0400. At 0400 hours our artillery opened up with a barrage on the enemy FDLs. On the opening of this barrage the transport which had been left in the FUP started up and followed in the rear of the Bn.

During the advance enemy defensive fire came down mostly from artillery from the right flank firing down the plain across which the Bn was advancing to the Roumana feature. Enemy mortars also opened up from behind Roumana. Shellfire however, was not in any way sufficient to impede the Bn advance though one shell landed by 'D' Coy HQ and wounded Capt CA Cameron (164901) the Coy Comd, who was evacuated. Lt JC Hamp, MC took over command of the Coy. Shortly after taking over command he was killed by a shell. Lt DML Ainslie then took over command of 'D' Coy. The two forward Coys reached the objective without difficulty though 'A' Coy lost direction to some extent and pls became too widely dispersed and contact was lost between Coy HQ and the pls of the Coy.

On arrival at the objective our artillery barrage was still landing on the slopes of the hill and the Bn had to wait for a few minutes while the last of our shells dropped. Owing to 'A' Coy losing direction Bn HQ found themselves against the side of the hill with none of our own troops actually in front though some were on the left and some were on the right. The Adjt therefore, went over to the left flank and got a platoon of

'C' Coy to come over and clear the hill in front of Bn HQ.

0530. By this time the objective was taken and some of 'A' and 'D' Coys, both of which were very scattered, were over the far side of the hill. The enemy offered little resistance, almost all of them being Italians and within about half an hour 200 prisoners had been sent back, this being quickly followed by another 200 within the next twenty minutes.

The Bn then settled down to collect itself together on the feature, Bn HQ being established in a small wadi on the reverse slope of the hill. 'A' and 'D' Coys (or what pls Coy Comds had been able to gather together) being on the forward slopes and 'C' Coy with one platoon forward with 'D' Coy and the remainder on the reverse slope of the hill.

0815. By now Coy HQ were in communication with Bn HQ by line and wireless. Communications with the Coys were at the time – 'A' Coy - runner only as the Coy Comd had become divorced from his wireless.
'B' Coy - runner and wireless.
'C' Coy - by line or runner.
'D' Coy - runner and wireless.
'B' Coy reported that they were through the gap made by the R.Es and as well as covering the Sappers were covering the advance of 50 Div on our left who were at that time held up.

The 5 Seaforth on our right appeared to have gained their objective but signs of a counter-attack from the north were apparent.
A message was received that Sherman tanks were expected to go through the minefield gap very soon.

0820. It was confirmed that Phase III of the attack would definitely take place at 0900 hours as previously ordered, the second phase having been the attack of the 2 Seaforth on Pt 112. On Phase III all three Bns were to advance to the Corps objective, a wadi north east of Roumana. Coys were informed to carry out Phase III with what pls of their Coys they could collect.

0930. 'A' and 'D' Coys moved forward on Phase III leaving 1 pl 'C' Coy on the forward slope of the hill. At this time many more prisoners were still coming in in such numbers that it was quite impossible to count them. Amongst these were many wounded and Capt RL Orchardson, RAMC, the Medical Officer was kept busy more with enemy wounded that with our own. Our casualties up to the present did not appear to be high although in addition to those already mentioned a number of officers were wounded and though only slightly had to be evacuated.

These were –

Capt J Elliot 'B' Coy Comd from whom Lt CF Burrows took over.

All the officers in 'C' Coy were wounded – Lieut A Sinclair, lt RN Roberts and Lt LW Campbell-Colquhoun. Lt HG Archibald, Bn I.O. took over commend of 'C' Coy.

At this time enemy resistance appeared to be stiffening and German troops in the north were making determined attacks. 2 Seaforth had apparently not been able to hold their objective and an intercept message on the wireless told that two of their Coys were being withdrawn although tanks of 50 R.T.R. were ordered to advance on the 2 Seaforth objective at the same time.

The enemy appeared to be infiltrating from the north towards high point of the Roumana hill, Pt 198. It appears that 5 Seaforth have not been able to advance on Phase III and our forward Coys are in danger of being attacked from 3 sides.

'A' and 'D' Coys were ordered to withdraw to their former positions. There was some difficulty in getting in touch with these Coys as 'A' Coy Comd had never found his wireless before leaving and 'D' Coy had left theirs behind – only communication therefore was runner.

'B' Coy were told to contact the tanks which were by now seen to be passing through the minefield gap, to ask them if they could fan out to the right and ease the situation of the two forward Coys.

Troops of 50 Div were also seen coming up to the minefield gap and it was suggested that part of this force could take on the enemy on the right of their line of advance which was the main track, and help our Coys to withdraw. The amount of sniping, both small arms and mortar, now going on on the hill and even on the reverse slope of Bn HQ area, made it apparent that the enemy were back on Pt 198. In view of this, although there was no immediate serious threat to the Bn HQ area, Major Malden organised local defence on top of the hill. This force consisted of a platoon of 'A' Coy which had not gone forward, spare signallers, and other personnel from Bn HQ and some of 'C' Coy.

1800. Capt D G Watson, CC 'A' Coy returned to Roumana with the portion of 'A' Coy that had gone forward. Lt GD Stewart was reported missing having been wounded and it is thought captured.

1815. M.T.O. brought up some reserve amn which was dumped at Bn HQ to replenish Coys.

1900 By now the situation appeared to have stabilised and although there was still a considerable amount of sniping and mortar fire the enemy did not appear to by trying to gain any more ground.

'A' and ' C' Coys were ordered to put out listening posts for the night and 'B' Coy was ordered to patrol at intervals along the front.

The Q.M. brought up a hot meal and the next day's rations after dark but it was considered that the situation did not permit of a hot meal being issued at that time so hard rations for the next day were dumped and the Q.M. went back to B Ech.

During the night Lt DH Cameron came up from B Ech and remained at Bn HQ preparatory to taking over 'B' Coy at first light.

At about midnight Lt DML Ainslie returned with the portion of 'D' Coy that had been forward with him during the day.

7 April. With the arrival of dawn the situation generally seemed to be quite quiet with no enemy fire of any sort and it appeared that the enemy had withdrawn. At first light the Adjt and Lt DH Cameron went out to look for the body of Lt JC Hamp, MC who had been reported killed.

No trace of Lt Hamp's body was found but the bodies of several O.Rs were discovered.

War Diary
5th Battalion Seaforth Highlanders
Commanding Officer:Lt Col JH Walford DSO & BAR
Place Date Time

Field, 5 April, 1700. The Commanding Officer gave out his orders to the 'O' Group.

1900. The battalion left the location at 204488 and moved by march route via 'HD' track of 153 Infantry Brigade to the FUP. Lieut. D Stuart Sutcliffe joined the battalion and was posted to 'C' Company. 6 April 0130 The battalion settled in FUP area, 1555.

0330. The battalion moved across the Start Line, 156556-152552 in the formation – 'A' Right forward, 'B' Right rear, 'C' Left forward, 'D' Left rear. Battalion headquarters with F.O.Os , M.G. Officer and L.O. from 152nd Infantry Brigade moved between 'B' and 'D' companies. An 'I' Group under Lieut. Houldsworth followed battalion headquarters laying tape along the axis of advance, 3180.

152 Infantry Brigade were ordered to attack the Roumana feature – 5

Seaforth Right and 5 Camerons Left. 2 Seaforth followed the 5 Seaforth axis in order to swing East along the feature towards Point 112 (1458) after Point 198 had been captured by 5 Seaforth. 50th Division were attacking the area of Point 85 (1254) on the left of 152nd Infantry Brigade. On the left flank, the 4th Indian Division were attacking the Fatnassa feature. When morning came, 154th Infantry Brigade were to attack on the right flank of 152nd Infantry Brigade. 201 Guards Brigade were to simulate an attack at 0415 hours on the coastal sector.

0335. Enemy aircraft dropped many flares.

0415. Artillery barrage came down along the line of the Roumana foothills.

0520. The battalion were in the wadis and foothills below Point 198.

0545. 2 Seaforth, following in the battalion axis, swing NE along the Eastern slopes of the feature.

0600. Heavy mortar and artillery fire on all parts of the battalion area until 0900 hours.

0900. 'D' Company moved over the top of Roumana towards Corp's objective, supported and followed by 'C' Company. 'B' Company stood by ready to move forward, to be supported and followed by 'A' Company.

0910. German infantry, approximately a company and a half strong, launched a counter-attack from the NE end of the feature along the Western slopes.

0920. 'D' Company organised a defensive position below Point 198. 'A', 'B' and 'C' Companies were forced to give ground off the main feature and later reorganised in the foothills.
0920 A force under the Adjutant and N° 4 Platoon Commander was established on the right of 'D' Company at approximately 135567 and two sections were established by the Intelligence Officer on the foothills at approximately 139569.

0930. Period of FireFight with counter-attacking enemy. Close fighting took place with mortars and L.M.Gs and the enemy were prevented from obtaining a permanent footing on the crest of the feature. Meanwhile, 5 Camerons on the battalion's left, had made the required minefield gaps at the South West end of the feature and A.F.Vs of the 23rd Armoured Brigade were beginning to pass through.

1215. Enemy Infantrymen occasionally succeeded in reaching to the crest of Roumana but the accuracy and the intensity of the shooting of the battalion Light machine-gunners, snipers and 3" mortarmen, aided by the 25-pdrs of 307 Battery, a New Zealand 'Honey' Tank giving independent support, the opening of the minefield gap on the battalion left and finally the arrival of 5 Black Watch as reinforcements, caused the enemy counter-attack to fail.

1400. Officer Commanding 5 Black Watch arrived on reconnaissance.
1430. Elements of 'B' Company regained the heights on their front.
1445. 'D' Company, which formed a position on Point 198 50-70 yds below the Roumana crest, were attacked at close quarters by the enemy with stick grenades. The enemy infantrymen were destroyed by the battalion snipers and 25-pdr fire.

1450. Elements of 'B' Company and 9 men from battalion headquarters reinforced 'D' Company.
1500. 5 Black Watch arrived and straightaway moved up the hill astride Point 198 and on to the Roumana crest with two companies up.

1600. The two Black Watch Companies were established and 'D' Company relieved.
1600. The enemy, unable to regain Point 198, again concentrated on severe mortar fire on the feature and the wadi below it.

1730. Battalion Headquarters moved to 135565. 1800 A force of two platoons under Captain PA Agnew, Commanding 'B' Company, was established at approximately 134565 to bridge the gap between 5 Black Watch and 5 Camerons. During dusk, the enemy concentrated shell fire chiefly on the minefield gap to the left of 5 Camerons. 2000 A hot meal arrived for the battalion.
It is considered that from approximately 2000 hours the enemy began to withdraw from Roumana. On the whole it was a quiet night.

During the day, the battalion suffered the following casualties:-
5 Officers killed – Captain DM Gordon, Commanding 'C' Company Captain ID Mackenzie, 'D' Company Lieut. WJD Gray, Commanding Mortar Platoon Lieut. J McGilvray, 'B' Company Lieut. GB Reed, 'A' Company
5 Officers wounded – Captain LG Begg, Commanding Carrier Platoon Captain AG Murray, Commanding Anti Tank Platoon Captain GA Willock, 'B' Company Lieut. DS Sutcliffe, 'C' Company Lieut. F Greenwood, 'C' Company

26 Other Ranks were killed and 81 were wounded while 11 Other Ranks were missing. Of those missing, 10 were later found to have been evacuated wounded, one of them fatally. 7 April Roumana feature was clear of the enemy. The pursuit by the 2nd New Zealand Division, 1st Armoured Division, 7th Armoured Division and "Spearforce" (23rd Armoured Brigade and 153rd Infantry Brigade) was begun.

The day was spent organising a cemetery in the foothills for personnel of the battalion and the 2nd Battalion killed on Roumana, collecting battalion equipment from the feature, locating and salvaging the equipment, stores, weapons and ammunition abandoned by the enemy.

War Diary
7th Battalion Argyll & Sutherland Highlanders
Commanding Officer: Lt Col LM Campbell
VC DSO and BAR, OBE – TD

Place Date Time 2. April. After three days rest the Battalion moved to a Brigade Concentration Area near the Oasis de Usseps, about 3 mils east of OUDREF. The harbour party, which left the old location before the main body, under the Comd of Lt W C Lees failed to turn off the main road at the correct place and ran on into the enemy's lines. Immediately fire of Artillery and small arms was brought to bear on the trucks which stopped and the party made for the ditch. An attempt to turn a truck was unsuccessful. The order was then given "every man for himself" and of the Argyll 3 O.Rs managed to make their way back through heavy fire to our own lines. The remainder of the party, consisting of Lts Lees and Robertson and a senior NCO failed to return and must be presumed prisoners. The keep which had been established on the 31st was withdrawn after four days and rejoined the Battalion. The keep itself had been in the Wadi RMEL about 2 to 3 miles from the Wadi Akarit and during the day pushed out O.Ps and at night, recce patrols did valuable work in investigating such things as steepness of banks of the Wadi Akarit and Oglet Es Smala and succeeding in finding the position and extent of the enemy's minefield. They were not able however, to penetrate as far as the anti tank ditch.

The few days at Oasis du Usseps were spent in resting, bathing and rehearsing for the coming attack. The type of the attack being explained to all ranks down to Pl Comds by means of sand models.
6 April Battle of Wadi Akarit The Officer casualties in this battle were as follows:- Killed : Captain DE Adamson, Lieuts TF McGill and PJ

Stewart-Bam Wounded : Lt Col LM Campbell DSO TD, Major JS Lindsay-MacDougall MC Capt IC Cameron, Capt MGJ Bate, Lieuts RD Marshall, AS Bowden and RF Kinghorn On the day following the battle, the following immediate awards were posted:-

Bar to DSO : Lieut Colonel LM Campbell DSO TD MC : Captain HDL Samwell DCM : 2986699 CSM Archibald M 2976509 CSM Gauld G MM : 298507 Cpl McColl W 2986308 L/Sjt Wallace J 299LO48 Pte Monaghan W Also announced previously was:- MM : 2986333 Cpl Macrae D The Battalion took at least seven hundred prisoners and captured 17 anti tank guns, 2 Lt AA guns, 2 Infantry guns, 8 Heavy Anti Tank rifles, 16 M.M.Gs, 17 L.M.Gs, 3 large mortars, 7 small mortars and a great deal of other equipment.
Casualties were:- Officers – Killed 3, Wounded 8 O.Rs – Killed 38, Wounded 100, Missing 5.

War Diary
7th Battalion Black Watch
Commanding Officer: Lt Col JA Oliver – DSO MBE
Place Date Time

Gabes, 4 April, 1030. Div conference attended by all Bn Commanders dealing with future operations.

5 April. Bn prepares for role in attack on Wadi Akarit line,which is to pass through gap in enemy line made by 7 A&SH, extend it to feature 112, H/R 1458, (74NE 1/50,000 Tunisia).
2000 Bn move to assembly area for the attack: M.R.

6 April, 0625. Bn moves forward through 7 A&SH gap and at 0815 hours forms up for attack in 112 area. 0915 Bn, having moved forward against the enemy, is in complete possession of ground to East of 112: no junction as yet with 2nd Seaforth on our left. 'B' and 'D' Coy are in forward positions: whole Bn is in a former Italian position with very deep trenches.

1000 to 1300 hours. Heavy shelling of Bn and considerable sniping.

1700. Enemy Counter Attack with infantry and tanks, engage by S.A. fire and artillery with great effect, but forward Coy overrun. Our tanks offer ineffective support.

1730. Air support called for by Bde, mistakes target and bombs Bn: no casualties. Throughout attack heavy shelling and occasional machine-gunning over Smala.

1830. One Coy of 1st Bn Black Watch arrives and eases situation by their presence up to 2300 hours. Bn standing-to ready for any enemy move.

2330. Bn moves 1,000 yards to the East, throughout the attack many prisoners were taken, 30 light field guns and 60 automatic weapons were captured, plus much enemy equipment. Casualties were : 10 officers wounded 1 killed (Lt JA Christison) 330 other ranks killed 77 wounded and 9 missing – a number of them prisoners

War Diaries : 1st Bn Gordon Highlanders
Commanding Officer : Lt Col Fausset-Farquhar
Place Date Time

5 April, 0900. Bn Strength 30 Officers - 709 Other Ranks.
'B' Coy had moved forward during the night and had taken two prisoners. During the day there was some shelling in the Bn area and in the late afternoon some enemy aircraft flew over the Bn area but did not take any offensive action.

0300. 'C' Coy had moved forward to a position within 150 yds of the enemy wire. The mortars took up a position behind 'C' Coy and their ammunition was carried forward by hand across a wadi. The enemy had made themselves very obvious at dusk, but in the evening they fired only a few bursts of machine gun fire.
Our front was very quiet during the early hrs of the morning. At 0415 the artillery barrage opened as the 152 Inf Bde went into the attack on our left flank. The enemy replied with a few shells, some of which landed in our area.

0800. From this hour onwards, throughout the day, many prisoners were taken, both German and Italian. The majority, by far, were Italians of the TRIESTE Division.

1750. In the late afternoon 3 enemy planes were shot down by A.A. fire in the rear of the Bn area. In the evening the firing began to die down and it was thought that the enemy might be withdrawing. 'B' Coy moved forward into a gap between two other units and 'D' Coy moved into the area which 'B' Coy had vacated. A Forward Bn HQ also moved into this area.

7 April, 0700. Bn Strength 30 Officers – 703 Other Ranks.

'C' Coy report that they have been forward with the tanks to the hills but saw no sign of the enemy. Reports from all other sources established the fact that the enemy has withdrawn once more. During the morning Spear Force passed through the Bn in pursuit of the enemy. Our carriers were at the head of this force in addition to the remainder of the carriers in the Division.

War Diary
5/7th Battalion Gordon Highlanders
Commanding Officer : Lt Col HWB Saunders
Place Date Time

6 April. The barrage was terrific – 3,000 rounds on Pt 85 alone in 15 minutes. By first light prisoners were already on their way to the POW cage. 688 passed through the Bn HQ alone, while 3,575 passed through Div. Moaning Minnie was active in the morning and the famous 18 came over in the afternoon. But 5 JU 88s, which endeavoured to bomb back area, two were shot down and the remaining three were seriously damaged. All that day there was bitter fighting and counter-attacks by the enemy, but the Bn had a grand-stand view of the battle and a few shells landed in our area.

The 152nd were seen to go in and they appeared to bear the brunt of the fighting. The Italians were surrendering at the rate of 1,000 per hour for a considerable time. The 5th B.W. moved through us at about 1400 hours to support the Seaforths and in the evening the Bn and the 1st Gordons moved forward by easy stages to enable us to be on the ridge by first light. By first light the Bn was safely in position on the hill and took it without firing a shot. Many more prisoners were taken. M.T. movement forward indicated the enemy were withdrawing.

7 April. The Bn has settled in in the Black Watch area and at about 0545 hours an O.P. is established on the top of Roumana overlooking 'A' Coy. One Italian was taken in at approx 0630 hours, he was from the Trieste Division and was found hiding in a hole. At various intervals more prisoners were brought in and formed into a pool, by about 0745 hours 48 prisoners had arrived, 10 of them being German and the remainder Italian : Trieste and P.G.R. The prisoners are used to act as stretcher

bearers and they bring in 2 Seaforths who lay out all night. In all 83 prisoners are taken and the other units represented are Boulonga and Spezia. The rest of the morning is employed collecting a vast amount of booty which was abandoned by the enemy.

BRIGADIER LORNE MACLAINE CAMPBELL.
VC. DSO AND BAR. OBE. TD.

BIOGRAPHICAL DETAILS

Lorne MacLaine Campbell was born in London on 22 July 1902, into a family with a proud military history in the Highland tradition. His uncle – Vice Admiral Gordon Campbell – was an expert on 'Q' ships and won the Victoria Cross in the First World War but refused a bar to it in favour of another nominee; he also won the DSO and two bars.

Young Lorne was educated at Dulwich and was a Postmaster (Scholar) at Merton College, Oxford. On coming down from university he worked in his father's wine shipping business. In 1921 he joined his father's regiment, the 8th Battalion Argyll & Sutherland Highlanders, as a Territorial Officer. He was promoted Lieutenant in 1923, Captain in 1931 and Major in 1938; 2 i/c 8th Battalion.

During the fighting in France, 1940 most of the 51st Highland Division was captured at St. Valery. However, Campbell managed to make his way through the German lines to find out what had become of his two leading companies; he found they had reached the coast and were sheltering in a lighthouse. Campbell rallied his men in their new position which was attacked by troops from Rommel's division, he led his men forward and forced their way out in a number of short sharp actions. The 8th Argylls marched for three nights and finally returned to England via Le Havre. In England he was hailed as the 'man who saved two hundred' and was awarded the DSO for his actions.

In Mid 1942, he was promoted Commanding Officer of the 7th Battalion Argyll & Sutherland Highlanders, part of the re-raised 51st Highland Division, in preparation for the North African Campaign. During the fighting at El Alamein he won a bar to his DSO. In the latter part of the Tunisian Campaign, Campbell won the Victoria Cross on 6 April 1943; his citation for this award describes in detail a memorable feat of arms:

VC CITATION
LONDON GAZETTE: 8 JUNE 1943

"On 6 April 1943, in the attack upon the Wadi Akarit position (before the Gabes Gap), the task of breaking through the enemy minefield and anti tank ditch to the east of the Roumana feature and of forming the initial bridgehead for a brigade of the 51st Highland Division was allotted to the battalion of the Argyll & Sutherland Highlanders commanded by Lt.-Colonel Campbell.

The attack had to form up in complete darkness and had to traverse the main offshoot of the Wadi Akarit at an angle to the line of advance.

In spite of heavy machine-gun and shell fire in the early stages of the attack, Lt.-Colonel Campbell successfully accomplished this difficult operation; captured at least 600 prisoners, and led his battalion to its objective, having to cross an unswept portion of the enemy minefield in doing so.

Later, upon reaching his objective, he found that a gap which had been blown by the Royal Engineers in the anti tank ditch did not correspond with the vehicle lane which had been cleared in the minefield. Realising the vital necessity of quickly establishing a gap for the passage of anti tank guns, he took personal charge of this operation.

It was now broad daylight and under very heavy machine-gun fire and shell fire, he succeeded in making a personal reconnaissance and in conducting operations which led to the establishing of a vehicle gap.

Throughout the day Lieut.-Col. Campbell held his position with his battalion in the face of extremely heavy and constant shell fire, which the enemy was able to bring to bear by direct observation.

About 1630 hours determined enemy counter-attacks began to develop, accompanied by tanks. In this phase of the fighting Lt.-Col. Campbell's personality dominated the battlefield by a display of valour and utter disregard for personal safety, which could not have been excelled. Realising that it was imperative for the future success of the army plan to hold the bridgehead his battalion had captured, he inspired his men by his presence in the forefront of the battle, cheering them on and rallying them as he moved to those points where the fighting was heaviest.

When his left forward company was forced to give ground, he went forward alone, into a hail of fire, and personally reorganised their position, remaining with the company until the attack at this point was held.

As reinforcements arrived upon the scene he was seen standing in the open, directing the fight under close range fire of enemy infantry, and he continued to do so although already painfully wounded in the neck by shell fire.

It was not until the battle died down that he allowed his wound to be dressed. Even then, although in great pain, he refused to be evacuated, remaining with his battalion and continuing to inspire them by his presence on the field.

Darkness fell with the Argyll's still holding their positions, though many of its officers and men had become casualties.

There is no doubt that but for Lieut.-Colonel Campbell's determination,

United Nations parade, Cairo, 14th June 1943. General Sir Henry Maitland Wilson, GBE. KCB. DSO. ADC. pinning the Victoria Cross ribbon on the chest of Lt. Colonel Campbell DSO, 7th Argylls.

splendid example of courage, and disregard of pain, the bridgehead would have been lost.

This officer's gallantry and magnificent leadership, when his now tired men were charging the enemy with the bayonet and were fighting them at hand-grenade range, are worthy of the highest honour, and can seldom have been surpassed in the long history of the highland Brigade."

The ribbon for the Victoria Cross was pinned to his chest by General Sir Henry Maitland Wilson, GBE, KCB, DSO, ADC, at a United Nations Day Parade in Cairo, 14 June 1943.

Following the desert battles, Campbell was given command of the 13th Infantry Brigade – part of the 5th Division, heading it through the campaigns in Sicily and Italy. In October 1944, he returned on leave to Auchendarroch, Argyll, his wife's family home, and received a hero's welcome. He arrived on the steamer Lock Tyne which was decked with flowers – pipes began to play as he set foot on land and cheer after cheer rang out across the loch. Troops of the Argylls marched past as Campbell took the salute in the local streets – a fine tribute to a brave man who was home at last.

Brigadier Campbell was decorated with his Victoria Cross on 21 October 1944, at Buckingham Palace by His Majesty King George VI. He was accompanied to the Palace by his wife Muriel and their two sons – Patrick and Alistair Lorne Campbell. His uncle, Vice Admiral Gordon Campbell, VC, DSO – TWO BARS, was also present to congratulate him.

When asked about his earlier decorations, Brigadier Campbell commented:

"DSO for walking with a couple of hundred other chaps through the Germans after being surrounded in France 1940.

Bar to DSO for the capture of Tel el Aqqaqir last day of."

It was typical of the man, that on being awarded the Victoria Cross, he was at pains to transfer the honour to his men:

"From El Alamein to Tunis every man of my battalion was simply magnificent, they never failed me, though sometimes I was almost apologetic when asking them to make attack after attack."

From 1944 to 1945 Campbell was on the General Staff in the Military Mission in Washington, subsequently, he served in Germany where he investigated the possibility of restarting the Boy Scout movement which had been abolished by Hitler.

After the war he returned to the family business which had been badly blitzed and rebuilt it. He went on to become elected Master of the Vintners Company and was also a Vice Lieutenant of the City of London. Campbell was six feet three inches tall and cut an impressive and athletic figure; in battle he was very controlled and was admired by all who knew him for his cool-headedness in a crisis; he had outstanding gifts of leadership.

Besides being awarded a VC, DSO and bar, he was mentioned in despatches four times; received the Territorial Decoration in 1941, was appointed OBE in 1968 and was an officer of the American Legion of Merit.

At the age of 88 years and after a varied and eventful life, Lorne MacLaine Campbell passed away in 1990.

CHAPTER FOUR
SUMMARY

Montgomery wrote in his diary regarding the Battle of the Wadi Akarit: "We had on this day the heaviest and most savage fighting we had had since I commanded the 8th Army. Certain localities changed hands several times, my troops fought magnificently".

The troops of the 4th Indian and 51st Highland Divisions had fought their first major action since El-Alamein, whereas the 50th Northumbrian Division had been badly mauled at Mareth two weeks earlier. Never-the-less this was a bold victory for the infantry of 30 Corps, 610 men were killed with 1,500 wounded and maimed.

By 0900 hours the attack along the whole front was in full swing, the Axis commanders, up until this time, had their eyes firmly fixed on Trieste Division's left flank until it dawned on them that the full weight of the assault was in the general areas of Trieste, Spezia and Pistoia Divisions' sectors. By 0800 hours they knew Roumana and Zouai had been lost and Panzer Grenadier Regiment 200 were ordered to counter-attack at Roumana, with Panzer Grenadier Regiment 361 and a battalion from Pistoia Division counter-attacking at Zouai. Two troops of 88mm guns and the 15th Panzer Division moved forward into Spezia Division's area. These moves exhausted all of the Axis Forces' reserves, but at 0930 hours the 10th and 21st Panzer Divisions facing Patton, some 80 tanks, were ordered across to the Akarit battle. Patton made no move to exploit the weakening opposition on his front.

By 0730 hours General Tuker knew from the reports coming in that his troops had achieved their objectives, 30 Corps HQ had received the message that Zouai, El-Aliz and El-Meida had fallen and that Tuker was eager to build on his success and press on. There began at this point a series of events about which the evidence is confusing; the details of what happened cannot with certainty be recovered and the overall view left is one of cross purposes caused by individuals' differing view points during the heat of the battle.

A crossing over the anti tank ditch had been hurriedly built by 0920 hours at the western end, the 4th Indian Division sat on their objectives and pressed the enemy constantly. At 0710 hours 10th Corps records that Horrocks left for the front, however, he is not mentioned again in their records until 1200 noon. Tuker states that at 0845 hours Horrocks arrived at 4th Indian Division HQ and that he told him (quote) "we had broken the enemy, that the way was clear for 10th Corps to go through and that immediate offensive action would finish the campaign in North Africa".

Tuker goes on to relate how Horrocks contacted Montgomery asking for permission to send in 10th Corps and so keep up the momentum of the assault before the enemy could recover, he then said that the armour would move at once over the crossings south-west of Roumana and at the western end of the anti tank ditch. Tuker goes on to state that Horrocks then got on the radio-telephone and alerted his HQ to the events taking place : Tuker's is the only traceable record of these negotiations.

The Division to lead 10th Corps was the New Zealanders and their historian, Freyberg; records that by 1100 hours they were still undecided whether to move east or west of Djebel Roumana.

Consumed with impatience General Tuker waited at his HQ and at 1045 hours General Leese directed the New Zealand Division to advance using the gap between the 50th (N) and 51st (H) Divisions, at 1110 hours the New Zealanders were placed under the command of 10th Corps. At noon Generals Horrocks and Freyberg were deep in discussion regarding the next move, no record of what passed between them has been recorded in any detail but by 1330 hours the Staffordshire Yeomanry were moving through the gap at the western end of Roumana, with the 3rd R.T.R. below Fatnassa. The Staffordshire Yeomanry ran into heavy, accurate and deadly fire from 88s that were concealed below the lower slopes of Roumana and were firing in enfilade, their forward move being checked. The 3rd R.T.R. were also stopped in their tracks and the high hopes which the advance of the 10th Corps had raised were quickly dashed.

The 50th (N) and 51st (H) Divisions had a complicated move forward in the dark; differences of approach marches, direction and the positions of start lines had involved intricate moves by large numbers of men. However, all was completed on time and the troops were in position with their supporting arms when the barrage began. The Highland Division attack went according to plan and by 0600 hours the 5th Camerons and 5th Seaforth of 152 Brigade were on Roumana; the 2nd Seaforth then passed through and fought their way along the ridge, Point 112 was reported captured an hour later and by this time the tanks of the 50th R.T.R. were passing through. 154 Brigade on the right had breached the enemy's defences and the 7th Black Watch pressed on to exploit the situation.

For the 50th (N) Division the assault did not go according to plan and the 69th Brigade found themselves on open ground and under a continuous hail of artillery, mortar and small-arms-fire. The 7th Green Howards took the outpost on Point 85, however, neither they nor the 5th

East Yorkshires could gain the anti tank ditch in the face of such severe opposition. Two commanding officers were wounded and casualties mounted steadily as both battalions became pinned down.

The check to this forward move by 69th Brigade would mean that, as the second phase of 30 Corp's plan came into operation, the troops of 152 Brigade would meet more serious opposition as it advanced down the north-western slopes of Roumana. No change was made to the existing plan by General Leese but it was decided that the 6th Green Howards and the squadron of 4th CLY attached to 69th Brigade should move in behind the enemy by passing through the gap which the Highland Brigade had made: all of this happened before 0900 hours.

At 0900 hours 152 Brigade attacked to the west; but even as they did so, Panzer Grenadier Regiment 200 launched a furious counter-attack, which was helped as dormant Italian positions sprang into life, and the Highlanders were thrown off their hard won gains on Roumana Ridge. They quickly re-grouped just below the crest, it was here the 5th Seaforth held their ground for three hours among the rocks and boulders in a vicious fight as the enemy tried valiantly to infiltrate their positions, to the north-east the 2nd Seaforth fought a bloody battle for Point 112 against the 15th Panzer Division. On the right the 154th Brigade held on to their final objectives, but between the Argylls and the Black Watch there was a dangerous gap of 1500 yards and the whole area was being swept by fire from three sides. The Valentine crews of the 40th R.T.R. moved to the front and engaged the enemy gunners but were picked off one by one, anti tanks guns reach the Argylls and a squadron of the 4th CLY joined the battle. The day was long and hard but the Highlanders held on to their positions.

In the sector held by the 50th (N) Division, events had taken a favourable turn. Shermans passed through a mine-field gap at the western end of Roumana at 0935 hours and the 6th Green Howards advanced over the anti-tank ditch and were soon at close quarters with the enemy, capturing some 400 Italians. The 5th Brigade of the 4th Indian Division pressed in rear of the enemy that were holding up the 50th (N) Division, and the 4th Rajputana Rifles took the El-Hachana hill and with it over 1,000 Italian prisoners. The 5th East Yorkshires of 69th Brigade crossed over to assist them as the Rajputanas prepared for their assault on Point 152. The 6th Green Howards pressed forward onto their final objective, following in their wake came engineers who made roads through the obstacles for anti-tank guns.

General Nichols was at this time on Point 85 observing events and could see that things were now going favourably for the badly mauled 69th Brigade, at 1225 hours he sent a message to 30 Corps HQ stating that resistance on the 50th (N) Division's front had been broken.

The German command however, did not have a clear picture of the situation. Messe believed that the Trieste Division had been deeply penetrated and that the Spezia Division was holding its own despite the fact that some of its units had been destroyed on El-Meida and El-Hachana. The German forces focus of attention was the fight for Roumana Ridge, between noon and 1530 hours Von Arnim, Gause and Cramer (Africa Corps Commanders) reach HQ AOK1 where they were informed by Bayerlein that all available reserves had been committed to the fight and that the counter-attacks may enable the front to hold on for a few extra days - but that the full force of the 8th Army had still to be felt. Cramer was of the opinion that the El-Guettar front could not be held indefinitely by his units and even as he spoke the advanced units of US 2nd Corps were driving towards Gabes after a week of holdups.

In the skies above the battlefield the Desert Air Force swept the area, one attempt by the Lufwaffe to interfere with the struggle below was driven off by fighters, and a second attempt defeated by the anti-aircraft gunners. Fighter bombers, fighters and Hurricane tank destroyers had flown 160 sorties into the battle area by noon.

At midday Montgomery, somewhat over-opportunistically, sent a message to Alexander to the effect that all of the main objectives had been taken on schedule and that 10 Corps would now press through the gap made by 30 Corps, who hung on grimly to their hard won gains. On the left the 4th Indian Division repelled vigorous counter-attacks by 361st Panzer Grenadier Regiment until late at night, in the centre the 50th (N) Division consolidated and mopped up, while on the right the 51st (H) Division fought a stubborn defensive battle - suffering heavy losses - against an enemy just as stubborn.

The Axis commanders tried desperately to find more reserves to throw into the battle, only the 164th Light Division was available and was ordered to move to the rear-centre in reserve. Von Arnim was convinced a retreat was not yet necessary, his colleague Messe said he could hold the front only until the evening of 7 April - but to hold it any longer would require every man to be thrown into the cauldron. All afternoon on 6 April the 90th Light Division and the 15th Panzer Division fought on; the unit commanders were increasingly unsure of the situation they found themselves in and had grave forebodings about the outcome. Around Point 152 in Spezia Division's sector only some anti-tank and field guns were left to oppose a break-through. Afrika Corp's tanks arrived at Akarit and moved swiftly to the area to reinforce the units there: however, when the fresh armour did counter-attack it was in a half-hearted manner and had little effect on the outcome of the battle.

The Desert Air Force met these counter-attacks with waves of bombers flying in formations of eighteen, Hurricane Tank Busters and fighter bombers. By 1700 hours the main Axis commanders were in agreement that their position was hopeless and that on 7 April the game would be up. Bayerlein received orders from Army Group to the effect that all units were to retreat after dark behind rear-guards: to a position which was in fact in very close proximation to 10th Corps objective. Messe, however, had a plan of his own and ordered what was left of Trieste and Spezia Divisions, plus his Army Artillery, to progress to Enfidaville with all haste. The Young Fascist Division collected transport for the rearward move and as soon as it was ready disengaged from the 8th Army and retreated to El-Djem - which is positioned between the towns of Sfax and Sousse. The conclusion of the withdrawal by the Axis Forces was that most of the German units, including those facing the 2nd US Corps, fell back on foot during the night of 6/7 April.

On the night of 6 April N° 205 Group; Desert Air Force, sent out 48 Wellington bombers to bomb transports using the Sfax-Mahares road. However, the main body of the retreating Axis Forces went undetected by the crews above them and had a lucky escape. The constant attacks by night and day by the Desert Air Force had a demoralising effect on the enemy troops, keeping them in a continual state of tension and apprehension.

As the order to withdraw was received by the Axis Forces, the 8th Army was preparing to renew the battle on 7 April, this fresh assault would be heralded by a saturation stonk on the area behind Roumana by the whole of 10th and 30th Corps artillery; with the hope of knocking out the 88s that had stopped the armoured advance so effectively on 6 April. 8th Armoured Brigade and the New Zealand Brigade would then break out aided by a heavy air-blitz to their front and flanks. In the early hours of 7 April, patrols reported that the enemy had gone and the meticulous planning made for the new assault proved unnecessary. A large number of Italian troops surrendered on 6 April and by 2000 hours 125 Germans and 5,211 Italians were accounted for in the cages, a number which rose on 7 April. Messe reported that the infantry units of the Spezia Division consisted of 1½ companies, while the Trieste Division was made up of only three incomplete battalions. 90th Light Division and Pistoia had lost heavily in the battle: losses that were to increase during the retreat. The artillery regiments at all levels suffered a similar fate.

The 8th Army had suffered roughly 2,000 casualties during the battle, 610 of which were killed; the bulk of the latter being in the 51st Highland Division. 80 tons of bombs had been dropped by the Desert Air Force and the British Artillery had fired 82,000 shells of all calibres, the infantry had added to this awesome fire power countless numbers of mortar bombs and small-arms rounds.

The 8th Army had won a great victory at Akarit and had given the old foe a severe mauling, yet once again the enemy slipped away, many believed then and still believe today that at Akarit there was an opportunity of disposing of the Axis Forces forever.

During the morning of 6 April the 10th and 21st Panzer Divisions facing Patton's forces were ordered to cross over to the Akarit front and help contain 8th Army's successful break in. Patton, after his failure to break into the Axis rear, did not take advantage of the now greatly weakened enemy forces on his front. He was urged on by Alexander and, despite the fact that under his command were 88,000 troops, he would not take the risk of further casualties. Had Patton taken the initiative and pressed on, his Corps would have taken the whole of the Akarit position in rear and brought the campaign to a swift and early end.

After 4th Indian Division's success in the early hours of 6 April the stage was set for the main assault, this made swift progress despite 50th Division's difficulties in the early morning. The developing situation soon seemed right for an armoured break-through, but as the tanks attempted to push through they came under fire from no more than three 88s firing in enfilade from the rear of Roumana and the attack ground to a halt. No attempt seems to have been made to subdue this fire even though the offending position was over-looked from Fatnassa, cooperation between tanks and artillery was found to be sadly lacking and the results were catastrophic for the whole 8th Army : a magnificent opportunity was lost.

CHAPTER FIVE

The End in Africa

(The 8th Army : April to May 1943)

Italian prisoners taken at Akarit. *(Courtesy of the Imperial War Museum)*

On 7 April 1943 8th Army patrols came into contact with the troops of the United States 2nd Corps which was advancing towards Gafsa in the east. Other meetings took place as the two armies converged after their different routes across Africa led them to link up on the Gabes Plain.

The contrasting dress and behaviour between the 8th Army and troops of the 1st Army was at once obvious, and many 8th Army men made wry comments as they saw their brothers in arms arrive in regulation dress and steel helmets.

Allan Moorhead was a war correspondent travelling with the 1st Army. He had been with the 8th Army at Alamein but had not seen them since; the sight of such a relaxed and confident desert army made a lasting impression on him which he described in a report:-

"The British desert soldier looked like no other soldier in the world, he looked at first sight like a rather rakish and dishevelled boy scout, the effect, I suppose, of his bleached khaki shorts and shirts and the paraphernalia of blackened pots and pans and oddments he carried round in his vehicle which was his home. He practically never wore a helmet, and had a careless loose limbed way of walking which came from walking in the open plains".

The 8th Army had become in effect an overseas army with its base in Cairo, cut off from Europe for years it had developed its own customs and expressions. These men considered themselves to be part of an elite fighting force and were indeed encouraged to do so by their commander. Any soldier who was not a part of this exclusive club was considered an outsider and it was from this viewpoint that the 8th Army soldiers viewed the strangely dressed 1st Army units.

However strong these first impressions must have seemed at the time, it was not long before the differences became blurred as units of the 1st Army became a part of the 8th and troops of all units were thrown together in rest areas; the easy going attitude that was the hallmark of Allied soldiers in the desert soon came into play and slowly the outsiders were accepted into this fraternity of fighting men.

The 8th Army's next task after Wadi Akarit was to break out and advance towards Tunis at speed, 8th Army troops entered the badly bombed port of Sfax on 10 April. Montgomery drove through the streets to a tumultuous reception from the inhabitants, behind him came the skirl of the pipes and the troops of the 51st Highland Division - kilts swinging, webbing white and brasses gleaming.

The kind of destruction that greeted the troops had not been seen before by many of the 8th Army, Sgt Green of the 6th Battalion Green

Howards commented:-

"Tunisia gave us our first glimpse of what war would be like in highly populated areas, it was a disturbing sight. In the desert war women and children would not be seen as two armies would fight it out like men in combat should, it seemed a more honourable conflict than what we would experience later".

On 11 April Kairouan was captured as the advance continued on a broad front with the invading forces converging upon this point. The advance up the east coast moved at an even faster rate into the steppe country, on the horizon appeared the amphitheatre of El- Djem which was built by the Romans and held 30,000 spectators.

About 100 kilometres north of Sfax lies Sousse which fell on 12 April, the town had been subjected to heavy bombardments and the port was a scene of terrible destruction with ships sunk, beached and blown apart scattered around; it was an apocalyptic sight. Many of the town's living areas suffered a similar fate, but whole sections of the town that had been well away from the port area were left untouched. The French population gave the men of the 8th Army and its commander a tumultuous welcome.

Alexander's combined Allied command was now a formidable force in both men and machines, though the 8th Army was now only a large cog in this mighty body. The Army Group's strength was 156 battalions with 43 of them being 8th Army units. The French provided 38 battalions and the Americans 22. The remainder being in the British 1st Army. The 8th Army tank strength was 460 out of an Army Group total of 1,193. Opposing this large fighting force were 90 German and Italian battalions who possessed a total tank strength of 143.

Alexander now began to plan his next move, in a dispatch of mid-April he wrote:-

"I decided for topographical reasons to make my main attack on the western front of this perimeter.

My intention was to break through to Tunis from the west and thereby split the enemy forces in two. I would then leave the smaller body of enemy to the north to be mopped up by the Allied troops on the spot and, turning southwards with the greater part of my forces, drive the larger body of enemy on the right flank of the penetration against the line finally held by 8th Army."

But before this grand plan could be initiated however, the 8th Army faced further trials on their own front, the coastal road which runs between Enfidaville and Sousse is overlooked by a hill which rises sharply out of the surrounding countryside.

The village of Takrouna sits on top of this feature and made a naturally strong position for the Germans, enabling them to bring down artillery fire over a wide and important area.

This was going to be a very difficult position to assault with its sheer cliffs and rocky overhangs; the job was given to the New Zealand Maori Battalion. The attack went in on the night of 20/21 April and was met by heavy defensive fire, there were many casualties as the men pressed upward - fighting for every yard gained. As daylight broke only Sgt Manahi and seven men were left to carry on the attack, this they did successfully and took seventy Germans prisoner. Senior officers who later visited the scene and ascended to the village above, looked in awe at the New Zealanders who had taken by force such a strongly held and steep sided position. Horrocks recommended that Sgt Manahi be awarded the Victoria Cross for such leadership: this recommendation was not accepted.

8th Army troops entered Enfidaville on 20 April shortly before the assault on Takrouna, but to the north of the town enemy forces were massing and resistance grew stronger. After consultations with Montgomery Alexander made changes to his original plan of future operations : in the new plan the 1st Army was given the task of taking Tunis, for this it would have under its command two of the most experienced infantry units in the 8th Army - 4th Indian Division and 201st Guards Brigade. As well as these two formations Montgomery had also agreed to release 7th Armoured Division to take part in this last victory : the Battle for Tunis.

The New Zealand Division's role in the new plan was to hold the front at Enfidaville and to assist the French 19th Corps by carrying out local operations. The formations of 30 Corps had by now been withdrawn to prepare themselves for 8th Army's next role in another theatre of war. To the north of Enfidaville the fighting was bitter - with the promise of worse to come.

Whilst the 8th Army units were in the process of uprooting themselves and moving out - the remainder of 8th Army were busy exerting strong local pressure in order to prevent enemy units being moved to 1st Army's front. And so it was, that after such a long triumphant march across North Africa from El-Alamein, the 8th Army was now at journey's end in this campaign.

Tunis was to be attacked directly from Medjez El-Bab through Massicault, the main attack would be made by 5th Corps, with the 9th Corps, with two armoured divisions, thrusting through them and on to Tunis - with the intention of forestalling any attempt by the Axis Forces to organise a defensive perimeter around the city and split the enemy forces in Tunisia in two. The 2nd US Corps would simultaneously advance towards Bizerta from the north.

The 4th British and 4th Indian Divisions stood on their start lines on the morning of 5 May, on 6 May the main assault was launched and by last light the troops had advanced half way to Tunis. The impetus of the attack was so great that enemy resistance, though desperate in places, was swept away : Alexander's strategy was successful, within a few hours of each other the 2nd US Corps entered Brizerta and the 1st Army entered Tunis on the afternoon of 7 May.

The last of the enemy troops were ejected from Tunis on 8 May and the 9th Corps was reconstituted to mop up left and right. On 12 May all organised resistance in Tunisia ceased. To the north of the Medjerda River all enemy units surrendered unconditionally to the 2nd US Corps on 9 May. Three days later there was mass surrenders in the south, and on 13 May the last of the Axis Forces laid down their arms at 1145 hours. At 1415 hours the same day General Alexander sent to Winston Churchill the message:-

"Sir, it is my duty to report that the Tunisian Campaign is over. All enemy resistance has ceased. We are masters of the North African shore".

So ended the fight for North Africa, some quarter of a million enemy troops laid down their arms in unconditional surrender - with less than seven hundred escaping to fight another day.

"In later years when a man is asked what he did in the war, it will be enough to say-
'I marched and fought with the Desert Army'."

Winston Churchill

Bibliography

Hayter A MBE MC	'The Second Step'	1962
Elliot JG Major Gen	'The Story of the Indian Army - 1939-45'	1965
Roe FG	'The Bronze Cross : A Tribute - 1940-45'	1945
Fergusson B	'The Black Watch and The King's Enemies : 1939-45'	Collins 1950
	'Register of The Victoria Cross'	This England Books 1988
Liddel-Hart BH	'History of The Second World War'	Cassel 1970
Official History	'The Mediterranean and The Middle-East' Vol 5 Destruction of the Axis Forces in Africa	
Anon	'Historical Records of 'The Queen's Own Cameron Highlanders' Vol VI	Blackwood 1953
Whiting C	'The Poor Bloody Infantry'	Paul 1987
Sandars J	'The 8th Army in The Desert'	Stephens 1976
Tuker F – Sir	'Approach to Battle'	Cassel 1963
Liddel-Hart BH	'The Tanks'	Cassel 1959
Sym J	'Seaforth Highlanders'	Gale & Polden 1962
Cameron I C	'History of The Argyll and Sutherland Highlanders 7th B'n El-Alamein to Germany'	Nelson 1946
Graham A	'Sharp Shooters at War' The 3rd, 4th and 3/4th County of London Yeomanry 1939-1945 The Sharp Shooters Regimental Association 1964	
Howarth P	'My God Soldiers : From Alamein to Vienna'	Hutchinson 1989
Stevens G R Lt Col OBE	'The Fourth Indian Division'	McLaren & Son 1948
Borthwick A	'Sans Peur' Republished in 1994 under the title of 'Battalion'	E Mackay 1946 Bâton Wicks Publications
Carell P	'The Foxes of The Desert : The Story of The Africa Corps'	MacDonald 1958
Hamilton S D	'50th Royal Tank Regiment : The Complete History'	The Lutterworth Press 1996
Brook S	'Montgomery and The 8th Army'	Bodley Head 1991
Ellis J	'Brute Force'	Andre Deutsch 1990

Ellis J	'The Sharp End' 1990	Windron & Greene
Blomfield-Smith D	'Fourth Indian Reflections : Memoirs of a Great Company'	Privately Published 1987
Lucas J	'Panzer Army Africa'	Purnell 1977
Mitcham S W	'Hitler's Legions'	Leo Cooper 1985
Moses H	'The Faithful Sixth'	County Durham Books 1995
Strawson J	'The Battle for North Africa'	Batsford 1969
Stevens G R Lt Col OBE	'A History of the 2nd King Edward VII's Own Gurkha Rifles (The Sirmoor Rifles) Volume III 1921-1948	Gale & Polden 1952
Hamilton N	'Monty-Master of The Battlefield 1942-1944'	Hamish Hamilton 1983
Montgomery FieldMarshall KG GCB DSO	'El-Alamein to the River Sangro'	Hutchinson Limited 1948
Clay E W Major MBE	'The Path of the 50th'	Gale & Polden 1950
Anon'	'The Tiger Kills : India's Fight in the Middle East and North Africa'	F Borton 1944
Salmond J B	'The History of The 51st Highland Division 1939-1945'	Blackwood 1953
Nightingale P R Lt Col	'A History of The East Yorkshire Regiment (Duke of York's Own) In The War of 1939-1945'	William Sessions Ltd 1952
Synge W A T Cpt	'The Story of The Green Howards 1939-1945'	The Green Howards 1952
Lucas-Philips C E	'Victoria Cross Battles of The Second World War'	Pan Books 1964
Martin T A	'The Essex Regiment 1929-1950' Association 1952	Essex Regimental
Barnet C	'The Desert Generals'	Allen & Unwin 1960
Douglas K	'Alamein to Zem-Zem'	Faber 1946
Horrocks B - Sir Lt Gen	'A Full Life'	Cooper 1974
Messenger C	'The Tunisian Campaign'	Allan 1982
Ministry of Information	'The 8th Army'	HMSO

| Verney G L
Maj Gen' | The Desert Rats' | Hutchinson 1954 |

Other Sources
The Commonwealth War Graves Commission
The Imperial War Museum
The Public Records Office – Kew
The American Battle Monuments Commission - Europe
Regimental Museums of All Units Involved
Old Comrades Associations - Nationwide

APPENDIX A
The Fallen – Notes Letters
and Photographs

" I wasn't at the sharp end – but I knew a man who was! " Miss Joan Barker

Scots troops look for fallen friends in the Highland Division cemetery.
On the right is Roumana Ridge.

150101Z PTE ANDREW COLQUHOUN ROLLIE
7th BN ARGYLL AND SUTHERLAND HIGHLANDERS

Andrew Rollie was born in 1918 in the village of New Cumnock, Ayrshire. This was a mining village and he lived in one of the numerous miner's terraced houses near the colliery. He was educated locally and when he left school he worked delivering milk for a nearby farmer until he was put out of business with the coming of bottled milk. After that he worked at the pit-head until he was called up into the Militia – three months before the outbreak of war.

He was later placed in a Welsh Regiment and stationed in Northern Ireland, when on leave in 1940 he married Miss Mary Morris in Kirkconnell Church; it was about this time he was transferred to the 7th Argylls.

Andrew fought with the Argylls at El-Alamein. In January 1943 he was one of the 1,000 kilted soldiers who represented the 51st Highland Division in the 'Victory Parade' through the main streets of Tripoli – watched by Churchill and Montgomery. But he was soon back at the front fighting in the action at Mareth and later Akarit where he lost his life at the age of 24 years.

The following letter was sent to Mrs Mary Rollie regarding his death.

"It is with deep sorrow that I have to inform you of the death of your husband. He was killed on 6th April 1943, during the battle for the Gabes Gap.

I am unable to give you any information about your husband's death but I can assure you he endured no pain or suffering in his end. May I offer you the sincere sympathies of the platoon and myself in yours, the greatest of all losses. Your husband was one of the most popular lads in the company and his courage and cheerfulness during the battle was an inspiration to us all. His death means a great loss to the platoon.

At the little service held in the battle-field cemetery near his grave all those of us who were left were present and not a few shed some tears. May the Lord bless and comfort you and help you understand. I am –

Yours sincerely,

R M Gibb (Lieut). "

Pte Andrew C Rollie's body was never found, he is commemorated on the Medjez-El-Bab Memorial to the Missing. FACE 22.

4396428 PTE JOHN EVERILL SPENCE
7th BN THE GREEN HOWARDS

Pte John E Spence was the eldest of a family of six – three boys and three girls. His other brothers also served in the army but he was the only one to be killed. In 1995 his sister Mrs Everill Squires wrote to the author and commented upon her elder brother:

"John was very shy and would never want his photograph taken. My mother, however, managed to get him to get one taken for her; how we laughed when it duly arrived to find he had taken two of his mates with him. After John was killed his friend – then in the army – wrote to my mother and told her John never ever wanted to fight and kill, but they had decided England, home and family were a worthy cause. Also they couldn't live without the food supply from the USA : which lads were risking their lives to bring. They used to stand on the bridge at Grinton and talk of the Swaledale they came home to.

The last time I saw John he told me his unit had been visited by the King and Queen, the lads stood for hours on a very hot day in full kit as no-one knew at what time the Royal Party would arrive. One by one lads fainted and were dragged behind a hedge. John said he thought 'what's all this for'! At last the King and Queen arrived, the Queen Mother smiled and like a flash he said he realised what was at stake – the England we knew and loved would be gone.

The enclosed photograph (John – back row, l/h side) is the only one we've got, we never even had it copied because John wasn't really a soldier. Our family have the happiest memories of a brother who was especially kind, with more humour than the rest of us put together.
Yours sincerely, Everill Squires. "

Pte John E Spence's body was never found, he is commemorated on the Medjez-El-Bab Memorial to the Missing. FACE 18.

10601987 PTE PATRICK FRANCIS MCDONALD
5th BN EAST YORKSHIRE REGIMENT

Copy of letter of condolence sent to Mrs McDonald by Cpt Fenwick, 27 December 1943.

"My Dear Mrs McDonald,

My mother sent me a cutting from a Newcastle-on-Tyne newspaper in the hope I might be able to help you. I knew McDonald very well – I took him out from England and was talking with him only a couple of days before the battle at Wadi Akarit where he so tragically died. The actual attack in which he was killed was a tremendous job and it was through the gallantry of his company that we managed to get over the anti tank ditch and in amongst the Italians. All his coy officers were killed and many brave lads too.

I have spoken to an NCO who tells me it was all over in a second – no suffering I assure you. He is buried in a little cemetery specially made for the East Yorkshiremen after the battle.

I know how terrible to you his loss must have been, for he was a delightful cheery boy of whom I was very fond. It isn't much that I can say, but it is because of such men that we are now in the wonderful position that we are today. You must be very proud of him,

Yours Most Sincerely,
T G Fenwick Cpt 5th Bn East Yorkshire Regiment."

Pte P E McDonald is buried in Sfax War Cemetery: 11.C.26, aged 20 years, under his real name which is spelt McDonnell.

3185204 CPL JOHN MCGRATH
2nd BN SEAFORTH HIGHLANDERS

Copy of letter of condolence sent to his wife, Mrs Edith Cavell McGrath on 10 April 1943.

"Cpt J M Anderson 2nd Seaforth. M E F

Dear Mrs McGrath It is with great sorrow I write to sympathize with you on the great loss you have suffered by the death of your husband. I knew him very well, he had served in 'B' Company for a long time and the more I got to know him the more respect I had for him. He had often been chosen, or had volunteered for particularly nasty jobs that had to be done, and no-one doubted his great efficiency or his amazing courage.

He was killed on the morning of 6th April in the attack on the Akarit positions on Hill 112 : which was our objective. He got there with a few men and his company commander was badly wounded and corporal McGrath killed. He was buried at the foot of the Roumana Ridge, with the dead of the two Seaforth Battalions, by the Padre Rev' Macrae and a lament was played by pipers of both battalions. It was by the courage of men such as he that enabled us to win that very fierce battle. Please believe me when I say that he will be greatly missed by everyone in the company and that I am only expressing the sentiments felt by all here when I write this letter,

Yours Sincerely, John Anderson. "

Cpl John McGrath is buried in Sfax War Cemetery. 11.F.20 aged 32 years.

2765466 CPL LAURENCE RAMSAY
5th BN THE BLACK WATCH

Copy of extracts from a letter written to the author by Miss Joan Barker in 1995.

'Dear Mr Barnes,

Seeing the name 'Wadi Akarit' in our local paper brings memories flooding back to me of a soldier who died there. His name was Laurence Ramsay of the Black Watch, I was only seventeen when I first met Laurence in London – 1937. He joined up at the beginning of the war and our family moved to Devon. Laurence and I corresponded during the war and in his last letter he asked me to wait for him until the war was over. The next letter was from his mother telling me he had been killed at Wadi Akarit, in his uniform pocket was my photo : next to his heart as his mother liked to believe. His father was Indian, married to an English woman, he had one younger brother and two sisters; all very attractive with dark skins. I wasn't at the sharp-end – but I knew a man who was! When you are next at Wadi Akarit I would be very pleased if you would put a cross on his grave in memory of a gentle and charming man. He was the only person I lost in the Second World War, his mother continued to write to me until she died. I often think of Laurence and wonder if he had come back whether I would have married him?

Most Sincerely, Joan Barker (Miss). "

Corporal Laurence Ramsey now lies in Sfax War Cemetery. 11.E.4.

7915543 CPL FREDERICK BOWERING 4th COUNTY OF LONDON YEOMANRY: RAC

Cpl Frederick Bowering was educated in the city of Hull, East Yorkshire, at the Lime Street School. For many years before the war he was employed at a garage on Holderness Road and married Francis Lillian Bowering, they lived at 22 Rosemead Street. Frederick was a keen sportsman and was well known in boxing and football circles in Hull.

Copy of a letter to Mrs Bowering from Cpt G G Briggs (4th cly regarding her husband's death.

" Cpt G G Briggs 4th County of London Yeo. M E F
June 24th 1943

Dear Mrs Bowering I am writing to you to express my most sincere sympathy in your loss. 'Tubby', as your husband was always known was a familiar and popular figure in this squadron and though he had been with us only a short time he was well liked by all ranks. His troop leader, Lt M Richie, thought particularly highly of him. Your husband was wounded on 6th April at the Wadi Akarit, his regiment has been in much of the fighting since Alamein but never in such a tough battle. In the middle of the fighting your husband had to assume command of another tank, getting out of his own to do this while under fire - continuous fire from the enemy. He displayed the utmost calmness and continued in command until he was wounded. A shell landed on the turret of his tank and smashed his left arm badly, the other members of his crew behaved magnificently, they bound him up and gave him morphia and brought him out of the damaged tank. I personally saw him evacuated to the RAMC. He was not suffering for the morphia had mercifully taken effect, he died later from his wounds. It was after dark when the whole incident occurred : and I would like to assure you everything was done for him that could be done. In the same action we lost his troop leader Lt Richie. Your husband did not die in vain, though we had casualties. We did our job at the Wadi Akarit that a break through the enemies position was made, enabling the Eight Army to link up with the First Army, with what result you know. The names of the other members of the crew who were with him were:- Corporal Adams, L/Cpl Hicks and Trooper Dally.

I do assure you they looked after Tubby very well. Again, I would like o express my sincere sympathy,

Yours Sincerely,
G G Briggs."

Cpl Frederick Bowering's body was never found after the battle and ie is commemorated on the Medjez-El-Bab Memorial to the Missing: ACE 4 aged 29 yrs.

T COL DERECK ANTHONY SEAGRIM VC 'th BN THE GREEN HOWARDS

Dereck Seagrim was born at Bournemouth on ?4 September 1903, where his father was a :urate at St Peter's Mancroft Church. He was ine of three brothers who were all educated at <ing Edward VI School – entering its portals in he latter days of the First World War. Dereck ioon proved himself to be a good all-round iportsman; excelling at cricket, football and the ialf-mile race, often he would represent his ichool at these events on the playing-fields of Norwich in the shadow of the Cathedral. He vent on to the Military Academy at Sandhurst and was commissioned nto the Green Howards in September 1923. After two years at Dover his iattalion was sent to the West-Indies, from there to Palestine and on to ihanghai for anti-pirate duty; finally he did a stint with the King's African Rifles in Kenya.

His early war years were spent chiefly behind a desk as an Air Liaison Officer until his big chance at El-Alamein when he was given command if the 7th Battalion Green Howards. His arrival was greeted with iuspicion by some who were sceptical of his staff background, but if any Joubts remained by March 1943 they were quickly swept away as the 7th itormed the Mareth Line on 20/21 of that month. For his actions here he vas awarded the Victoria Cross, the official citation for his actions read is follows:-

" On the night of the 20/21st March 1943, the task of a battalion of The Green Howards was to attack and capture an important feature on the eft flank of the main attack on the Mareth Line. The defence of this 'eature was very strong and it was protected by an anti tank ditch twelve feet wide and eight feet deep with minefields on both sides. It formed a new part of the main defences of the Mareth Line and the successful capture of this feature was vital to the success of the main attack. From the time the attack was launched the battalion was subjected to the most intense fire from artillery, machine-guns and mortars and it appeared more than probable that the battalion would be held up entailing failure of the main attack. Realising the seriousness of the situation, Lieutenant Colonel Seagrim placed himself at the head of his battalion which was at the time suffering heavy casualties and led it through the hail of fire. He personally helped the team which was placing the scaling ladder over the anti tank ditch and was himself the first to cross it. He led the assault firing his pistol, throwing grenades, and personally assaulting two machine-gun posts which were holding up the advance of one of his companies. It is estimated that in this phase he killed or captured twenty Germans. This display of leadership and personal courage led directly to the capture of the objective.

When dawn broke the battalion was firmly established on the position which was of obvious importance to the enemy, who immediately made every effort to regain it. Every post was mortared and machine-gunned unmercifully and movement became practically impossible, but Lieutenant Colonel Seagrim was quite undeterred. He moved from post to post organising and directing the fire until the attackers were wiped out to a man.

By his valour, disregard for personal safety and outstanding example he so inspired his men that the battalion successfully took and held its objective thereby allowing the attack to proceed."

Lt Colonel Seagrim was never to know of his award as he was mortally wounded at the head of his men as he led them over the anti tank ditch at Akarit where they were held up; dying of his wounds the same day.

His brother, Lt Colonel Cyril Livian Seagrim OBE commented on Dereck in 1966:-

"Dereck was good at games and with his men, but over apprehensive and somewhat over-sensitive and diffident, not really a conventional hero at all, but he gained confidence in the rush of war".

His second brother Major Hugh Paul Seagrim GC DSO MBE served behind enemy lines in the hills of Burma, he was executed by the Japanese on 22 September 1944 and awarded the George Cross posthumously.

The War Memorial in Whissonsett Churchyard, Norfolk, bears the names of the Seagrim brothers and in 1985 the villagers of Whissonsett raised £1,000 to have a sign made dedicated to Dereck and Hugh. This was unveiled on Saturday 29 June by the last surviving brother and stands proudly in the village as a tribute to two brave men.

Lt Colonel Dereck Anthony Seagrim is buried in Sfax War Cemetery. XIC.C.21
Aged 39 years.

4387081 CSM JAMES GRAHAM OLIVER MM 6th BN THE GREEN HOWARDS

Copy of letter from CSM Oliver to his Aunt, in which he expresses his views on the German Nation and the reasons why he is fighting.

"4387081 CQMS J G Oliver   'B' Company 6th Bn Green Howards   M E F 6.4.42

Dear Auntie
It is Easter-time, a time when we should be thinking of the man who many years ago gave his life for the people of this earth that they should be free to enter the Kingdom of God, and today 2000 years later men are fighting and dying in the hope that this world may be freed from the scourge of a people who have proven time and time again, that they like to be lead by this type of evil men (Hitler). I'm beginning to think that the German people are all painted with the same brush, the atrocities that they have committed in Poland, Russia and other countries were committed by German Soldiers and Airmen they call themselves Nazis, we call them Bosche and many other names.

People who have not met them and seen some of the things that they have done and are doing every day, say it is not the wish of the German masses, the German masses like to read and hear about it and say nothing to their heathen masters, I call them heathen, but I make a mistake a heathen wouldn't do the things they do heathens do have a morality phrase in their religion and mode of living.
I hold no hate for the German Nation my feelings towards it are just the same as they would be for a mad dog 'destroy it before it bites again'.

When this war is over and if I do get out of it alive, I hope to start my life over again, it will be impossible for me to pick up where I left off, my

children are growing up and work will not be plentiful, I for one, wan
to see a Germany split up in such a manner that she will not be able to
cause for my children the misery and horror that she has caused for this
generation.

This is the thing that I for one am fighting for, and if in this fight
should be killed my death and many more will not, if this Germany is
split up, have been in vain, like all those men who in the last war gave
their lives to end war.

I've written this, it's been on my mind all this weekend and I just had
to get it off. I would like to have gone to church but circumstances would
not permit. I thought of you and uncle and all the people at home and
pray, that the scourge of this war should not reach the door-steps of
home as it has done for the Poles and Russians.

I received an augraph from you today, I'm so sorry I haven't written
to you in answer to all the letters I have received from you so I hope you
will forgive me.

How are things keeping? Does Mary appear to have altered since she
got married or is she just the same old Mary.

I had ideas in my head that when Mary got married you would come
down to the milder weather of the South and live with me when all this
war is settled with, but your last letter sounds as if you would rather
stay there in Sheffield and the home that you love.

Well Auntie this is all for the present so I will close with all my love
and one wish and this is, that God may spare us so that I meet again the
Auntie who has been both a mother and a friend to me.

Love Jim xxxxxx xxxxxx "

Copy of letter from CSM Oliver to Muriel and Eddie : February 1943,
two months before his death.

"CSM J G Oliver 'B' Company 6th Bn Green Howards M E F 7.2.43

Dear Muriel and Eddie

Here's to a speedy return, 'do you remember that toast', we were all
surprised to meet again the following weekend, I'm afraid it may be
quite a while before we do meet again. A lot has happened since then,
you have had Air Raids, I've seen death, stared it in the face, wondered
if it hurt when you did get your ticket. I have always managed to
wriggle out, covered thousands of miles by sea and land but never do I
seem to get any nearer to home, but who knows one of these days I'm

going to walk in on you when least expected, one never knows ones luck does one. Well Eddie, how's the beer situation? Its rank here, I've had about five bottles since November and now when we do manage a bottle we are drunk at the smell of it. How are things at home, Is Ivor called up yet? I wouldn't half smarten him up if he came to my company. Well I think this is all at the present, so I wish you love and best wishes, hoping that you and the children are in the best of health. Jim. "

Copy of letter from Cpt R Lofthouse, 6 June 1943 in which he comments on the circumstances of CSM Oliver's death.

"I am in receipt of your letter dated 2 June 1943 reference the late CSM Oliver MM. Sgt Maj Oliver was killed in the action fought by his Battalion at Akarit on April 6 1943 by a shell which dropped in Coy HQ during the attack. The CSM was killed outright and I can assure you that he did not suffer. He was given a burial service by our Army Padre in the Wadi Akarit and subsequently we had a cross made upon which was placed his badge of rank.

I can hardly express how deeply grieved the officers and men of this Company were at his death and he was a great loss to us. At that time I was second in command of the company, but previously I was in command at Mareth with him and he put up a magnificent show.

Please convey my feelings of deepest sympathy to Mrs Oliver in her great loss, the Company Commander at the time did write to her and I trust she received that letter.

Yours faithfully, R Lofthouse "

───────────────

In 1992 Mrs Oliver was contacted by Mr Bill Vickers MM who also served with the Green Howards at the Wadi Akarit. His version of CSM Oliver's death differs somewhat from Cpt Lofthouse's version.

"CSM Jim Oliver, your father, was our company Sgt Major. He was a very nice man, and quiet in spite of being a Sgt Major. Your father was killed at Wadi Akarit Tunisia 6th April 1943. His runner and the signaller were also killed, I forget their names. My mate, Sgt Rufty Hill was his nickname, and I where nearby and went to give what assistance we could to the three of them. Your father was still alive when we reached them. These were the only words he spoke before he died, 'tell my wife, tell my wife'. So he must of loved your mother very much for him to think about her at a time like that. We buried them where they had fallen, I suppose that later they would have been reinterred at a war cemetery."

CSM James G Oliver MM is buried in Sfax War Cemetery. 30.II.D.21 Aged 30 yrs.

APPENDIX B

The Highland Division Cemetery at Akarit, April 1943. In the forground can be seen
the steep sides of the Wadi-Akarit and to the rear stands Roumana Ridge.

List of the Fallen

gives Name, Rank, Number, Awards, Date of Birth, Unit, Age, Home
Address and Place of Burial or Commemoration.

SFAX WAR CEMETERY

ABBEY, Private, BERNARD WILLIAM 4399176. 7th Bn. Green Howards (Yorkshire Regt.) 6 April 1943 Age 23. Son of Walter and Elizabeth Abbey, Husband of Gertrude Abbey, of Middlesbrough, Yorkshire. M.C.8

ADAMS, Private, JOHN, 4346941. 5th Bn. East Yorkshire Regt. 6 April 1943 Age 26. Sonof Alfred and Alice Adams, of Hull II.D.18

ADAMSON, Captain, DOUGLAS EDGAR, 219912. 7/10th Bn. Argyll and Sutherland Highlanders. 6 April 1943 Age 34. Son of William Charles and Emmie Adamson; Husband of Pamela Mary Adamson, of High Wycombe, Buckinghamshire. II.A.7

AFFLECK, Driver, SAMUEL, T/139723. 523 Gen. Transport Coy., Royal Army Service Corps. 5 April 1943 Age 26. Son of Thomas and Agnes Affleck, of Crosshill, Glasgow. XI.C.16.

AINSCOUGH, Sapper, GEORGE, 1948625.276 Field Coy., Royal Engineers. 7 April 1943 Age 21. Son of George and Elizabeth Ainscough, of Marshside, Southport, Lancashire. II.B.7.

AISBITT, Private, GEORGE DESMOND, 3322719. 7th Bn. Black Watch. 6 April 1943 Age 23. Son of William James Aisbitt and Eunice Aisbitt, of West Hartlepool, Co. Durham III.A.8

ALEXANDER, Private, JAMES ALLAN, 2930983. 5th Bn. Queen's Own Cameron Highlanders. 6 April 1943 Age 23. Son of William R and EM Alexander, of Walton, Liverpool. II.A10

ALEXANDER, Private, THOMAS, 2754385. 5th Bn. Black Watch. 7 April 1943 Age 33. Son of David and Agnes Alexander; Husband of Jamesina Barbara Carol Alexander, of Aberdeen. III.B.1.

ALLEN, Private, GEORGE ANDERSON, 2761963. 7/10th Bn. Argyll and Sutherland Highlanders. 6 April 1943 Age 20. Son of Albert and Mary Allen, of Edinburgh. III.B.23

ALLEN, Private, THOMAS HEWLETT, 6021779. 1/4th Bn. Essex Regiment. 6 April 1943 Age 26. Son of Thomas Hewlett Allen and Kitty Alice Allen, of Highams Park, Essex. XI.B.10

ALLISON, Private, JOHN, 2827214. 2nd Bn. Seaforth Highlanders. 6 April 1943 Age 31. Son of John and Agnes Allison, of Paisley, Renfrewshire; Husband of Jean T. W. Allison of Paisley. III.E2

ANDERSON, Private, ERIC, V C, 4347754. 5th Bn. East Yorkshire Regt. 6 April 1943 Age 27. Son of George and Mary Ann Anderson, of Fagley, Yorkshire; Husband of Irene Anderson, of Fagley. IIIC.14

ANDERSON, Private, FREDERICK, 7043739. 2nd Bn. Seaforth Highlanders. 6 April 1943 Age 25. III.D.17.

ANDERSON, Private, GEORGE, 2753272. 7th Bn. Black Watch. 6 April 1943 Age 39. Son of George and Jane Hogg Anderson; Husband of Catherine Anderson, of Hill of Beath, Crossgates, Fife. III.A.2

ANGUS, Lance Corporal, JOHN ROBINSON, 2828699. 2nd Bn. Seaforth Highlanders. 6 April 1943 Age 32. Son of Joseph and Sarah Angus, of Bedlington, Northumberland; Husband of Alice Angus, of Bedlington. III.B.7.

ARCHIBALD, Private JOHN, 2984898. 7/10th Bn. Argyll and Sutherland Highlanders. 6 April 1943 Age 22. Son of William Hugh and Catherine Archibald, of Possilpark, Glasgow. II.B.2.

ATKINSON, Lieutenant, JOHN ALLEN, 235334. East Yorkshire Regt. Border Regiment. 6 April 1943 Age 32. Son of George Frederick and Dorothy Norah Atkinson, of Blackpool, Lancashire. Chartered Accountant. VII.A.13

BAHADUR SINGH, Sapper, 27845. KGVs O. Bengal Sappers & Miners. 6 April 1943 Age 19. Son of Mangal Singh, of Bunga Amir Singh, Atari, Montgomery, India. H.D.7

BAILEY, Private, ARTHUR, 3860624. 5th Bn. East Yorkshire Regt. 6 April 1943 Age 25. Nephew of Annie Bailey, of Bolton, Lancashire. III.E.20.

BAILEY, Sergeant, NORMAN HENRY, 4384264. 6th Bn. Green Howards (Yorkshire Regt.) 6 April 1943 Age 38. Son of Walter Ernest and Lilly Bailey; Husband of Lily Sophia Bailey, of Middlesbrough, Yorkshire VII.E.8.

BAINES, Private JOHN WILLIAM, 3322727. 7th Bn. Black Watch. 6 April 1943 Age 23. Son of William and Ellen Baines, of Shildon, Co. Durham. III.A.5.

BAIRD, Private, ALAN GEORGE, 3654042. 7th Bn. Green Howards (Yorkshire Regt.) 6 April 1943 Age 22. Son of James and Jane Harvest Raynes Baird, of Grappenhall, Cheshire, VII.A.17.

BALDWIN, Lieutenant, JOHN ROWLAND SCHOLFIELD, M.C. 182558. Attached to King George's Own Sappers & Miners. Royal Engineers. 6 April 1943 Age 22. Son of Edwin and Gladys Baldwin, of Burscough, Lancashire. VII.A.1.

BALE RAM, Rifleman, 23212. 6th Rajputana Rifles. 4 April 1943 Age 23. Son of Harkey, of Baland, Rohtak, India; Husband of Sh. Bharto, of Baland. H.D.2.

BARON, Private, JOHN, 4349366. 5th Bn. East Yorkshire Regt. 6 Apri 1943 Age 31. Son of John D Baron and Mary Baron (nee Cottingham), o: Hull; Nephew of Alice Lawson, of Hull. II.C.19.

BARRETT. Corporal, EDWARD FRANCIS, 6021794. 1/4th Bn. Esse× Regiment. 6 April 1943 Age 28. Son of Edward and Lillian France: Barrett, of Catford, London. VII.E.13.

BARWICK, Private, VICTOR LANCELOT, 4802106. 2nd Bn. Seaforth Highlanders. 6 April 1943 Age 23. Son of Mrs RL Barwick; Stepson of R Childs, of Grantham, Lincolnshire. III.D.6.

BEACHY-HEAD, Gunner, MICHAEL ERIC, 1095847. 102 Northumberland Hussars. 6 April 1943 Age 19. Son of Eric Beachy-Head and Marguerite Beachy-Head, of Salisbury, Southern Rhodesia. III.E.18.

BEATTIE, Private, JAMES, 2828322. 2nd Bn. Seaforth Highlanders. 6 April 1943 Age 29. Son of James and Jeanie Beattie, of Kilbirnie, Ayrshire. III.D.5.

BEATY, Lt. James Herbert. 64454. The King's Rgt. (Liverpool), Attd. 5th Bn. East Yorkshire Rgt. 6th April 1943. Age 28. Son of Richard Herbert and Grace Gertrude Beaty of Rhyl, Flintshire.

BELL, Major, O M, MBE, 134777. 31 Road Constr. Coy., S. African Engineer Corps. 7 April 1943 Age 37. Son of William H and Helen M Bell; Husband of Eileen PC Bell, of Port Elizabeth, South Africa. (B.Sc Eng.), A.M.I.C.E. VI. E.23.

BENNETT, Private, GEORGE MCLEOD COURTNEY, 2930570. 5th Bn. Queen's Own Cameron Highlanders. 6 April 1943 Age 22. II.A.17.

BENZIES, Gunner, ALEXANDER STEWART, 2885534. 149th A/Tk Regt (Lancs Yeo), R.A. 6 April 1943 Age 27. Son of Alexander and Lillie Benzies, of Aberdeen. II.D.14

BERTENSHAW, Private, EDWARD, 4459959. 7th Bn. Green Howards (Yorkshire Regt.) 8 April 1943 Age 25. XIV.F.14.

BHUPAL THAPA, Jemadar, 15295/IO. 1st Bn. 9th Gurkha Rifles. 7 April 1943 Age 34. Son of Dhanbahadur and Chame, of Sallyan, Chandrakot, Gulmi, Nepal; Husband of Somatri, of Sallyan. H.B.9.

BISH, Lance Corporal, EDWARD VICTOR, 6402426. 1st Bn. Royal Sussex Regiment. 6 April 1943 Age 31. Son of Edward James Bish and Phoebe Ellen Bish; Husband of Daisy Clara Bish, of Portslade, Suzzed. VII.E.24.

BLACKMORE, Private FRANK, 2762311. 5th Bn. Black Watch. 7 April 1943 Age 29. Son of Frank Ernest and Alice Blackmore, of Moston, Manchester; Husband of Irene Blackmore, of Moston. III.E.3.

BLACKWELL, Captain, ALAN ARTHUR, Mentioned in Despatches, 137958. 5th Bn. East Yorkshire Regt. 6 April 1943 Age 26. Son of Frederick and Annie Elizabeth Blackwell, of Whitton, Middlesex; Husband of Marjorie Joan Blackwell. VII.A.14.

BLAKEMAN, Private, RICHARD HERBERT, 6009542. 1/4th Bn. Essex Regiment. 6 April 1943 Age 28. Son of Richard William and May Amelia Blakeman; Husband of Ivy Henrietta Blakeman, of Southend-on-Sea, Essex. VII.E.14.

BLUNDELL, Lieutenant Colonel, JOHN HIGHT, DSO, 17207 Attached to King George's Own Sappers & Miners. Royal Engineers. 6 April 1943 Age 41. Son of Maj. Alfred Hubert Blundell and Amelia Woodward Blundell, of Appletreewick, Yorkshire. XIII.A.6

BLYTH, Lt. Benjamin Hall. 113739. The Royal Scotts. (The Royal Rgt). Attd. 2nd Bn, Seaforth Highlanders. 6th April, 1943. Age 23. Son of Benjamin Hall Blyth and Agnes Tullis Blyth of Edinburgh.

BOARER, Private, VICTOR, 6402685. 1st Bn. Royal Sussex Regiment. 6 April 1943 Age 24. Son of Luke and Emily Boarer, of Shortgate, Sussex. VII. E.23.

BODLEY, Corporal ERIC ANGUS, 2819810. 2nd Bn. Seaforth Highlanders. 6 April 1943 Age 24. Son of Fred and Christina Bodley. II.F.3.

BOLAS, Private, ALBERT, 4467643. 2nd Bn. Seaforth Highlanders. 6 April 1943 Age 32. II.F.21.

BOLTON, Private, ERNEST, 4345937. 5th Bn. East Yorkshire Regt. 6 April 1943 Age 33. Son of John Fennel Bolton and Sarah Jane Bolton, of Hull; Husband of Madge Bolton, of Hull. III.E.26.

BOOTH, Private, PERCY, 3132831. 5th Bn. Queen's Own Cameron Highlanders. Royal Scots Fusiliers. 6th April 1943 Age 25. Son of Herbert and Emma Booth, of Ossett, Yorkshire. II.A.24

BOOTH, Private, SIDNEY ROBERT FRAMWELL, 4391006. 7th Bn. Green Howards (Yorkshire Regt.) 6 April 1943 Age 33. Son of Thomas Ernest and Sarah Helen Booth; Husband of Hilda Booth, of Scarborough, Yorkshire. VII.A.26.

BOUCH, Private, JOHN REX, 14201323. 5th Bn. Queen's Own Cameron Highlanders. 6 April 1943 Age 21. Son of Ernest and Hilda Bouch, of Billingham, Co. Durham. III.D.36.

BREMNER, Lance Corporal, ALEXANDER, 2822888. 5th Bn. Seaforth Highlanders. 6 April 1943 Age 22. Son of Alexander and Jessie Bremner, of Wick, Caithness-shire. II.F.13.

BRENNAN, Sergeant, THOMAS MICHAEL, 2933136. 5th Bn. Queen's Own Cameron Highlanders. 1 April 1943 Age 27. Son of T and Gertrude Brennan, of Batley, Yorkshire. VII.C.10.

BRETT, Private, JOHN STEPHEN, 4399539. 7th Bn. Green Howards (Yorkshire Regt.) 6 April 1943 Age 20. Son of Olive Brett, of Stockton-on-Tees, Co. Durham. VII.A.21

BROAD, Private, CYRIL ALBERT, 6022965. 1/4th Bn. Essex Regiment. 6 April 1943 Age 27. Son of John Frederick and Florence Elizabeth Broad, of Paddington, London. XIII.E.2.

BROWN, Private, HARRY, 4344541. 5th Bn. East Yorkshire Regt. 6 April 1943 Age 27. Son of Mr & Mrs John William Brown, of Thurscoe, Yorkshire. II.C.21.

BROWN, Private, JOHN PETER, 4350930. 5th Bn. East Yorkshire Regt. 6 April 1943 Age 21. Son of Arthur Brown and Emma Brown, of Bentley, Doncaster, Yorkshire. II.C.24.

BROWN, Lance Corporal, JOHN WILSON, 2825466. 2nd Bn. Seaforth Highlanders. 6 April 1943 Age 26. Son of Peter and Catherine Brown, of Paisley, Renfrewshire. III.E.1.

BROWNLEE, Lance Corporal, WALTER RENWICK, 3191704. 5th Bn. Queen's Own Cameron Highlanders. 6 April 1943 Age 24. Son of James and Dora Matilda Brownlee, of Selkirk. II.A.14.

BULLOCK, Lance Corporal, JOSEPH, 4349870. 5th Bn. East Yorkshire Regt. 7 April 1943 Age 32. XIV.D.26.

BURGESS, Private, GEORGE, 2821864. 2nd Bn. Seaforth Highlanders. 6 April 1943 Age 24. Son of Myles Burgess and Sarah Burgess, of Elderslie, Renfrewshire. II.F.24

BURNETT, Private, ALEX, 3193255. 2nd Bn. Seaforth Highlanders. 6 April 1943 Age 31. Son of William Finlayson Burnett and Helen Yates Burnett; Husband of Jeannie Burnett. II.F.6

BURNS, Private, GEORGE, 4392273. 7th Bn. Green Howards (Yorkshire Regt.) 6 April 1943 Age 24 VII.A.25.

BUTLER, Lance Corporal, JULIUS LANGTHURNE, 6470919. 5th Bn. Seaforth Highlanders. 6 April 1943 Age 28. Son of Julius Cogan Butler and Rose Elizabeth Butler; Husband of Caroline Rose Butler, of Brentford, Middlesex. II.E2.

BUTTERY, Private FRANK, 4539649. 5th Bn. East Yorkshire Regt. 6 April 1943 Age 24. Son of Mr & Mrs Frank Buttery, of Leeds, Yorkshire. II.C.10.

CAIN, Private, ALEXANDER, 3191783. 7/10th Bn. Argyll and Sutherland Highlanders. 6 April 1943 Age 24. Son of Daniel and Isabella Cain; Husband of Annie Mary Cain, of Whityorn, Wigtownshire. III.B.18

CALEY, Private, ALBERT, 4396519. 7th Bn. Green Howards (Yorkshire Regt.) 6 April 1943 Age 20. Son of Joseph and Alice May Caley, of Redcar, Yorkshire. II.C.2.

CAMPBELL, Gunner, JAMES, 1945149. 102 Northumberland Hussars. 5 April 1943 Age 29. Son of Hugh and Jessie Campbell, of Crieff, Perthshire. III.E.19.

CAMPBELL, Sergeant, JAMES, 2987318. 7/10 Bn. Argyll and Sutherland Highlanders. 6 April 1943 Age 26. Son of Hugh and Elizabeth Campbell, of Glasgow; Husband of Rose Campbell. II.E.24.

CAMPBELL, Corporal, STEPHEN MCLEAN, 3318791. 7th Bn. Black Watch. 6 April 1943 Age 25. III.A.26.

CAMPION, Sgt. Ronald. 7891637. 40th (7th Bn The King's Rgt ; Liverpool) Royal Tank Rgt, RAC. 6th April 1943. Age 30. Son of John and Margaret Campion of Liverpool; Husband of Lillian May Campion of Kirkdale, Liverpoool.

CARTER, Private, JAMES GERALD, 4132074. 2nd Bn. Cheshire Regiment. 6 April 1943 Age 21. Son of Samuel and Catherine Carter, of Liverpool. XIV.F.6.

CHANAN SINGH, Signalman, a/4644. Indian Signal Corps. 5-6 April 1943 Age 20. Son of Inder Singh and Santi, of Chak Hira Singh, Pakka, Patiala, India. H.B.4.

CHANDLER, Guardsman, JOHN ANSON, 2663365. 3rd Bn. Coldstream Guards. 7 April 1943 Age 24. XIV.F.18.

CHRISTISON, Lieutenant, JOHN ALISTAIR, 197228. 7th Black Watch. 6 April 1943 III.A.14.CHURCHILL, Private, ERIC SIDNEY, 2824327. 5th Bn. Seaforth Highlanders. 6 April 1943 Age 24. Son of Arthur Robert and Ethel Churchill; Husband of Elizabeth Churchill, of Boston Spa, Yorkshire. III. B.11.

CLARK, Corporal, Alexander Lang, 2825469. 5th Bn. Seaforth Highlanders. 6 April 1943 Age 29. Son of Alexander and Jane GL Clark, of Greenock, Renfrewshire. II.F.26.

CLARK, Private, ROBERT, 2762006. 1st Bn. Black Watch. 6-7 April 1943 Age 29. II.B.19.

CLARK, Corporal, THOMAS FREDERICK, 4345396. 6th Bn. Green Howards (Yorkshire Regt.) 6 April 1943 Age 24. VII.E.7.

CLARK, Private WILLIAM MCKINLAY, 2828437. 2nd Bn. Seaforth Highlanders. 6 April 1943 Age 23. Son of James A & Jean McKinley Clark, of Beith, Ayrshire. III.D.1.

CLARKE, Private, THOMAS, 4920802. 7th Bn. Green Howards (Yorkshire Regt.) 6 April 1943 Age 27. II.C.1.

COOK, Sergeant. NORMAN FRANCIS, 1060277. 242 Bty. 61st Anti Tank Rgt Royal Artillery. 4 April 1943 Age 39. Son of Frank Henry and Alice Cook, of Caerphilly. XIII.C.14.

COOK, Private, THOMAS, 7948425. 5th Bn. East Yorkshire Regt. 6 April 1943 Age 20. Son of Thomas and Annie Cook, of Sheffield. II.C.13

COPPING, Private, ERNEST, 4344223. 5th Bn. East Yorkshire Regt. 6 April 1943 Age 27. XIV.C.24.

COUBROUGH, Private, ARCHIBALD CLACHER, 3191279. 2nd Bn. Seaforth Highlanders. 6 April 1943 Age 23. Son of James and Agnes Coubrough, of Glasgow. III.D.15.

COWAN, Private, WILLIAM GEORGE, 2822703. 5th Bn. Seaforth Highlanders. 6 April 1943 Age 28. Son of Alexander and Annabella Cowan; Husband of Williamina Cowan, of Sanday, Orkney. III.D.25.

CREARIE, Corporal, WILLIAM, 2827289. 2nd Bn. Seaforth Highlanders. 6 April 1943 Age 28. Son of John and Jane Crearie, of Glasgow; Husband of Elizabeth Crearie, of Glasgow. III.B.3.

CRUMP, Private, FREDERICK GEORGE, 5628824. 6th Bn. Green Howards (Yorkshire Regt.) 6 April 1943 Age 22. Son of Augustus John and Beatrice Maude Crump, of Exminster, Devon. II.D.22.

DALTON, Private, THOMAS, 2933816. 5th Bn. Queen's Own Cameron Highlanders. 6 April 1943 Age 25. Son of T & Margaret Dalton, of Eastriggs, Dumfriesshire. III.B.9

DEAN, Private, JAMES, 2825793. 2nd Bn. Seaforth Highlanders. 6 April 1943 Age 29. Son of Thomas and Matilda Dean, of Greenock, Renfrewshire. III.B.2.

DEANS, Private, JOHN, 2829039. 2nd Bn. Seaforth Highlanders. 6 April 1943 Age 21. Son of Michael and Bessie Deans, of Gallowhill, Paisley, Renfrewshire. II.F.4.

DERRY, Lance Corporal, JOHN, 3318235. 5/7th Bn. Gordon Highlanders. 5 April 1943 Age 23. VI.B.15.

DEWBERRY, Private, ARTHUR LESLIE, 2764705. 5th Bn. Black Watch. 7 April 1943 Age 33. Husband of Amy Ada Dewberry, of Stoke Newington, London. II.F.2.

DICK, Corporal, EBENEZER, 2821827. 2nd Bn. Seaforth Highlanders. 6 April 1943 Age 24. Son of Ebenezer and Agnes Dick, of Greenock, Renfrewshire. III.D.4.

DRUMMOND, Lance Corporal, JOHN, 2986559. 7/10th Bn. Argyll and Sutherland Highlanders. 6 April 1943 Age 25. Son of John and Annie Drummond, of Alva, Clackmannanshire. II.B.1.

DUCK, Private, RICHARD BOWMAN, 4272419. 1/7th Bn. Middlesex Regiment. 6 April 1943 Age 21. Son of George and Annie Duck, of Robin Hood's Bay, Yorkshire. II.E.14.

DUNBAR, Private, ROBERT SUTHERLAND, 2820926. 5th Bn. Seaforth Highlanders. 6 April 1943 Age 23. Son of Ben and Jean Dunbar, of Watten, Caithness-shire. III.D.22.

DUNNETT, Private, ALEXANDER, 2829431. 2nd Bn. Seaforth Highlanders. 8 April 1943 Age 28. Son of John and Alison Dunnett, of Bowermadden. Caithness-shire. XIV.F.21.

DURRAND, Lance Corporal, JAMES BRENNAR, 2822255. 5th Bn. Seaforth Highlanders. 6 April 1943 Age 22. III.D.24.

EDGELL, Private, EDWIN GEORGE, 6014457. 1/4th Bn. Essex Regiment. 6 April 1943 Age 24. Son of Charles and Mary Edgell, of Dagenham, Essex. VII.E.12.

EDNEY, Private, JAMES, 4749266. 7th Bn. Green Howards (Yorkshire Regt.) 6 April 1943 Age 24. Son of James and M Edney, of Greenford, Middlesex. II.C.3.

EDWARDS, Private, WILLIAM HENRY JAMES, 14200427. 2nd Bn. Seaforth Highlanders. 6 April 1943 Age 20. Son of Alfred and Catherine Louisa Edwards, of Ryde, Isle of Wight. II.F.9.

EVERIN, Private, EDGAR, 3860146. 7/10th Bn. Argyll and Sutherland Highlanders. 6 April 1943 Age 28. Son of Fred and Emily Gertrude Everin; Husband of Gladys Everin, of Horwich, Lancashire. III.B.15.

FAIRHURST, Private JOHN, 2934672. 5th Bn. Queen's Own Cameron Highlanders. 6 April 1943 Age 23. Son of John and Olive Fairhurst, of Cadishead, Lancashire. II.A.9.

FARMELO, Signalman, ERNEST, 2583549. Royal Corps of Signals. 7 April 1943 Age 22. Son of Ernest and Edith Farmelo, of Plumstead, London. XIV.D.21.

FARRELL, Private, PETER, 14201648. 5th Bn. East Yorkshire Regt. 6 April 1943 Age 21. Son of Francis and Edith Farrell, of Birmingham. II.C.11.

FISHER, Captain, EDWARD MASON, 87275. 'A' Sqdn., 40th (7th Bn. The King's Regiment) Royal Tank Rgt. RAC. 6 April 1943 Age 22. Son of William Edward and Margaret Noel Fisher, of Liverpool. II.B.18.

FISHER, Private, WILLIAM, 2766766. 7th Bn. Black Watch. 6 April 1943 Age 32. Son of William and Catherine Fisher, of Dundee; Husband of Isabella Lamond Fisher, of Mid Craigie, Dundee. III.A.24.

FITZSIMMONS, Private, HENDRY CROMBIE, 2823296. 5th Bn. Seaforth Highlanders. 6 April 1943 Age 23. Son of Quintin and Mary Fitzsimmons, of Bishopton, Renfrewshire. III.B.13.

FLUGEL, Lieutenant JOHN FRANCIS, 189543. 2nd Bn. Seaforth Highlanders. 6 April 1943 Age 31. Son of Bernard John and Mabel Kate Flugel; Husband of Mary Flugel, of Hendon, Middlesex. III.E.13.

FOGGIN, Private, JACIE, 4392850. 7th Bn. Green Howards (Yorkshire Regt.) 6 April 1943 Age 24. Son of Thomas William and Alice Maud Foggin, of Middlesbrough, Yorkshire. VII.A.12.

FORBES, Lance Corporal, GILBERT, 2762034. 1st Bn. Black Watch. 6-7 April 1943 Age 27. Son of Andrew and Mary Forbes, of Dundee. II.B.20.

FOX, Private, LESLIE, 4390834. 7th Bn. Green Howards (Yorkshire Regt.) 6 April 1943 Age 23. Son of John and Sarah Ann Fox, of Beverley, Yorkshire. VII.A.19.

FRASER, Private, ALISTER, 2880691. 5th/7th Bn Gordon Highlanders. 4 April 1943 Age 27. Son of William McIntosh Fraser and Flora McDonald Fraser; Husband of Margaret Fraser, of Dyce, Aberdeenshire. VI.B.18.

FRASER, Private, MALCOLM, 2824520. 5th Bn. Seaforth Highlanders. 6 April 1943 Age 25. Son of John and Annie Fraser, of Inverness. III.D.7.

GARDNER, Sapper, WILLIAM THOMAS, 1877305. 505 Field Coy., Royal Engineers. 7 April 1943 Age 25. Son of Fredrick Henry and Edith Katherine Gardner, of Stockingford, Nuneaton, Warwickshire. II.E.17.

GARNISH, Private, ARTHUR, 28160143. 2nd Bn. Seaforth Highlanders. 6 April 1943 Age 38. III.D.16.

GAVIN, Private, WILLIAM TERENCE, 2983033. 7/10th Bn. Argyll and Sutherland Highlanders. 8 April 1943 Son of James and Mary Gavin, of Stirling. III.B.26.k

GAYLARD, Captain, DERRICK WILLIAM, MC, 99819. 1st Bn. Royal Sussex Regiment. 6 April 1943 Age 30. Son of William Frederick and Caroline Jessie Gaylard, of South Croydon, Surrey. VII.E.20.

GILCHRIST, Sergeant, JOHN, 7654215. 61st Anti-Tank Regt., Royal Artillery. 6 April 1943 III.B.19.

GILL, Private, GEORGE QUAYLE, 4127275. 2nd Bn. Cheshire Regiment. 6 April 1943. Son of Robert and Hannah Mayers Gill, of Birkenhead. VII.E.5.

GIVENS, Lt. William Logie. 180034. The Royal Scotts . (The Royal Rgt) Attd. 2nd Bn. Seaforth Highlanders. 6th April, 1943. Age 31. Son of Peter and Margaret Logie Givens, of East Wymiss, Fife. Husband of Jean Givens, of Wymiss.

GLOVER, Private, LESLIE, 4547536. 5th Bn. East Yorkshire Regt. 6 April 1943 Age 20. II.C.16.

GODFREY, Private, JAMES WILLIAM HENRY, 4384642. 6th Bn. Green Howards (Yorkshire Regt.) 6 April 1943 Age 38. II.E.11.

GOODWIN, Lance Corporal, CHARLES LESLIE, 6014881. 1/4th Bn. Essex Regiment. 6 April 1943 Age 21. Son of George Charles and Minnie Goodwin, of Dagenham, Essex. VII.E.11.

GORDON, Captain, DOUGLAS MALCOLM, 194920. 5th Bn. Seaforth Highlanders. 6 April 1943 Age 25. Son of Mr & Mrs Alexander Paterson Gordon, of Portmahomack, Ross and Cromarty. III.E.4.

GORMLEY, Private, JAMES, 3716041. 5th Bn. Queen's Own Cameron Highlanders. 6 April 1943 Age 28. Son of James and Charlotte Gormley, of Blackburn, Lancashire; Husband of Margaret A Gormley, of Blackburn. II.A.18.

GORRIE, Private, JAMES CHRISTOPHER, 2760349. 7/10th Bn. Argyll and Sutherland Highlanders. 6 April 1943 Age 29. Son of Robert and Christina Gorrie, of Lochee, Dundee. II.E.23.

GRAY, Private, ALEXANDER, 2759781. 7th Bn. Black Watch. 6 April 1943 Age 26. Son of Elizabeth Gray, of Edinburgh; Husband of Ann Jane Gray, of Edinburgh. III.A.4.

GRAY, Lieutenant, WILLIAM JOHN DUFF, 184823. 5th Bn. Seaforth Highlanders. 6 April 1943 Age 22. Son of George Alexander Gray and Jessie McNaughton Gray, of Edinburgh. III.E.6.

GREEN, Trooper, HARRY, 3456346. 40th (7th Bn. The King's Regiment) Royal Tank Regiment. 6 April 1943 Age 28. Son of Harry and Sarah Alice Green; Husband of Nora Green, of Greenfield, Lancashire. II.E.19.

GREEN, Lance Corporal, JOHN, 4394014. 7th Bn. Green Howards (Yorkshire Regt.) 6 April 1943 Age 24. Son of Mrs A Brookes, of Sandhill, Rotherham, Yorkshire. VII.A.22.

GREEN, Private JOHN, 345830. 7th Bn. Green Howards (Yorkshire Regt. 6 April 1943 Age 26. XIV.C.26.

GREEN, Signalman, RONALD BRUNTON, 2381094. Royal Corps o Signals. 7 April 1943 Age 20. Son of Ralph and Ada Green, of Shiney Row, Co. Durham. XIV.D.25.

GREGORY, Private, ALFRED, 4350865. 5th Bn. East Yorkshire Regt. (April 1943 Age 23. Son of Henry and Mary Emma Gregory, of Sheffield II.C.20.

GRIFFITHS, Private, WILLIAM HENRY, 3325252. 7th Bn. Black Watch 6 April 1943 Age 21. Son of William E and Ada Griffiths, o Middlesbrough, Yorkshire. III.A.11.

GUNNINGHAM, Private, WILLIAM HENRY, 13048250. 1st Bn. Roya Sussex Regiment. 6 April 1943 Age 29. Son of Laura Gunningham Stepson of Thomas Harris, of Bridgwater, Somerset. VII.E.21.

GUTHRIE, Major, BRUCE CAMPBELL, 180229. 5th Bn. Black Watch. 1 April 1943 Age 28. Son of Ernest Fairbairn Guthrie and Dorothy Leigh Guthrie. VII.C.23.i

HADDEN, Lance Sergeant, ARCHIBALD MITCHELL, 3323790. 7th Bn Black Watch. 6 April 1943 Age 30. Son of Alexander and Elizabeth Hadden, of Edinburgh; Husband of Ethel Hadden, of Edinburgh. III.A.19

HALL, Private, JOHN, 2990357. 7/10th Bn. Argyll and Sutherland Highlanders. 6 April 1943 Age 23. Son of Thomas Bird Hall and Isabella Redpath Hall, of Edinburgh. II.A.3.

HALL, Lance Corporal, WALTER, 4395545. 6th Bn. Green Howards (Yorkshire Regt.) 6 April 1943 Age 28. Son of John Mather Hall and Jane Hall, of Dinnington Colliery, Northumberland. II.E.7.

HAMILTON, Private, JAMES, 2829281. 7th Bn. Black Watch. 6 April 1943 Age 20. Son of William and Jeanie Hamilton, of Glasgow. III.A.21.

HAMP, Lieutenant, JOHN COLIN, M.C., 153410. 5th Bn. Queen's Own Cameron Highlanders. 6 April 1943 Age 25. Son of John and Jessie Hamp; Husband of Mary Hamp, of Leighton Buzzard, Bedfordshire II.A.25.

HANN, Private, ROBERT, 5052379. 1st Bn. Black Watch. 6-7 April 1943 Age 26. Son of Charles and Elizabeth Hann, of Endon, Staffordshire Husband of Renee Hann, of Endon. II.B.21.

HARDING, Private, TURNER, 4395369. 6th Bn. Green Howards (Yorkshire Regt.) 6 April 1943 Age 26. VII.E.9.

HARRIS, Corporal, GERALD PERCIVAL SETH, 6012265. 1/4th Bn. Essex Regiment. 6 April 1943 Age 31. Son of William Seth and Daisy Catherine Harris, of Teddington, Middlesex. XI.B.11.

HARRISON, Private, JOSEPH, 4131034. 1/7th Bn. Middlesex Regiment. 6 April 1943 Age 23. Son of Joseph and Catherine Harrison, of Skerton, Lancaster. II.E.15.

HARRISON, Sergeant, STEPHEN, MM, 402213. 40th (7th Bn. The King's Regiment) Royal Tank Rgt. RAC. 6 April 1943 Age 31. Son of Alfred and Teresa Harrison; Husband of Irene E Harrison, of Gipsyville, Hull. XIV.D.10.

HART, Private, FRANCIS JOSEPH, 2990366. 7/10th Bn. Argyll and Sutherland Highlanders. 8 April 1943 Age 28. Son of Ernest Edward Hart and Rose Buckell Hart, of Possilpark, Glasgow; Husband of Anna Hart. III.B.25.

HAWKSWORTH, Private, WILLIAM, 14209356. 2nd Bn. Seaforth Highlanders. 6 April 1943 Age 22. Son of Horace R and Mary J Hawksworth, of Moor End. Cleckheaton, Yorkshire. III.E.15.

HEAVISIDE, Private, THOMAS WILLIAM, 44566678. 7th Bn. Black Watch. 6 April 1943 Age 22. Son of John and Margaret Heaviside, of Evenwood, Co. Durham. III.A.22.

HEMMINGS, Corporal, ROBERT EDWARD, 5118840. 5th Bn. East Yorkshire Regt. 6 April 1943 Age 28. II.C.23.

HENDERSON, Lance Corporal, THOMAS MORRISON, 2885200. 5/7th Bn. Gordon Highlanders. 5 April 1943 Age 27. VI.B.16.

HILL, Private JOHN, 3975682. 5th Bn. Queen's Own Cameron Highlanders. 6 April 1943 Age 19. Son of James and Alice Hill, of Heaton Norris, Stockport, Cheshire. II.A.16.

HILL, Private, JOHN ROLAND, 7538050. 2nd Bn. Seaforth Highlanders. 6 April 1943 Age 25. Son of Charlie and Jane Hill, of Cleethorpes, Lincolnshire; Husband of Eileen Hill, of Cleethorpes. II.F.23.

HILLCOATE, Corporal, NORMAN FINDLAY, 2823400. 5th Bn. Seaforth Highlanders. 6 April 1943 Age 24. Son of Daniel G and Jeanie EF Hillcoat, of Renfrew. III.B.12.

HOBBS, Private, WILLIAM LANGDON, 4395371. 5th Bn. East Yorkshire Regt. 7 April 1943 Age 29. Son of Thomas John and Elizabeth Hobbs, of Stockton-on-Tees, Co. Durham. XIV.F.13.

HODGSON, Private, JOHN, 4463596. 7th Bn. Black Watch. 6 April 1943 Age 28. Son of Robert Morrell Hodgson and Margaret Ann Hodgson, of South Church, Co. Durham. III.A.18.

HOGG, Bombardier, FRANK,4278585. 149th A/Tk Regt (Lancs Yeo), R A. 6 April 1943 Age 35. Son of James and Alice Renton Hogg, of Chirnside, Berwickshire; Husband of Mary Hogg. II.D.16.

HOGG, Private, JOHN HERBERT, 14209360. 5th Bn. Queen's Own Cameron Highlanders. 6 April 1943 Age 26. Son of Joseph Henry and Ada Hogg, of Sheffield; Husband of Jenny Hogg, of Walkley, Sheffield. III.D.23.

HOLDSWORTH, Private, LEONARD, 4349996. 5th Bn. East Yorkshire Regt. 6 April 1943 Age 32. Son of Leonard and Eleanor Holdsworth, of Leeds, Yorkshire; Husband of Alice Holdsworth, of Leeds. II.C.15.

HOOTON, Trooper, PAUL REGINALD, 7952069. 50th Royal Tank Regt R A C. 6 April 1943 Age 20. Son of Frederick Reginald and Olga Agnes Hooton, of Rushden, Northamptonshire. XIV.C.25.

HORNIBROOK, Lance Corporal, ROBERT, 6410122. 2nd Bn. Seaforth Highlanders. 6 April 1943 Age 31. Son of Robert and Margaret Hornibrook, of Cork, Irish Republic; Husband of Charlotte Hornibrook, of Cork. III.B.4.

HOWARD, Private, EDWARD WILLIAM, 4749400. 7th Bn. Green Howards (Yorkshire Regt.) 6 April 1943 Age 23. Son of George and Mary Anne Howard, of Edmonton, Middlesex. II.C.4.

HOWARD, Private, STANDLEY VICTOR, 6027780. 1/4th Bn. Essex Regiment. 6 April 1943 Age 30. Son of Albert and Catherine Howard, of Grays, Essex; Husband of Marjorie Howard, of Grays. XI.B.6.

HUBBARD, Private, EDWARD, 4538993. 5th Bn. East Yorkshire Regt. 6 April 1943 Age 27. Son of Sarah Ann Parker, of Leeds, Yorkshire. II.C.25.

HUDSON, Private, CLIFFORD, 2940065. 5th Bn. Queen's Own Cameron Highlanders. 6 April 1943 Age 23. II.A.19.

HUDSON, Private, RICHARD, 4389349. 7th Bn. Green Howards (Yorkshire Regt.) 6 April 1943 Age 26. Son of Richard and Maud Mary Hudson, of Thirkleby, Yorkshire. XIV.D.12.

HUGHES, Staff Sergeant, ERNEST WILLIAM, 23332. 6 Field Regt. N.Z. Artillery. 5 April 1943 Age 35. Son of William David Hughes and of Mabel Hughes (nee Luke), of Wellington City, New Zealand; Husband of Phyllis Hughes, of Auckland City. X.C.1.

HUKAM DAD, Rifleman, 22151 4th Bn. 6th Rajputana Rifles. 8 April 1943 Age 18. Son of Allah Dad and Begum Ji, of Mowara, Rawalpindi, Pakistan. M.D.9.

JACK, Lance Corporal, ANDREW, 3196111. 7/10th Bn. Argyll and Sutherland Highlanders. 7 April 1943 Age 27. Son of Andrew and Mary D Jack, of Possilpark, Glasgow. II.B.6.

JAMES, Lieutenant and Quartermaster, ARTHUR SEDGWICK, 254581. 5th East Yorkshire Regt. 6 April 1943 Age 38. Son of John Walton James and Alice Maud James; Husband of Beryl James, of Rhyl, Flintshire. VII.A.11.

JAMES, Corporal, CHARLIE CECIL, 2763156. 7th Bn. Black Watch. 6 April 1943 Age 26. Son of Cecil John and Anne Mary James; Husband of Hilda Gladys James, of Leighbeck, Canvey Island, Essex. III.A.6.

JANGIR SINGH, Sapper, 24936. KGVs O. Bengal Sappers & Miners. 6 April 1943 Age 18. Son of Harnam Singh and Sant Kaur, of Nathu Wala, Moga, Ferozepur, India; Husband of Bachan Kaur, of Nathu Wala. H.D.9.

JENKINS, Private, JOHN BAXTER, 2986646. 7/10th Bn. Argyll and Sutherland Highlanders. 6 April 1943 Age 26. VI.B.14.

JENNINGS, Gunner, CLIFFORD Robert, 1110545. 11 Field Regt., Royal Artillery. 5 April Age 34. Son of Robert James Jennings and Emma Lena Jennings; Husband of Jane Elizabeth Jennings, of Sutton, Surrey. XI.B.15.

JOBSON, Private, ROBERT HENRY, 14201995. 7/10th Bn. Argyll and Sutherland Highlanders. 6 April 1943 Age 20. II.B.26.

KANE, Private, EDWARD, 2987187. 7/10th Bn. Argyll and Sutherland Highlanders. 6 April 1943 Age 26. Son of John and Margaret Hill Kane, of Renton, Dunbartonshire. II.B.11.

KEEFE, Corporal, JOHN RYDER, 2824130. 5th Bn. Seaforth Highlanders. 6 April 1943 Age 25. Son of Frank and Alice Pemberton Ryder Keefe. III.D.9.

KEENAN, Lieutenant, PATRICK, 220971. 274 Field Coy., Royal Engineers. 6 April 1943 Age 24. Son of Patrick and Florence Keenan; Husband of Irene Joan Keenan, of West Bromwich, Staffordshire. II.B.12.

KEIR, Private, GEORGE, 2761972. 7th Bn. Black Watch. 6 April 1943 Age 20. Son of George and Betsy Keir, of Dundee. III.A.3.

KENNEDY, Private, JOHN, 4393657. 6th Bn. Green Howards (Yorkshire Regt.) 7 April 1943 Age 26. Son of John and Ann Kennedy, of Gateshead, Co. Durham. XIV.D.3.

KERR, Private, ALEXANDER, 2763345. 7th Bn. Black Watch. 6 April 1943 Age 23. Son of John D and Letitia Kerr, of Glasgow. III.A.16.

KIRKHAM, Private, JOHN ROBINSON, 4394104. 7th Bn. Green Howards (Yorkshire Regt.) 6 April 1943 Age 28. Son of William and Mary Annie Kirkham, of Liverpool; Husband of Doris Eva Kirkham, of Kirkdale, Liverpool. XIV.D6.

KIRKWOOD, Private, JAMES, 2825826. 5th Bn. Seaforth Highlanders. 6 April 1943 Age 28. Son of William and Elizabeth Kirkwood, of Port Glasgow, Renfrewshire. III.E.9.

LAKIN, Private, GEORGE FREDERICK, 4397091. 7th Bn. Green Howards (Yorkshire Regt.) 6 April 1943 Age 32. Son of Arthur and Annie Lakin, of Burton-on-Trent; Husband of Marjorie Noreen Lakin, of Burton-on-Trent. II.E.5.

LANGSTAFF, Private, GEORGE, 4350251. 5th Bn. East Yorkshire Regt. 6 April 1943 Age 36. Son of Frank and Nellie Langstaff; Husband of Ellen Langstaff, of York. III.E.25.

LAURENCE, Private, ALFRED WILLIAM, 6200395. 2nd Bn. Cheshire Regiment. 6 April 1943 Age 30. Son of Thomas Francis and Louise Laurence; Husband of Georgina Mary Laurence, of Shepton Mallet, Somerset. VII.A.10.

LEYSHON, Sergeant, ROBERT ALFRED, 4341034. 5th Bn. East Yorkshire Regt. 6 April 1943 Son of Philip and Ann Leyshon; Husband of Jane Ann Leyshon, of Bradford, Yorkshire. II.C.18.

LILLY, Private, GEORGE VINCENT, 2987384. 7/10th Bn. Argyll and Sutherland Highlanders. 6 April 1943 Age 23. Son of Owen and Catherine Lilly, of Langside, Glasgow. II.B.9.

LIVESEY, Lieutenant, JOE TAYLOR, 2225657. 4th County of London Yeo. (Sharpshooters), RAC. 6 April 1943 Age 29. Son of Richard and Clarissa Livesey, of Redcar, Yorkshire. II.B.5.

LOMAS, Sapper, CHARLES, 2125323. 276 Field Coy., Royal Engineers. 7 April 1943 Age 28. II.E.16.

LOVE, Private, JOSEPH SMITH, 3318337. 2nd Bn. Seaforth Highlanders. 6 April 1943 Age 23. Son of Joseph Smith Love and Margaret Dewar Love, of Glasgow; Husband of Elizabeth Love, of Glasgow. III.D.2.

LYNCH, Private, JOHN WILLIAM, 4751945. 7th Bn. Green Howards (Yorkshire Regt.) 6 April 1943 Age 27. Son of Ellen Kate Lynch, of Wanstead, Essex. VII.A.23.

MACFARLANE, Corporal, JAMES ROLLAND, 2982716. 7/10th Bn. Argyll and Sutherland Highlanders. 6 April 1943 Age 21. Son of James Rolland MacFarlane and Mary Lamont Spiers MacFarlane, of Polmont, Stirlingshire. II.B.22.

MACFARLANE, Sergeant, JOHN, 2986091. 7th Bn. Argyll and Sutherland Highlanders. 7 April 1943 Age 24. Son of John and Annie MacFarlane; Stepson of Mary MacFarlane, of Rutherglen, Lanarkshire. XIV.F.20.

MACKAY, Private, ANGUS, 2822337. 5th Bn. Seaforth Highlanders. 6 April 1943 Age 22. Son of Angus and Elizabeth Mackay, of Golsary, Caithness-shire. III.D.12.

MACKENZIE, Captain, IAN DRUMMOND, 121645. Reconnaissance Corps, attd. 5th Bn. Seaforth Highlanders. 6 April 1943. Son of John Edwin and Jean Villiers Mackenzie; Husband of Rosemary Mackenzie, of Tain, Ross and Cromarty. III.E.5.

MACKINNON, Private, CHARLES, 2933728. 5th Bn. Black Watch. 7 April 1943 Age 26. Son of Murdo and Marion Mackinnon, of Broadford, Isle of Skye. II.F.18.

MACKLER, Captain, ARTHUR, Mentioned in Despatches, 103549. Royal Army Medical Corps. 5 April 1943 Age 27. Son of Joseph and Regina Mackler, of Hackney, London. L.R.C.P., M.R.C.S. VII.C.11.

MACLEOD, Private, KENNETH, 2828397. 2nd Bn. Seaforth Highlanders. 6 April 1943 Age 34. Son of Kenneth and Isabella MacLeod, of Portnalong, Isle of Skye. II.F.5.

MACPHERSON, Private, WILLIAM JOHN SHEARER, 2822947. 5th Bn. Seaforth Highlanders. 6 April 1943 Age 25. Son of William John Sherer MacPherson and Roberta Irene MacPherson (nee Sutherland), of Thurso, Caithness-shire. II.F.11.

MACRAE, Warrant Officer Class II (C.S.M.), IAN, 2930292. 5th Bn. Queen's Own Cameron Highlanders. 6 April 1943 Age 21. Son of John and Mary MacRae; Husband of Helen MacRae (nee Duguid), of Aberdeen. II. A.20.

MALLEN, Signalman, ANTHONY, 2329607. Royal Corps of Signals. 6 April 1943 Age 21. Son of John and Mary Mallen, of Dovecot, Liverpool. II.D.15.

MARSHALL, Sergeant, THOMAS, 4341038. 4th County of London Yeo. (Sharpshooters), RAC. 6 April 1943 Age 32. Son of Charles and Katherine Marshall; Husband of Laura Mary Marshall, of Gipsyville, Hull. II.B.15.

MASLEN, Private, JAMES, 4622182. 7th Bn. Green Howards (Yorkshire Regt.) 6 April 1943 Age 30. Husband of Elaine Maslen, of Manningham, Bradford, Yorkshire. II.E.6.

MASSON, Private, GEORGE, 2820513. 5th Bn. Seaforth Highlanders. 6 April 1943 Age 23. Son of Alexander and Susan Masson, of Cromdale, Morayshire. II.F.14.

MAUNDER, Major, REGINALD SAMUEL, 105808. 61 Anti-Tank Regt., Royal Artillery. 6 April 1943 III.B.14.

McADAM, Lance Corporal, ROBERT William, 6211184. 1/7th Bn. Middlesex Regiment. 8 April 1943 Age 25. Son of John James McAdam and Mary Elizabeth McAdam, of Leamside, Co. Durham. XIV.F.16.

McALLISTER, Private, WILLIAM, 2827524. 2nd Bn. Seaforth Highlanders. 6 April 1943 Age 29. Son of Peter and Margaret McAllister, of Muir of Ord, Ross and Cromarty. II.F.8.

McBRIDE, Sergeant HUGH, 2751981. 5th Bn. Black Watch. 8 April 1943 Age 31. Son of Thomas and Margaret McBride; Husband of Annie McBride, of Worthing, Sussex. XIV.A.15.k

McCALL. Bombardier, ROBERT STEWARD, 918334. 128 Field Rgt. Royal Artillery. 6 April 1943 Age 30. Son of Robert Stewart McCall and Grace Agnes McCall, of Glasgow; Husband of Margaret McCall, of Southampton III.D.14.

McCOLL, Private, ALEXANDER, 2818135. 2nd Bn. Seaforth Highlanders. 8 April 1943 Age 30. XIV.F.22.

McDONNELL, Private, PATRICK FRANCIS, 10601987). 5th Bn. East Yorkshire Regt. 6 April 1943 Age 20. (served as McDONALD), Son of Thomas and Annie McDonnell, of Jarrow, Co. Durham. II.C.26.

McDOUGALL, Bombardier, JAMES, 907655. 126 Field Regt. Royal Artillery. 6 April 1943 Age 22. Son of Robert and Margaret McDougall, of Greenock, Renfrewshire. III.B.22.l

McGILL, Lieutenant, THOMAS FRANCIS, 228437. 7/10th Bn. Argyll and Sutherland Highlanders. 6 April 1943 Age 24. Son of Hugh and Margaret McGill, of Glasgow. A.R.I.B.A. II.A.6.

McGILVRAY, Lieutenant, JOHN, 269356. 5th Bn. Seaforth Highlanders. 6 April 1943 Age 27. Son of Charles and Margaret McGilvray; Husband of Elsie McGilvray, of Darlington, Co. Durham. III.E.7.

McGLADE, Private, JAMES, 2935914. 7/10th Bn. Argyll and Sutherland Highlanders. 6 April 1943 Age 30. Son of John and Jane P McGlade, of Parkhead, Glasgow. II.B.8.

McGRATH, Corporal, JOHN, 3185204. 2nd Bn. Seaforth Highlanders. 6 April 1943 Age 32. Son of Thomas and Anne McGrath; Husband of Edith Cavell McGrath, of Kirkcudbright. II.F.20.

McGRATH, Private, WILLIAM PAISLEY, 2940006. 5th Bn. Queen's Own Cameron Highlanders. 6 April 1943 Age 25. III.D.21.

McGUIRE, Gunner, WILLIAM BARLAM, 1591050. 171 Bty., 57 Lt. A.A Rgt. Royal Artillery. 6 April 1943 Age 28. Son of Walter and Helen McGuire; Husband of Vera McGuire, of Spennymoor, Co. Durham. XIII.E.1.

McKIM, Private, DANIEL, 2825316. 2nd Bn. Seaforth Highlanders. 6 April 1943 Age 27. III.D.18.

McKINTOSH, Corporal, JOHN, 2825855. 5th Bn. Seaforth Highlanders. 6 April 1943 Age 28. Son of Donald and Mary Ann McKintosh; Grandson of Flora Campbell, of Paisley, Renfrewshire. III.D.8.

McLEOD, Private, WILLIAM THOMPSON, 2987346. 7/10th Bn Argyll and Sutherland Highlanders. 6 April 1943 Age 26. Son of William Thompson McLeod and Susan McLeod, of Glasgow. II.A.4.

McMAHON, Private, THOMAS KELLY, 2979426. 7/10th Bn. Argyll and Sutherland Highlanders. 6 April 1943. Son of John and Mary McMahon, of Lochore, Fife. II.E.22.

McMULLAN, Private, JAMES, 3660961. 7th Bn. Black Watch. 7 April 1943 Age 29. Son of William and Catharine McMullan, of Heaton Norris, Stockport, Cheshire. XIV.F.17.

McNAIR, Private, THOMAS WILLIAM, 4754502. 2nd Bn. Seaforth Highlanders. 6 April 1943 Age 27. Son of James C and JE McNair, of Wembley, Middlesex. III.D.19.

McPHERSON, Private DONALD, 5959087. 7/10th Bn. Argyll and Sutherland Highlanders. 6 April 1943 Age 33. Son of Alexander and Jane McPherson; Husband of Evelyn Beatrice McPherson, of Wheathampstead, Hertfordshire. II.E.26.

MESSER, Private, WILLIAM WILSON, 2823513. 5th Bn. Seaforth Highlanders. 6 April 1943 Age 24. Son of James and Jeanie Neil Messer. II.E.1.

MILES, Private, GEORGE, 4129686. 2nd Bn. Cheshire Regiment. 6 April 1943 Age 26. Son of John and Anne Miles. VII.E.2.

MITCHELL, Private, JAMES MCGLASHAN, 2819499. 2nd Bn. Seaforth Highlanders. 6 April 1943 Age 26. Son of Mr & Mrs Robert Mitchell; Husband of Doris Grace Joan Mitchell, of Harford Bridge, Hampshire. II.F.7.

MOCHAR, Private, ANDREW, 2990972. 7/10th Bn. Argyll and Sutherland Highlanders. 6 April 1943 Age 33. Son of Charlotte Mochar; Stepson of David Mann; Husband of Isabella Mochar, of Maddiston, Stirlingshire. II.B.16.

MOOR, Private, JAMES, 2759478. 7th Bn. Black Watch. 6 April 1943 Age 25. Son of James and Isabella Moor, of Dundee. III.B.20.

MOORE, Lance Corporal, JAMES WATSON BARROW, 4341313. 5th Bn East Yorkshire Regt. 6 April 1943 Age 34. Son of Joseph Moore and Emily Moore (nee Sillet), of Howden-Le-Wear, Co. Durham; Husband of Hilda Moore, of Howden-Le-Wear. II.C.17.

MOORE, Private, PATRICK, 2993056. 7/10th Bn. Argyll and Sutherland Highlanders. 6 April 1943 Age 22. Son of Mr & Mrs Walter Moore, of Netherton, Wishaw, Lanarkshire. III.B.17.

MORGAN, Lance Corporal, JOSEPH, 4465540. 2nd Bn. Seaforth Highlanders. 6 April 1943 Age 29. Son of Joseph and Margaret Morgan, of Fishburn, Co. Durham. III.B.8.

MORGAN, Lance Corporal, LEONARD 2076085. 42 Field Regt., Royal Engineers. 6 April 1943 Age 24. Son of William John and Selina Morgan, of Huntington, Staffordshire. VII.E.6.

MORRIS, Corporal, STANLEY, 6897863. 2nd Bn. Cheshire Regiment. 7 April 1943 Age 23. Son of Ernest and Annie Eleanor Morris, of Blackpool, Lancashire. XIV.D.11.

MORRISON, Sergeant, GEORGE, 2873214.149th A/Tk Regt (Lancs Yeo), R.A. 6 April 1943 Age 33. Son of Richard and Margaret Morrison, of Aberdeen; Husband of Grace Morrison, of Woodside, Aberdeen. II.D.17.

MORTIMER, Private, CYRIL DOUGLAS, 4751125. 5th Bn. Queen's Own Cameron Highlanders. 6 April 1943 Age 27. II.A.26.

MUHAMMAD HANIF, Sapper, 73748. Queen Victoria's Own Madras, Sappers & Miners. 5 April 1943 Age 22. Son of Khader Batcha and Pathambi, of Kolakombai, Coonoor, Nilgiri, India. M.B.10.

MULHOLLAND, Lance Corporal, JOHN 2825886. 5th Bn. Seaforth Highlanders. 6 April 1943 Age 30. Son of Robert J and Agnes MulHolland, of Barrhead, Renfrewshire. II.F.10.

MULLAN, Private, OWEN, 3318207. 7th Bn. Black Watch. 6 April 1943 Age 24. Son of William and Elizabeth Mullan, of Dennistoun, Glasgow. III.A.25.

MUNRO, Corporal, DUNCAN, 3135480. 7/10th Bn. Argyll and Sutherland Highlanders. 6 April 1943 Age 28. Son of George and Jessie Munro, of Forres, Morayshire; Husband of Alice Munro, of Forres. II.A.2.

MURPHY, Private, JOHN WILLIAM, 867301. 1/4th Bn. Essex Regiment. 6 April 1943 Age 22. Son of John Murphy and Annie M Murphy, of Southend-on-Sea, Essex. XI.B.9.

MURPHY, Corporal, PETER HENRY, 2758210. 7th Bn. Black Watch. 6 April 1943 Age 24. Son of Patrick and Mary Murphy. III.B.21.

MURRAY, Major, WILLIAM JAMES ADAMSON, M.C. 130332 attached to King George's Own Sappers & Miners. Royal Engineers. 6 April 1943 Age 32. Son of William Robert Murray and Jeanie Caldwell Murray (nee Adamson), of Stirling. A.M.I.E.E. VII. A.2.

NAR BAHADUR GURUNG, Havildar, 1622. 1st Bn. 2nd King Edward VII's Own Gurkha Rifles (The Sirmoor Rifles). 7 April 1943 Age 28. Son of Jaharsing and Kali, of Gaurapani, Mirlungkot, No. 3 West, Nepal. H.B.7.

NAR BAHADUR SAHI, Rifleman, 96921. 1st Bn. 9th Gurkha Rifles. 6 April 1943 Age 21. Son of Garnbhir, of Limgha, Gulmidarbar, Gulmi, Nepal; Husband of Boukumari, of Limgha. H.B.10.

NUGENT, Private, RICHARD, 4614537. 5th Bn. Queens Own Cameron Highlanders. 6 April 1943 Age 21. Son of James and Catherine Nugent, of Pellon, Yorkshire. II.A.12.

O'HALLORAN, Major, DENIS NORTH EAST 34484. 11 Field Regt., Royal Artillery. 7 April 1943 Age 36. Son of Sylvester NN and Annie E O'Halloran; Husband of Betty Zoe O'Halloran, of Bembridge, Isle of Wight. XIV.D.22.

OAKES, Private, WALTER, 4129228. 2nd Bn. Cheshire Regiment. 6 April 1943 Age 22. Son of Owen and Emma Oakes, of Anderton, Cheshire. VII.E.4.

OLIVER, Warrant Officer Class II (C.S.M.), JAMES GRAHAM, M.M. 43887081. 6th Bn. Green Howards (Yorkshire Regt.) 6 April 1943 Age 30. I.D.21.

ONGERI, Private, MARIO, 4751964. 6th Bn. Green Howards (Yorkshire Regt.) 6 April 1943 Age 26. Son of Giovanni and Leododa Ongeri, of Barrow-in-Furness, Lancashire. II.D.25.

ORANGE, Gunner, ERIC AUBREY, 1115605. 102 Northumberland Hussars. 6 April 1943 Age 21. Son of Arnold Henry William and Sarah Ann Orange, of Leamington Spa, Warwickshire. II.E.9.

ORR, Private, ALEXANDER, 14205461. 5th Bn. Queen's Own Cameron Highlanders. 6 April 1943 Age 20. Son of Alexander Orr and Margaret Orr, of Port Charlotte, Isle of Islay. III.D.11.

OXLEY, Private, ARTHUR, 4396391. 6th Bn. Green Howards (Yorkshire Regt.) 6 April 1943 Age 29. Son of William Arthur and Anna Oxley, of Norton-on-Tees, Co. Durham. II.D.26.

PADAM RANA, Rifleman, 26746. 1st Bn. 2nd King Edward VII's Own Gurkha Rifles (The Sirmoor Rifles). 7 April 1943 Age 19. Son of Satal and Surma, of Namjakot, Husekot, Palpa, Nepal. H.B.5.

PARKER, Bombardier, EDWARD, 920914. 126 Field Regt., Royal Artillery. 6 April 1943. Son of William Murray Parker and Jessie Robertson Parker; Husband of Agnes Scott Parker, of Bankhead, Aberdeenshire. II.B.13.

PARRY, Lance Sergeant, ROBERT JOHN, 2929127. 5th Bn. Queen's Own Cameron Highlanders. 6 April 1943 Age 25. Son of Robert and Martha Parry, of Liverpool; Husband of Elisabeth Margaret Parry, of Anfield, Liverpool. II.A.11.

PATERSON, Corporal, WALTER, 2823289. 2nd Bn. Seaforth Highlanders. 7 April 1943 Age 24. Son of Thomas and Agnes Paterson, of Kirkmuirhill, Lanarkshire. XIV.D.17.

PATTERSON, Private, JAMES, 2766131. 1st Bn. Black Watch. 8 April 1943 Age 21. Son of Stewart James Patterson and Norah Catherine Patterson, of Rattray, Perthshire. XIV.F.5.

PEACE, Lance Corporal, ROBERT WILLIAM, 3318431. 1st Bn. Black Watch. 6-7 April 1943 Age 23. Son of Robert L and Catherine J Peace, of Edinburgh; Husband of Janet MW Peace, of Edinburgh. II.B.24.

PEARSON, Private, WILLIAM, 4696921. 5th Bn. East Yorkshire Regt. 6 April 1943 Age 31. Son of Thomas and Mary Ann Pearson, of Shildon, Co. Durham; Husband of Philomena Pearson, of Shildon. XIV.D.24.

PHIPPS, Lance Corporal, HENRY, 4390770. 6th Bn. Green Howards (Yorkshire Regt.) 6 April 1943 Age 23. Son of Henry and Lily Phipps, of Cargo Fleet, Middlesbrough, Yorkshire. XIV.F.7.

PHIZACKERLEY, Corporal, VERNON, 29311251. 5th Bn. Queen's Own Cameron Highlanders. 6 April 1943 Age 23. Son of Eric and Annie Gertrude Phizackerley, of Whiston, Lancashire. II.A.15.

PLAYFORD, Trooper, FRANK, 7905140. 4th County of London Yeo. (Sharpshooters), RAC. 6 April 1943 Age 32. III.B.24.

PRATT, Lieutenant, FRED HARTLEY, 184729. 6th Bn. Green Howards (Yorkshire Regt.) 6 April 1943 Age 21. Son of Hartley Turner Pratt and Gertrude Amelia Pratt, of Worcester Park, Surrey. II.D.23.o

PRESCOTT, Private, ALFRED ERIC, 2933600. 5th Bn. Queen's Own Cameron Highlanders. 6 April 1943 Age 26. Husband of Florrie Prescott, of St. Helens, Lancashire. II.A.23.

PURNA NAND, Lance Naik, 21388. KGVs O. Bengal Sappers & Miners. April 1943 Age 21. Son of Manorath and Sodha Devi, of Molgad, Pithora Garh, Almora, India; Husband of Radhka Devi, of Molgad. H. D.3.

RAJ SINGH, Rifleman, 30425. 4th Bn. 6th Rajputana Rifles. 6 April 1943 Age 19. Son of Kashmira Singh and Ganga Devi, of Hajipur Romi, Jasoi, Muzaffarnagar, India. H.B.6.

RAMASWAMI, Signalman, A/2757. Indian Signal Corps. 6 April 1943 Age 22. Son of Ramanjalu and Andalamma, of Maleshwaram, Bangalore, India. H.D.4.

RAMSAY, Corporal, LAURENCE, 2765466. 5th Bn. Black Watch. 7 April 1943 Son of Florence M Ramsay, of Upper Holloway, London, II.E.4.

RASHID ALI, Ambulance Sepoy, H/903941B. 17 Ind. Field Ambulance. April 1943 Age 19. Son of Hamid Ali. M.B.7.

RAYNER, Sergeant, LEONARD HENRY GEORGE, 4618051. 5th Bn. East Yorkshire Regt. 6 April 1943 Age 23. Son of Arthur and Florence Jeanette Rayner, of Penge, Kent. His brother Ronald Arthur also fell. II.C.12.

REED, Lieutenant, GEORGE BAXTER, 269935. Seaforth Highlanders. Queen's Own Cameron Highlanders. 6 April 1943 Age 23. Son of Isaac and Annie Reed, of Irthington, Cumberland. III.E.8.

REES, Private, EDWARD WALMSLEY, 2824364. 5th Bn. Seaforth Highlanders. 6 April 1943 Age 25. Son of Edward W Rees and Jennie Rees, of Keighley, Yorkshire, III.B.10.

REESE, Private, CHARLES, 6399455. 1st Bn. Royal Sussex Regiment. 6 April 1943 Age 28. Son of Harry and Margaret Jane Reese, of Hollington, St. Leonards-on-Sea, Sussex. VII.E.22.

REID, Private, WILLIAM, 2762588. 7th Bn. Black Watch. 6 April 1943 Age 23. Son of Alexander and Jane Reid; Husband of Georgina Reid. III.A.17.

REYNOLDS, Private, RONALD, 4127189. 2nd Bn. Cheshire Regiment. 5 April 1943 Age 23. Son of Edward and Rose Reynolds, of Liverpool. VII.E.3.

RICHARDS, Private, WALTER, 5889991. 7th Bn. Green Howards (Yorkshire Regt.) 6 April 1943 Age 28. Husband of Lily Richards, of Hyson Green, Nottingham. II.C.6.

RIDLEY, Private, LESLIE, 4397434. 7th Bn. Green Howards (Yorkshire Regt.) 6 April 1943 Age 35. Son of Thomas H Ridley and Sarah Ridley, of Ferryhill, Co. Durham. II.C.7.

RIFKIN, Lance Corporal, SIDNEY, 2934076. 5th Bn. Queen's Own Cameron Highlanders. 6 April 1943 Age 26. Son of Soloman and Hetty Rifkin, of Leeds, Yorkshire. II.A.21.

RIGBY, Private, JOSEPH JAMES, 2827042. 5th Bn. Seaforth Highlanders. 6 April 1943 Age 27.   Son of Joseph James Rigby and Ellen Rigby, of Manchester; Husband of Elizabeth Alice Rigby, of Beswick, Manchester. III.E.17.

RITCHIE, Lieutenant, MICHAEL ALAN, 172922. 4th County of London Yeo. (Sharpshooters),

RAC. 13th/18th Royal Hussars, RAC. 6 April 1943 Age 22. Son of Sir James William Ritchie, M.B.E., Bt., and Lady Ritchie (nee Emerton), of Crick, Northamptonshire. II.B.14.

ROBERTS, Corporal, LAWRENCE, 2825995.   5th Bn. Seaforth Highlanders. 6 April 1943 Age 28. Son of Samuel Lawrence Roberts and Sarah Roberts, of Liverpool; Husband of Margaret Roberts, of Holt Road, Liverpool. II.F.17.

ROBERTSON, Private, GAVIN CHAPMAN, 2991002. 7/10th Bn. Argyll and Sutherland Highlanders. 6 April 1943 Age 20. Son of Joseph Cowdell Robertson and Catherine McCann Robertson, of Paisley, Renfrewshire. II.B.17.

ROBERTSON, Sergeant, IAN, 2821746. 2nd Bn. Seaforth Highlanders. 8 April 1943. Son of John and Marion Robertson, of Shettleston, Glasgow. XIV.F.19.

ROBERTSON, Private, JOHN HATTON, 2824234. 2nd Bn. Seaforth Highlanders. 6 April 1943   Age 24. Son of Ernest and Mary Ann Robertson, of Nairn. III.B.6.

ROBINSON, Captain, JAMES MAIRS, 160770. 1st Bn. Black Watch. 6 April 1943 Age 35. Son of David JM and Annie Mairs Robinson; Husband of Frances Perioli Robinson, of Kells, Co. Antrim, Northern Ireland. II.B.25.

RODGERS, Lance Corporal, RICHARD, T/69283. 288 Gen. Transport Coy., Royal Army Service Corps. 6 April 1943 II.A.13.

ROSS, Lance Corporal, MALCOLM BLACK, 2932151. 5th Bn. Queen's Own Cameron Highlanders. 6 April 1943 Age 23. Son of Thomas and Marion Ross, of Inverness. II.A.8.

ROWELL, Lance Corporal, PETER NORTON, 421252 'A' Sqn., 4th County of London Yeo. (Sharpshooters), RAC. 7 April 1943 Age 22. Son of Alan Edward and Elsie Rowell, of Brighton, Sussex.

RYAN, Private, RICHARD LAWRENCE, 3191831. 7th Bn. Black Watch. 5 April 1943 Age 39. Son of George and Mary Ryan, of Peebles; Husband of Agnes Ryan, of Peebles. III.A.20.

SARDAR KHAN, Rifleman, 26641. 6th Rajputana Rifles. 7 April 1943 Age 21. Son of Niaz Ali and Bakhat Bhari, of Mulian, Talagang, Attock, Pakistan; Husband of Mehar Bhari, of Mulian. M.B.6.

SAUNDERS, Sergeant, NORMAN, 2819552. 2nd Bn. Seaforth Highlanders. 6 April 1943 Age 25. Son of Roderick and Mary Saunders, of Borve, Isle of Lewis. III.D.3.

SAVORY, Lieutenant, LESLIE WILLIAM, 233947. 4th County of London Yeo. (Sharpshooters), RAC. 6 April 1943 Age 21. Son of Frank and Ethel Violet Savory, of Ashton Gate, Bristol. II.B.10.

SCARROTT, Private, EDWARD ALBERT, 6028773. 5th Bn. East Yorkshire Regt. 6 April 1943 Age 30. Son of Charles Henry and Louisa Scarrott, of Cheltenham, Gloucestershire; Husband of Florence Hilda Scarrott, of Cheltenham. III.F.24.

SEAGRIM, Lieutenant Colonel, DEREK ANTHONY, V.C. 26914. Cdg. 7th Bn. Green Howards (Yorkshire Regt.) 6 April 1943 Age 39. Son of Charles Paulet Cunningham Seagrim and Annabel Emma Halsted Seagrim, of East Dean, Sussex. XIV.C.21.

SEAWRIGHT, Private, THOMAS, 7014284. 5th Bn. Black Watch. 7 April 1943 Age 21. Son of Thomas G and Louise D Seawright, of Dungannon, Co. Tyrone, Northern Ireland. II.F.15.

SHANKAR SINGH, Lance Naik, 21745. KGVs O. Bengal sappers & Miners. 6 April 1943 Age 18. Son of Jagat Singh and Jiwan Kaur, of Gill, Khan Pur, Jullundur, India; Husband of Karam Kaur, of Gill. H.D.8.

SHAW, Private, JOHN JOSEPH, 3658331. 7th Bn. Green Howards (Yorkshire Regt.) 6 April 1943 Age 28. Husband of Marion Shaw, of Warrington, Lancashire. VII.A.18.

SHEO CHAND RAM, Jemadar, 27795110. 4th Bn. 6th Rajputana Rifles. 5 April 1943 Age 24. Son of Mehar Chand and Bhuri, of Chhilro, Narnaul, Patiala, India. H.D.1.

SIGLEY, Private, NORMAN, 5344005. 7/10th Bn. Argyll and Sutherland Highlanders. 6 April 1943 Age 24. Son of Abraham Sigley and Emma Sigley, of Uttoxeter, Staffordshire. II.E.25.

SIMMONDS, Gunner, JAMES, 1128076. 61 Anti-Tank Regt., Royal Artillery. 5 April 1943 Age 34. Son of William and Edith Simmonds; Husband of Lily Gwendoline Simmonds, of Catshill, Worcestershire. III.B.16.

SINGLE, Lieutenant, GEOFFREY ROBERT CHARLES, 109539. 1/4th Bn. Essex Regiment. 6 April 1943 Age 22. Son of Samuel Robert and Beatrice Elizabeth Single, of Brighton, Sussex. XI.B.12.

SMITH, Private, CLIFFORD WALTON, 4618035. 5th Bn. East Yorkshire Regt. 7 April 1943 Age 23. Son of John Robert and Maggie Smith, of Rochdale, Lancashire; Nephew of Mrs E Hudson of Rochdale. XIV.D.

SMITH, Private, DOUGLAS HAIG, 4399330. 7th Bn. Green Howards (Yorkshire Regt.) 6 April 1943 Age 23. Son of George and Susannah Smith, of Wingate, Co. Durham; Husband of Mary Smith, of Wingate. II.C.8.

SMITH, Private, JAMES GRANT, 2815153. 2nd Bn. Seaforth Highlanders. 6 April 1943 Age 32. Son of Robert Wighton Smith and Jeannie Warnock Smith, of Glasgow. III.E.16.

SMITH, Private, JOHN NEAVE, 2759019. 7th Bn. Black Watch. 6 April 1943 Age 24. Son of John and Elizabeth Smith, of Dundee. II.B.3.

SMITH, Gunner, VERNON, 805457. 31 Field Regt., Royal Artillery. 6 April 1943 Age 30. Son of William James Smith and Elizabeth Smith. Husband of Dorothy Mary Smith, of Derby. II.D.13.

SMITH, Private, WILLIAM BENNETT, 6982666. 5th Bn. Seaforth Highlanders. 6 April 1943 Age 27. Son of William Bennett Smith and Mary Ann Smith; Husband of Muriel Joyce Edna Smith, of Wallington, Surrey. II.F.12.

SMITH, Private, WALTER HENRY, 6711615. 5th Bn. Black Watch. 7 April 1943 Age 30. Son of Mr & Mrs Walter Henry Smith; Husband of Kathleen Smith, of Watford, Hertfordshire. III.D.13.

SMYTHE, Corporal, TERENCE, 4458488. 9th Bn. Durham Light Infantry. 6 April 1943 Age 23. VII.A.16.

SPREULL, Captain, WILLIAM HARVEY, 180320. 2nd Bn. Seaforth Highlanders. 6 April 1943 Son of Maj. Andrew Spreull, D.S.O., T.D., D.L., M.R.C.V.S., and Effie Moncur Spreull, of Dundee. III.E.11.

STANFIELD, Sergeant, WILLIAM GEORGE, 806551. 61st Anti-Tank Regt., Royal Artillery. 6 April 1943 Age 29. Son of George Thomas Stanfield and Ada Stanfield; Husband of Rosina Stanfield, of Hackney, London. XIV.D.8.

STARMER, Private, KENNETH, 5891697. 5th Bn. East Yorkshire Regt. 6 April 1943 Age 20. Son of Frederick and Nellie Starmer, of Northampton. II.D.19.

STEPHENSON, Private, JOHN, 6024894. 1/4th Bn. Essex Regiment. 6 April 1943 Age 28. Son of Joseph and Sarah Isabel Stephenson, of Branthwaite, Workington, Cumberland. XI.B.17.

STEWART-BAM, Lieutenant, PATRICK JOHN, 153426. 7/10th Bn. Argyll and Sutherland Highlanders. 6 April 1943 Age 22. Son of Lt.-Col. Sir Pieter Canzius Van Blommestein Stewart-Bam of Ards, O.B.E., and Lady Stewart-Bam, of Connel, Argyllshire. II.A.5.

STONE, Lance Corporal, CYRIL RICHARD EVANS, 4348611. 5th Bn. East Yorkshire Regt. 6 April 1943 Age 27. Son of Samuel and Lillian Stone, of Hull; Husband of Miriam Stone, of Hull. VII.E.16.

STORIE, Private, WILLIAM, 2990499. 7/10th Bn. Argyll and Sutherland Highlanders. 6 April 1943 Age 30. Son of James and Margaret Storie, of Leith, Edinburgh; Husband of Susan Storie, of Leith. II.B.23.

STRAITON, Corporal, THOMAS, 2888935. 1st Bn. Gordon Highlanders. 8 April 1943 Age 29. Son of James and Grace Copeland Straiton, of Glasgow; Husband of Mary Bain Straiton, of Cardonald, Glasgow. XIV.B.5.

STROWGER, Private, GORDON ARTHUR, 3195155. 5th Bn. Seaforth Highlanders. 6 April 1943 Age 27. Son of Ernest and Elizabeth Freeman; Husband of Ivy Strowger, of Lower Broughton, Salford, Lancashire. III.D.10.

STURMEY, Private, WILLIAM GEORGE VICTOR, 4749333. 7th Bn. Green Howards (Yorkshire Regt.) 6 April 1943 Age 23. Son of George and Ada Sturmey, of Harlesden, Middlesex. II.C.5.

TALLACK, Private, FREDERICK HARRY, 3133279. 5/7th Bn. Gordon Highlanders. 5 April 1943. Husband of Katie Nellie Tallack, of Hayes, Middlesex. VI.B.17.

TAYLOR, Private, ALFRED, 3775401. 1st Bn. Gordon Highlanders. 6 April 1943 Age 34. Son of John Henry and Matilda Taylor, of Liverpool. VI.B.13.

TAYLOR, Private, WILLIAM, 3322296. 2nd Bn. Seaforth Highlanders. 6 April 1943 Age 28. Son of William and Annie Taylor, of Glasgow; Husband of Elizabeth Taylor, of Renton, Dunbartonshire. II.F.1.

THOMPSON, Private, CHARLES KNIGHT, 3456331. 7th Bn. Black Watch. 6 April 1943 Age 28. Son of David and Phoebe Alice Thompson, of Blackburn, Lancashire. III.A.10.

THOMSON, Private, HUGH, 2755712. 7th Bn. Black Watch. 6 April 1943 Age 26. Son of Robert and Mary Ann Thomson, of Dundee; Husband of Georgina Thomson, of Dundee. III.A.23.

THRAXTON, Private, JOHN, 5343963. 7/10th Bn. Argyll and Sutherland Highlanders. 6 April 1943 Age 28. Son of William and Mary E Thraxton, of Jarrow, Co. Durham, II.E.21.

TODD, Private, HUGH, 14211764. 2nd Bn. Seaforth Highlanders. 6 April 1943 Age 20. Son of William and Georgina Todd, of Dennistoun, Glasgow. III.B.5.

TOPLIFFE, Lance Sergeant, JOHN EDWARD, 4391307. 7th Bn. Green Howards (Yorkshire Regt.) 6 April 1943 Age 23. Son of Henry and Florence Topliffe, of Dormanstown, Redcar, Yorkshire. II.E.18.

TWEDDLE, Private, HEBERT, 4396907. 6th Bn. Green Howards (Yorkshire Regt.) 6 April 1943 Foster-Son of Sophia Pimlott, of Middlesbrough, Yorkshire. XI.B.13.

URQUHART, Private, WILLIAM, 6475694. 5th Bn. Seaforth Highlanders. 6 April 1943 Age31. Son of William and Elizabeth Ann Urquhart, of Dundee. II.F.25.

VALLANCE, Lance Sergeant, ROBERT, 3190429. 7/10th Bn. Argyll and Sutherland Highlanders. 6 April 1943 Age 21. Son of Robert and Ethel Vallance, of Eastriggs, Dumfriesshire. II.B.4.

WADE, Private, HARRY, 7928455. 5th Bn. East Yorkshire Regt. 6 April 1943 Age 36. Son of Harry and Ruth Wade, of Sheffield; Husband of Annie Wade, of Sheffield. XIV.D.23.

WAINWRIGHT, Private, JOSEPH, 2824383. 2nd Bn. Seaforth Highlanders. 6 April 1943 Age 24. Son of Ernest and May Wainwright, of Bolsterstone, Yorkshire. III.E.14.

WALKER, Private, ALEXANDER BLAIR, 3196580. 7th Bn. Black Watch. 6 April 1943 Age 29. Son of John Oswald and Julia Hugo Walker, of Scotstoun, Glasgow. III.A.15.

WALKER, Lance Corporal, CYRIL KENNETH, 4346411. 5th Bn. East Yorkshire Regt. 6 April 1943 Age 23. Son of John and Annie Walker, of Swallownest, Yorkshire. VII.A.15.

WALKER, Corporal, ERNEST WILLIAM, 791811. 7th Bn. Green Howards (Yorkshire Regt.) 6 April 1943 Age 30. Husband of Edith Emily Walker, of Puttenham, Surrey. VII.A.24.

WALKER, Private, WILLIAM, 4395985. 7th Bn. Green Howards (Yorkshire Regt.) 6 April 1943 Age 23. Son of John Richard and Jane Walker, of Leeds, Yorkshire. II.C.9.

WALLACE, Major, HERBERT NOEL, M.C. 63581. 5th Bn. East Yorkshire Regt. 6 April 1943 Age 28. Son of Jeremiah Thomas Wallace and Elizabeth Wallace, of Bangor, Co. Down, Northern Ireland. II.D.20.

WALLACE, Private, WILLIAM, 6021758. 1/4th Bn. Essex Regiment. 6 April 1943 Age 26. Son of William John and Mary Eunice Wallace, of Acton, Middlesex. XIII.A.8.

WALLINGTON, Gunner, RAYMOND ARTHUR, 11255584. 102 Northumberland Hussars. 6 April 1943 Age 20. Son of Christopher and Ruth Wallington, of Luton, Bedfordshire. II.E.10.

WALMSLEY, Private, SIDNEY PERCY, 6211876. 1/7th Bn. Middlesex Regiment. 6 April 1943 Age 25. Son of Percy Alfred and Evelyn Maud Walmsley, of Notting Hill, London. VII.A.9.

WARD, Private, SYDNEY ROY, 5961237. 6th Bn. Green Howards (Yorkshire Regt.) 6 April 1943 Age 20. Son of Frederick Ward and Florence Ward, of Hoddesdon, Hertfordshire. VII.E.10.

WATSON, Private, ROBERT, 4397967. 7th Bn. Green Howards (Yorkshire Regt.) 7 April 1943 Age 35. Son of Robert and Jane Watson, of Seaham Harbour, Co. Durham; Husband of Gladys Mary Watson, of Seaham Harbour. XIV.D.5.

WEBB, Private, RICHARD, 4805515. 2nd Bn. Seaforth Highlanders. 6 April 1943 Age 26. Son of Arthur and Hannah Webb; Husband of Ethel Webb, of Ruddington, Nottinghamshire. III.D.20.

WEBSTER, Private, JOHN WILLIAM, 4394456. 6th Bn. Green Howards (Yorkshire Regt.) 7 April 1943. Son of Samuel and Mary Webster; Husband of Nancy Webster, of West Hartlepool, Co. Durham. XIV.D.4.

WHITEHEAD, Private, RICHARD, 4542104. 5th Bn. East Yorkshire Regt. 6 April 1943 Age 33. Son of Charles and Eleanora Whitehead. III.E.23.

WHITFIELD, Private, EDWARD, 4754623. 7th Bn. Green Howards (Yorkshire Regt.) 6 April 1943 Age 27. Son of James and Alice Elizabeth Whitfield, of Custom House, Essex. II.E.8.

WIGGS, Private, JAMES HENRY, 6408530. 1st Bn. Royal Sussex Regiment. 6 April 1943 Age 21. Son of James Henry Wiggs and Daisy Ellen Wiggs, of Paddington, London. XIII.E.14.

WILLIAMS, Private, SIDNEY PRICE, 4924409. 6th Bn. Green Howards (Yorkshire Regt.) 4 April 1943 Age 23. Son of Sidney and Elsie Williams, of Bilston, Staffordshire. XIV.D.16.

WILSON, Private, HUGH KELSO, 2993122. 7;/10th Bn. Argyll and Sutherland Highlanders. 6 April 1943 Age 20. Son of Hugh Kelso Wilson and Elizabeth Wilson, of Glasgow. III.A.1.

WILSON, Private, JOHN DUTHIE, 2767016. 7th Black Watch. 6 April 1943 Age 25. Son of Matthew and Jean Duthie Wilson; Husband of Marion Thomson Wilson, of Crossgates, Fife. III.A.9.

WOOD, Captain, GREGORY DILLON, 105266. 5th Bn. East Yorkshire Regt. 6 April 1943 Age 32. Son of WGS and G Alice Wood, of Whitstable, Kent. III.E.22.

WOOD, Private, JAMES, 2759395. 5th Black Watch. 7 April 1943 Age 26. Son of Hugh and Agnes Wood, of Glasgow. II.F.16.

WOOD, Trooper, JOHN HENRY, 87918114. 4th County of London Yeo. (Sharpshooters), RAC. 6 April 1943 Age 32. Son of John and Elizabeth Wood; Husband of Evelyn Wood, of Oswestry, Shropshire. II.E.13.

WOOD, Private, JOHN WARRENDER, 2757562. 7th Bn. Black Watch. 6 April 1943 Age 30. Husband of Margaret Gibb Wood, of Dysart, Fife. III.A.7.

WOOD, Private, WILLIAM, 2990423. 7/10th Bn. Argyll and Sutherland Highlanders. 6 April 1943 Age 27. Son of Alex and Catherine Wood, of Plean, Stirlingshire. II.A.1.

WOODS, Private, RONALD, 2933651. 5th Bn. Queen's Own Cameron Highlanders. 6 April 1943 Age 26. Son of Richard and Margaret Woods, of Liverpool; Husband of Irene Julia Woods, of Liverpool. II.A.22.

WRIGHT, Private, JAMES, 2757661. 7th Bn. Black Watch. 6 April 1943 Age 22. Son of Benjamin George and Elizabeth Wright, of Whitley Bay, Northumberland. III.A.13.

YOUNG, Private, ANDREW, 2755107. 7th Bn. Black Watch. 6 April 1943 Age 27. Son of William Young and Annie Young, of Dunfermline, Fife. III.A.12.

ENFIDAVILLE WAR CEMETERY

CHALLENGER, Private. GEORGE, 4394798. 6th Bn. Green Howards. (Yorkshire Regt.) 6 April 1943 Age 35. Son of George and Georgina Challenger, of South Church, Co. Durham.

CHALMERS, Cpl. JAMES A.G. 2933790. 5th Bn. The Queen's Own Cameron Highlanders. 23 March, 1943. Son of James and Elizabeth Allan, of Elgin, Morayshire. V.A.11.

COUPLAND, Private, HARRY, 43399651. 6th Bn. The Green Howards (Yorkshire Regt.) 6 April 1943 Age 19. Son of Francis W and Hilda Coupland, of Leeds, Yorkshire. V.E.29.

DON, Private, JOHN, 2760631. 7/10th Bn. The Argyll and Sutherland Highlanders. 7 April, 1943. Age 30. Son of John and Bridget Don, of Dundee. VI.F.6.

DOUGLAS, Lt. JAMES, 162673. 2nd Bn. Seaforth Highlanders. 8 April, 1943 Age 27. Son of David and Mary Elizabeth Douglas, of Morpeth, Northumberland. VI.F.4. Died of wounds received at Akarit.

GRIFFIN, Private, WILLIAM, 4858373. 6th Bn. The Green Howards (Yorkshire Regt.) 7 April, 1943 Age 24. Son of Michael and Mary Jane Griffin; Husband of Winifred May Griffin, of Bawtry, Yorkshire. VI.F.7.

INCH, Lieutenant, CHARLES BAYLISS REID, 198591. 50th Royal Tank Regt., RAC. 5 April, 1943 Age 28. VI.F.13.

JACKSON, Spr. DAVID, 2118625. 276 Field Coy., Royal Engineers. 7 April, 1943 Age 29. Son of Christopher and Janet Jackson, of Torrance, Stirlingshire; Husband of Mary D S Jackson, of Torrance. VI.F.20.

JACKSON, L. Cpl. DAVID WEIR, 2993186. 7/10th Bn. The Argyll and Sutherland Highlanders. 6 April 1943 Age 20. VI.F.9.

KISCH, Brigadier FREDERICK HERMANN, C.B., C.B.E., D.S.O., Officer de la Legion d'Honneur, Croix de Guerre (France) avec Palme. Royal Engineers and Commands and staff. 7 April, 1943 Age 54. Son of Hermann Michael and Alice Kisch; Husband of Ruth Laura Kisch, of Aldingbourne, Sussex. VI.F.22.

LAIRD, Gdsmn. SAMUEL, 2764252. 2nd Bn. Scots Guards. 6 April, 1943 Age 21. Son of John and Lillian Laird, of Motherwell, Lanarkshire. VI.F.11.

LIDDELL, Pte. ROBERT, 2989733. 7/10th Bn. The Argyll and Sutherland Highlanders. 7 April 1943 Age 22. VI.F.21.

MORRISON, Cpl. GEORGE CHARLES PHIMISTER, 2822410. 2nd Bn. Seaforth Highlanders. 7 April 1943 Age 27. Son of William and Davidina Morrison of Wick, Caithness-shire; Husband of Mary Elizabeth Morrison, of Wick. VI.F.3.

MCLELLAND. Pte. ROBERT, 7368957. 175 Fld Ambulance. 7 April 1943 Age 23. Son of Charles and Catharine Donoghue McLelland. VI.F.10.

MITCHELL, Pte. PERCY, 4750152. 6TH Bn. The Green Howards (Yorkshire Regt.) 6 April 1943 Age 26. Son of Thomas and Mary Ann Mitchell, of Rotherham, Yorkshire. V.E.27.

OGSTON, Pte. WILLIAM, 2935637. 5th Bn. The Queen's Own Cameron Highlanders. 6 April 1943 Age 26. Son of James Ogston and Margaret Ogston, of Blantyre, Lanarkshire. VI.F.8.

OSTICK, Dvr. JIM, T/286478. R.A.S.C., attd. 176 Field Amb., R.A.M.C. 7 April 1943 Age 32. Son of James and Emily Ostick, of Horsforth, Yorkshire. VI.F.19.

PETRIE. Cpl. JAMES. 2762115. 1st Bn. Black Watch. 7 April 1943 Age 29. Son of James and Williamina Petrie, of Dundee; Husband of Isabella Forest Petrie, of Dundee. VI.F.5.

PURSER, Major. David Merlin. 69731. 3rd Field Squadron, Royal Engineers. 6th April 1943. Age 26. Son of Edmund George and Edith Merle Purser of Salwarpe Worcestershire.

SHANNON, Colonel S.B., 133676V, C.B.E., M.C. South African Engineer Corps. 7 April, 1943. VI.F.23.

SMITH, Pte, ALBERT, 7370362. 176 Field Amb., R.A.M.C. 6 April 1943 Age 24. Son of John and Helen Smith, of Aberdeen. VI.F.18.

SMITH, Cpl. JAMES ANDERSON, 2754756. 7th Bn. The Black Watch (Royal Highland Regt.) 7 April, 1943 Age 26. Son of James A and Isabella Smith, of Guthrie, Angus. VI.F.15.

VOIGT, Capt. F.C.M., 134505, M.C. 31 Road Constr. Coy., South African Engineer Corps. 7 April 1943 Age 27. Son of Frederick CM and Susanna M Voigt, of Rondesbosch, Cape Town, South Africa. B.Sc. (Engineering). VI.F.24.

WEIR, Pte. GEORGE LINDSLEY, 5260313. 6th Bn. The Green Howards (Yorkshire Regt.) 6 April 1943 Age 21. Son of George and Ellen Weir, of Wednesfield, Wolverhampton. V.E.31.

WHYTE, Sergeant, VICTOR, 2091825. 2765 Field Coy., Royal Engineers. 6 April 1943 Age 23. Son of Charles S and Elizabeth Whyte, of Paisley, Renfrewshire. VI.F.17

WILLIAMS, Pt. WILLIAM John, 3967972. 6th Bn. The green Howards (Yorkshire Regt.) 6 April 1943 Age 23. Son of William and Charlotte Ann Williams, of Rhyd-y-Felin, Glamorgan. V.E.30.

WILSON, Pte. JAMES, 4393416. 6TH Bn. The Green Howards (Yorkshire Regt.) 6 April, 1943 Age 25. Son of William and Ellen Wilson, of Billinge, Lancashire. V.E.28.

MEDJEZ-EL-BAB MEMORIAL TO THE MISSING

AITHWAITE, Private, WILLIAM, 4399179. 6th Bn. Green Howards (Yorkshire Regt.) 6 April 1943 Age 24. Face 18.

BAHADUR SING GURUNG, Lance Naik, 2058. 1st Bn. 2nd King Edward VII's Own Gurkha Rifles (The Sirmoor Rifles). 6 April 1943 Age 23. Son of Dhan Bahadur and Bhaimata, of Digaon, Nepal. Face 43.

BAIRD, Private, GEORGE, 2762374. 7 10th Bn. Argyll and Sutherland Highlanders. 6 April 1943 Age 28. Son of Mr & Mrs George Baird; Husband of Helen Scott Cramb Baird, of Kennoway, Fife. Face 31.

BANYARD, Trooper, HERBERT RICHARD, 787358. 40th (7th Bn. The Kings Regt., Liverpool) Royal Tank Regt., RAC. 7 April 1943 Age 30. Husband of DM Banyard, of Pool, Dorsetshire. Face 4.

BAZ KHAN, Rifleman, 21445. 4th Bn. 6th Rajputana Rifles. 6 April 1943 Age 18. Son of Khuda Bakhsh. Face 41.

BENTLEY, Trooper, GEORGE ARTHUR, 7940692. 40th (7th Bn. The King's Regiment) Royal Tank Rgt. RAC. 6 April 1943 Age 34. Son of George H and Ellen Bentley; Nephew of Alice Hextall, of Lenton, Nottingham. Face 4.

BHAKAT RAM PUN, Rifleman, 26301. 1st Bn. 2nd King Edward VII's Own Gurkha Rifles (The Sirmoor Rifles). 6 April 1943 Age 21. Son of Sete and Saina, of Dangsi, Nepal. Face 43.

BIR BAHADUR GURUNG, Lance Naik, 25979. 1st Bn. 2nd King Edward VII's Own Gurkha Rifles (The Sirmoor Rifles). 6 April 1943 Age 26. Son of Biraj Gurung and Sirkumari, of Ghalel, Nepal. Face 43.

BIR BAHADUR THAPA, Rifleman, 25164. 1st Bn. 2nd King Edward VII's Own Gurkha Rifles (The Sirmoor Rifles). 6 April 1943 Age 21. Son of Kirta Bahadur and Somitra, of Archale, Nepal. Face 43.

BIS RAM GURUNG, Rifleman, 26413. 1st Bn. 2nd King Edward VII's Own Gurkha Rifles (The Sirmoor Rifles). 6 April 1943 Age 19. Son of Som Bahadur and Jhejaple; Husband of Kamini, of Kharchok, Nepal. Face 43.

BOWERING, Corporal, FREDERICK, 7915543. 4th County of London Yeo. (Sharpshooters), RAC. 6 April 1943 Age 29. Son of John and Charlotte Bowering; Husband of Frances Lillian Bowering, of Hull. Face 4.

BUCK, Trooper, MICHAEL JOSEPH, 408715. 4th County of London Yeo (Sharpshooters), RAC. 6 April 1943 Age 24. Son of Michael and Johanna Buck, of Adamsdown, Cardiff. Face 4.

BUTCHER, Trooper, FREDERICK, 7943269. 40th (7th Bn. The King's Regiment) Royal Tank Rgt. RAC. 6 April 1943 Age 40. Son of Alfred and Caroline Butcher. Face 4.

CARR, Private, GEORGE RILEY, 3322183. 7th Bn. Black Watch. 6 April 1943 Age 27. Son of Robert and Millicent Carr; Husband of Dorothy Carr, of Doncaster, Yorkshire. Face 24.

COPLAND, Trooper, JAMES DAVIDSON, 7920954. 40th (7th Bn. The King's Regiment) Royal Tank Rgt. RAC. 6 April 1943 Age 31. Son of David and Ellen Lavinia Copland; Husband of Eileen Louise Copland, of Cleethorpes, Lincolnshire. Face 4.

COUGHLAN, Lance Corporal, LESLIE NOEL, 4389604. 6th Bn. Green Howards (Yorkshire Regt.) 6 April 1943 Age 23. Son of Mr & Mrs AE Coughlan, of Eston, Yorkshire. Face 17.

DIN MUHAMMAD, Lance Naik, 11978. 4th Bn. 16th Punjab Regiment. 6 April 1943 Age 22. Son of Ghulam Muhammad and Barkat Bibi, of Paikhel, Mianwali, Pakistan. Face 41.

DIWAN ALI, Lance Havildar, 13996. 5th Bn. 6th Rajputana Rifles. 6 April 1943 Age 18. Son of Budha Khan; Husband of Razia Begum, of Sarsala, Gujrat, Pakistan. Face 41.

DONALDSON, Private, JOHN FERGUSON, 2756956. 5th Bn. Black Watch. 7 April 1943 Age 24. Face 24.

DOST MUHAMMAD, Naik, 13799. 6th Rajputana Rifles. 6 April, 1943. Face 41.

ELLIS, Trooper, GEORGE, 3770222. 40th (7th Bn. The King's Regiment) Royal Tank Rgt. RAC. 6 April 1943 Age 28. Face 4.

FRASER, Lance Sergeant, ALEXANDER, 2879538. 5/7th Bn. Gordon Highlanders. 6 April 1943 Age 29. Son of Hugh and Janet Fraser; Husband of Jean Fraser, of Torrance, Stirlingshire. Face 30.

GANGE THAPA, Rifleman, 2707. 1st Bn. 2nd King Edward VII's Own Gurkha Rifles (The Sirmoor Rifles). 6 April 1943 Age 20. Son of Gore and Bishna, of Charchare, Nepal. Face 44.

GARDNER, Sergeant, WILLIAM, 2983078. 7/10TH Bn. Argyll and Sutherland Highlanders. 6 April 1943 Age 22. Son of William Gardner and Mary Gardner, of Denny, Stirlingshire. Face 31.

GHULAM NABI, Lance Naik, 17278. 4th Bn. 6th Rajputana Rifles. 6 April 1943 Age 20. Son of Muhammad Khan and Fatema Bibi; Husband of Amena Bibi, of Bhota, Gujrat, Pakistan. Face 41.

GLENDINNING, Private, FREDERICK LAMBERT, 2058558. 1/7th Bn. Middlesex Regiment. 6 April 1943 Age 23. Face 27.

GORNALL, Trooper, ALBERT ERNEST, 3459336. 10th Royal Hussars, RAC., 6 April 1943 Age 22. Son of Albert Ernest and Sarah Ann Gornall, of Fleetwood, Lancashire. Face 2.

GUMAN SING RANA, Naik, 1394. 1st Bn. 2nd King Edward VII's Own Gurkha Rifles (The Sirmoor Rifles). 6 April 1943 Age 31. Son of Tilbir and Mati; Husband of Manrupi, of Soraghari, Nepal. Face 43.

HARAK BAHADUR THAPA, Naik, 2197. 1st Bn. 9th Gurkha Rifles. 6 April 1943 Age 29. Son of Lachhuman and Khaisari; Husband of Lalitkumari, of Balachaur, Nepal. Face 42.

HARKA SING GURUNG, Naik, 1694. 1st Bn. 2nd King Edward VII's Own Gurkha Rifles (The Sirmoor Rifles). 6 April 1943 Age 29. Son of Bhakte Sing and Kirbuli; Husband of Sarkhani, of Batase, Nepal. Face 43.

HARMSWORTH, Private, CYRIL THOMAS, 6201261. 1/7th Bn. Middlesex Regiment. 6 April 1943 Age 28. Face 27.

HARTLEY, Private, ALBERT, 4399761. 7th Bn. Green Howards (Yorkshire Regt.) 6 April 1943 Age 26. Son of Emma Hartley, of Wombwell, Yorkshire. Face 18.

HORN, Lance Corporal, FREDERICK GEORGE, 2659107. 3rd Bn. Coldstream Guards. 7 April 1943 Age 23. Son of Frederick and Kate Horn, of Finedon, Northamptonshire. Face 12.

HORNER, Private, JOHN, 2765771. 1st Bn. Black Watch. 6 April 1943 Age 23. Son of William and Ann Horner, of Burnley, Lancashire; Husband of Louisa Horner, of Burnley. Face 24.

HUNT, Private, JOHN, 6200473. 1/7th Bn. Middlesex Regiment. 6 April 1943 Age 29. Face 27.

JACKSON, Sergeant, WILLIAM, 3769287. 40th (7th Bn. The King's Regiment) Royal Tank Regt. RAC. 6 April 1943 Age 28. Son of William and Ellen Jackson; Husband of Elizabeth Patricia Jackson, of Bickerstaffe Lancashire. Face 4.

JACKSON, Corporal, WILLIAM MCLEOD, 2763039. 5th Bn. Black Watch. 7 April 1943 Age 28. Son of William McLeod Jackson and Jessie Brown Guthrie Jackson, of Glasgow. Face 23.

LJHAP BAHADUR RANA, Rifleman, 2226. 1st Bn. 2nd King Edward VII's Own Gurkha Rifles (The Sirmoor Rifles). 6 April 1943 Age 21. Son of Nar Bahadur and Mati, of Taksar, Nepal. Face 44.

KAY, Private, LEONARD, 4920917. 7/10th Bn. Argyll and Sutherland Highlanders. 6 April 1943 Age 23. Face 32.

KEANE, Trooper, ANTHONY, 7895869. 10th Royal Hussars, RAC. 6 April 1943 Age 21. Son of Mr & Mrs Andrew Keane, of Oldham Lancashire. Face 2.

KEMP, Private, WILLIAM, 2829435. 2nd Bn. Seaforth Highlanders. 6 April 1943 Age 30. Son of John and Margaret Kemp; Husband of Rose Kemp, of Broom of Moy, Forres, Morayshire. Face 29.

KISHAN BAHADUR KARKI, Rifleman, 95519. 1st Bn. 9th Gurkha Rifles 6 April 1943 Age 21. Son of Durja Bahadur and Lachmi, of Soryek, Nepal. Face 43.

LAL DHOJ GURUNG, Lance Naik. 2032. 1st Bn. 2nd King Edward V11'S Own Gurkha Rifles. (Sirmour Rifles). 6th April 1943. Age 23. Son of Dhanjit and Putali; Husband of Baki, Of Nepal.

LAWRIE, Private, WILLIAM, 2993046. 7/10th Bn. Argyll and Sutherland Highlanders. 6 April 1943 Age 20. Son of Alexander Lawrie and Mary Lawrie (nee Livingstone), of Ballachulish, Argyllshire. Face 32.

LAY, Private, ERIC ALFRED, 5337565. 2nd Bn. Cheshire Regiment. 6 April 1943 Age 22. Son of George and Alice Lay, of Tottenham, Middlesex. Face 19.

McDERMOTT, Private, JOHN, 2991492. 7/10th Bn. Argyll and Sutherland Highlanders. 6 April 1943 Age 21. Son of George and Jenny McDermott, of Johnstone, Renfrewshire. Face 32.

McGREGOR, Private, MURRAY ANDERSON, 2759217. 7th Bn. Black Watch. 6 April 1943 Age 24. Son of John and Andrewina McGregor; Husband of Betsy McGregor, of Thornton, Fife. Face 24.

MILLS, Sergeant, DAVID, 2934321. 5th Bn. Queen's Own Cameron Highlanders. 6 April 1943 Age 26. Son of George and Elsie Mills, of Edinburgh. Face 30.

MORRELL, Lance Corporal, MALCOLM MAURICE, 2762194. 1st Bn. Black Watch. 6-7 April 1943 Age 26. Son of Alfred Jones Morrell and Selina Morrell; Husband of Irene Morrell, of Urmston, Lancashire. Face 23.

NADIR KHAN, Water carrier, 55. 4th Bn. 16th Punjab Regiment. 7 April 1943 Age 41. Son of Noor Din and Alam Bi; Husband of Begman, of Adrana, Jhelum, Pakistan. Face 42.

OSBORNE, Private, FREDERICK WILLIAM, 5833323. 5th Bn. East Yorkshire Regt. 6 April 1943 Age 29. Son of Henry and Martha Osborne, of Luton, Bedfordshire; Husband of M Osborne, of Tunbridge Wells, Kent. Face 16.

PAINDA KHAN, Jemadar, 14932/IO. 4th Bn. 16th Punjab Regiment. 6 April 1943 Age 36. Son of Mehdi Khan and Suba Bi; Husband of Anar Begum, of Maira, Jhelum, Pakistan. Face 41.

PERKINS, Lance Bombardier, NORMAN HENRY, 1131758. 128 Field Regt., Royal Artillery. 6 April 1943 Age 21. Son of Harry and Edith Maud Perkins, of Herne Hill, London. Face 6.

POUND, Private SAMUEL, 3`136864. 7th Bn. Black Watch. 6 April 1943 Age 30. Son of Thomas and Isabel Pound, of Burnley, Lancashire. Face 24.

PURAN SINGH, Sapper, 21447. KGVs O Bengal Sappers & Miners. 6 April 1943 Age 19. Son of Waryam Singh and Atri, of Paranewala, Ferozepore, India. Face 41.

RAJ WALI, Rifleman, 18572. 4th Bn. 6th Rajputana Rifles. 6 April 1943 Age 19. Son of Sharaf Din. Face 41.

RESHAM SINGH, Naik, 21735. KGVs O Bengal Sappers & Miners. 6 April 1943 Age 19. Son of Naurang Singh and Chinti; Husband of Kartar Kaur, of Doaba Bolinna, Jullundur, India. Face 41.

RICHARDSON, Corporal, HENRY FREDERICK, 2992386. 1st Bn. Black Watch. 6-7 April 1943 Age 28. Son of Henry and Florence Ada Richardson; Husband of Phyllis Daphne Richardson, of New Cross, London. Face 23.

RICKARD, Sergeant, SIDNEY EDWARD, 3133703. 5th Bn. Black Watch. 8 April 1943 Age 25. Son of Sidney E and Florence Rickard; Husband of Doris Rickard, of Totton Hampshire. Face 23.

RIKHI RAM ALE, Rifleman, 26305. 1st Bn. 2nd King Edward VII's Own Gurkha Rifles (The Sirmoor Rifles). 6 April 1943 Age 18. Son of Narain and Fattu; Husband of Mani, of Danrapur, Nepal. Face 44.

ROLLIE, Private, ANDREW COLQUHOUN, 1501012. 7/10th Bn. Argyll and Sutherland Highlanders. 6 April 1943 Age 24. Face 32.

SAYID AKBAR, Sapper, 27332. KGVs O Bengal Sappers & Miners. 6 April 1943 Age 24. Son of Muhammad Hassan and Begum Bibi, o Rakka, Rawalpindi, Pakistan. Face 41.

SCOTT, Sergeant, THOMAS WHITE, 2823577. 2nd Bn. Seafortl Highlanders. 6 April 1943 Age 38. Son of Thomas White Scott and Amy Scott; Husband of Mary Scott, of Newlands, Glasgow. Face 29.

SHILLCROSS, Trooper, GEORGE WILLIAM, 7939650. 50th Royal Tank Regt. RAC., 6 April 1943 Age 33. Son of George Shillcross and Rutl Shillcross, of Kegworth, Leicestershire. Face 3.

SMART, Private, THOMAS, 6209775. 1/7th Bn. Middlesex Regiment. 6 April 1943 Age 24. Face 27.

SMITH, Trooper, ARTHUR CHARLES, 7912189. 4th County of Londor Yeo. (Sharpshooters), RAC. 6 April 1943 Age 22. Face 4.

SMITH, Sergeant, GEORGE, 2077859. 274 Field Coy., Royal Engineers 6 April 1943 Age 26. Son of Alex and Isabella Smith; Husband of Helen Smith, of Lerwick. Zetland. Face 10.

SMITH, Sergeant, HENRY WILLIAM, 7347138. 176 Field Ambulance. 6 April 1943 Age 34. Son of George and Annie Smith; Husband of Rose Smith, of Old Meldrum, Aberdeenshire. Face 37.

SPENCE, Private, JOHN EVERILL, 4396428. 7th Bn. Green Howards (Yorkshire Regt.) 6 April 1943 Age 28. Son of John and Everill Mary Spence. Face 18.

SPRIDDELL, Squadron Sergeant Major (WO.II), GODFREY TREVELYAN, M. M, 420579. 4th County of London Yeo. (Sharpshooters), RAC. 6 April 1943 Age 32. Face 4.

STARKEY, Trooper, ARTHUR, 7945090k. 4th County of London Yeo (Sharpshooters), RAC. 6 April 1943 Age 22. Son of Henry and Annie Starkey, of Tamworth, Staffordshire. Face 4.

TEK BAHADUR THAPA, Rifleman, 2826. 1st Bn. 2nd King Edward VII's Own Gurkha Rifles (The Sirmoor Rifles). 6 April 1943 Age 20. Son of Bankabal and Sambarn, of Argali, Nepal. Face 44.

WALLER, Lance Corporal, JOHN LEWIS, 48652098. 7th Bn. Black Watch. 6 April 1943 Age 18. Son of Adelaide Waller; Stepson of Albert Garris, of Hull. Face 24.

WHETTON, Trooper, EDWARD BADEN, 7944880. 10th Royal Hussars, RAC. 6 April 1943 Age 22. Son of Annie E Bennett, of Dunstall, Staffordshire. Face 2.

WYKES, Lieutenant, CLIFFORD, 184006. 50th Royal Tank Regt. RAC. 5 April 1943 Age 25. Son of George and Emily Wykes; Husband of Ruth Murthwaite Wykes, of Shildon, Co. Durham. Face 3.

YAQUB MASIH, Ambulance Sepoy, 97578. 17 Field Ambulance. 6 April 1943 Age 18. Son of Attah Ullah, of Talauranadi Rama, Gurdaspur, India. Face 44.

MEDJEZ-EL-BAB WAR CEMETERY

BRETT, Driver, EDWARD, T/5056733. Royal Army Service Corps. 6 April 1943 Age 29. Son of Ernest Edward and Caroline Brett, of Hurstmonceaux, Sussex; Husband of Anna Maria Brett, of Hurstmonceaux. 16. D.4.

BROUGHTON, Private, CHARLES ALFRED, 4346669. 5th Bn. East Yorkshire Regt. 6 April 1943 Age 26. Son of Alfred and Sarah Ann Broughton, of Wortley, Leeds, Yorkshire. Sp. Mem. "C". 17.H.17.

CARROLL, Private, BERNARD, 4349577. 5th Bn. East Yorkshire Regt. 6 April 1943 Age 33. Son of William J and Sarah Carroll, of Bradford, Yorkshire. Sp. Mem. "C".17.H.18.

COLEMAN, Sergeant, EDWARD ARTHUR, 1644522. Royal Artillery. 5 April 1943 Age 24. Son of George and Lillian May Coleman; Husband of Tamar Coleman, of Lewisham, London. 16.E.8.

HALL, Gunner, ALAN ERNEST, 20807. N.Z. Artillery. 6 April 1943 Age 24. Son of Harold John and Winifred Daisy Hall, of Mangapehi, Taranaki, New Zealand. 14.A.4.

HYATT, Gunner, JOHN FRANCIS, 998988. 127 Field Regt. Royal Artillery. 6 April 1943 Age 31. Spec. Mem. "C". 17.H.14.

LEATHER, Guardsman, WALLACE, 2619151. 5th Bn. Grenadier Guards. 7 April 1943 Age 29. Son of Thomas and Vivien Leather; Husband of Bessie Leather, of Blackburn, Lancashire. 3.F.2.

LLOYD, Guardsman, PERCY, 2736975. 3rd Bn. Welsh Guards. 5 April 1943 Age 28. Son of John and Elizabeth Lloyd, of Holywell, Flintshire; Husband of Olwen Lloyd, of Holywell. 14.B.20.

PARRY, Lance Corporal, RALPH, 3962040. 2nd Bn. Cheshire Regiment. 6 April 1943 Age 26. Son of Arthur and Jessie Parry, of Ystrad Mynach, Glamorgan. Sp. Mem. "C." 17.H.16.

SMITH, Gunner, CHARLES, 1139646. 124 Field Regt., Royal Artillery. April 1943 Age 21. Son of Fredrick and Winifred Ann Smith, of Exeter Sp. Mem. "C." 7.H.19.

SPENCER, Lance Sergeant, ARTHUR VICTOR SYDNEY, 4858097. 5th Bn. Grenadier Guards. 7 April 1943 Age 24. 9.E.19.

BEJA WAR CEMETERY

BOUSFIELD, Private, JOHN WILLIAM, 4399852. 5th Bn. East Yorkshire Regt. 6 April 1943 Age 19. Son of William and Annie Bousfield, of Stockton-on-Tees, Co. Durham. SP.MEM "C." 2.0.11.

FLYNN, Gunner, 970431. 166 (Newfoundland) Regt. Royal Artillery. April 1943. 2.F.A.

JAMAN KHAN, Sepoy. 17246. 4th Bn. Punjab Rgt. 8 April 1943 Age 23 Son of Yar Muhammad and Bakhat Bi, of Uchalli, Shahpur, Pakistan 2.B.4.

MISON, Corporal, JOHN FREDERICK, 4387848. 5th Bn. East Yorkshire Rgt. 6 April 1943 Age 29. Son of Frederick John and Daisy Mison, of Boston Spa, Yorkshire. Sp MEM. "C." 2.O.1.

SMITH, Corporal, ERNEST, 4391492. 5th Bn. East Yorkshire Rgt. 6 April 1943 Age 22. Son of Albert Ernest and Lillian Smith, of Middlesborough, Yorkshire; Husband of Edith Olga Smith, of Middlesborough, Sp MEM "C." 2.O.9.

NORTH AFRICA AMERICAN CEMETERY: TUNISIA (CARTHAGE)

ALLEN, 2 Lieutenant. CARL, A. Ninth Air Force Head Quarters. 6 April 1943. Plot F. Row 19. Grave 6.

ALAMEIN MEMORIAL TO THE MISSING: EGYPT

ANNAKIN, ARTHUR, R. 7921088. Trooper. 1st Scorpion Regiment, RAC. 6 April 1943 Age 22. Son of Arthur H and Winifred Annakin of Harrogate, Yorkshire. Column 13 (Trooper Annakin was mistakenly placed on this memorial, his correct place should be on the Medjez-El-Bab Memorial to the Missing).

APPENDIX C

HONOURS AND AWARDS

30 Corps

Gallantry Awards for the 'Battle of the Wadi Akarit' 6 April 1943

These are listed by Division and Battalion. A few awards were given for a number of actions that included 'The Wadi Akarit'. These are shown by a star (*) after the date it was 'gazetted'.

As far as I know, this list is complete. However, if I have missed out any individual I apologise to him and his family.

VC : Victoria Cross

DSO : Distinguished Service Order

MC : Military Cross

DCM : Distinguished Conduct Medal

IDSM : Indian Distinguished Service Medal

IOM : Indian Order of Merit

MM : Military Medal

MID : Mentioned in Dispatches

KIA : Killed in Action (indicated in unit column)

If a bar to any medal is indicated, it denotes a second award of the same medal, this bar is worn on the ribbon of the first medal.

50th Northumbrian Division

Award	Name and Rank		Date Gazetted	Unit
VC.	Anderson. E.	Pte.	29.07.43	5th East Yorks. (KIA: 06.04.43)
MM.	Carter. T.	Pte.	08.07.43	5th Bn East Yorks Reg.
MM.	Gouldsborough. T.	Cpl.	08.07.43	5th Bn East Yorks Reg.
MM.	Clayton. J.	Sgt.	25.11.43	6th Bn Green Howards.
MM.	Harper. H.	Pte.	08.07.43	6th Bn Green Howards.
BAR to MC.	Hull. C. M.	Major. MC.	08.07.43	6th Bn Green Howards.
MM.	Smith. R. W.	L/Cpl.	08.07.43	6th Bn Green Howards.
MM.	Winterbottom. A.	Pte.	08.07.43	6th Bn Green Howards.
BAR to MM.	Craddock. C.	Sgt. MM.	22.07.43	7th Bn Green Howards.
MC.	Hay. I. T. R.	Cpt.	22.07.43	7th Bn Green Howards.
MC.	Mansell. J. B.	Major.	25.11.43	7th Bn Green Howards.
MM.	O'Rourke. J.	Cpl.	22.07.43	7th Bn Green Howards.
MM.	Ebdon. J. E.	L/Sgt.	17.06.43	50 Div Signals.
MM.	Gough. H.	L/Sgt.	26.08.43*	42nd Fld Coy: RE.
DSO.	Keeling. S. V.	Lt-Col.	17.06.43	2nd Cheshire Reg.
MM.	Thorpe. H.	Sgt.	14.10.43	7th Med Reg: RA.

51st Highland Division

Award	Name and Rank		Date Gazetted	Unit
BAR to DSO.	Murray. G.	Brig. DSO. MC.	08.07.43	O.C. 152 Bde.
MC.	Ainsley. D. M. L.	Lt.	17.06.43	5th Camerons.
MM.	Darling. W.	Pte.	22.07.43	5th Camerons.
MM.	Gordon. J. D.	Sgt.	17.06.43	5th Camerons.
MM.	MacDougal. N.	Sgt.	14.09.43	5th Camerons.
MC.	Sim. J. R.	Lt.	14.09.43	5th Camerons.
MM.	Wilson. P.	Pte.	08.07.43	5th Camerons.
MM.	Anderson. M. G.	Pte.	08.07.43	2nd Seaforth.
MM.	Black. J.	L/Cpl.	08.07.43	2nd Seaforth.
MC.	Barclay. P. S.	Cpt. (MO)	17.06.43	2nd Seaforth.
MM.	Donnolly. L.	Sgt.	14.09.43	2nd Seaforth.
MC.	Grant. I. J. C.	Cpt.	17.06.43	2nd Seaforth.
BAR to MC.	Gilmour. A. M.	Major. MC.	17.06.43	2nd Seaforth.

Award	Name and Rank		Date Gazetted	Unit
MM	McGeachie. H. J. L.	Sgt.	14.09.43	2nd Seaforth.
MC.	McHardy. W. G.	Major	17.06.43	2nd Seaforth.
DSO.	Horne. R. D.	Lt-Col.	17.06.43	2nd Seaforth.
MM.	McWilliam. G.	Pte.	14.09.43	2nd Seaforth.
BAR to MM.	Bridges. D. M.	Pte. MM.	-	5th Seaforth.
DSO.	Davidson. J.H.	Major.	17.06.43	5th Seaforth.
MM.	Kennedy. D.	L/Sgt.	08.07.43	5th Seaforth.
MM.	McGachie.	Sgt.	22.07.43	5th Seaforth.
MM.	Polson. A.	Sgt.	17.06.43	5th Seaforth.
MC.	Wilcock. G. A.	Cpt.	17.06.43	5th Seaforth.
MM.	Wilcockson. S. W.	L/Cpl.	08.07.43	5th Seaforth.
DCM.	Baddeley. R. M.	Sgt.	22.07.43	1st Black Watch.
DCM.	Elliot. E. R.	Pte.	22.07.43	1st Black Watch.
MM.	Sutherland. W.	L/Cpl.	22.07.43	1st Black Watch.
DCM.	Craig. R. H.	Sgt.	22.07.43	7th Black Watch.
MM.	Davidson. D. B.	Sgt.	22.07.43	7th Black Watch.
DSO.	Hopwood. J. A.	Cpt.	22.07.43	7th Black Watch.
MM.	Jordan. W.	L/Cpl.	22.07.43	7th Black Watch.
MC.	Watson. J. P.	Lt.	22.07.43	7th Black Watch.
MM.	Archibald. J. M.	CSM. DCM.	22.07.43	7th Argylls.
VC.	Campbel. L. M.	Lt-Col. DSO+BAR	08.06.43	7th Argylls.
MC.	Faid. N. E.	Lt.	14.09.43	7th Argylls.
MM.	Ginty. J.	Cpl.	14.09.43	7th Argylls.
MM.	Hemphill. W.	Sgt.	22.07.43	7th Argylls.
DSO.	Lindsay-MacDougal. J.S.	Major. MC.	22.07.43	7th Argylls. (D.O.W.: Sicily)
DSO.	Mathieson. R.	Major. TD.	14.09.43	7th Argylls.
MM.	Snaddon. J.	Pte.	14.09.43	7th Argylls.
MM.	Watson. J.	Pte.	14.09.43	7th Argylls.
MM.	Williamson. J.	Pte.	14.09.43	7th Argylls.
MM.	Clark. G.	Pte.	22.07.43	5th Black Watch.
MC.	Crichton-Melville. H. R.	Lt.	22.04.43	5th Black Watch.
MM.	Dewar. A. B.	Sgt.	22.07.43	5th Black Watch.
MC.	Dunn. G. W.	Major.	19.08.43	5th Black Watch.
MM.	Ketchen. R.	L/Sgt.	22.07.43	5th Black Watch.
MM.	Murray. R. G. H.		22.07.43	5th Black Watch.

MC.	Nicol. T. J. T.	Reverend	22.07.43	5th Black Watch.
MM.	Ramsay. F.	Cpl.	14.09.43	5th Black Watch.
MM.	Ross. A. D.	Pte.	22.07.43	5th Black Watch.
MM.	Wilson. W. W.	Pte.	22.07.43	5th Black Watch.
DSO.	Buckwell. B. A.	Major.	25.11.43*	3rd Reg: RHA.
DSO.	Hildebrand. G. L.	Lt-Col.	08.07.43	149 A/Tk Reg: RA.
MC.	Henderson. J. R.	Lt.	22.07.43	128 Fld Reg: RA.
MM.	Nuttall. H.	Gnr.	26.08.43	127 Fld Reg: RA.
MM.	Mathens. K. W. F.	Gnr.	26.08.43	127 Fld Reg: RA.
DSO.	Bishop. B.	Cpt.	26.08.43	126 Fld Reg: RA.
MM.	Hamilton. A.	Gnr.	26.08.43	126 Fld Reg: RA.
MM.	Gray. A.	Gnr.	19.08.43	58 Fld Reg: RA.
MM.	Hone. K.	Bdr.	19.08.43	58 Fld Reg: RA.
MM.	Blackman. J. H. C.	Cpl.	14.09.43	275 Fld Coy: RE.
MM.	Duffy. R. J.	Sapper.	14.09.43	275 Fld Coy: RE.
MM.	Ross. F. J. B. P.	Sapper.	22.07.43	275 Fld Coy: RE.
MM.	Marren. P.	Cpl.	22.07.43	275 Fld Coy: RE.
MM.	Foster. F.	Sapper.	14.09.43	274 Fld Coy: RE.
MC.	Patullo. A.	Cpt.	22.07.43	274 Fld Coy: RE.
MM.	Shireffs. J. R.	Cpl.	22.07.43	274 Fld Coy: RE.
MC.	George. I. B. W.	Lt.	22.07.43	275 Fld Coy: RE.
MM.	Nicol. F. W.	L/Bdr.	22.07.43	128 Fld Coy: RE.
MM.	Avery. G. V.	Cpl.	14.09.43	1st / 7th Middlesex
MM.	Rosskilly. J. G.	L/Cpl.	22.07.43	1st / 7th Middlesex
M.	Wiltshire. L.	Cpl.	22.07.43	1st / 7th Middlesex
MM.	Coull. W. W.	Cpl.	22.07.43	Signals.
MM.	Hunter. D.	Pte.	22.07.43	Signals.
MC.	Locke. R. F.	Cpt.	22.07.43	(HQ) Signals.
MM	Mackenzie. T.	Sgt.	17.06.43	Signals.
MC.	McCormick. J. O.	Lt.	17.06.43	Signals.
MC.	Wright. F. A.	Cpt.	25.11.43	(CRA) Signals.
DSO.	Kerr. C. H.	Lt-Col.	08.07.43	176 Fld. Amb.
MM.	Buchanan. J. W.	Pte.	22.07.43	175 Fld. Amb.
MM.	Gracie. J. M.	Dvr.	08.07.43	R.A.S.C.
MM.	McCloy. W. S.	Dvr.	08.07.43	R.A.S.C.
MM.	Stewart. R.	Dvr.	19.08.43	R.A.S.C.

4th Indian Division

Award	Name and Rank		Date Gazetted	Unit
I.D.S.M.	Dalbir. G.	L/Naik.	22.07.43	1st / 2nd Gurkhas.
MC.	Fraser. J. N.	Cpt.	Not Found	1st / 2nd Gurkhas.
I.D.S.M.	Ghale. D.	L/Naik.	22.07.43	1st / 2nd Gurkhas.
I.D.S.M.	Gurung. B.	Jemadar	22.07.43	1st / 2nd Gurkhas.
I.D.S.M.	Gurung. H.	Pte.	22.07.43	1st / 2nd Gurkhas.
I.D.S.M.	Gurung. S.	Naik.	22.07.43	1st / 2nd Gurkhas.
I.D.S.M.	Rana. B.	Jemadar.	22.07.43	1st / 2nd Gurkhas.
DSO.	Lovett. Ode T.	Brigadier.	17.06.43	OC. 7 th Brigade.
I.D.S.M.	Pun. B.	Havildar.	08.07.43	1st / 2nd Gurkhas.
I.D.S.M.	Pun. I.	Rifleman.	22.07.43	1st / 2nd Gurkhas.
I.O.M.	Pun. L.	Pte.	22.07.43	1st / 2nd Gurkhas.
BAR to MC.	Ramsay-Brown. MC. Cpt.		17.06.43	1st / 2nd Gurkhas.
DSO.	Showers. L. J. G.	Lt-Col.	17.06.43	1st / 2nd Gurkhas.
MC.	Stubbs. P. L.	Cpt.	Not Found	1st / 2nd Gurkhas.
I.D.S.M.	Thapa. J. A.	Jemadar.	22.07.43	1st / 2nd Gurkhas.
I.D.S.M.	Thapa. M.	Havildar.	08.07.43	1st / 2nd Gurkhas.
I.D.S.M.	Thapa. N.	L/Naik.	22.07.43	1st / 2nd Gurkhas.
VC.	Thapa. L.	Subedar.	15.06.43	1st / 2nd Gurkhas.
MC.	Walcot. S. W.	Major.	17.06.431	st / 2nd Gurkhas.
BAR to MM.	Bungard. J.	Sgt. MM.	Not Found	1st Royal Sussex.
MM.	Coppard. D. R. G.	Sgt.	08.07.43	1st Royal Sussex.
MM.	Greenfield. J.	CSM.	08.07.43	1st Royal Sussex.
MC.	Reilly. T.	Cpt.	08.07.43	(RAMC) Royal Sussex.
MC.	Hawkes. G. W.	Cpt.	08.07.43	1st Royal Sussex.
MM.	Hickman. J. H.	L/Cpl.	08.07.43	1st Royal Sussex.
DSO.	Firth. C. E. A.	Lt-Col.	17.06.43	1st Royal Sussex.
MM.	Jubb. W.	Pte.	Not Found	RE
MM.	Ives. B.	Pte.	08.07.43	1st Royal Sussex.
MM.	Mackinlay. N. W.	Pte.	08.07.43	1st Royal Sussex.
MC.	Philips. F. W.	Cpt.	08.07.43	(RACD) Royal Sussex.
MM.	Peacock. E. G.	Pte.	08.07.43	1st Royal Sussex.
MM.	Rossiter. E.	Pte.	08.07.43	1st Royal Sussex.
MC.	Upton. S. J. F.	Cpt.	08.07.43	1st Royal Sussex.
MC.	Weeks. L. W.	Cpt.	08.07.43	1st Royal Sussex.
I.D.S.M.	Aslam. M.	Havildar.	08.07.43	4th / 16th Punjab.

Award	Name and Rank		Date Gazetted	Unit
I.D.S.M.	Mian. M.	Subedar.	08.07.43	4th / 16th Punjab.
I.D.S.M.	Niwaz. M.	Sepoy.	22.07.43	4th / 16th Punjab.
MC.	Perkin. R. A.	Cpt.	08.07.43	4th / 16th Punjab.
I.D.S.M.	Ram. K.	Sepoy.	26.08.43	4th / 16th Punjab.
I.D.S.M.	Sakir. M.	Havildar.	08.07.43	4th / 16th Punjab.
I.D.S.M.	Singh. L.	L/Naik.	26.08.43	4th / 16th Punjab.
MC.	Amoore. D. M.	Cpt.	22.07.43	1st / 9th Gurkhas.
I.D.S.M.	Khattri. K.	L/Naik.	22.07.43	1st / 9th Gurkhas.
I.D.S.M.	Khattri. B.	Naik.	22.07.43	1st / 9th Gurkhas.
I.O.M. (2nd Cl)	Khan. A.	Subedar.	22.07.43	4th / 6th Rajputana.
MM.	Khushi. M.	L/Naik.	22.07.43	4th / 6th Rajputana.
MM.	Niwaz. M.	Havildar.	22.07.43	4th / 6th Rajputana.
I.D.S.M.	Ram. R.	Havildar.	08.07.43	4th / 6th Rajputana.
I.D.S.M.	Ram. G.	Jemadar.	08.07.43	4th / 6th Rajputana.
I.O.M. (2nd Cl)	Singh. D.	Havildar.	22.07.43	4th / 6th Rajputana.
MC.	Riddick. G. R.	Cpt.	08.07.43	Rajputana-Machine Gun Bn.
MM.	Brewer. H. T.	Cpl.	02.07.43*	1st / 4th Essex.
DCM.	Rose. C. J.	RSM.	25.11.43*	1st / 4th Essex.
MC.	Jephson.	Major.	Not Found	11th Fld Regt. RA.
MM.	Teeder. J. S.	L/Cpl.	25.11.43 *	1st / 4th Essex.
MC.	Wily. B. P.	Cpt.	25.11.43	1st / 4th Essex.
I.D.S.M.	George. A.	Naik.	25.11.43	Signals.
DSO.	Gray. F. P.	L.Lt-Col.	08.07.43*	Signals.
I.D.S.M.	Singh. K.	Havildar.	17.06.43	Signals.
I.D.S.M.	Singh. J.	Naik.	17.06.43	Signals.
I.D.S.M.	Singh. J.	L/Naik.	17.06.43	Signals.
I.D.S.M.	Singh. P.	Pte.	17.06.43	Signals.
I.D.S.M.	Ullah. H.	Sepoy.	08.07.43	R.I.A.S.C.
MC.	Dadir. A.	Cpt.	22.07.43	26th Fld Amb.
I.D.S.M.	Sundra-Bab U. C. R.	Sepoy.	08.07.43	17th Fld Amb.
DSO.	Thorne. H. J. R.	Lt-Col.	08.07.43	17th Fld Amb.
MM.	Bonney. W. F.	L/Bdr.	08.07.43	31st Field Reg: RA.
MC.	Calvert. W. H.	Cpt.	08.07.43	31st Field Reg: RA.
MC.	Colenette. D. B.	Cpt.	08.07.43	31st Field Reg: RA.
MC.	Galetti. A.	Major.	17.06.43	KIA: 04.43
MM.	Newsham. H.	Gnr.	22.07.43	KIA: 04.43

Award	Name and Rank		Date Gazetted	Unit
DSO.	Norton. G. H.	Lt-Col.	26.08.43	KIA: 04.43
MM.	Smailes. C. C.	Bdr.	08.07.43	KIA: 04.43
MC.	Ward. D. J.	Major.	26.08.43	(KIA: 20.04.43)
MM	Sellars. W.	Gnr.	25.11.43	11th Fld Reg: RA.
MC.	Huntley. J. F. B.	Major.	17.06.43	11th Fld Reg: RA.
MM.	Sales. T. W.	L/Cpl.	17.06.43	11th Fld Reg: RA.
MC.	Galbraith. A.	C.Lt.	08.07.43	149 A/Tk Reg: RA.
MM.	Walker. J. J.	L/Bdr.	22.07.43	57 L.A.A. Reg: RA.
I.D.S.M.	Duraimuthu.	Havildar.	17.06.43	12th Fld Coy: RE.
I.O.M.	Krisnnan.	Naik.	17.06.43	12th Fld Coy: RE.

Armoured Units
New Zealand Engineers (Mine-Field Task Force)
30 Corps Staff

Award	Name and Rank		Date Gazetted	Unit
MM.	Allison. D. st C.	L/Cpl.	22.07.43	4th Cly.
DSO.	Cameron. A. A.	Major.		
		MC + BAR.	22.07.43	4th Cly.
MM.	Kirkley. J. N.	L/Sgt.	22.07.43	4th Cly.
MM.	Moore. R. A.	Sgt.	22.07.43	4th Cly.
MM.	Samuel. V. D.	Cpl.	22.07.43	4th Cly.
BAR to DSO.	Scott. H. B.	Lt-Col. DSO.	22.07.43	4th Cly.
BAR to MC.	Scott. P. M. R.	Major. MC.	22.07.43	4th Cly.
MC.	Foot. F. W.	Major.	22.07.43	40th Rtr.
M.I.D.	Sowden. H. J.	Sgt.	22.07.43	40th Rtr.
DSO.	Russel. G. E.	Lt-Col.	22.07.43	50th Rtr.
MC.	Venn. D. P.	Major.	22.07.43	50th Rtr.
DSO.	Hanson. F. M. H.	Lt-Col.		
		OBE. MM.	22.07.43	New Zealand C-R-E.
MC.	Morris. R. W.	Lt.	25.11.43	New Zealand C-R-E.
MC.	Blackburn. J. D.	Lt.	08.07.43*	4th Survey Reg. RA.
BAR to DSO.	Steward. R. H. R.	Lt-Col. DSO.	25.11.43*	30 Corps Sig's.
MM.	Thorpe. H.	Sgt.	14.10.43*	REME: Lad.
MM.	Bunce. G. A.	L/Cpl.	14.10.43	113 Provost Coy.
MC.	Hall. W.	Cpt.	22.07.43*	(AAIPU) R-E.
MC.	Nixon. S.	Lt.	Not Found	50th RTR. (Kia: Sicily. 1943)

APPENDIX D

The Battle of the Wadi Akarit – 6 April 1943 : Order of Battle : 8th Army

30 CORPS

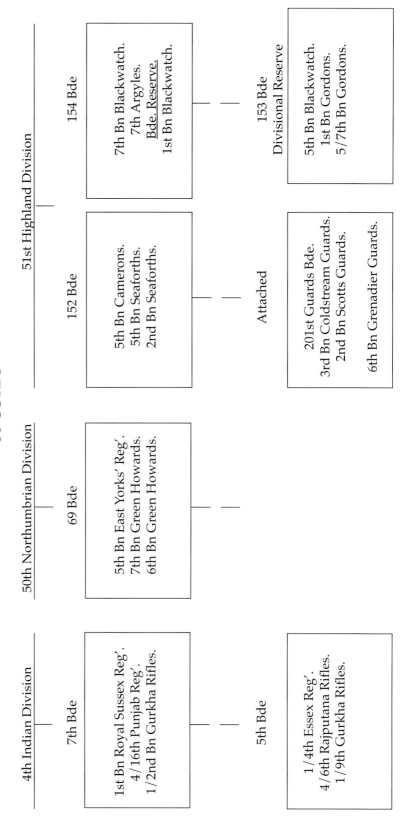

4th Indian Division

7th Bde
1st Bn Royal Sussex Reg'.
4/16th Punjab Reg'.
1/2nd Bn Gurkha Rifles.

5th Bde
1/4th Essex Reg'.
4/6th Rajputana Rifles.
1/9th Gurkha Rifles.

50th Northumbrian Division

69 Bde
5th Bn East Yorks' Reg'.
7th Bn Green Howards.
6th Bn Green Howards.

51st Highland Division

152 Bde
5th Bn Camerons.
5th Bn Seaforths.
2nd Bn Seaforths.

Attached
201st Guards Bde.
3rd Bn Coldstream Guards.
2nd Bn Scotts Guards.
6th Bn Grenadier Guards.

154 Bde
7th Bn Blackwatch.
7th Argyles.
Bde. Reserve.
1st Bn Blackwatch.

153 Bde
Divisional Reserve
5th Bn Blackwatch.
1st Bn Gordons.
5/7th Bn Gordons.

APPENDIX E

Axis Forces Order of Battle at the Wadi Akarit : 6 April 1943

(On this date 15th Panzer Div' had 26 Serviceable Tanks : 4 of these were Italian)

21 CORPS   **20 CORPS**

Pistoia Division

> I Bn / 36 Regiment.
> II Bn / 36 Regiment.
> I Bn / 35 Regiment.
> II Bn / 35 Regiment.
> III Bn / 35 Regiment.
> DET : 15 Panzer

Spezia Division

> III Bn / 125 Regiment.
> Tobruk Bn.
> 39 Bersaglieri

90th Light Division

> I Bn / 155 Regiment.
> II Bn / 155 Regiment.

164th Light Division

> (Saharan Group)
>
> I Bn / 382 Regiment.
> II Bn / 125 Regiment.

Reserves

> 361st Panzer Gremadier Regiment
> 190th Anti Tank Unit : 90th Light Div'.
> (Fatnassa Sector).
> 15th Panzer Division : Less DET'.
> 200th Panzer Grenadier Regiment :
> 90th Light Div'.
> (North of Roumana)

Trieste Division

> I Bn / 126 Regiment.
> II Bn / 126 Regiment.
> Gran Bn.
> Folgore Bn.
> I Bn / 65 Regiment.
> II Bn / 65 Regiment.

APPENDIX F

BBC Broadcast from Wadi Akarit
6:15am - 6 April 1943 Mr Gillard

It's just after sunrise on the morning of Tuesday 6 April and I'm standing here at the side of a track not very far south of the Wadi Akarit (gun-fire in background). The lull, which has lasted some days down here in southern Tunisia, was broken at a quarter past four this morning. It was still dark then, all night long we've heard the rumble of our planes roaring overhead towards the enemy lines, all night long we heard the thudding of their bombs as they found their target, but by four o'clock things were still again, everything seemed quiet and peaceful (explosions in the distance) in the dim light of the stars which were stirring in a deep grey sky.

But it was a deceptive stillness, there in the darkness all over the Gabes Plain the men of the 8th Army in their thousands and tens of thousands were standing to, waiting for the moment. The infantrymen who were to advance across the fifteen hundred yards of no-mans land were waiting, wearing their steel helmets, each man grasping his rifle or automatic or preparing to handle those deadly three inch mortars as they move forward through the mine-fields to attack the enemy positions.

Further back in the line the tank-crews were standing by their tanks ready to crash through the breach once the infantry had captured their objectives, whilst in the gun-pits the artillery were waiting - every shell fused, every gun calibrated, waiting for the signal to open fire. (More explosions). At 4:15 precisely that signal came and suddenly the peace of the Gabes Plain was shattered with a roar and a blast. Great yellow flashes of light blazed out from the muzzles of our guns from all over the front. The whole air and sky became a fury - a searing inferno of fire and steel for two hours, now that barrage has been kept up, you can still hear it in the background as I speak here. At times it's dropped for a moment and you can hear the sound of the larks - the calling of the curlew overhead and the braying of terrified donkey in the countryside around, then the guns have opened up again. We have seized on a comparatively quiet moment to record this, with the barrage at its height, you'd scarcely hear a word of what I'm saying.

Well once again the 8th Army is on the move, we can't say yet how the attack is going but we can say everyone here is in high spirits and full of expectation. And now I'll leave the last word in this dispatch to the guns of the 8th Army, those guns which are blasting the enemy at this very moment out of his strong positions across the Gabes Gap and softening the tough shell of Axis resistance and covering the advance of our own forces as they go forward to make a bridgehead in the enemy positions.

APPENDIX G

AN ACCOUNT OF THE 7th BN ARGYLL & SUTHERLAND HIGHLANDERS' PART IN THE BATTLE OF THE WADI AKARIT
BY BRIGADIER (THEN LT.COL.) LORNE MACLAINE CAMPBELL. VC. DSO. AND BAR. OBE. TD.

An interesting and very detailed account by a battalion commander who was always in the thick of the action, with typical modesty he makes no mention of his own deeds here that won him the Victoria Cross. The actions of other individuals are described in detail; Major Mathieson, keen to enter the battle but ordered to keep out of it. Doc Wilson's work in aiding the wounded without thought for his own safety. CSM Archibald's keenness to return to his own company. Major Maunder's disregard for his own safety as he sat calmly on the parapet smoking his pipe and directing operations until he was killed and Lt. Lindsay-MacDougall, though twice wounded, leading a desperate bayonet charge to restore a failing situation, for this he was awarded the DSO.

Many such deeds of bravery are enclosed in this most illuminating story as seen from the centre of the battle by the officer directing operations in the front line.

After being driven from the Mareth Line, Rommel retired as expected, to the Gabes Gap which provided, in Monty's words "an extremely strong natural defensive position". A large area of lakes and marshes which prevented any wide outflanking movement, narrowed the coastal plain to a width of twelve to fifteen miles. Across the narrowest part saw the Wadi Akarit, which, reinforced by an anti tank ditch, formed an obstacle to tanks and vehicles. Some steep-sided hills, of which one of the principle was Roumana, afforded dominant observation and strong points to which the defence could be locked.

Monty decided that he must attack quickly in order to prevent the position being still more strongly fortified and hoped by not waiting for the full moon to achieve a measure of surprise, his first instruction was to make the attack with the 51st and New Zealand Divisions. But, he soon realised that this would not be enough and decided to use three Infantry Divisions - 51st, 50th and 4th Indian - attacking side by side, as he said 'like a piston driving up a cylinder'.

The Highland Division was allotted the right hand sector of the attack, from the coastal road area up to and including Roumana, with orders to seize and hold a bridgehead over the Wadi Akarit.

In the Divisional sector, South of the wadi, a ridge of hill ran across from East to West. The direction of attack was approximately due North. From the top of it a long, open slope of a mile ran down to the wadi. On the far side of the wadi, in the right half of the sector, the bank rose in a slope of about six hundred yards, falling away to the level of the wadi on either flank. Elsewhere, the North bank was more or less level with the South. All the way along the West side of this sector, and stretching into the distance as far as the eye could see, ran a high brier of hill, which immediately on the far side of the wadi rose into an enormous, steep-sided, rocky lump which was Roumana itself. The whole area was sand-strewn and bare, except for a little occasional found cover; of all vegetation.

It was obvious that the place for their bridgehead was where the bank of the wadi rose on the far side, a reverse slope and some degree of command of the surrounding country. It was equally obvious that, if it was to be taken and held, Roumana must be captured, as it dominated the whole area, which must be laid out like a map below it. So the Divisional plan was for 154 Bde to make and hold the bridgehead, and 152 Bde to capture Roumana; and 153 Bde, who had made the first contact with the enemy and been holding the transverse East to West ridge, referred to above, to be in measure.

Meanwhile, the area of the coastal road was held by 201 Guards Brigade, who were not taking part in the attack, but were ordered to keep the men of the German 90th Light Division opposite them quiet by 'making faces at them'.

The plan for 154 Bde was that 7 Argyll should take and hold the bridgehead. 7 B.W. would be ready either to reinforce them if they were in difficulties in securing the bridgehead or, if they were successful, to launch an attack on their left and enlarge the bridgehead by clearing the North bank of the wadi as far as the foot of Roumana.

Before proceeding further with this account, which will henceforth deal only with the action of 7 A.S.H., it is desirable to describe what happened to the other units engaged. 7 B.W. duly launched their attack westwards from the left flank of 7 A.S.H. and enlarged the bridgehead considerably, but met within very stiff resistance and were unable to extend it to the foot of Roumana. 152 Bde reached the top of Roumana and seized a large part of it, but, though they got very close to it, were never able to capture the highest point. It was not for lack of trying. They attacked again and again over difficult rocky ground, with very fierce fighting and heavy casualties : but the enemy were obviously determined to hold the highest point at all costs and 152 could not dislodge them.

Our attack in 7A.S.H. was to start just before dawn. All descriptions in this account are taken from right to left.

Our start-line was the top of the transverse East to West ridge to which I have already referred. We then had to go down the mile of forward slope to the wadi which was about two hundred yards wide at this point and quite dry at this season. The front of our attack, which covered the slope on the far bank which was to form the bridgehead, was of a thousand yards westward from the point on the right where a tributary, the Oglet El Smala, joined the main wadi. This tributary, which was now towards us diagonally across our line of advance, was an undesirable feature, as troops crossing our obstacles are apt to walk off at right-angles to it and so lose direction. On the right half of our front the steep bank of the wadi on the far side had been scarped into a high perpendicular wall, on the left half, and starting almost exactly in the middle of the front, where the bank was lower, the anti tank ditch began and ran all the way to Roumana.

An air-photo gave us a very good idea of the enemy dispositions. The slopes which we intended to seize were obviously strongly held with numerous positions. The scarped wadi bank was estimated to be six to eight feet high. Earlier patrols had found no minefield, but a patrol sent out shortly before the attack reported that one about a hundred yards deep had been laid across the front. It also reported that the holding troops were Italians.

The air-photo showed the principle enemy positions to be two large ones on the right of the slope, one half way up and one at the top, and two rather smaller ones, similarly placed on the left. There were many smaller ones in between. The plan, accordingly, for the battalion attack was:- 'B' and 'A' Coys in the front line and 'C' and 'D' in the second, 'B' to take the position half way up on the right and 'C' to pass through, turn and take the position at the top, while 'A' took both the two smaller positions on the left in succession.

'D' Coy to follow 'A' and establish themselves near the wadi as battalion reserve. All companies to dig themselves in to hold their objectives when secured.

We left our assembly area on the evening before the battle, as soon as the light faded enough for our movement not to be spotted from the air and marched the seven miles to our Forming-Up Place, which was on the rear of the transverse ridge, first below our start line on the crest. Trenches had already been dug by 153 Bde and we were able to take up our attack formation and settle into them for the night. We were undisturbed until 0415 hours when actions began and their guns opened up. It was a rather ominous sound bringing the realisation that in an hour's time it would be our turn. So I took a walk round some of our trenches to see how our chaps were taking it. But, I need not have worried as they were also in great form, laughing and joking. We were further cheered by a hot breakfast produced by the battalion cooks and carried up in containers and every man had with him twenty-four hour ration and a full water-bottle for the day ahead.

Forming a bridgehead was the main object of 51 Div. and Divisional HQ gave us every possible help to achieve it, guns, machine-guns, tanks, sappers etc. To start with, at 0415 hours, an hour before we began our attack, a strong party of sappers with 'Scorpion' flail-tanks, covered by the artillery, tanks of the Royal Tank Regiment and our own mortar platoon with some of our signallers, went down to spend half an hour clearing two gaps through the minefield and the anti tank obstacles on our front.

At 0515 the battalion crossed the start-line, 'B' and 'A' Coys leading with 'C' and 'D' and Bn HQ following seven hundred yards behind. It was still dark when we started and, to begin with, there was very little hostile fire. They probably could not see us, and anyhow their attention was probably diverted by what was going on elsewhere on the 8th Army front. But as we advanced down the long, open slope to the wadi, the light quickly became clearer and clearer, and with it the fire increased in volume and the casualties began.

Just as I was getting into my jeep to follow the battalion up to the Forming-Up Place, a cheerful young officer from Div. HQ had driven up with an envelope which he handed me, saying they thought I might like to see the latest air-photo of the enemy positions. I did not like it at all. I had already decided that we had to deal with about as much as one battalion could tackle, and here was the enemy still just about doubled with several positions on our side of the wadi which had not been shown before. For good measure, the scarped bank of the wadi which had previously been estimated as six to eight feet high, was now shown as ten to twelve. It was too late to alter our plan ('Order, Counter-order, Disorder'). I told only Maj Lindsay-MacDougall, O.C. 'C' Coy and warned him not to start his men to pass through 'B' Coy until he heard from me, as he might be needed for something different if the enemy urned out to be as strong as the new photo showed. In fact, I need not have worried. As the second line, with Bn HQ, came down the slope we could see in the growing light the enemy positions appearing as shown in the original photo, each marked by a group of Italians with their hands in the air; and I was able to tell Major MacDougall to carry on as planned.

We gained the bridgehead with unexpected ease. The wire was thin and the minefield, though fairly deep, was laid with large, flat mines off which the wind had blown the covering sand so that most of them could be easily seen; and it caused us little trouble.

The Italians, having been heavily bombarded during our gapping operation and now, half an hour later, bombarded again by our guns supporting our attack, had for the most part lost all interest in the battle. Some made a brief show of resistance, but very soon all had surrendered. 'B' Company in their approach had swung too far to their left and crossed the wadi in 'A' Coy's area. They should have been guided correctly by the navigating party: but the navigating officer, Capt Cameron, had been hit on the slope and his deputy may have got his bearings wrong. Or it may have been due to that notorious source of misdirection, the Oglet El Smala running diagonally across the line of advance. But, I think the cause may, most probably, have been something which we had not appreciated, the lie of the land. The transverse ridge, which was running East to West on the Start Line, gradually edged forward to North East until it finally died out just to the right of our area.

Anyone trying to walk straight across the grain of such country, if, in the half light, he could not clearly see his final objective, but knew he had to go downhill, would be continually nudged by the tilt of the ground to go half left; and I think this is probably what happened. In the event it forced a fortunate reconnaissance because the Company missed the scarped bank, which they would otherwise have had to cross, and were able to attack their objective, the strongest of the enemy positions, from the flank. 'C' Company, who followed them and could see better where they were going in the growing light, had to climb the bank and found it a serious obstacle. Some of them were helped up by the Italian prisoners!

We now had the bridgehead. All the companies had taken their objectives and the job was to hold it throughout the day. Bn HQ was in a ditch in the wadi, picked off the air-photo. It turned out to be shallower than it looked in the photo and in the middle of the minefield with mines along the edge of it. Not the ideal position, but everyone had been told that that was where it would be, so there it remained. Bell, my batman,

dug a very good trench for me, but after a short time I decide that if
stayed in it much longer I would never want to get out of it again. So
left it and never went back again. Soon after we had arrived, the
prisoners started coming back. Streams of them. They cried out with
horror when they found they had to run through the minefield and I had
to post a couple of men with fixed bayonets to prevent them dashing
through our HQ. The last to come, all alone, was a magnificent figure
probably an R.S.M. A big, tall, upright man in a beautiful uniform and
with a large black moustache, who trotted slowly, with great dignity and
no complaints, through the wire and the mines. The prisoners al
gathered in a great mass in the wadi behind us, where they were shelled
by their own guns. Major Mathieson at Rear Bn HQ counted them as
they went through. He counted up to eight hundred. Major Mathieson
was not at all happy. An order had come from Division that all seconds-
in-command were to be 'left out of Battle', as a reserve for any C.O. who
was knocked out, and that did not suit him a bit. He wanted to be in it
with everyone else; and he pretty well was. He was all over the place
not far behind us and even came up to Bn HQ and had to be asked to go
away again. He did a magnificent job keeping us supplied with
everything we wanted, brought up by the carriers. We never lacked
anything. Even an ambulance or two came down, though many of the
wounded had to stay where they were until it got dark.

The shelling and small arms fire, which had increased in volume all
the time we were advancing down the slope to the wadi, continued with
the same intensity the whole day.

Just two or three times there was a short pause in the shelling, possibly
when 152 Bde was making another attack on Roumana; but then it
resumed on the same scale as before. Most of our lay-out must have been
clear to the observers on Roumana and Bn HQ though sheltered from
their small-arms fire, naturally had a particular attraction for their
shelling. The Signallers had dug a large square hole in which they set up
their exchange, and one of the enemy guns kept putting its shell just over
the back of it. At last it scored a direct hit and caused many casualties,
including the acting Signals Officer, Stewart-Bam, and the Carrier
Platoon Commander, both killed. The Signals, though now without an
officer, put up a very good show indeed. There were occasional failures
chiefly with wireless sets, but the communications were remarkably
good and their efficiency one of the memorable features of the day. As
usual, we used telephones to the rear and the wires kept being cut by
the shelling, every time this happened Signallers went out and repaired
the gap. The shell which burst in the exchange produced a display of
bravery by another branch of the battalion, the medical. Where the gun

at last hit its mark, the inclination of anyone who had seen what had been happening was to wait for a moment to see if it was going to do the same again. But not 'Doc' Wilson - without a moment's hesitation he at once plunged in and started dealing with the casualties.

An early visitor to Bn HQ was CSM Archibald from 'B' Coy. In fact, the only one I remember seeing from the forward companies. He came to report that 'B' Company was in position and to collect some more ammunition. To do so he had had to cross a great expanse of open ground with no cover and he had a bullet hole through his helmet from a shot which had somehow managed to miss his head. I suggested he should stay where he was and wait until things got a bit quieter before going back. But shortly afterwards I found he had gone. They hit him on the way back, but he went on fighting for the rest of the day.

The first enemy reaction came soon after we arrived, when 'B' Company reported that Germans were making a very determined attempt to work round their right flank and they had not enough men to stop them. This was serious, as they had not far to go to infiltrate the wadi and if they could do that and make it untenable they would endanger our whole show. So I sent a platoon of 'D' Coy to reinforce 'B' and put a section of the Middlesex machine–gunners, who had just arrived, on the job and the movement was halted, though they continued to harass 'B' Company all day.

The rifle companies were all much below strength. Our losses in previous operations had not yet been fully made up by reinforcements, and the position was not helped by a party of two or three officers and a number of selected men, led by the Signals Officer, having a day or two earlier overshot the mark on the coast road and driven into the German lines, where they were captured. I have not got further details but the following figures, taken from Company Commanders' reports, give some idea of the situation. 'A' Coy at noon, 2 Officers, 42 O.Rs, 'B' Coy at start 80, at finish 38; 'C' Coy at start 3 Officers, 74 O.Rs, 15 casualties, incl 2 Officers, before reaching objective (one of them on start line), at finish 52. 'B' Coy was particularly short of men to man their position as several of them had followed the barrage and carried on with 'C' Coy, and they suffered heavily from the small-arms fire of the German 90 Light Division on their flank.

The gapping operation carried out in darkness, for a limited time and under fire, had only half succeeded. On the right the bank had been levelled out, there was no passage through this minefield; on the left a way had been cleared through the mines but there was no way over the anti tank ditch. The work was continued in daylight and an R A Major Maunder was particularly noticeable sitting calmly on the parapet of the ditch, in full view smoking his pipe and watching some Italian prisoners whom he had requisitioned to fill it in. He was unfortunately killed.

It was 1200 hours before a passage had been effected and the R.T.R. tanks, who had been waiting in the wadi, were able to come through into the rear of the bridgehead. At 1400 hours more tanks towing the guns of two troops of 241 A-Tk Bty. came through and towed the guns up to their positions on the front, where the gunners had a very hard job trying to dig them in on the rocky ground and under fire.

At 1345 hours a squadron of tanks of the 4th County of London Yeoman came down the long slope to the wadi to take over the tank defence of the bridgehead. It is interesting to read their account of the battle in their Regimental History. They had been in the Desert a year before us and taken part in the big battles before El-Alamein, but they describe Akarit as 'one of their more memorable and costly battles'. On the way down the slope they attracted very heavy fire, including an 88. When they entered the bridgehead they went forward to the front of our position and lined up along the crest, where they remained for the rest of the day being shelled and sniped at without cease. They describe the noise as being as great that you had to shout to make yourself heard. At the time we took a very poor view of their performance. I don't know what we expected them to do: but they seemed to be doing nothing except that every now and then a tank crew baled-out and made for the rear. Of course we were quite wrong, as one realised in afterthought and as is made clear by their history. They attracted a tremendous amount of fire, but engaged with their guns the tanks which took part in the counter-attack and spent the rest of their time in continued efforts to spot and eliminate the machine-guns and snipers which were harrying us and them. The latter they found difficult as it was hard to see from exactly where the fire was coming, a task made more difficult by the fire being so heavy that they had to keep their turrets closed and observe by periscope. One recently joined officer, who wanted a better view of a target, did open his turret and looked out and was killed. Nine of their tanks were put out of action, but the remainder still held firm and continued to shoot. Finally, as it got dark, the seven surviving tanks came down and drove away. They had done excellent work for us, though we did not appreciate it at the time. Their main presence must have had a very cooling effect on the enthusiasm of anyone thinking of a counter-attack.

Both 'C' and 'A' Coys, after capturing the final objectives, had had to go further forward than was anticipated in order to secure good defensive positions. This was not realised at once. It was disclosed to 'C' Coy by the first defensive fire for which they called falling upon themselves. This was at once corrected and there was no further trouble. In the case of 'A' Coy the disclosure was rather more dramatic . I was with them at the time when half a dozen of our aeroplanes appeared over the skyline coming from the direction of the enemy and suddenly dropped their bombs on us - Not a pleasant experience. No one was hit, but Capt. Robertson, the Company Commander, declared that the whole of his equipment which he had on and buckled up had been blown off him. It sounds incredible, but he was not one for fairy stories and he certainly had no equipment on when I saw him.

I had realised in walking out to them that they were too far forward and told him, when it was dark and things were quiet, to come back about three hundred yards.

The first enemy counter-attacks, bodies of men emerging and moving in our direction, were quickly taken up by our artillery and never came anywhere near us. At about 1600 hours a more serious attempt was made. Eight tanks appeared and infantry climbed on to them while more infantry started advancing around them.

They were again engaged by our artillery and tanks, who got right on to them almost immediately, and first the infantry and later the tanks drew back to where they had come from. At about 1800 hours the real thing came, about two battalions with tanks and a hurricane of shelling on Bn HQ. Then came a most alarming sight, 'A' Coy withdrawing rapidly down the slope. It looked like the worst thing that can happen during an enemy attack because once troops start running away there is often no stopping them and it is apt to be infectious. What had happened was that Capt. Roberts had seen about a battalion of the enemy moving across his front which had suddenly turned and come straight for him. He was worried about the poor field of fire which his men, only about thirty all told, had. He probably had at the back of his mind my talk of withdrawal. This was the last time at which I would have suggested it being made, but we had spoken first after the air-bombing and neither he nor I were probably at our clearest and calmest at the time. Anyway I should have had more confidence in the discipline and courage of 7 A.S.H. Capt. Bate, who had been sent ahead to choose the place to which they should withdraw, had been wounded but they came back fast and in good order, and, when they reached a suitable place turned about and opened fire with their Brens and rifles on any enemy who came over the skyline to such effect that the attack on that front was completely halted.

But their withdrawal worried 'C' Coy, who wondered if a general withdrawal had been ordered. But, as no orders had reached them, they decided to stay put. About two companies with tanks came at them and it looked as if they were done for. Major Lindsay-MacDougall had been twice wounded, but was determined they should die fighting. He climbed with difficulty out of his trench and shouted "No Surrender, 'C Coy Charge'. The five men of his company, HQ and some of 13 Platoon who were nearby, got up and charged; and he hobbled along behind them, determined to die with them. Then the miraculous happened. Confronted by this show of defiance, the enemy turned and fled. Shortly afterwards I got on to him on the wireless and the conversation was as follows, I asking the questions - 'How many were in that attack?' 'About two battalions'. 'How many attacked you?' 'About two companies with tanks'. 'Where are they now?' 'The infantry are about three hundred yards away and the tanks a bit closer'. 'How many men have you got?' 'My Coy HQ and 13 Platoon, and I think the remains of Archie MacVicar's platoon is somewhere on my left'. Myself, rather incredulously 'Are you alright?' Major L M, quite indignantly 'Of course we are alright. We only have to look at them and they run away'.

Shortly after that, darkness fell and the fighting and shelling stopped. Both sides patrolled rigorously and there were several encounters. One large patrol which got in behind 'D' Coy and was busy altering the tapes marking the passage through the minefield, was seen off by Capt Corcoran. But when daylight came the enemy had gone. We sent out a patrol of three carriers to go as far as the Wadi Ereth, about three miles ahead, and see if they could see them.

Shortly after they had gone, we got an order from Division that we were to send out a patrol and we were able to tell them that we had already done so. They sounded shocked when they heard how far they were trying to go. But, it turned out that we were not far wrong as they reached the Wadi Ereth, the next big wadi ahead, in time to see the last enemy vehicle just going over the crest on the far side.

So ended the Battle of Wadi Akarit - After the final counter-attack and before it got dark, 'B' Coy of 1 Black Watch had men sent down to reinforce us. They had all their officers knocked out on the way down the long slope and were commanded by the CSM. They went to support 'B' Coy. Later 'C' Coy, 1 B.W. followed and they made us feel much more secure. The enemy position had been a strong one and, besides prisoners we captured 17 A-Tk guns, 2 Lt. AA. guns, 2 Infantry guns and many A-Tk rifles, 16 M.Gs (Medium), 17 M.Gs (Lighter), 3 large mortars, 7 small mortars and a lot of other equipment. Our casualties were:- Officers- 3 killed, 8 wounded; O.Rs- 38 killed, 100 wounded, 5 missing.

The battle brought much honour to 7 A.S.H. The task given by 8th Army to the Highland Division was to make and hold a bridgehead over the Wadi Akarit. We were detailed to do the job and we did it. But that cannot belittle the achievement of the others, 7 Bn and 152 Bde, who were engaged in the action. The object of their attacks was to give all help possible to ensure that our object, which was the Division's object, was attained, and this they most gallantly did. The fact that neither attack reached it's final objective, though they got close to it, is immaterial. By keeping the pressure and the threat on the enemy, at great loss to themselves, all day, they diverted a very large part of the attention which would have otherwise been all turned on the bridgehead. Once we had got the bridgehead I felt pretty confident that we would hold it. But if the enemy had been allowed to bring his undivided effort against us, he might well have overcome us by sheer weight of numbers. It was a first-class Divisional plan, successfully executed by all concerned. For us it was far and away the hardest battle we had in the Desert. The behaviour of the battalion throughout was magnificent. The attack to secure the bridgehead was carried out with great efficiency and complete success, and, as it turned out, unexpected ease; and the counter-attacks, on 'B' Company's flank and on 'C' and 'A' Companies' front, were held. But the most memorable feature of the battle was the shelling and sniping, which began soon after we had crossed the Start Line and continued almost without a break from dawn to nightfall, with an intensity which we had never encountered before and, in my own case, never since. And the battalion never faltered. Finally came the supreme honour. The 7th Territorial Battalion had 'Wadi Akarit' chosen as one of the honours to be embroidered forever on the colours of The Argyll and Sutherland Highlanders.

Lorne Campbell
1 Dec 1982

INDEX.

Baldwin. J. R. S. Lt. 4th Field Coy. RE: 32,73.

Baron. A. G. Cpt. 4/6th Rajputana Rifles: 42.

Bacon. G. Sgt. 1/4th Essex: 59.

Bateman. Brigadier. CO 5th Brigade: 28.

Bate. Cpt. 7th Argylls: 147, 231, 327.

Begg. L. G. Cpt. 5th Seaforths: 229.

Beaty. Lt. 5th East Yorks: 133.

Bell. O. M. Maj. South African RE: 199, 201.

Bentley. G. A. 40th RTR: 115, 116, 118, 187.

Beech. W. A. Signaller. 1st Field Regiment. RA: 50.

Bhian. Bahadur. Ichathi .Rifleman. 1/9th Gurkha Rifles: 76.

Bhupar.Thapa. Rifleman. 1/9th Gurkha Rifles: 76.

Blackwell. H. N. Maj. 5th East Yorks: 134.

Black. Lt. 2nd Seaforth: 219.

Black. F. Pte. RA: 114

Blyth. B. H. Lt. 2nd Seaforth: 152, 220.

Blundell. J. Lt Col .OBE. CO Royal Engineers : 32, 73.

Bimbahadur. Rana. Rifleman. 1/2nd Gurkha Rifles: 24.

Bishanbahadur. Gurung. Rifleman. 1/2nd Gurkha Rifles: 26.

Bibanbahadur.Pun. Rifleman. 1/2nd Gurkha Rifles: 24

Bowering. F. Cpl. 4th CLY: 55, 262.

Bowden. A. S. Lt. 7th Argylls: 231.

Bodnick. P. Pte. 7th Argylls: 202.

Bonney. L/Bdr. 31st Field Rgt RA: 50.

Brazendale. MQM. MM. 4th CLY: 175.

Briggs. G. G. Cpt. 4th CLY: 262, 263.

Brennan. Pte. 7th Green Howards: 87.

Bremner. Pte. 5th Seaforths: 161.

Bull. L/Cpl. 6th Green Howards: 90.

Burrows. C. F. Lt. 5th Camerons: 226.

Cab - Malden. Maj. 1st Blackwatch: 219, 224.

Caden. H. D. Lt. 7th Green Howards: 97.

Cameron. I. Cpt. 7th Argylls: 145,231.

Cameron. D. H. Lt. 5th Camerons: 227.

Cameron. C. A. Cpt. 5th Camerons: 224.

Cameron. Maj. 1st Sussex: 63.

Cameron. Major. MC and Bar. 4th CLY: 170.

Campion. Sgt. 40th RTR: 185.

Campbell-Colquoun. L. W. Lt. 5th Camerons: 226.

Campbell. L. M. Lt Col. VC. DSO and Bar. TD. CO 7th Argylls: 145, 170, 179,185, 190,203,204, 230, 231, 235 to 239, 319 to 329.

Campbell. G. VC. Vice Admiral: 236, 239.

Caldbeck. R. Lt Col. CO 1st Black Watch: 148.

Carnduff. Sgt. 5th Seaforths: 162.

Calvert. Cpt. MC. 31st Field Rgt. RA: 50.

Chapman. E. Sgt. 1/4th Essex: 56.

Chappel. L.W.A. Maj. 1/4th Essex: 74.

Cheal.W. Cpl. 6th Green Howards: 120.

Church. Cpl. 5th East Yorks: 122.

Churchill. Winston: 253.

Clark. W. A. S. Cpt. 1st Sussex: 68.

Clayton. J. Sgt. 6th Green Howards: 119.

Crichton-Melville. H. R. Lt. 5th Black Watch: 155, 222.

Cummings. A. Pte. 175 Field Ambulance: 188.

Connel. Cpt. 308 Battery. RA: 221.

Cooke-Collis. Brigadier. DSO. CO 69 Brigade: 84,96, 119, 134.

Cornford. D. R. Gunner. 31st Field Rgt. RA: 50.

Corrie. J. A. G. Cpt. 2nd Seaforth: 152, 220.

Cotgreave.E. Signals. 201st Guards Brigade: 208.

Cramer: Ais Commander: 245.

Cruickshank. J. S. Lt . 2nd Seaforth: 220.

Curran. J. Gunner-Signaller. 31st Field Rgt. RA: 37.

Cumming-Bruce. H. Maj. 5th Seaforth: 165.

Christison. J. A. Lt. 7th Argylls:232.

Dalbir.Ghale. 1/2nd Gurkha Rifles: 33.

Dally. Trooper.4th CLY: 262.

Davidson. J. Maj. 5th Seaforth: 150, 158, 159, 162, 167.

Dalton. B. Cpt. DSO. OBE. 1st Sussex: 44.

Deans A. Pte. . REME Att 40th RTR.: 183.

Depoix. Lt. 7th Green Howards: 135.

Dixon. Sgt. 7th Green Howards: 87.

Donovan. D. H. Cpt. 1/9th Gurkha Rifles: 75.

Douglas. J. Lt. 2nd Seaforth: 220.

Donaghue. P. Pte. 7th Green Howards: 123, 125.

Draycott. A. Cpl. 5th East Yorks: 112.

Drummond. J .Pte. 7th Argylls: 204.

Edgar. Maj. Appointed CO 7th Green Howards after Seagrims death: 135.

Edwards. Maj. 1/2nd Gurkha Rifles: 65.

Elliot. J. Cpt. 5th Camerons: 226.

Fairclough. Cpt. 6th GreenHowards: 136.

Fausset-Farquhar. Lt Col. CO 1st Gordons: 232.

Fenner. Lt Col. 6th DLI: 127.

Fenwick. T. G. Cpt. 5th East Yorks: 260.

Findlay-shirras. Adj. 5th Seaforth: 162.

Finnegan. J .Lt Col. 40th RTR: 110.

Firth. Lt Col. CO 1st Sussex: 27.

Flugel. J. F. Lt. 2nd Seaforth: 152, 220.

Forth. Harry. Pte . MID. 5th East Yorks: 108.

Fox. CSM. 7th Black Watch: 197.

Fox .P. 7th Green Howards : 105.

Freyberg. General. CO New Zealand Forces: 243.

Galletti. Maj. 31st Field Rgt. RA: 33,52, 38.

Gallie. A. K. Lt. 2nd Seaforth: 220.

Gauld. G. CSM. DCM. 7th Argylls: 231.

Gause. Axis Commander: 245.

Garret. Dickie. 50th RTR: 177.

Garner. William. 7th Argylls: 204.

Gaylord. D. W. Cpt. MC. 1st Sussex: 69.

Glennie. I. Maj. 5/7th Gordons: 206.

George. Lt. 275 Field Coy. RE: 221.

Gordon. Douglas. Cpt. 5th Seaforths: 162,229.

Green. A, Sgt. MM. 40th RTR: 116.

Green. Trooper. 40th RTR: 184.

Greenwood. F. Lt. 5th Seaforth: 229.

Graham. B. Sapper. RE: 201.

Graham. D. A. H. Brigadier. CO 153 Brigade: 213, 222.

Gray. W. J. D. Lt. 5th Seaforth: 161, 163, 229.

Green. Sgt. 6th Green Howards: 250, 251.

Girardot. Lt. 1/2nd Gurkha Rifles: 65.

Gillard. BBC broadcast from Akarit: 318.

Gilmer. D. Cpl. 4th CLY: 53.

Gilmour. A. M. Maj. MC. 2nd Seaforth: 152, 219, 220.

Givens. L. Cpt. 2nd Seaforth: 151,220.

Haddon. Teddy: 200.

Hall.A. 25th Light Anti Aircraft Rgt. RA: 113.

Hamp. J. C. Cpt. MC. 5th Camerons: 224, 227.

Hanson. F. M. H. Lt Col. New Zealand RE: 121.

Harley. Lt. 1/2nd Gurkha Rifles: 65.

Hailwood. S. Pte. 5th Seaforth: 158.

Harrison. Cpt. 5th East Yorks: 122.

Harrison. S, Sgt. MM. 40th RTR: 111.

Harakbahadur. Gurung. Rifleman. 1/2nd Gurkha Rifles: 25.

Head. P. Pte. 7th Argylls: 194.

Henderson. Lt. 308 Battery. RA: 221.

Honeyman. Cpt. 7th Green Howards: 96,136.

Horrocks. General: 4,8,242,252.

Horne. R. D. Lt Col. DSO. CO 2nd Seaforth: 150, 219.

Houldsworth. Lt. 5th Camerons: 227.

Hicks. L/Cpl. 4th CLY: 262.

Hill. W. A. Sgt. 6th Green Howards: 94.

Hiscock. Ken. 4th CLY: 170.

Hudson. D. W. Cpt. 2nd Seaforth: 151, 220, 221.

Hughes. W. R. Maj. 40th RTR: 110, 187.

Hughes .Lt Col. CO 4/16th Punjab Rgt : 28.

Hull. Maj. 6th Green Howards: 136.

Hunwicks. V. Anti-tank gunner: 51.

Hyde. J. Pte. RASC: 53.

Inrabahadur. Gurung. Rifleman. 1/2nd Gurkha Rifles: 25.

James. R. B .Lt Col. CO 5th East Yorks: 88, 132, 133.

Jackson. R. J. L. Maj. 6th Green Howards: 119.

Jackson. Bill. SQMS. 40th RTR: 188.

Jackson. T. Sgt. Anti-tank gunner. ScottsGuards. 201st Guards Bde .: 207.

James. S. H. Lt. 1/9th Gurkha Rifles: 76.

Jarvis.T 4th CLY: 170 to 173.

Jephson. Maj. MC. TD. 11th Field Rgt. RA: 48.

Jenner. H. J. L/Bdr. RA: 178.

Jon. The two types: 14.

Jones. Ted, Bdr.31st Field Rgt. RA: 52.

Jones. M. P. F. Cpt. 1/9th Gurkha Rifles: 75.

Jones. Ken. Sgt. 50th RTR: 177.

Johnson. H .Pte. 7th Black Watch: 195.

Jubb . William. Pte. MM. 42nd Field Coy. RE: 54.

Khar. Bahadur. Ichathi. Rifleman. 1/9th Gurkha Rifles: 76.

Kinghorn. Lt. R. F. 7th Argylls: 231.

Kirby. Cpt. 6th DLI: 129.

Kisch. F. H. Brigadier: 199, 200.

Kennedy. D. Pte. MM. 5th Seaforth: 175.

Lachlan-Taylor. Pte. 7th Argylls: 189.

Laidler. L/Sgt. 6th GreenHowards: 90.

Lalbahadur. Pun. Rifleman. 1/2nd Gurkha Rifles: 33, 45.

Lalbahadur. Thapa. Subedar. VC. OBI. 1/2nd Gurkha Rifles: 25, 65, 78 to 81.

Lamb. Larry 1st Black Watch mascot: 198.

Lance. G. Lt Col. CO 6th Green Howards: 89, 119, 128, 136.

Law. D. B. Cpt. 2nd Seaforth: 151, 220.

Lees. W. C. Lt. 7th Argylls: 230.

Leese. General: 4,10,243.

Levine. Lt. 6th Green Howards: 136.

Lee. S. J. S. Cpt. 2nd Seaforth: 151, 202.

Lindsay-MacDougal. Maj. DSO. 7th Argylls: 147, 231, 319, 322, 328.

Limer. H. Lt. 40th RTR: 110.

Lisle. G. CQMS. MC. 2nd Seaforth: 168.

Lloyd. Maj. RE: 210.

Lofthouse. Cpt. 6th Green Howards: 136, 267.

Lovett. Brigadier. CO 7th Brigade: 22.

Lumby. J. B. Maj. 40th RTR: 187.

Lyons. Sgt. 149th Anti Tank Rgt. RA: 49.

Lymberley. Lt. 40th RTR: 115.

Mackay. G. Sapper. RE: 191.

Mackenzie. I. Cpt. 5th Seaforth: 161,229.

Macleod. Sgt. 5th Seaforth: 161.

Macdonald. R. T. Sgt. 61st Anti Tank Rgt. RA: 185.

Macdonald. D. C. Maj. MC. 6th Green Howards: 118, 136.

Macrae. CSM. 5th Camerons: 154.

Macrae. D. Cpl. MM. 7thArgylls: 231.

Manahi. Sgt. Maori Bn: 252.

Mansell. Cpt. 7th Green Howards: 86.

Manilal. Thapa. Havildar. 1/2nd Gurkha Rifles: 25, 45.

Maitland. H. Sir. GBE. KCB. DSO. ADC: 238.

Marley-Clarke. Cpt. 1/2nd Gurkha Rifles: 26.

.Martin. Cpt. REME: 184.

Martin. QMS. REME. att 40th RTR.: 183.

Marshal. R. D. Lt. 7th Argylls: 231.

Marshal. T. Sgt. 4th CLY: 172.

Markham. G. W. Reverend. 124th Field Rgt. RA: 98.

Mason-Fisher. Cpt. 40th RTR: 110, 117, 187.

Mather. Pte. 7th Green Howards:125, 126.

Mathieson. Major. 7th Argylls: 324.

Mackenzie. Sgt. 5th Seaforths: 159.

Maunder. R. Maj. RA: 180, 319, 326.

Macrory. Father. 7th Argylls: 204.

McDonald. P. F. Pte. 5th East Yorks: 260.

McGilvray. J. Lt. 5th Seaforth: 229.

McGrath. J . 2nd Seaforth: 260.

McLaren. Maj. 40th RTR: 187.

McLelland. Pte. 7th Black Watch: 197.

McMillan. W. Pte. 1st Black Watch: 195.

McCann. C. Pte. 5th Camerons: 191.

McGill. T. F. Lt. 7th Argylls: 230.

McHardy. W. G. Cpt. 2nd Seaforth: 151.

McPhail. BSM. MM. 241/61st Anti Tank Rgt. RA: 179.

Messe. Axis Commander: 8, 13, 245.

Meiklejohn. Cpt. 7th Argylls:146.

Miers. R. D. M. C. Lt Col. DSO. CO 5th Camerons: 153, 166, 223.

Monahan. W. MM. 7th Agylls: 231.

Moore. Sgt. MM. 4th CLY: 175.

Montgomery. Field Marshal: 1, 3, 7, 9, 11, 143, 215, 242, 245, 252, 319.

Morgan. Cpt. 6th Green Howards: 136.

Moorhead. A. War Correspondent: 250.

Mount. C. Official WarArtist. RA: 18,46.

Murray. J. A. Maj. MC. 4th Field Coy. RE: 32, 73.

Morgan. L/Cpl. 42nd Field Coy. RE: 54.

Murray. A. G. Cpt. 5th Seaforth: 229.

Murray. G. Brigadier. DSO. MC. CO 152 Bde: 148, 165, 168, 210, 222.

Mulhern. Lt Col: 199, 200, 201.

Nare. Thapa. Lance Naik. 1/2nd Gurkha Rifles: 32.

Nairn. P. Sir. MC. Int Officer. 5th Seaforth: 160, 182.

Napier. A. G. Lt. 2nd Seaforth: 220.

Nethercoat. F. Sgt. 1/4th Essex: 57.

Newmarch. A. Pte. 5th East Yorks: 122.

Nichol. Cpt. 1/2nd Gurkha Rifles: 25.

Nichols. J. S. Maj General. DSO. MC. CO 50th Division: 83, 127, 244.

Nixon. Sam . Lt. 50th RTR: 176 to 178.

Noble. Lt Col. CO 1/4th Essex: 29, 73.

Nosotti. Lt. 7th Green Howards: 87.

O'Donoghue. J. E. Cpl. MM. 1/4TH Essex: 58.

Oliver. J. A. Lt Col. DSO. CO 7th Black Watch: 148, 231.

Oliver. J. CSM. MM. 6th Green Howards: 94, 265 to 268.

O'Neill. Pte. 5/7th Gordons: 181.

Orchardson. R. L. Cpt. RAMC: 225.

O'Toole. Cpl. RA: 114.

Overmont J. 74th Field Rgt, RA. Att 7th Green Howards.: 115.

Owen. Maj. 128 Field Rgt. RA: 222.

Oxley. A. Pte. 6th Green Howards: 121.

Patton. General: 8, 242, 247.

Payne. R. E. Lt. 2nd Seaforth: 220.

Penton. S. C. L/Cpl. 42nd Field Coy, RE. Att Green Howards : 105.

Pennington . Sam. 4th CLY: 170.

Perkin. R. Cpt. MC. 4/16th Punjab Rgt: 39.

Perkins. Max. Spitfire pilot. 601 Squadron.RAF: 12.

Perry.C. Cpt. 2nd Seaforth: 220.

Pierce. C. Lt Col. 4th CLY: 169.

Priest. Pte. 7th Green Howards: 87.

Pringle. Sgt. 1st Black Watch: 198.

Popple. Cpt. 4/16th Rgt: 28.

Power. J. P R. Maj. 126 Field Rgt, RA: 185.

Pullinger. Maj. 6th Green Howards: 91.

Purser. D. M. RE: 199, 201.

Ramsay-Brown. Cpt. MC. 1/2nd Gurkha Rifles: 16, 22, 36.

Rankin. K. M. 1ST Black Watch: 190.

Reed. G. B. Lt. 5th Seaforth: 229.

Reynolds. A. Pte. 2nd Seaforth: 205.

Richie .Mike .Lt. 4th CLY: 170, 262.

Rickwood. R. L. Pte. 7th Green Howards: 123.

Roberts. Cpt. 7th GreenHowards: 87.

Roberts. R. N. Lt. 5th Camerons: 226

Robertson. Lt. 7th Argylls: 230, 327.

Robertson. Cpt. 7th Argylls: 147.

Robinson. Maj. REME: 184.

Roche. Lt Col. CO 1/9th Gurkha Rifles: 28, 74.

Rollie. A. C. Pte. 7th Argylls: 258, 259.

Rommel. Erwin. Field Marshal: 3, 6, 236.

Roller. Maj. 7th Black Watch: 196.

Roper-Caldbeck. Lt Col.   DSO. CO 1st Black Watch: 219.

Ross. Sgt. 7th Black Watch: 196.

Rutherford. Ken. L/Sgt. 5th East Yorks: 111.

Rude. Cpt. RA: 180.

Runmey. Cpt. RAMC: 129.

Ryan. Gunner. 4th CLY : 173.

Samwell. H. D. L. Cpt. 7th Argylls: 231.

Saunders. H. W. B. Lt Col. CO 5/7th Gordons: 233

Scott. Lt Col. CO 4/6th Rajputana Rifles: 29, 76.

Scott. P. Maj. MC. 4th CLY: 170.

Scott. Sgt. 2nd Seaforth: 153.

Stewart-Sutcliffe. D. Lt. 5th Camerons: 227.

Stirling. J. E. Brigadier. DSO. MC. CO 154 Bde: 144, 215.

Strachan. Cpt. REME. Att 40th RTR : 183.

Stubbs. Cpt. 1/2nd Gurkha Rifles: 24.

Sutton. Dick. 4th CLY: 174.

Sutcliffe. D. S. Lt. 5th Seaforth: 229.

Tandy. C. Maj: RE. 201.

Thomson. Lt Col. CO 5th Black Watch: 154, 221.

Thornton. J. Int Officer. 5th Seaforth: 166.

Topcliffe. Sgt. 7th Green Howards: 87.

Tucker. F. I. S. Major. General. CB. DSO. OBE. CO 4th Indian Division: 10, 15, 31, 76, 242.

Turner. A. Gnr. 72nd Anti Tank Rgt. RA: 187.

Underlay. Lt. 7th Green Howards: 86.

Vickers. F. W. Pte. MM. 6th Green Howards: 94, 267.

Von Arnim. Jürgen. Axis Commander: 6, 245.

Voight. F. C. M. Cpt. South African RE: 199, 201.

Von Sponeck. Axis Commander: 13.

Walford. J. H. Lt Col. DSO and Bar. CO 5th Seaforth: 149, 162, 167, 181, 227.

Walton. Cpt. 6th DLI: 128.

Wallace. Maj. 5th East Yorks: 133.

Wallace. J. L/Sgt. MM. 7th Argylls: 231.

Watt. J. Cpt. DSO. MC. 1/4th Essex: 55.

Watson. D. G. Cpt. 5th Camerons: 226.

Watson. W. I. Col. 6th DLI: 127.

Wharton. Cpt. 25th Light Anti Aircraft Rgt, RA: 113.

White. L. Pte. 7th Green Howards: 105.

Whittle. L. CSM. 5th East Yorks: 101.

Wood. Cpt. 5th East Yorks: 133.

Wimberley .D. N. Major General. CO 51st Highland Division: 10, 143, 144, 160, 189.

Willcock. Cpt. 5th Seaforth:150, 160, 229.

Wilson. R. A. Cpt: 116.

Wilson. Doc. 7th Argylls: 319.

Wykes. T. 50th RTR: 116.

Wynne. L. CQMS. 1/4th Essex: 58.

Yeoman. R. 241/61st Anti Tank Rgt. RA: 179.

Young. G. M. Maj. MC. 7th Green Howards: 95.

Young. R. E. Pte. 7th Green Howards: 106.

UNITS.

Anti Tank Battery. 241st : 144, 146, 326.

Argylls. 7th Bn : 144, 189, 204, 216, 230, 236, 319.

Armoured Brigade. 8th : 135, 137, 246.

Armoured Brigade. 23rd : 221, 228, 230.

Armoured Division. 1st :9, 11.

Armoured Division. 7th : 5, 212, 214, 30, 252.

Army.1st: 250.

Army. British .1st: 5.

Army Group. 18th : 6.

Australian Division. 9th : 2.

Brigade. 5th : 28,71.

Brigade. 69th : 84, 134, 213, 243.

Brigade. HQ. 7th : 62.

Brigade .152: 144, 148, 190, 210, 222, 243, 320.

Brigade 154: 144, 148, 160, 170, 179, 188, 190, 215, 243, 320.

Brigade.153: 144, 168, 212, 213, 230, 320.

Black Watch. 7th Bn: 144, 146, 148, 195, 216, 231, 243.

Black Watch. 5th Bn: 154, 160, 182, 214, 221, 229.

Black Watch. 1st Bn: 144, 147, 190, 197, 216, 219.

Bersaglieri. Italian unit : 96, 129.

Camerons. 5th Bn: 144, 149, 153, 189, 191, 210, 223.

Cheshires. 2nd Heavy Machine Gun Bn: 106, 119, 134.

Corps. 9th : 253.

Corps.10th : 242, 245, 246.

Corps.30th : 244, 245, 246.

County of London Yeomanry. 4th : 91, 134, 147, 211, 217, 244, 326.

Durham Light Infantry. 6th Bn: 91, 135, 136.

East Yorkshire Rgt. 5th Bn: 86, 88, 100, 132, 134, 136, 244.

Essex Rgt. 1/4th Bn: 29, 3.

Green Howards. 7th Bn: 86, 89, 100, 134, 136, 243, 263.

Green Howards. 6th Bn: 85, 89, 100, 134, 136, 244.

Guards Brigade. 201st : 11, 144, 145, 207, 208, 213, 228, 252, 320.

Gordons. 1st Bn: 165, 214, 232.

Gordons. 5/7th Bn: 206, 214, 233.

Greek Brigade: 2.

Gurkha Rifles: 1/9th : 28, 74.

Gurkha Rifles. 1/2nd : 23, 32, 62, 64, 70.

Hussars. 11th Bn: 4.

Light Division. 90th . German : 8, 36, 129, 154, 163, 172, 211, 218, 245, 320.

Light Division: 164th .German: 11, 245.

Middlesex. 1/7th Machine Gun Bn: 146, 150, 221, 325.

New Zealand Division. 2nd : 135, 149, 164, 167, 168, 212, 215, 230, 243, 246, 252.

Northumberland Hussars: 134.

Order of Battle. Axis: 317.

Order of Battle. 8th Army: 316.

Panzer Division. 10th: 8,247.

Panzer Division. 15th: 9, 129, 218, 218, 242, 244.

Panzer Division. 21st : 8, 9, 242, 247.

Panzer Grenadier Rgt. 200: 242, 244.

Panzer Grenadier Rgt. 361: 242,245.

Pistoia Division: 28, 77, 129, 242.

Punjab Rgt. 4/16th : 28, 70.

Rajputana Rifles. 4/6th : 29, 76, 244.

Royal Sussex. 1st Bn: 27, 62, 68.

Royal Tank Rgt 3rd Bn: 243.

Royal Tank Rgt. 40th Bn: 144, 183, 187, 217, 244.

Royal Tank Rgt. 50th Bn: 176, 183, 187, 210, 226, 243.

Seaforths. 2nd Bn: 144, 148, 150, 161, 164, 205, 210, 219, 224, 243.

Seaforths. 5th Bn: 144, 149, 154, 164, 168, 175, 181, 210, 222, 224, 227, 243.

South African Division.1st: 2.

Spearforce: 213, 223, 230.

Spezia Division: 77, 129, 134, 136, 161, 211, 234, 242, 245.

Staffordshire Yeomanry: 243.

Triest Division: 232, 233, 242, 245.

United States 2nd Corps: 5, 8, 245, 246, 253.

Young Fascist Division: 243.

PLACE NAMES.

Kasserine: 5.

Kairouan: 251.

Le Havre: 236.

Libya: 5.

Marble Arch: 2.

Maknassy: 8.

Massicault: 253.

Matmata Hills: 6.

Mareth: 5, 6, 7, 8, 176, 179, 183, 242, 263, 319.

Medanine: 6.

Medjerda River: 253.

Mersa Matruh: 1, 3.

Medjez El Bab Memorial to the Missing: 301.

Medjez El Bab War Cemetery: 307.

Medjez El Bab: 253.

North Africa American Cemetery. Tunisia. (Carthage): 308.

Oudref: 16, 18, 132, 174, 230.

Point 85.The Pimple or Cutie: 85, 87, 132, 134, 136, 228, 243, 244.

Roumana: 9, 10, 73, 89, 127, 144, 146, 148, 160, 165, 177, 190, 194, 222, 224, 226, 242, 319.

Sfax War Cemetery: 270.

Sfax: 214,223,246,250.

Sollum: 1.

Sousse: 246,251.

St Valery: 236.

Takruana: 252

Tel El Aqqaqir: 239.

Tobruk; 1,2.

Tripoli: 4,160,167.

Tunis: 250,252,253.

Tunisia: 5,6,160,251.

Zouai: 9,24,26,32,62,242.